VIET-NAM

THE FIRST FIVE YEARS

An International Symposium

VIET-NAM
THE FIRST FIVE YEARS

●●●●●

AN INTERNATIONAL SYMPOSIUM

Edited and Introduced by
RICHARD W. LINDHOLM

MICHIGAN STATE UNIVERSITY PRESS
1959

★
★
★
★
★

CONTENTS

v

INTRODUCTION

FROM THE TIME of their subjugation by the French in the 1860's until the state of Free Viet-Nam was created in 1954, the Vietnamese engaged in one effort after another to regain their political freedom. During these years of resistance they exhibited an ability to develop leaders of considerable courage and skill. Ngo Dinh Diem, leader of south Viet-Nam, and Ho Chi Minh, leader of north Viet-Nam, are both exceptionally capable men. Although the similarities and differences in the development of both states under these two strong leaders are worthy of study, our concern is only with the Viet-Nam of which Ngo Dinh Diem is President.

Today Diem* is considered a dictator by some observers and a strong leader by others; a person who has made few errors of judgment by some, and one who has developed major policy errors by others. On Diem's leadership, William Henderson has this to say: "By the middle of 1956, after two years of power, Diem had still to prove that his professed devotion to the democratic cause represented anything more than a façade to disguise the increasingly plain reality of stern dictatorship." Expressing admiration for Diem's leadership, Ellen Hammer writes: "Since that time [independence] Diem has set about building a regime, step by step, on foundations that go deep into what in the past was legitimate and decent for an Asian country, namely Confucianist ethics. . . . In this development of a political credo which draws its deepest roots from traditions of which Asia can legitimately be proud, the service rendered by Diem to free Asia may well extend beyond the frontiers of his Republic of Viet-Nam." In Diem's elimination of the politico-religious sects, David Hotham says critically: "far from being the triumph it was acclaimed, the breakdown of negotiations and degeneration of the situation into open war was, at best, a failure of leadership." Supporting Diem's move is Joseph Buttinger, who writes: "It is part of Ngo Dinh Diem's political greatness not to have succumbed to the deceptive magic of unity, to have refused to enter into

* To address President Ngo Dinh Diem as either Diem or President Diem would be, to the Vietnamese, as familiar a form of address as Dwight or President Dwight would be to the present President of the United States. However, so widely has this form been used in English-speaking periodicals, it was felt wise to leave this usage in this book and thus not confuse the interested English-speaking layman.

it with elements of national dissension, and to have understood that the sects, unhealthy products of the colonial past, could not be appeased and had to be destroyed."

This wide difference of opinions on Diem and his policies reflects the general uncertainty in the Free World of the best program to be followed in developing the base for a viable democratic nation. The Communists, quite the contrary, seem to be much more confident of the correct program to achieve their ends. However, United States experience in underdeveloped areas—and it is becoming considerable—leads one to doubt if the procedures successful in one culture can ever be successfully transplanted to another culture. If this is true, President Diem must be judged on how well he reflects his own culture and how well he has used this base to adapt what the West has to offer.

Because national development is multisided, the contributors to *Viet-Nam: The First Five Years* vary from a foreign minister of Australia, who is deeply interested in preserving freedom in Viet-Nam, to a Vietnamese bureaucrat, who has just completed what is more than likely one of the world's most successful refugee resettlement programs.

Free Viet-Nam is now entering the beginning phases of reconstructing, modernizing, and expanding its basic institutions, and reorienting its economy from a colonial supplier of raw materials to the economy of an independent state. In carrying out this program, Viet-Nam can be expected to blend the methods of the Orient with those of the Western democracies. Most likely a political oligarchy will make the most progress in achieving this "blend," with the government providing technical information and certain social and venture capital, as well as conditions that encourage private ownership and the development of human and natural resources. The primary object must be to encourage the expansive cultural and economic forces that will break the frame of the stationary society.

Economic planning and development is a prerequisite to developing a higher per capita income and a self-sustained growth process. The basic requirement of an economic development program for Viet-Nam seems to be dependent upon the farming class, which makes up about 80 percent of the population, which must be willing and able to respond to possibilities opened up by: (1) new political and educational opportunities, (2) new production techniques, (3) land taxation, providing funds for local social investment, (4) leasehold and ownership arrangements stimulating investment of effort and funds, (5) cheap and safe transportation facilities adequate toward making a single market out of the country, and (6) a credit organization which facilitates planning and development throughout the nation. Progress can be hastened by a purposeful elite in government and in the private sector, but real progress must wait until there is a change in the outlook of the people toward new techniques and opportunities.

Activities such as the refugee leaders developed in education and production, and the program of foreign trade and use of domestic raw materials to replace imported finished goods, as advocated by Huyn Van Lang, are indications of the progress that can be made by Vietnamese leaders. These projects establish conditions of external economy (lower costs other than the internal costs of production), and change emphasis from buying and selling to producing and selling.

Free Viet-Nam is in a good position to bring about a higher per capita income—that of Viet-Nam is already higher than other countries in Southeast Asia, as David C. Cole points out. This somewhat higher per capita income is vital, for it permits support of the educational, social, and health agencies that a nation producing at a mere existence level cannot provide. More than likely these agencies must function effectively if the citizens of a country are to carry forward their activities as effective producers of goods and services. Perhaps the failure of experts to emphasize this point in the consideration of economic development possibilities of poorer countries has raised false hopes. This shortcoming might have been avoided by more careful study of economic history, for historical economic data indicate that nations which have experienced an industrial development have started from a per capita income base that was considerably higher than that existing in many countries striving to make a similar industrialization program effective today.

Viet-Nam: The First Five Years started out to include all aspects of all development efforts in Free Viet-Nam. One cannot help but register disappointment in failing to reach that goal. However, in every case a sincere effort was made to induce persons who had worked in Free Viet-Nam to write a basic article, or to comment on one, so that the varied viewpoints of the people of the Free World would be represented.

In many instances detailed, frank analyses were made by very busy persons; and it was their willingness to describe and discuss publically their accomplishments, problems, and observations which has made this book possible. Those who were unable or unwilling to do this must bear some of the responsibility for any "slant" that may be detected in a section or in the entire book.

R. W. L.

Eugene, Oregon
March, 1959

PART ONE

A NEW STATE
IN SOUTHEAST ASIA

In 1954 newspaper headlines around the world blazoned the name of a small mountainous village in Southeast Asia. Most Westerners became familiar with that name—Dien Bien Phu—long before they knew much about the country in which it was located—Viet-Nam. For the struggle at Dien Bien Phu was dramatic and tragic: Ten thousand of France's best soldiers were encircled and besieged by three times their number of Viet-Minh forces, in what the French had thought was an impregnable fortress, despite its isolated position three hundred miles from supply bases.

On the other hand, the name of Viet-Nam, along with Cambodia and Laos, was virtually buried in another place name, French Indochina. For eight years, between 1946 and 1954, the French and the Communists had been protagonists in the Indochina war: Viet-Nam and the non-Communist Vietnamese received little notice as such. "Standing between the two armed parties, a helpless victim of their equally ruthless methods of warfare," writes Joseph Buttinger, "the Vietnamese peasant was neither indifferent nor impartial. He had love for neither, feared them both, but practiced a passive solidarity with the Viet-Minh, who were after all compatriots at war with the peasant's oldest and most easily identifiable enemy: armed foreigners on Vietnamese soil."

With the fall of Dien Bien Phu, colonialism was dead in Viet-Nam. And with the Geneva Conference, Viet-Nam was divided at the 17th parallel, with communism the victor in the northern part of the country. And what of the southern part? Ellen Hammer answers this question: "The decision to divide Viet-Nam, although it placed the country in the same unhappy position as Germany and Korea, at least gave international recognition to a state where a truly nationalist, and non-Communist, regime could be consolidated. Thereby, the Geneva Conference registered international acceptance of the importance of Viet-Nam in the competition between the Communist bloc and the Free World in Asia."

In this "created" free nation, the Vietnamese face many problems as to what to do with their independence, as Ton That Thien points out: "During these years [of French rule], the Vietnamese acquired a new mentality: that of the revolutionary nationalist—bitter, uncompromising, destructive. The Vietnamese learned how to destroy—materially, mentally, socially. Having no responsibility for the running of their country, they had no opportunity to learn how to preserve, to develop, to build—in a word, to think and act constructively."

Now this new state in Southeast Asia, with the help of the Free World, is learning to preserve, to develop, to build. Indeed, it must do so, and rapidly, if it is to survive against the Russian and Chinese efforts to "draw economically underdeveloped countries into the Communist camp."

I. Nationalism vs. Colonialism and Communism

ELLEN J. HAMMER[1]

On the outskirts of Hue, beyond hills dotted with pine trees and on the far side of the Perfumed River, is the tomb of Minh Mang, the great emperor who, more than a hundred years ago, ruled over the country of Viet-Nam, which his father had reunited under the Nguyen dynasty. Today the country has been split in two: Only a few miles to the north of Hue is the 17th parallel, which divides the southern Republic of Viet-Nam from the Communist state in the north. But the tombs of the Nguyen emperors, which have been carefully preserved by the southern republic, have become national monuments, reminders of the long and remarkable history of the Vietnamese people, whose vigor and ability have set them apart from the other peoples of Southeast Asia.

Not all of the most impressive episodes in Vietnamese history date back to the remote past. Quite the contrary, one of the most dramatic periods began only when World War II ended, and it is still going on. It has been marked by the renascence of the Vietnamese nation, and this despite the conjunction of a number of adverse circumstances arising from a peculiarly intricate international situation.

In this period Viet-Nam, alone of all the countries of Southeast Asia, won its independence, and won it by years of resistance, much of that time without any aid from abroad. In 1945 British military authorities made the mistake of bringing back the French colonial administration to Viet-Nam, without making clear to their allies beforehand the extent to which the Vietnamese situation had altered during the Japanese occupation, necessitating a farsighted change of policy such as the British themselves were about to make in India. And when the Vietnamese resisted the re-establishment of the colonial regime, the American people, for many years, did not realize the impact of this event on the future of Southeast Asia. If the Chinese sometimes took a hand in their neighboring nation's affairs at this time, it was less for the sake of Vietnamese independence than to further their own interests and those of the large Chinese minority in Viet-Nam.

The Vietnamese resistance to colonialism was that of a whole nation, and its military successes should be credited more to the masses than to the handful of Communists who tried to exploit this revolutionary situation for their own ends. In fact, the presence of Communists in key positions in the resistance movement immensely complicated the struggle and delayed the attainment of independence. At many a possible turning point during these years, the merits of the nationalist cause were obscured by the Communist threat, losing for Viet-Nam the friendship of foreigners

[1] Author of *The Struggle for Indochina.*

3

who otherwise might have helped to shorten the war. And ultimately the Vietnamese Communists, led by Ho Chi Minh,[2] who claimed to be fighting for independence and geographic unity, demonstrated their readiness to sacrifice both these national objectives to their own ideological interests. They abandoned their claim to independence when they compelled that part of the country which they controlled to be absorbed into the Communist bloc. And in 1954, at the Geneva Conference, they forsook their claim to geographic unity when they preferred to see the country divided so that they could ensure exclusive Communist rule north of the 17th parallel.

Representatives of the United States, France, the United Kingdom, the Soviet Union, Communist China, Laos, Cambodia, Viet-Nam, and the Viet-Minh movement met at Geneva in April, 1954. The settlement finally reached by the Geneva Conference in July provided for the division of Viet-Nam along the 17th parallel of latitude, for a cease-fire between the French Union and the Viet-Minh forces, and for the withdrawal of those forces south and north of the 17th parallel respectively. An International Commission for Supervision and Control, comprising representatives of India, Canada, and Poland, was established to supervise the truce arrangements. Separate administrations were to continue on either side of the 17th parallel, and consultations between the north and the south were to begin in July, 1955, with a view to holding free nation-wide elections a year later to re-establish the unity of the country.

The decision to divide Viet-Nam, although it placed the country in the same unhappy position as Germany and Korea, at least gave international recognition to a state where a truly nationalist, and non-Communist, regime could be consolidated. Thereby, the Geneva Conference registered international acceptance of the importance of Viet-Nam in the competition between the Communist bloc and the Free World in Asia.

In a truncated country, menaced on its northern frontier by a ruthless Communist political and military threat, the new southern Republic of Viet-Nam needed all the material aid it could muster from abroad, as well as understanding and sympathy from the Free World. And this it has received: Many individuals of good will, from many countries, have come to work in and for Viet-Nam since 1954.

Both in its scope and in the fact that it represents the collective effort of people from a number of countries, the foreign aid program in Viet-Nam has been one of the most interesting anywhere in the postwar world.

[2] Ho Chi Minh was the founder of both the Indochinese Communist Party and the Viet-Nam Doc Lap Dong Minh Hoi, popularly known as the Viet-Minh. In September, 1945, the Viet-Minh was still a united front movement, but the Communists gradually eliminated all non-Communist elements and eventually dominated it entirely.

Its magnitude and the degree of effectiveness which it has achieved have been directly conditioned by the unique qualities and history of the Vietnamese people.

The Vietnamese nation, throughout its long history, has never been slow to fight back when it believed itself threatened. By the same token, it has been remarkably responsive and hospitable to legitimate foreign influences, while at the same time preserving its own identity. This was certainly true during the early centuries when the country grew up in resistance to Chinese domination and, after almost a thousand years of Chinese administration, won its independence in 939. Thereafter, with the exception of a short period in the fifteenth century, the Vietnamese maintained their freedom, although only at the price of periodic battles with Chinese invaders, of which the most famous were their victories against the Mongol armies of Kublai Khan in the thirteenth century, and their most recent, which occurred late in the eighteenth century. During all this time the Vietnamese borrowed generously from the Chinese culture, blending it with their indigenous traditions to make it their own: During the course of the national struggle against the Chinese, a distinctive Vietnamese culture took shape.

Slowly but relentlessly, the Vietnamese moved southward from their birthplace near the Chinese frontier until, in the seventeenth century, they reached the southern tip of what came to be known to the West as Indochina.[3] The name was apt, not because the Indochinese peninsula lies between the two great cultures of Asia, nor even because, in contrast to the Chinese-influenced Vietnamese, their neighbors in sparsely populated Cambodia and Laos are impregnated with Indian cultural influence, but because Viet-Nam itself also had important links with the Indian world, specifically of a religious nature. Buddhism was a vital force in Viet-Nam, superimposed on the popular animism and coexisting with the Confucian code of social morality which had spread from China.

The daily life of the Vietnamese peasant has been a perpetual battle against the forces of nature in the hot Vietnamese plains; he lives in the shadow of disaster, either from the floods which often overflow the banks of the multitude of coastal rivers or from the recurrent drought, both of which threaten the rice crop upon which he and his family depend mainly for subsistence. Remote as these preoccupations may be from issues of high politics, the peasant could not always take refuge in his village from the ravages of the struggles for power which sporadically used to plague

[3] According to popular usage, the term "Indochina" designates Viet-Nam, Cambodia, and Laos. These, in turn, are regarded as constituting the eastern part of the Indochinese peninsula, which also includes Burma, Thailand, and Malaya.

the country. Generally, these were wars among local leaders, but some-times, as during the wars with the Chinese, the Vietnamese was called upon to defend his country against the foreign invader. In the nineteenth century, for the first time, the foreign invader came from Europe.

At the start the Europeans had come as friends; but in the 1820's, when the first French consul to Viet-Nam was rebuffed by the Emperor Minh Mang and left the country in disgrace, Viet-Nam stood at the crossroads of its history. Minh Mang's father, Gia Long, had put down the Tay Son uprising,[4] bringing internal peace to Viet-Nam, and to accomplish this, had enlisted a small group of Frenchmen as allies. Minh Mang directed his considerable talents to further consolidating Vietnamese unity, de-veloping the national administration and constructing extensive public works, among them the Mandarin Road which was to link the country from north to south and along which modern travelers still drive from Saigon to Hue. But there remained the question of how to deal with the West. French Catholicism, by the time of Minh Mang, had made con-siderable progress. To the emperor, it seemed to threaten the traditional unity of the state, in which supreme religious and secular authority were combined in his person, the Son of Heaven. Minh Mang, therefore, turned against the Catholics, as against the French; for the greater part of his reign he acted as if Viet-Nam could safely turn its back on Europe. In this, he clearly miscalculated. Viet-Nam was still an independent nation when Minh Mang died in 1841; but his fatal error in judgment opened an era of war for his successors as they tried, unsuccessfully, to stand firm against the Europeans.

In the course of the spread of European political control over large areas of Asia and Africa which marked the nineteenth century, the French came back to Viet-Nam. This time they came with armed force. They first seized three southern provinces in 1862; five years later they oc-cupied the entire southern part of the country which they transformed into the colony of Cochinchina, under direct French rule. Emperor Tu Duc, the grandson of Minh Mang, fought the invaders at every point, but without success, and in 1884, a year after his death, the French imposed a protectorate over central (Annam) and north (Tonkin) Viet-Nam. When, the following year, Emperor Nam Nghi, in his turn, raised the nation against the French, he was defeated and exiled. This was the most spectacular of a series of popular revolts against French colonial rule, which ended only with the re-establishment of Vietnamese independence in 1954.

----

[4] An uprising led by three brothers, which arose as a local rebellion of the landless and miserable peasants in Tay Son, and spread successfully throughout south Viet-Nam. The Tay Son brothers, whose historical name comes from their native village, after gaining control in the south, marched northward and united north and south Viet-Nam.

If the era of colonial rule in Asia is still too recent to lend itself to proper evaluation, one fact at least seems clear in regard to Viet-Nam. The Third Republic committed a cardinal error when it failed to realize that Viet-Nam was by far the most advanced member of its colonial empire, and did not take the decisive political and economic steps necessary to give that highly civilized people a special status which could have led to some sort of free association between Viet-Nam and France. Nor were the historic economic problems of Viet-Nam solved by the colonial system which, according to the classic pattern, was grounded on the export of raw materials and the import of manufactured goods; all trade and banking were in foreign hands, both French and Chinese, as were the few local industries which were permitted to develop. In central Viet-Nam, where the superficial forms of the traditional administration were allowed to continue, some members of the mandarinate struggled to preserve even a little of the substance of freedom from the incursions of the colonial regime; and in 1916 the courageous young Emperor Duy Tan led an abortive revolt against the colonial administration. He was sent into exile and replaced by Khai Dinh, a hand-picked candidate of the colonial regime. It was the latter's son who became the Emperor Bao Dai.

The Vietnamese population never really accepted colonial rule; that is the evidence of the variety of nationalistic outbreaks, all more or less quickly repressed, which characterized the colonial period. Nationalist leaders faced the problem of translating this popular anticolonial feeling into effective political action, and to do so they needed a drastic change in the international situation. For this, they had to wait until the outbreak of World War II. Only then did the colonial administration, which was cut off from France and thrown on its own resources, alter in some degree the tightness of its control; and in March, 1945, the Japanese brought that control to an abrupt end by taking over the country outright.

The Vietnamese were not deceived by the Japanese proclamation of the "independence" of Viet-Nam, which came too late to be of any practical use and, in any case, was limited largely to words. However, they were more than ready to exploit the opportunity created by the overthrow of the French administration. They waited only for the Allied defeat of Japan to declare, in September, 1945, the independence of Viet-Nam.

In the early flush of national freedom, Bao Dai was frightened into abdicating unconditionally in favor of the new revolutionary regime headed by the Viet-Minh leader, Ho Chi Minh. After the outbreak of war with the Vietnamese late in 1946, the French decided to take advantage of the former emperor's weakness of character and to bring him back as Chief of State of an opposition regime, which was established in 1949. Bao Dai's total inability to assume leadership of the nationalist movement at this late date was not due wholly to his own personality; it was made inevitable by the refusal of the still powerful colonial administrators, along with certain other influential Frenchmen, to allow his government any real independence. As a result, the attempt made by these men to use Bao Dai to split the resistance ended in failure. The fighting lasted for eight years, terminating in the battle of Dien Bien Phu. Its consequences extended beyond Southeast Asia into France itself, where the effects of the long frustrating Vietnamese war are still being felt.

In Viet-Nam the end of the war, far from ending Western influence in this part of the world, signaled the rebirth of a vigorous, independent nation, one place in Southeast Asia where an ancient and firmly established civilization has welcomed and assimilated many of the elements of Western culture. For example, French cultural influence, now that it is no longer associated with colonial rule, is assuming a new vitality. And in the field of religion, the Catholic faith is prospering among more than a million Vietnamese now that it is no longer regarded as a means of Western penetration. Perhaps most remarkable of all, and certainly of particular significance for the future, is the emergence of an elite highly qualified in the field of science and technology. That elite, on which the Viet-Minh had relied so heavily for technical help during the first, national front period of the resistance, can now turn its efforts to the peaceful development of Viet-Nam. A recent survey of the number and quality of scientific contributions ranks the Republic of Viet-Nam, despite its small population, directly after Japan and India. If only for that one reason, this courageous and dynamic people is entitled to substantial and continuous aid from abroad, in all domains. The contribution to science and culture to be made by the people of the Republic of Viet-Nam, along with the other nations of Asia, is the more indispensable in a century when some counterbalance to the scientific and technological development of Communist China must be found by the Free World.

II. The Miracle of Viet-Nam

JOSEPH BUTTINGER[5]

WHEN THE REPUBLIC of Viet-Nam was created in July, 1954, even friendly and hopeful observers said that the new nation could not last for more than two years. So strong was the belief of its early demise that its existence today is frequently referred to as a political miracle—as if the survival of this new state were not so much an unexpected as an essentially inexplicable event.

To speak of this event as a political miracle would be misleading if no effort were made to relate the existence of a non-Communist Viet-Nam to the circumstances and forces that determine the course of present-day history. The survival of Free Viet-Nam, one of the major contemporary political developments, is far from being a closed subject. Not only does it touch upon issues as painfully alive as the ongoing struggle between the Western colonial powers and the restless people they still rule; it is also closely related to present Russian and Chinese attempts to draw all economically underdeveloped countries into the Communist camp. Indeed, the "miracle of Viet-Nam" may turn into one of the West's brief political consolations if it is not understood what brought it about.

What led to the Geneva Conference and made France, after waging eight years of an ugly and costly war, accept the loss of Indochina? Is it true that the Communist-led Viet-Minh armies had become unbeatable, and the Communist movement irresistible, by the time the great powers agreed to settle the Indochina war? Correct answers to these questions will go far toward explaining why the regime set up in Free Viet-Nam was expected to be overthrown as soon as the Communist leaders should decide to give the signal. Luckily, post-Geneva developments went contrary to this sad prognosis. So far Americans and the Western world have been spared another one of the disasters on which their political defeatism has been feeding ever since the end of World War II. But if this "miracle of Viet-Nam" is to become a permanent gain for the Vietnamese people, the circumstances that made it possible must be known and the forces and policies that produced it must be understood.

The bewildering spectacle of Indochina before the Geneva Conference will long remain a rich source of historical controversy, but there will probably always be general agreement about one important point: At the beginning of the Indochina war, in December, 1946, the French, with less than fifty thousand men, were stronger than they were seven years later when they had at their disposal a total of over 400,000 European, African, and Vietnamese soldiers. The steady decline in French military

---

[5] Author of *The Smaller Dragon: A Political History of Vietnam* (Praeger, 1958).

effectiveness was borne out by the whole course of the war, but it was brought to light only in the spring of 1954, during the famous battle of Dien Bien Phu, which, through Communist political strategy, will forever remain associated with the Geneva Conference and the birth of the new state of Free Viet-Nam.

More important, however, than to recognize France's deteriorating military position is to know what caused this fatal trend. It was neither lack of troops nor insufficiency of equipment. In numbers of regular army units and modern arms, the French were greatly superior to the Viet-Minh.[6] Their military weakness had purely political reasons: the unrelenting hostility of the whole people for the French, expressed either in lack of co-operation or in active support of the Viet-Minh. And co-operation of the people was indispensable to success. In this respect, all advantages were on the side of the Viet-Minh, who, through the ubiquity of their armed agents, were able to extract co-operation even from people who wished they had never seen a Viet-Minh guerrilla near their homes.

One notable item of evidence for French military weakness prior to the fall of Dien Bien Phu is a slender book by the French journalist, Robert Guillain. Largely a day-to-day account of the fateful battle, this report outweighs everything written on the subject before or after.[7] To his dispatches from Hanoi, Saigon, and Luang Prabang (the capital of Laos), Guillain added a few uncensored articles, written in Paris, in which he pleaded for a compromise peace with the Viet-Minh before all should be lost. The book is written in the vivid style of reports based on direct experience, deeply felt and immediately communicated, and it is as informative and exciting today as its separate articles must have been to the French newspaper readers during the tragic weeks of the Dien Bien Phu battle in 1954.

In one of his dispatches Guillain describes how difficult it was for the French to find and destroy, all over the country, the rice kept by the Viet-Minh in secret depots, so that they would have a food supply for their guerrillas and regular troops wherever they chose to send them into action. Frequently, the French had a clue as to the location of these depots, but they rarely found, among the many who knew, the one man who would act as informer. If they were lucky enough to discover the rice, their problem was still not solved. Rice in large quantities makes a poor fuel, and no amount of gasoline or napalm makes sure that it will all burn. The fire, Guillain writes, "sometimes goes out, which means

[6] Although the Viet-Minh was absorbed by the Lien-Viet in May, 1946, the term Viet-Minh is still in general use. It shall be used here to designate both the Communist-controlled movement and the regime headed by Ho Chi Minh.

[7] Robert Guillain, *La Fin des Illusions,* Centre d'Études de Politique Étrangère, Paris, 1954.

that the enemy could recuperate part of his provisions. One of the best means of destruction is to slaughter a buffalo on the heap, to let its blood run over the rice and to leave the perished animal on it. But one does not always have the time . . . nor the buffalo."[8]

The whole drama of the Indochina war—human, military, and political —is reflected in this brief book. In the midst of a people living for years on the edge of starvation, a major concern of the French was the destruction of food. The people's lack of co-operation, however, thwarted most measures designed to embarrass the Viet-Minh, whom the French could no longer stop from attacking at almost any place in the country. However, no matter what Guillain and other perplexed reporters may have written about this united national front of Vietnamese noninformers, it did not rest on any love of the Vietnamese for the Communists. The Communists did not really expect the peasants, who make up 80 percent of this people, to believe in communism. For their part, the peasants would have remained unaffected by Communist propaganda had they been exposed to it. Ho Chi Minh, however, had already put a stop to Communist party propaganda before 1945: The only avowed aim of the Viet-Minh was national independence, established through a victory of the "Democratic Republic of Viet-Nam" over the French.

To defeat the French and achieve national independence was an aim on which, with very few exceptions, all Vietnamese agreed; even those who hated the Viet-Minh could not but sympathize with this cause. Standing between the two armed parties, a helpless victim of their equally ruthless methods of warfare, the Vietnamese peasant was neither indifferent nor impartial. He had love for neither, feared them both, but practiced a passive solidarity with the Viet-Minh, who were after all compatriots at war with the peasants' oldest and most easily identifiable enemy: armed foreigners on Vietnamese soil.

The Geneva Conference resulted after the French, who at last perceived their hopeless military position, told their Western allies, while their army was being besieged at Dien Bien Phu, that they were no longer able to carry on the Indochina war. Nothing illustrates better how far the position of the French had deteriorated than a description of the siege, battle, and fall of Dien Bien Phu.

Dien Bien Phu, a village in a small valley surrounded by densely wooded mountains, was occupied by the French army on November 26, 1953.[9] The French moved into Dien Bien Phu to threaten the flank of

[8] Guillain, *op. cit.*, p. 22.
[9] It is interesting to note that Prince Henri d'Orléans in his book *Autour du Tonkin* remarked sixty years before these events that the post of Dien Bien Phu had no strategic value.

strong Viet-Minh forces marching from Tonkin (the north, where the French still held most of the populated delta) toward upper Laos. They hoped to stop Nguyen Van Giap, Ho Chi Minh's leading general, who apparently intended to storm Luang Prabang. A Japanese-built airstrip at Dien Bien Phu enabled the French to fly in their troops, equipment, and supplies. Ten thousand crack soldiers quickly transformed the place into a seemingly impregnable fortress. Men and officers alike looked forward to the day when the Viet-Minh forces would attack, confident that they would repulse and subsequently destroy them in the first great open battle of the war.

As expected, the Viet-Minh stopped before Dien Bien Phu on their way to Laos and surrounded the fortress, but did not attack. They dug in and soon increased their numbers to an estimated 30,000-40,000, looking down on and aiming their Chinese-supplied artillery at their enemies, while remaining invisible themselves even during the few hours when French air observation was not obstructed by long daily fogs.

The French were greatly surprised when the Viet-Minh, instead of launching the attack expected on January 25, 1954, and without lifting the siege of Dien Bien Phu, resumed their invasion of Laos by marching with one of their best divisions toward Luang Prabang. General Navarre, the French Supreme Commander, lacked both the men and the means to stop Giap's threat to the capital of Laos. With his best troops tied down in Dien Bien Phu and others engaged in an ill-conceived operation in central Viet-Nam, Navarre could never have prevented the fall of Luang Prabang had the Viet-Minh really wanted to take it. When Giap's troops had almost reached their pretended aim, he suddenly ordered them to return and rejoin his contingents around Dien Bien Phu.

There the French soldiers and officers became daily more restless, waiting for the inevitable battle. It started, after an unexpectedly heavy barrage by Viet-Minh artillery, on the evening of March 13, but was mysteriously called off on March 15, after the two most horrible nights of the Indochina war.

It was then that the French, full of premonition, suddenly realized the extent of their military plight, to deny which had long been a condition for their continuing the struggle. It was now too late to listen to General Cogny, who had protested the "folly" of concentrating the cream of the army and the best of its equipment at an isolated point in the mountains, three hundred miles from their supply bases. Cogny had said Dien Bien Phu would lose Tonkin for the French, "and the loss of Tonkin means that all will be lost." But General Navarre, when he sent his best troops to Dien Bien Phu, had had the backing of Paris, where the real situation was unknown—because of military censorship and the ability for self-deception common to discomposed military and political leaders, and always greatest just before some disaster reveals the truth.

"The fate of the whole Indochina war is at stake at Dien Bien Phu," wrote Guillain on March 16. The French brought in a battalion of parachute troops, poured a deluge of napalm on the invisible Viet-Minh positions, even counterattacked once, and dug new and deeper trenches in anticipation of the next Viet-Minh blow. But the enemy remained strangely inactive. Only antiaircraft guns, another weapon received from the Chinese, continued to interfere with the efforts of the French to supply their encircled troops.

The Viet-Minh were apparently unaware of the fact, revealed later by the French themselves, that Dien Bien Phu would have fallen on March 16 if they had kept up their attacks for another day. Had their heavy losses broken their offensive power? Or was Viet-Minh military action subordinated to Russian and Chinese action in the diplomatic field, where the outcome of the Indochina war would be decided and was, in fact, already being prepared? The Geneva Conference, agreed upon by the Big Four in Berlin, met on April 26. Hell was let loose again at Dien Bien Phu during the opening sessions of the conference, and the fortress was overwhelmed and taken on May 8, precisely the day on which, in Geneva, the discussion on Indochina began.

If the fall of Dien Bien Phu had left the slightest hope for the notorious "final victory" predicted at every previous moment of crisis, the French would probably have tried to continue the Indochina war. But the blow they had suffered, apart from reducing their strength, had broken their will. Dien Bien Phu thus opened the way for a political solution of the Indochina struggle.

The chances for such a solution had been seriously debated ever since Ho Chi Minh, in an interview with a Swedish newspaperman on November 29, 1953, had announced that he was willing to start peace negotiations. But only weeks before the Geneva Conference, in March, 1954, the French had made one further attempt to bring about a favorable military decision. They had asked the United States to intervene directly in the Indochina war. This request had divided not only the United States and England, but also had split Washington into two opposing camps. However, those who demanded that the American Air Force and Navy prevent a Communist victory in Indochina—Vice President Nixon, Admiral Radford, Senator Knowland, and apparently also Secretary of State Dulles—were blocked by Congress when Churchill and Eden emphatically stated that England would not go along.

The near-collapse of the French army after the fall of Dien Bien Phu precipitated the evolution of Western policy toward positions that no longer threatened the compromise solution envisaged soon after the Geneva Conference had been agreed upon by the Big Four. In France, the government of Laniel-Bidault was replaced by one formed by

Mendès-France, expressly for the purpose of bringing the fighting in Indochina to a quick end. For the sake of peace, France was apparently getting ready to accept the loss of her "richest colony." This meant that it was willing not only to let the Communists harvest their substantial gains but also to grant genuine independence to whatever regions of Indochina could be prevented from falling into Communist hands. The United States, although opposed to the compromise that began to take shape in Geneva, had dropped the illusion that all could still be saved by reverting to the catastrophic French notion of settling the matter by force. To save the entire country from communism at this stage was possible only by means that would have destroyed the whole Vietnamese people, together with their buffaloes and rice. It would have required the razing of all inhabited places, as every village and town was infested by well-armed Viet-Minh guerrillas.

Communist strength forced the West into accepting a compromise through which the world's scarred political landscape was defaced once again by the creation of two violently opposed political regimes for one and the same nation. The compromise was concluded not only between France and the Viet-Minh, but also—and this in spite of United States reservations—between the combined powers of the East and West. But whereas the Communists, as a result of the military situation, gained the whole northern half of the country and *de facto* recognition of their regime, the people in the southern half could now look forward to the day when political independence ceased being a mere fraud. Western opinion, French political evolution, and, almost paradoxically, American political firmness, by helping to make Vietnamese independence a reality, had at last also created the conditions under which the anti-Communist wing of Vietnamese nationalism could become a dominant political force.

Opinions may differ as to the role played by Western policy in the unexpected survival of an anti-Communist regime in south Viet-Nam. But in order to check the danger of a Communist-fostered collapse, considerable strength was required in south Viet-Nam itself, a strength that was not military but political and of a decidedly nationalist and anti-Communist complexion. The revival of anti-Communist nationalism as an active and preponderant element in Viet-Nam's political life is indeed the main reason why the Communists failed to conquer the south.

Because it saved the south, this unhoped-for upsurge of forces long thought of as either moribund or extinct must be regarded as a turning point in the modern history of Viet-Nam. The Communist project, embodied in the Geneva Agreement, had been to complete the victory they had won in war through a peacetime annexation of the south. They had every reason to believe that Geneva had settled the fate of the whole country. After Dien Bien Phu the Communists did not feel compelled to make concessions likely to spoil their hard-won success. All they conceded to the French was to let them save face and salvage their armies. The French knew this as well as the Viet-Minh, as was shown by their post-Geneva policy, which for almost a year was based on the view that Geneva had given to the Bao Dai state only a short lease on life. But anti-Communist nationalism, gathering strength while removing the remnants of colonial power, transformed the feeble and disjointed state of Bao Dai into a unified and strong republic. It was this transformation that made the south invulnerable to propaganda and subversion from the north.

There can be no doubt that the Communists were as surprised over south Viet-Nam's obstinate refusal to collapse as were most pro-Western and "neutralist" observers. The triumphant propaganda of the Viet-Minh after Geneva had depicted the elimination of their opponents in the south as an almost accomplished fact. Had not the Viet-Minh suppressed, ever since 1945, all nationalist forces opposed to Communist leadership? Had not resistance to the French, and the glory derived from the military defeat of France, been a Viet-Minh monopoly? And had not what had once existed of anti-Communist nationalism committed political sucide by co-operating with the French under the odious regime of Bao Dai?

Not until the spring of 1956 did the Communists realize that something had gone wrong with their calculations. They were unable to pressure the south into holding the "elections" for unification promised, in the Final Declaration of the Geneva Conference, for July, 1956. What could their now irreparable error have been?

The tactical error of the Communists was not that they had agreed to withdraw their troops from the positons they had held in the south when the cease-fire was signed. They had counted on winning the south with political rather than military weapons. Their main mistake was that they had not foreseen the revival of political forces not subject to Viet-Minh control. The Communist leaders had counted on the French (and the United States) to continue the inglorious Western policy of pseudo-independence for Viet-Nam, a policy that had stymied all earlier attempts to take the cause of national independence away from the Viet-Minh. At Geneva the Viet-Minh had made their agreements only with the French; nothing at all was agreed upon between the Viet-Minh and the newly installed Saigon government of Premier Ngo Dinh Diem. Almost two years after Geneva, Hanoi still demanded that Paris see to it that the election agreement be honored, ignoring the fact that French rule had become as nonexistent in the south as in the north. It is true that colonialism fought a desperate rear guard action. Had it succeeded, this would have perpetuated the conditons under which anti-Communist nationalism had been unable to grow. But bold leadership in the south and United States support of true Vietnamese independence spoiled the Communist scheme. Independence permitted the forces of anti-Communist nationalism to march into the political arena and at last become a match for the Communist-led Viet-Minh.

Seen in this light, the course of recent Vietnamese history, along with its present results, loses some of the aspects that have puzzled so many observers. The events can be shown to conform to the universal pattern created by the conflicting historical tendencies of the present.

The secret of Communist success in Viet-Nam lies in the upsurge, after World War II, of the forces of a genuine national revolution. There is no way of understanding the Indochina war if one sees it only as a step in a Communist scheme to conquer the world. The forces on the Vietnamese side were not created by Communist propaganda. They were the product of history. The Communists merely recognized the unusual strength of these forces and knew how to use them to promote their own cause.

The strength of Vietnamese nationalism is rooted in both the ancient and the modern history of Viet-Nam. This history shows that Viet-Nam does not conform to the Western-made image of colonies as primitive countries unable to progress unless guided and protected by a more civilized nation of the West. The Viet-Nam of whose destinies France began to take charge in the 1800's was a country with a known history of over two thousand years. A Vietnamese state had already existed in the third century B.C. It was conquered by China, but before this event, the Vietnamese people had developed a separate culture and their own distinct way of life. The Chinese, whose higher civilization had spread early into the Red River Valley, ruled the Vietnamese for more than one thousand years, from 111 B.C. to A.D. 939.

Chinese domination is responsible for one strong and unfading component in the national mentality of the Vietnamese: their abhorrence of foreign rule. This deep-rooted attitude explains why the struggle for national independence became the main source of glory in the long history of Viet-Nam. Armed resistance to foreign rule derived its repute as an exalted national virtue from a long series of rebellions that ended in the expulsion of the Chinese, and from the many wars to prevent their return after independence was achieved.

Vietnamese national pride was deeply hurt when the country, between 1858 and 1883, again fell under foreign rule, after it had grown to twice its former size during the nine hundred years of independence. Long before the French started their protracted invasion, the Vietnamese had surpassed all other Indochinese peoples in numbers, and were still expanding their country's territory by their devotion to work and their ability to fight. Except for the more recent technical inventions brought forth by the development of modern Western science, the Vietnamese lacked none of the marks denoting an old civilization, and were in some respects more civilized than a number of nations in the West. Like their Chinese mentors, the educated Vietnamese of the nineteenth century called the Western intruders barbarians, a designation that French behavior during the twenty-five years of conquest and the subsequent fifteen years of pacification did little to contradict. It is significant that Vietnamese armed resistance during these forty years, and up to the end of the nineteenth century, was led chiefly by scholars, and that the names of these men are today celebrated with equal fervor in both parts of divided Viet-Nam.

The old resistance movements, inspired if not actually led by the scholars, were defeated, but the twentieth century had hardly gotten under way when it became evident that Vietnamese nationalism would lose nothing of its virulence as a consequence of the changes inaugurated by the colonial regime.

Some of the causes for this were beyond the control of the French. In spite of French precautions, Western ideas of social progress and political freedom spread among the Vietnamese and increased their awareness of their own miserable lot. Japan, by defeating Russia, had shown that Asia, through the adoption of Western science and technology, could in a short time become as strong as the West. The Chinese revolution influenced Vietnamese nationalism in a similar way: It increased the ranks of those who knew that success in the struggle for national freedom required a rapid modernization of thinking, and that old habits of mind and venerable institutions could hinder progress as effectively as most features of the colonial regime.

However, these developments abroad could give no more than additional inspiration to the fervent nationalism predominant in Viet-Nam. Its main well of strength was the colonial regime itself: the changes it produced in Vietnamese society, the prospects for a better life which it opened but was unwilling to advance, the unrelieved economic exploitation and its ugly twin, political repression. There is no doubt that economic progress was made under the colonial regime, but its speed, direction, and purpose were determined, and its benefits reaped, by the French, and, apart from some Chinese businessmen, by the small number of Vietnamese supporters of the French. The mass of the peasants owned too little land when the French took over; they owned even less when the colonial regime came to an end. Sixty-three percent of all taxpayers in the north were peasants without land. In the south, where land was abundant, three fourths of all peasants were landless. The surface of rice land has increased enormously under the French, but the new land was given to a class of Franco-Vietnamese landowners created by the colonial regime. More than half the nation lived in abject misery, always close to starvation. Impressive statistics showing that the colonial regime had raised the yearly rice exports from nothing to 1,500,000 tons neglected to mention that this was possible only because the peasants ate less than before. They were not permitted by the colonial regime to fight the great landowners, greedy moneylenders, profit-seeking merchants, and rice exporters for a small share in the country's increasing wealth.

Misery was coupled with humiliation. A largely literate country was transformed into one where 80 percent of the people could not read or write. The old Confucian scholars, who had been the intellectual and political leaders of Viet-Nam, were fated to disappear, but a modern scientific education was withheld from the Vietnamese for several decades, and later given only in poor quality and to ridiculously small numbers. In order to get the higher education to which they had always aspired, many young Vietnamese were forced to take the road of political exile. For a long time those who were able to complete their studies were excluded from most positions in the French-staffed administration. When more "liberal" policies led to a change, a Vietnamese professor or higher official had to be content with a smaller salary than the French help in his office or school.

The humiliation of the educated produced the new revolutionary leaders of Vietnamese nationalism. The wretched life of the peasants and later the misery of those who had become workers in mines and on plantations explain why the militant nationalists were always able to renew their attacks after every one of their many defeats.

When the growth of national consciousness in Asia began to make the anticolonial rebellion universal and irresistible, the French were given a golden opportunity—by the turn history took during World War II—to transform their colonial relationship to the Vietnamese people into one of democratic alliance beneficial to both sides. A look at Vietnamese history and at the evolution of nationalism in more recent times might have taught the French that such a people could not be held down forever. However, the men who governed France and commanded in Indochina were not the ones who had given to the world some insight into the history and the national charatcer of the Vietnamese. So the French insisted on returning to Indochina from which they had already been ousted by the Japanese. They decided to undertake the historically hopeless task of suppressing the movement for national liberation at the very moment when the people of Viet-Nam had in fact already been freed by the circumstances surrounding the end of the war.

Thus began the long struggle during which the Communists became the leading faction of the Vietnamese movement for national liberation.

There is nothing mysterious in the development of a Communist wing within the Vietnamese national movement. Anticolonial propaganda and action was organized by Moscow on a large scale soon after the Bolshevik revolution. After the Vietnamese Communists had adjusted their tactics to the existing historical situation, they did not appear as an alien force on the national scene. Their claim to fight only against economic misery and for national liberation could be doubted only by people with exceptional political insight or education. During the 1930's Moscow tactics began to favor the creation of united and popular fronts based on non-Communist programs. To the Vietnamese nationalists, the Communists could offer a vast store of experience in illegal politics. They provided badly needed training to young men whose sole qualification for revolutionary work was their good will. Many were sent to Moscow, others were schooled and used in China, where, ever since 1902, a large community of political exiles had formed various groups. Several nationalist factions were numerically stronger, but the Communists had more money for their organizations, more economic security for their leaders, and more international connections and support. Their Leninist recipe for tactics in colonies made it easy for them to adapt their propaganda and action to changing conditions quickly, as they did for instance in 1940, after the Japanese moved into Viet-Nam with Vichy-French consent. With all these advantages, the League for the Independence of Viet-Nam (Viet-Minh), which the Communists created in 1941, would have become a major group in the nationalist camp even without the support it later received from the Allies, at war with Japan.

The growth of the Viet-Minh was no doubt also partly due to the personality of the Communist leader, Ho Chi Minh, but it would be misleading to assume that he did more than exploit the conditions created by others for his extraordinary success. There was probably never a Communist, however, who played the role of nonpartisan national leader as well as Ho Chi Minh. His assets were his good temper, his personal inclinations, and even his physical appearance. An inborn feeling for the efficacy of friendliness, a natural desire to please, an ever-ready willingness to compensate with soothing words and pleasing gestures for the pain inflicted by action sums up his much-admired technique of political manipulation. His "kind eyes," his famous "openness," his apparently genuine distress whenever political necessity spoiled friendly personal relations, his fatherly concern for the well-being of the masses—all were honest with him, but were also consciously and effectively used to promote his party's aims. Ho Chi Minh would be a remarkable Communist in any situation, because he is a remarkable man; but how simple an "enigma" he becomes if judged only by his deeds. And how useless would all his talents in human relations have been if circumstances, historical

forces, and political opponents had not lent themselves to being exploited
by these well-proven means.

Nor can Communist strength in Viet-Nam be explained by the money
the Viet-Minh received from Nationalist China and by the American
equipment given them during the war against Japan. It had deeper and
infinitely less transparent reasons. The Communists rose to hegemony
because all powers involved in the affairs of Indochina after World War
II co-operated in the ruin of anti-Communist nationalism. The French,
the Chinese, and the Japanese promoted the Viet-Minh cause by active
interference, and Americans, on whom so much of the world's future
depended at that time, did so through ignorance and by default.

Some of the forces harmful to non-Communist nationalism in Viet-
Nam have succeeded in remaining historically anonymous to this very
day. For a long time after the war it would indeed have been difficult to
prove the thesis that Japanese, Chinese, and French policy makers in
Viet-Nam prepared the ground for all the Viet-Minh victories. Yet this
was the combined effect of their variously motivated actions, almost as
if they had plotted the ruin of all parties opposed to the Viet-Minh.

The role of the Japanese is in particular need of reappraisal in any
attempt to describe the circumstances in which the Viet-Minh were able
to come to power in August, 1945. After having tolerated the French
administration for more than four years, the Japanese, on March 9, 1945,
suddenly disarmed and interned all French troops and dismissed the
entire French administration. This, and their apparent promotion of a
Vietnamese national government, were naturally interpreted as a final
and well-calculated blow against French power in Viet-Nam. But why
did the Japanese refuse to bring Prince Cuong De, who had been their
candidate for a Vietnamese government for several decades, from Japan?
Why did they prevent the appointment of Ngo Dinh Diem, whom the
Vietnamese themselves wanted to head their first administration not
dominated by the French? And why, after a government was formed in
April at the old imperial capital, Hue, did the Japanese see to it that it
did not become effective? They withheld from it all means of communication, they denied it the necessary minimum of arms, and they interfered
with its freedom of action. The whole south, for example, where most
of the wealth of Viet-Nam was concentrated, was directly administered
by the Japanese until a few days before their capitulation.

The government of Tran Trong Kim has been wrongly described as
a tool of the Japanese. The men who formed it were genuine nationalists
whose chief and immediate concern was the welfare of the Vietnamese
people. But Tran Trong Kim and his team aimed also at having the
foundation for total independence laid by the time the generally expected

Japanese collapse occurred. Bao Dai himself lived then through one of his brief periods of serious political endeavor. The Hue government could certainly have used a few stronger and politically more gifted men, but the main reason for its failure was that it lacked the means to realize its immediate objectives. The Japanese were obviously not interested in promoting Vietnamese independence; if this had been the purpose of their move of March 9, 1945, they would have made sure that a functioning Vietnamese administration supported by an adequate army existed before the French could attempt to return.

The action that the Japanese took against the French only a few months before their surrender had other motives. One was their fear of being at the mercy of the French in their own hour of defeat. By the spring of 1945 most Frenchmen in Indochina were already leaning toward the Free French, whose agents began to move into Viet-Nam from their headquarters in southern China; those Vichy-French in Viet-Nam who had the blackest record of collaboration with the Japanese were naturally most eager to rehabilitate themselves by demanding drastic measures against the Japanese. The Japanese were well aware of the danger that this attitude constituted for them. But fear of French revenge was not the only reason why they disarmed and interned the French army before the war came to the anticipated end. By holding on to the essence of power, the Japanese, far from making Vietnamese independence a post-war *fait accompli,* meant, on the contrary, to keep the door open for whatever arrangements the Allies would make in regard to Viet-Nam, including the possible restoration of the evicted colonial regime.

One immediate effect of their policy was a rapid deterioration of the Hue government's authority and morale; another, a political deflation of all nationalist leaders and organizations that had collaborated with the Japanese. The Cao Dai sect was by far the strongest among the few groups whom the Japanese had persuaded that one of their aims was an independent Viet-Nam. But pro-Japanese sentiment had always been weak among the Vietnamese, most of whom knew that the Japanese had cultivated Vietnamese nationalism not for its own sake but only to serve the interests of Japan. The visible decline of Japanese power in 1945, together with the double-faced Japanese policy in Viet-Nam, increased the authority of those who had opposed the Japanese from the beginning. Independence was not expected to result from the victory of Japan, in which no one any longer believed, nor from the help the Japanese would still be able to give the Vietnamese nationalists before the old colonial regime could be reinstated. In the summer of 1945 independence was universally expected to result from the rapidly approaching Allied victory.

This attitude of the Vietnamese was naively expressed by Emperor Bao Dai himself, who privately announced his intention to hold a great feast the very day Japan went down. *"On va tuer le porc"*—"we shall slaughter a pig"—was the expression he used. Bao Dai could hardly wait for the moment when the first American soldier would land on Vietnamese soil. Japan's defeat would reveal to the world that the independence of Viet-Nam had become an historical reality. In the eyes of the Vietnamese, the colonial regime had definitely come to an end. Besides, whatever claim the French may have had was extinct since they had been unable to protect the country from being exploited for the Japanese war effort. True, Bao Dai's declaration of independence in March had found no more than a negative response by the provisional French government in London, and his desperate pleas in August to the world's political and spiritual authorities for support of a free Viet-Nam were completely ignored. But the war aim of the Allies, all Vietnamese felt, excluded a return to the old colonial conditions, even if France tried to stop history's inexorable course. The United States, the great champion of a Free World, would make sure that freedom's imminent triumph was not spoiled by continual lack of freedom for Viet-Nam.

These high expectations were cruelly smashed. President Roosevelt's idea of paving the way for Vietnamese independence by replacing French rule with an international trusteeship was dropped when he died. The Potsdam Conference agreed on an Allied occupation of Viet-Nam, with British in the south, Chinese in the north—but only to disarm the Japanese and to maintain order until the French could return.

While the government of Tran Trong Kim fought desperately to bring the country under its administrative and political control before the Allies arrived, the Viet-Minh, with allied support, stepped up their sabotage and guerrilla attacks against the Japanese. In one appeal after another they asked the people to destroy the "Japanese fascists" and to take the future of Viet-Nam into their own hands. In the far north, near the Chinese border, where Japanese control was weak, the Viet-Minh were able to create several "liberated zones." On August 7, the day after the bomb was dropped on Hiroshima, they baptized their guerrillas "Army of Liberation." For the same day Ho Chi Minh had called a National Congress to elect a Viet-Minh controlled "Committee for the Liberation of the Vietnamese People." On August 10 the Communist leaders ordered a general insurrection in Viet-Nam.

But their well-advertised activity and clever scheming to outstrip their nationalist opponents would never have succeeded if they had not also accomplished one of the century's greatest feats of political deception. Ever since they had founded the Viet-Minh in 1941, the Vietnamese Communists had presented it not only as a suprapartisan national front, but also as one standing firmly in the Allied camp. What they said and did was determined by their two main propaganda objectives. One was to persuade the Allies that the Viet-Minh was the only group capable of doing damage to the Japanese army, the other was to convince the Vietnamese people that of all the nationalists active in exile the Allies recognized and supported only the Viet-Minh.

With this propaganda the Viet-Minh did surprisingly well with the Allies. The Chinese supported them with money, the Americans with arms, and the French by releasing many Vietnamese Communists imprisoned in other French colonial territories. But Viet-Minh propaganda succeeded even better with the Vietnamese people, who considered Allied support essential to the liberation of Viet-Nam. It was evident that the hamstrung Vietnamese government at Hue enjoyed no such support; the Allies probably regarded it only as an instrument of Japanese policy. The Viet-Minh had convinced the people that they were the party of the Allies long before American officers publicly fraternized with them in Hanoi. Most Vietnamese felt that they would certainly fare better with leaders who had consistently fought the Japanese and had sided with the victors from the beginning when the war came to an end. It was under the pressure of these sentiments that the discouraged government of Tran Trong Kim gave up its hopeless struggle shortly after the Viet-Minh appeared legally on the Vietnamese national scene.

The Viet-Minh started their lightning campaign to exploit the pro-Allied sentiments of the people on August 17, 1945, only two days after the surrender of Japan. The population of Hanoi and other cities were given a daily opportunity to express these sentiments in huge demonstrations. The many powerful currents of joy, hope, and determination released by the end of the war all swelled the Viet-Minh tide. In less than a week the Communists had put their hands on the entire Tonkin administration. All over the country, people demanded a government by the men who promised to get the victorious Allies behind the cause of Vietnamese freedom. At Hue even the emperor and his entourage were swept off their feet. On August 22 Bao Dai asked Ho Chi Minh to form a new national government, and on August 24 he gave up his throne to make way for the Communist-inspired "Democratic Republic of Viet-Nam."

The nationalist leaders who were aware of the Viet-Minh's true political character were quite helpless against this tide. Whatever opposition the Viet-Minh encountered was denounced as hostility to the Allies, co-operation with the Japanese, a breach of the existing national unity, and a threat to the cause of Vietnamese independence. The prevailing political climate made it impossible to prove that the Viet-Minh leaders were pursuing other than their loudly proclaimed objectives. Many of the leading nationalists knew what went on in the "liberated zones," where the tragedy of a Communist-dominated Viet-Nam was already being rehearsed. But they had learned that, for them, the Viet-Minh was a more dangerous enemy than the French had ever been. To silence their opponents, the Communists employed not only their public cheerleaders but also their secret assassins.

However, only a look at the foreign powers that were politically engaged in Viet-Nam can fully reveal why all the strong winds of the moment blew into the sails of the Viet-Minh. The Japanese, after their surrender to the Allies, openly began to support Vietnamese independence precisely when their change of policy could only favor Ho Chi Minh. Their army remained helpfully neutral while the Communists took power and drove all other nationalists from the streets of Hanoi. The Japanese had done nothing to strengthen the anti-Communist government at Hue between March and August; now they did nothing to weaken the Communist-dominated government at Hanoi. On the contrary, they helped it by handing over the arms of the old Indochinese guard to the Viet-Minh.

The anti-Communist parties fared even worse with the Chinese Nationalists, who were generally regarded as their supporters and friends. It is true that the Viet-Minh tide was temporarily stemmed when the Chinese armies of occupation arrived in Viet-Nam. But for cash and gold supplied by the Viet-Minh, Chiang Kai-shek's generals soon betrayed their Vietnamese allies, and China itself, after concluding a most advantageous treaty with France, no longer supported the cause of Vietnamese independence. When the Chinese agreed to evacuate the north in the spring of 1946, thereby removing the last obstacle for a return of the French, the stage was set for the great Franco-Vietnamese duel. Through what seemed like a conspiracy of blind circumstances and conscious action, the fate of anti-Communist nationalism, and with it the future of Viet-Nam, was now determined by the forces least qualified to promote political freedom and national independence: communism and colonialism.

From the beginning, these two intransigent antagonists had one common aim: to weaken and, if possible, destroy the non-Communist parties of Vietnamese nationalism; the Viet-Minh, because this was a condition for the continuance of Communist rule; the French, because the non-Communist nationalists were as violently opposed to their return as were the Viet-Minh and, in addition, more likely than the Communist to get China, then still ruled by the nationalists, to support the cause of Vietnamese independence.

When the French, in September, 1945, opened their struggle against the Vietnamese national revolution by using force against the new Vietnamese regime in the south, they did not in the least pretend that their aim was to keep communism out of the country. Their undisguised purpose was to reinstate themselves in their former position, and they would have acted as they did even if no Communist had existed in Viet-Nam. They would, of course, have preferred to do in Hanoi exactly as they had done in Saigon, but the north, unlike the south where the French had been reinstated by the British army of occupation, was occupied by the Chinese, who, although they did not like the Viet-Minh, strongly sympathized with the Vietnamese national revolution. As long as the Chinese remained in Viet-Nam, the French could not risk entering the north by force.

Because Chinese support for a non-Communist government at the head of the Vietnamese revolution might have prevented their return to the north forever, the French preferred a Vietnamese government controlled by the Viet-Minh and at odds with China. A pro-Chinese government, from fear of the French, would probably have induced the Chinese to stay on another year. And even after the French had paid off China with the agreement of February 28, 1946, their scheme of returning through a deal with the Vietnamese would have failed if Hanoi had had a government backed by Chiang Kai-shek's China, instead of one determined to eliminate all parties allied to the Chinese. The sympathy of the Chinese for the cause of Vietnamese independence and their desire to help the parties opposed to the Viet-Minh thus explain the apparent anomaly that the French and the Viet-Minh, although engaged in a mortal struggle against each other, nevertheless co-operated against the Chinese and their Vietnamese allies up to and even beyond December, 1946, when they jointly unleashed the Indochina war.

What the French gained by this policy was easy to see. Viet-Minh persecution of the pro-Chinese parties immobilized large numbers of uncompromising enemies of the French, reduced the danger of Chinese support for the "Democratic Republic of Viet-Nam," and freed Ho Chi Minh's hands for the agreement of March 6, 1946, through which he permitted the French, in exchange for a qualified recognition of his Communist-dominated regime, to move an army into north Viet-Nam.

The return of the French army to the north was a frightful blow to Vietnamese freedom. It cleared the way for the French to extend their policy of reconquering Viet-Nam by force to the north; it was also the main reason why the Indochina war became unavoidable. But the cause closest to Ho Chi Minh's heart, which was the victory of his party, did not suffer at all from the return of the French army to the north. On the contrary, the deal of March, 1946, between the French and the Communists was as much a condition for the eventual triumph of Vietnamese communism as was the treaty of Brest-Litovsk for the victory of the Bolshevik revolution.

Ho Chi Minh, like the Frenchmen with whom he concluded his hazardous agreement, always knew that there would be a final Franco-

Vietnamese showdown by force. Rather than avoiding this showdown, his policy aimed at securing a Communist monopoly of leadership for the time when the inevitable clash would occur. The alternative to this course would have been to secure Chinese support for Vietnamese independence, which would have required concessions to the pro-Chinese nationalists that excluded a Communist-dominated regime both in peace and in war. As long as the Chinese remained in the country, the Viet-Minh were always in danger of being forced by them into doing what fear of the French could not induce them to do: give up their monopoly of power. Rather than share power with their nationalist opponents, the Viet-Minh risked being ousted by the French, confident that the ensuing war, which they knew might last five to ten years, would end with a French defeat. Ho Chi Minh preferred a war-torn Viet-Nam to one not controlled by his party, and a long war for independence under Communist leadership to a short struggle led by the opponents of the Viet-Minh. After the war had begun, the Communists fought fiercely for national independence, but only because they believed that their efforts would produce a Communist Viet-Nam.

As the war went on, it became evident that the strategy of the Communists prior to the outbreak of the war had been superior to the strategy of the French. The Communists were now safely installed at the head of a great movement of national resistance, which the French had mistakenly expected to suppress in a short time. The Viet-Minh succeeded in mobilizing the best energies of the Vietnamese people, while the French, contrary to their predictions, faced not a handful of Communist rebels but an entire nation, openly or secretly devoted to the cause of national liberation, which in this century no longer succumbs to greater military force. This is indeed the key to the entire problem: no matter how much the struggle for Indochina developed into a war against Indochinese communism, supported by Moscow and later also by Peiping, it still remained to the very end also a war against the national aspirations of the peoples of Viet-Nam, Cambodia, and Laos.

For this reason alone, all later French efforts to win Vietnamese support against the Communist-led Viet-Minh were doomed in advance. No nationalist leader could co-operate with the French without being considered a traitor to his country's political independence. The various Bao Dai governments after 1949 remained totally ineffective, because the actions of the French continued to reveal their real intentions—to hold on to their colonial privileges—even after France had promised full freedom for Viet-Nam as soon as the war was won.

French policy, determined by small groups with strong interests and narrow views, never cleared the ground on which the loudly demanded bastion of Vietnamese anti-communism could have been erected. Men such as Ngo Dinh Diem would have acted long before Geneva had not action for them, under French auspices, been so manifestly identical with political suicide. They opposed communism as much as, if not more than, the French. Their severely criticized *attentisme* (attitude of waiting) was said to have been the reason why they were politically ineffective. But they were inactive not because they were neutral, and they were ineffective not because they did not act—much of their "waiting" was done in Communist and French prisons or in exile; "waiting" was not their position of choice. Under the conditions of national unfreedom perpetuated by the French, it was all they could do. Those who were active under the tutelage of the French not only discredited and further weakened the nationalist groups opposed to the Viet-Minh; they also reduced the chances of anti-Communist nationalism to become effective in the future.

The French, because they could not arrest the steady growth of Viet-Minh power either by military or political means, would have collapsed long before the spring of 1954 if diplomacy and propaganda, for the sake of preventing another victory for communism in the Far East, had not prevailed upon the United States to support their cause, already widely recognized as hopeless.

Of American policy in Indochina up to Bao Dai's reinvestiture by the French in 1949, the best one could say was that it did not exist. It began to take shape while the Chinese Communists completed their victory over Nationalist China, intervened in Korea, and decisively strengthened the Viet-Minh through massive military aid. These events, combined with the negative results of French policy in Viet-Nam, produced the situation that eventually led to Dien Bien Phu and Geneva, but not without first having enabled the French to obtain enough American support to continue the Indochina war for another three years. The French were now at last in a position to denounce all attacks on their policy in Indochina as aid and comfort to the forces that stood for a Communist Viet-Nam. Thus, when Washington finally became active in the affairs of Indochina, the policy it adopted was not American but French.[10]

There had been no lack of American good intentions toward Viet-Nam, even if no real policy, before Washington became overwhelmed by the complexity of the problem of how French colonialism could be repudiated without increasing the much-discussed danger of a Communist advance, via Indochina, into the entire Southeast Asian world. United States leaders, whether Democratic or Republican, have on the whole disliked what the French did in Indochina, but a policy based on such sentiments

[10] The United States recognized the French-sponsored state of Bao Dai on February 7, 1950.

never developed beyond the embryonic stage of expressions of sympathy for the French-controlled Indochinese countries, and it survived after 1950 only in the form of a bad conscience over United States support for the French and their Indochina war. No serious attempt was ever made, under either Secretary of State Dean Acheson or John Foster Dulles, to get France to grant independence to Viet-Nam, Cambodia, and Laos as a condition of American aid, although it was clear that without this aid the French could not have continued the war beyond 1952. With what amounted to almost intentional ignorance, Washington said it was satisfied with the French formula of "Independence within the French Union"—equating the French Union with the British Commonwealth, as if the French Union had been created in order to free the French colonies and not for the purpose of keeping them within the old colonial French empire.[11]

Once engaged in the affairs of Indochina, Washington was always eager to strengthen Vietnamese nationalism against the Communists, and was sometimes even inclined to strengthen it against the French. Unfortunately, ignorance of, and indifference toward, Indochina had made America miss the great hour in which it could have solved the problem of Viet-Nam, saved France a hopeless war, and spared the West a peace that was to become a Communist triumph. The cause that Americans later desired to support in Viet-Nam had made its appearance in 1945, under the anti-Communist government at Hue, which preceded the Communist-led government at Hanoi. But Americans were unaware of the fact that this government, at least in August, 1945, represented the cause of the West: They never knew that its life or death depended on their action. And they still have not recognized that their indifference in 1945—when they decided so much by deciding nothing—was as great an element in the emerging drama as were French blindness and Communist deceit. Then and later, they permitted a militant Vietnamese nationalism to perish under the combined blows of the Communists and the French, trying vainly to revive it during the four years preceding Dien Bien Phu, sometimes suspecting, but never fully realizing that the cause they intended to support could be reborn only when both the substance and semblance of French rule had vanished from Viet-Nam.

This had long been the contention of a man whom the French and the Communists hated with equal passion, Ngo Dinh Diem, today's President of the Republic of Viet-Nam. The crisis that led to the Geneva

[11] In May, 1950, Dean Acheson said that Viet-Nam, Cambodia, and Laos are now "enjoying independence within the French Union." John Foster Dulles used the same words in July, 1953.

Agreement tossed Ngo Dinh Diem from political exile into the premiership of the emerging non-Communist state.

After the dramatic interlude of American flirtation with force, in March and April, 1954, the evolution of Western policy toward Viet-Nam entered its final phase on June 16, 1954, the day Bao Dai appointed as premier the nationalist leader who most prominently personified the idea that communism could be checked in Viet-Nam only after colonialism had come to an end. This, to be sure, was a radical change of French policy, but it gave anti-Communist nationalism not more than a last chance. The evolution of Western policy from colonial supremacy to democratic alliance, still incomplete, had unfortunately been due less to growing insight than to the pressure of circumstances—that sad and costly substitute for courageous political action. French colonialism, forced to give in to Communist pressure, was still reluctant to give way to nationalist demands long after Ngo Dinh Diem had taken office. The Communists, jubilant over continued French obstacles to the expansion of anti-Communist forces in the south, were so sure of their imminent victory over Ngo Dinh Diem that they stopped the mass exodus of civilians from the north only when its unexpected proportions threatened Hanoi with catastrophic political consequences.[12] The world looked on while the struggle for Indochina continued through the winter and spring of 1955, not at all anticipating the "miracle" that was in the making, but being convinced that nothing less than a miracle could now interfere with the consummation of Ho Chi Minh's long-pursued aim.

The stage was set for the "miracle of Viet-Nam" when the United States, soon after Geneva, made a surprisingly clean break with the policy of the French, who were still busy stifling the growth of the only forces capable of defeating the Communist threat. A bad American conscience, as it were, aided Washington in adopting the policy needed if Viet-Nam were to survive. But the indispensable "miracle" could be performed only by the Vietnamese nationalists themselves. Geneva, when it gave the nationalists their one great opportunity since the end of World War II, had also provided them with a stupendous historical task. The new regime, in order to lay the ground for stability and lasting strength, had to repair the damage done by colonialism and communism to the body and soul of Viet-Nam. It was hampered by addiction to force as a means of solving political problems, by illegality as a habit of political action, by immoderate political feelings, by extremist views, as well as by accommodation to the existing powers, venality as a means of political advancement, and cynicism in regard to the future, which admittedly looked anything but bright. These were magnified by the disruption of the state, due to

[12] Article 14 of the Geneva Agreement stipulated that the people of the two zones were free to choose in which they wished to live.

colonialist patronage of autonomous territories and realms of public administration under the control of the so-called sects.

"Nothing short of political genius," one observer wrote, "would be enough to cope with the situation."[13] Genius or not, Ngo Dinh Diem was the leader whose record and talents made him most fit for the task of building a new state out of chaos before anti-Communist nationalism completely expired. His untainted integrity, his tenacious refusal to compromise with colonialism, and his profound insight into the political nature of his enemies were topped only by the courage he displayed toward friend and foe in creating the truly independent and strictly unified administration that his country then needed more than food and arms.

Next to the survival of his political strength and personal integrity during the corrupting and debilitating times of pseudo-independence under Bao Dai, it is this re-establishment of administrative and political unity that must be regarded as Ngo Dinh Diem's major contribution to the "miracle of Viet-Nam." No one disagreed that the task was urgent; everyone demanded that all unite, lest all should perish; but he alone had the insight, rare among the contestants in any national crisis, that unity is an empty word unless the conditions are accepted that can bring it about. To spell out the terms on which the opposing forces are willing to unite is bound to bring to light, as it did in Saigon in 1955, that unity can come about only through the elimination of all elements incompatible with the existence of a healthy state. It is part of Ngo Dinh Diem's political greatness not to have succumbed to the deceptive magic of unity, to have refused to enter into it with elements of national disruption, and to have understood that the sects, unhealthy products of the colonial past, could not be appeased but had to be destroyed.

It was on the basis of his achievements in building and consolidating the Republic of Viet-Nam that Ngo Dinh Diem was able, before July, 1956, to reject all offers to discuss the problem of Viet-Nam's unification and later to ignore the threats against his government emanating from Hanoi. Today Free Viet-Nam has the strength to withstand all pressures the Communists may bring to bear on the government, and as long as Diem and his successors are unwilling to co-operate in their own destruction, it will not succumb to its sworn enemies in the north.

In view of this, it would be a serious understatement to say that prospects for an early unification of Viet-Nam are bad—such prospects do not exist at all! Whether and when they will come about, no one can predict. The unification presupposes an end to the division of the world into two hostile and politically irreconcilable camps. Neither Ho Chi Minh

[13] Ellen Hammer, *The Struggle for Indochina Continues,* Supplement to the *Pacific Spectator,* Summer, 1955, p. 26.

nor Ngo Dinh Diem is able to advance the day when this will occur, because neither can bring about a change in Communist aims and tactics radical enough to make the West feel that it is no longer threatened in its own half of the world by the existence of communism in the other half.

Frozen into unchangeability by the low temperatures of the cold war, the two Viet-Nams now stand solidly before a divided world, the north a symbol of Communist strength, the south a symbol of Communist failure. Both are products of the policies pursued by the West since the end of World War II. The West's denial by force of Viet-Nam's justified national aspirations produced the Communist regime, which fortunately remained confined to the north, but only because the West finally recognized and supported full independence for Viet-Nam. Thus, south Viet-Nam was saved from communism when America and France began to practice in Indochina what they had long loved to preach.

But this change by the West turned out to be much more than a mere test of new tactics designed to halt the steady progress of communism in Southeast Asia. It has not only had immediate good effects; it has also become irreversible, and is no doubt one of the reasons why the old trust in force as a means of preserving colonial domination has been fading away so rapidly during the last few years. When the Communist tide was broken in Viet-Nam, not by the protracted use of force but because force was abandoned in favor of political weapons, a new chapter opened in the history of Viet-Nam. If it is read correctly, it may also become the beginning of a new chapter in the relations of the West to colonial, postcolonial, and other economically underdeveloped countries. Force has served the Communists well wherever circumstances or Western policy gave them an opportunity to use it. Communist power in the world has been built on force ever since communism began to spill over the borders of Russia, both toward East and West. And given an opportunity, the Communists will use force again, in spite of their present preference for economic weapons. It will depend largely on Western policy whether the Communists will find new and successful opportunities.

In Viet-Nam the Communists are now being deprived of total victory because the West is applying policies consonant with the principles of a democratic world. Should this not also lead us to revise defeatist views about the advantages the Communists allegedly possess over the West in the struggle for the underdeveloped and largely still uncommitted nations of the world? If there is a lesson in the "miracle of Viet-Nam" it can indeed be only this: Western policy toward nations suffering from economic misery and lack of political freedom will remain inferior to Communist policy only if actions are contrary to the principles free Western nations profess.

III. A Vietnamese Looks at His Country

TON THAT THIEN[14]

INDEPENDENCE for Viet-Nam marked the beginning of many difficulties, quite unlike those encountered during the near century of French rule. When the French ruled Viet-Nam, the problem for the Vietnamese was relatively simple: How to get rid of the French. Since French rule provided neither any procedure for peaceful change nor tolerated opposition, the problem of independence resolved itself into one of violent revolution to overthrow foreign rule. And, among the Vietnamese, this universally accepted aim resulted in a sense of national unity and a willingness to sacrifice for the cause.

However, the problem of the postindependence period is of a different kind. It is a problem of the choice between various alternatives, both in regard to aims and means. And it is precisely on this question that the Vietnamese differ and are divided.

It is not surprising that such division should occur. Under foreign rule, it mattered little which policy was adopted by the government. Any policy was considered *ipso facto* bad and not binding, at least mentally, on the Vietnamese, merely because it emanated from a foreign government. Now, with the Vietnamese themselves making the policies, the habitual attitude of opposition must be changed to one of evaluating every policy as to whether it is right or wrong, or the most practical under the circumstances, for Viet-Nam.

The basic choice the Vietnamese have to make is what to do with independence. It is a problem of reorientation, which cannot mean a complete break with the past. It is impossible for a nation to wipe out the influence of its past, either recent or distant and, of course, Viet-Nam will have to take into the account the fact of French rule. It will have to charter a new course for its national life in the light of the Vietnamese traditions and of the impact of the French, that is, of Western presence within its boundaries for nearly a hundred years.

This reorientation problem resolves itself into one of what and how much to reject of each, or how to correct the ill effects of one system or the other, or of both. There is also the problem of the choice of the means to achieve the ends, once these ends have been chosen.

At the time of the French conquest, Viet-Nam's intellectual, spiritual, and social life was based on the teachings of Confucius and Buddha. Its political institutions were those of an absolute monarchy. Its economy was in the early stages of capitalism.

Power—legislative, executive, and judicial—was concentrated in the hands of the Emperor, and exercised through his officials, the mandarins.

---

[14] Lecturer at the National Institute of Administration, Saigon, Viet-Nam.

There was no democratic government in the Western sense of the word. But the choice of mandarins was made through competitive examinations, open to all without discrimination in regard to birth or fortune. Intellectual ability was the only criterion. There was no divorce of the intellect from the moral: The scholar was expected to show as much moral as intellectual perfection. For direction the people looked to the Emperor and to his mandarins, whose duty was to educate the people. There was no system of checks and balances: The only restraint was that of a possible rebellion. The accepted principle was that government was a people's trust, and if good government should fail to obtain, then the people were entitled to withdraw their trust and give it to someone else.

Society was based on three basic relationships: Emperor-subject, husband-wife, and father-son. The subject was expected to show submission and loyalty to the Emperor, the wife to the husband, and the son to the father. Moral life was based on the observance of the five virtues— Jen, Li, I, Chi'i, Hsing (Generosity, Politeness, Steadfastness, Reason, Trust).

In addition to Confucianism, there was Buddhism, imported into Viet-Nam as early as the tenth and eleventh centuries. The Vietnamese were strongly influenced by the Buddhist doctrine that everything is transitory, and nothing is worth desiring but the nirvana, or complete absence of human desire. The Vietnamese were equally strongly influenced by the Buddhist teaching that compassion was a fundamental virtue, even if it might conflict with the exercise of justice.

Both Confucian and Buddhist doctrines reject material possessions as the aim of life. The only aim worth striving for is either moral or intellectual perfection.

Prior to the French conquest, there were indications that Viet-Nam was experiencing a beginning of capitalism. Mining, for example, was done along capitalist lines. An enterprising mandarin leased a mine from the state and worked it with his own capital, with the help of both native and imported, or Chinese labor. Trade was developing, and commercial relations existed with China, Japan, the Philippines, the South Sea Islands, and Europe, through fixed ports such as Faifo or Qui Nhon. Silk, copper, and iron were among Viet-Nam's exports.

Combined with a strong intellectual and moral structure, the Vietnamese had some organizational ability. This, indeed, made them capable of resisting Chinese absorption and, later, French assimilation. For example, it showed itself in Viet-Nam's fight against Chinese invasion. The Trans generals, who defeated the Chinese in the fourteenth century, had to maneuver on a front extending from the Chinese border to the pass of Deo Ngang, on the 20th parallel, that is on a front of more than three hundred miles in depth, both by land and sea. Again, more than an ordinary sense of organization was required for the Ly generals to plan and carry out military operations, both on land and sea, against the Chams at Qui Nhon in the twelfth century.

However, nearly two hundred years of internal strife and warfare in the sixteenth and seventeenth centuries exhausted the country, and even if unification was achieved at the end of this period, the country was too weak to resist French conquest in the middle of the nineteenth century.

After their conquest the French broke up the political unity of the country, but retained its social foundations. They discovered that continuing the monarchy, subject to their regulation, and the Vietnamese social system were effective means of enforcing their rule.

Thus, the tendency toward absolutism and away from democracy was reinforced. Instead of one absolute government, the Vietnamese were subjected to two. Viet-Nam, under French rule, contrasted strongly with the experience of India, for example, which, as well as the Philippines under American rule, received a grounding in parliamentary government.

At the same time, French rule resulted in the elimination of the Vietnamese from the effective running of the country. Thus, the people's sense of organization, leadership, and responsibility were lost, or at least blunted.

Economically, the capitalist development was arrested, and enterprise, that fundamental factor in the economic development of a nation, was also lost little by little. French economic policy in Viet-Nam, the two main tenents of which were the French Tariff Law of 1887, reinforced by the Tariff Law of 1891, and the Doumer program of 1895, produced a kind of specialization in which farming along traditional lines was reserved to the Vietnamese, while industry, trade, transport, banking, and modern farming were all in French hands. Indeed, a French exchange economy was grafted on to a Vietnamese subsistence economy. Only two careers were open to the Vietnamese: they could become peasants—that is, subsistence farmers—or functionaries—that is, mandarins of the lower echelons.

Consequently, for nearly a hundred years, Viet-Nam remained outside the world movement toward industrialization and technical development; and the training of people who could think, plan, and execute, with a sense of responsibility, was nonexistent.

In fact, during these years, the Vietnamese acquired a new mentality: that of the revolutionary nationalist—bitter, uncompromising, destructive. The Vietnamese learned how to destroy—materially, mentally, socially. Having no responsibility for the running of their country, they had no opportunity to learn how to preserve, to develop, to build—in a word, to think and act constructively.

Such was the situation of the Vietnamese when they gained their independence. In a world which each day imposes heavier burdens on the state and its officials, Viet-Nam found itself greatly handicapped. As already pointed out, Viet-Nam's exertions for decades have been largely of a revolutionary and destructive nature. If one adds to this the intellectual and social legacy of Viet-Nam, one realizes the magnitude of the problem facing the government today, with its lack of trained officials and leaders.

In a situation where communism is capitalizing on the weakness of a new independent nation, it is all the more serious. Much money, time, and energy have to be diverted to the struggle against communism. Further, instead of reacting against the "revolutionary" mentality, the Communists seek to develop it among both the officials and the masses. Whatever is done is therefore done in a climate of emergency.

Further, the partition of the country has brought with it many other difficulties. It has separated the industrial and heavily populated north from the agricultural and sparsely populated south. Too, it has imposed on the country an excessive military burden. The combined armed forces of Red and Free Viet-Nam, which have a total population of about twenty-five million, equal the size of the army of India and its nearly four hundred million people—that is, half a million men: 350,000 for Red and 150,000 for Free Viet-Nam.

Partition has also had the effect of splitting in two the meager body of officials of the country. Much resources, both in material and personnel, are therefore wasted. As a consequence, Viet-Nam is deprived of the co-operation of a number of Vietnamese trained at home or abroad. Many of them cannot decide whether to support Red or Free Viet-Nam, and therefore "sit on the fence," which means, for all practical purposes, choosing the life of exile in the West, where their marginal value is small. In so doing they deny the country of much-needed competence. Or, if they are at home, they spend their time in the concentration or labor camps of the north or in idleness in the south, while the capable men who take a stand are overworked and less efficient because they have too many jobs to do at the same time.

Partition has also had its financial consequences. Viet-Nam needs external aid, especially in the form of loans to accelerate its economic development. But, as long as Viet-Nam is divided, it is difficult for it to obtain capital from abroad, it being a well-known fact of banking that the lenders often prefer security to a high rate of profit. Viet-Nam, therefore, has to depend on grants, a very unsatisfactory method of financing its economic development, because it is not completely free to dispose of these grants and because the necessary complicated administrative procedures slow down the work of development.

One cannot write or talk about Viet-Nam without touching upon the problem of reunification. Disregarding the *if,* when and how the country will be reunified cannot be predicted. In this regard, it may be said that the will to unity is strong in the Vietnamese people, and that Viet-Nam has been divided and reunified in the past.

In Vietnamese history, the unifier of a divided Viet-Nam has always come from the south. There are reasons for this. The occupier of north Viet-Nam always has disadvantageous factors working against him. The north, being close to China, cannot easily escape Chinese control or influence. China is also north Viet-Nam's source of supplies and support. The Vietnamese people, however, look upon China as the traditional enemy and threat to their national existence, and distrust any association or connection with their northern neighbor.

Secondly, the North is overpopulated, and food is scarcer there than in the south. In a time of tension the government has to impose heavy taxes to maintain large armed forces and to enforce strong discipline. Both of these measures are bound to be unpopular. The south is not subject to these disadvantages, nor is its national existence threatened by a big neighbor. It has wide access to the sea, that is to supplies and aid from friendly countries in case of emergency. If it overthrows the northern authorities, it will enjoy the great advantage of being looked upon as the liberators of the country from Chinese rule. Lastly, it has climatic advantages. Northern armies moving southward are subject to a warmer, harsher climate and to diseases of it. In fact, in their fights against Chinese invasions, the Vietnamese have had "general summer" on their side, just as the Russians have had "general winter" on theirs.

Again disregarding the *if,* once Viet-Nam is unified, what will be its place in the world, and especially in Asia? Situated as it is at the point of convergence of migrations and cultural contacts between East and West, and between North and South Asia, Viet-Nam can play an important role in bringing nations together. Unlike Singapore and Hong Kong, which are important international centers but have no culture of their own, Viet-Nam has a culture which is Asian. Through France, it has had intimate cultural contacts with the West. With independence regained, the cultural contacts will broaden and include Western culture centers other than Latin. Viet-Nam can show the way in which a synthesis of Western and Eastern civilizations may be achieved.

Such is the background against which the Vietnamese situation and the efforts of the Vietnamese to build a better Viet-Nam should be appraised and gauged. Such is also the background of the problems which face the Vietnamese leaders in their search for a proper reorientation of Viet-Nam. The Vietnamese may ignore these historical, social, and psychological factors, as is being done in the north, where an attempt is being made to force communism on the people. Or they may give a great importance to these factors and seek solutions that would maintain some continuity with the past, as is being done in Free Viet-Nam.

IV. The Political Background of Ngo Dinh Diem

ELLEN J. HAMMER

THE YEAR 1931 was a time of despair and unrest in Viet-Nam. A nationalist uprising was put down by the French colonial administration at the cost of much blood and suffering among the Vietnamese population; thirteen nationalist leaders were beheaded at Yen Bay, with the forbidden name of "Viet-Nam" on their lips before they died.[15] The throne had been virtually empty since 1925, with the death of the unpopular Khai Dinh, who had been named emperor by the French colonial administration in 1916 after nationalist uprising had been repressed and its leader, the Emperor Duy Tan, sent to join two other Vietnamese emperors in exile.

In 1932 a new optimism swept the country when Bao Dai, Khai Dinh's son, arrived from France to actively succeed his father. In view of his education in France, the Vietnamese expected Bao Dai to bring home the modern ideas of the West, to strengthen and renovate the ancient system inherited from their ancestors.

To his side in 1933 was summoned a thirty-two-year-old man, a member of one of the great families of the country, who had been rigorously trained in the mandarinal system. As Minister of Interior, he stood ready to safeguard the rights and practices of the Vietnamese against the encroachments of the colonial system. His name was Ngo Dinh Diem.

It took only a few months for the optimism that the new regime had generated to collapse in disillusionment. Not only were Diem's plans for a nationalist revival and a limited monarchy rejected by the French Governor General, but the young minister himself was forced to resign by the Emperor, who went so far as to strip him of all his decorations. In the Emperor's abject surrender to the French colonials, Bao Dai was also to surrender his nationalist leadership. But the status that Bao Dai lost would be regained in the future by the other person in this incident. Ngo Dinh Diem spent some twenty years in voluntary retirement, part of it in self-imposed exile. In 1954 he returned to power as Prime Minister, to preside over the first independent state which had existed in Viet-Nam in some seventy years. Becoming President a year later, he, more than anyone else, links the old Viet-Nam with new.

The dramatic experiences of the Vietnamese in recent years have received such publicity as to obscure this political background which shaped the struggle against both colonialism and communism. This background is of far more than merely academic interest; it explains many of the key political problems confronting the Viet-Nam republic in its formative

---

[15] Under the colonial regime, the country was divided into three parts, the protectorates of Annam and Tonkin, and the colony of Cochinchina. The historic designation of "Viet-Nam" was used by nationalists to symbolize national unity and independence.

years. It will have a determining effect on the adaptation to the Vietnamese scene of such important and distinctively Western concepts as
political parties, a written constitution, and democracy. And it is of
special significance because of the underlying continuity of Vietnamese
political and cultural history. Individuals from the United States and
Europe who visit Viet-Nam have sometimes been misled by superficial
evidence of westernization, by the wide acquaintance of educated people
with French culture and the French language, to the point that Vietnamese men, although not women, have adopted the wearing of European
dress.

In reality, during the period of French rule, Vietnamese society remained surprisingly unaltered. Social and cultural contacts between the
two peoples were kept to a bare minimum. Although the displacement
of political power to French hands inevitably disrupted certain aspects of
Vietnamese life, the political traditions of old Viet-Nam managed to survive through the family which, voluntarily or involuntarily, became the
guardian of the national traditions.

Because the old Viet-Nam had little in common with Western society,
the language of Western politics cannot be transposed to Vietnamese life
without the greatest caution, and then only at the risk of confusion and
misunderstanding. Vietnamese society was characterized by both a highly
developed autocracy and a remarkable degree of democracy. Although all
power reposed in the Emperor, who had absolute authority over his subjects, every aspect of his life, as with the least of his subjects, was regulated
according to the moral precepts of Confucius. The Confucianist teaching, which was grounded solidly on humanism and characterized by
moderation, minutely regulated the behavior of the individual; it provided
that the role of the citizen in government was only one facet of a carefully
organized network of social relations and obligations. Thus, the spirit and
the relationships which contributed to the creation of the state were an
extension of those at the root of the family; they were endowed with the
same permanence and the same profound duty to obedience. For this
reason, the Communists in north Viet-Nam, in seeking to impose their
absolute rule over the population, had first to break down the sanctity of
the family, a fact which explains much of the cruelty of the Viet-Minh
regime.

It should be emphasized that the Confucianist system took for granted a
pre-existing society which was already old and settled, even static, in
which each individual knew his place and his duties. Whatever rights an
individual might have had were in no way absolute or inherent in his
person, but derived largely from his functions and from the role which
he was called upon to play in the social system. Confucianism was not a

religion but a way of life which impregnated the entire culture of Viet-Nam. It left an indelible imprint upon the Vietnamese, regardless of their religion, upon Catholics and Buddhists, as well as animists; and in its emphasis on the responsibilities of the individual to society, it acted as a valuable counterpose to the prevailing Buddhism, which was essentially other-worldly and indifferent to social or political relations.

In this Confucianist world, political behavior was logically deduced from a set of ethical equations which any servant of the state had to assimilate before he could qualify for a position in the governing hierarchy. There was thus no place for the concept of the right of the minority to become a majority, which is at the root of Western political democracy, nor of "majority rule." As to political parties, which are so vital a part of Western life, these could only be regarded as undesirable sources of factionalism and disorder in a society in which government was not only an indissoluble part but, actually, the summit of the social order. There was no hereditary aristocracy to stand between the Emperor and the people. With the Vietnamese state recruiting its governing elite, or mandarins, entirely through educational channels by a system of triennial examinations open to the entire population, its officials were selected to a striking extent on ability.

This intricately hierarchical society was permeated by a profound sense of popular sovereignty, for all that it was expressed in ways unknown to the West. It affected even the Emperor, who governed according to "the mandate of heaven." In ordinary times this doctrine had the effect of lending a religious sanction to the imperial authority. But if the Emperor were to break with the Confucianist ethical laws and fall into tyrannical ways, then it could be assumed that the heavenly mandate had been withdrawn from him and he could therefore be removed. Drastic and rare though such a doctrine might be, it provided, under the proper circumstances, a legal, and even a religious, sanction for revolution.

The ultimate right of revolution thus joined with the omnipresent rules of Confucianist doctrine to impose both a practical and theoretical check on the abuse of power. At the lowest levels of the pyramid of administration, the village organization (the village was the basic unit of Vietnamese social, political, and economic life) had the same effect. Within the framework of the imperial government, each village directed its own affairs through its leading citizens, who were organised in a Council of Notables. They were not popularly elected, but chose their own members through a system of co-option, to insure that they did in reality comprise the individuals in the villages who were best acquainted with the Confucianist ethical equations. Nor did they operate by majority rule: They arrived at decisions by discussion and general agreement.

Inevitably this delicate structure of checks and balances, which characterized the old Viet-Nam, was dislocated by the colonial regime. At the same time that the authority of the Emperor and his officials was replaced by that of the colonial administration, the moral principles of the old system and their practical implementation in daily life tended to degenerate. In place of the old obligation of responsibility to society which had been imposed on every Vietnamese, the mandarins fell prey to widespread corruption. Although the administration, in north and central Viet-Nam at least, was still nominally headed by the Emperor, no ruler was tolerated by the colonial administration who to any degree represented the popular feeling or felt bound by any of the traditional duties to his people. From the puppet Emperor at Hue to the superficially Gallicized officials who drew their power from the colonial regime, the colonial administration thus used the forms of the traditional institutions, while stripping them of their substance. It created an artificial and misleading screen of Franco-Vietnamese collaboration, behind which distinguished mandarins such as Ngo Dinh Diem, as well as the younger generation of intellectuals, many of whom had studied in the West, tried to stave off the chronic encroachments of colonial administrators upon their authority and their freedom of action. It was understood in this colonial period that there was no possibility for the formation of political parties; least of all were there any legitimate channels through which a political minority group could form itself into a majority.

Under the colonial system, in striking contrast with the old Viet-Nam, established authority itself fell into disrepute. No foreigner or individual subservient to the foreigner could legitimately demand the obedience of the people. Out of the wreckage of the old political and social morality, there emerged instead the obligation to disobey, to resist passively or (depending upon the individual and the occasion) actively the foreign occupier.

Eventually, it is true, one political party did develop, in the 1930's and 1940's, with a certain popular following and a detailed program embracing both the means of winning control of the machinery of the state and a political system to be established once the state was taken over. However, this party, which was the Communist Party, was opposed not only to political democracy in any form, but also to any political or social morality. For this reason, certain nationalists, notably Diem, found it impossible to collaborate with the Communists under any circumstances, even during the first years of the war with France, when the latter temporarily took over leadership of the nationalist movement. Only after Vietnamese independence was finally achieved in 1954, and when it became clear that no elections would be held to unite the country (as had been proposed by the Geneva Conference which ended the war), did the great majority of the population south of the 17th parallel give their open adherence to Diem's lifelong policy of opposition to communism.

These various factors go far to explain many of the difficulties and apparent contradictions confronting the new regime when Diem returned to power. The old Vietnamese state, embedded in an organized society and grounded on certain accepted values and on a traditional and efficient administration, no longer existed. In 1954 there was, as a matter of fact, no state at all. The duty of obedience to established authority had long since been undermined; there was little agreement among the population as to political principles or practices, and little notion of political morality. The most active elements were small groups and individuals whose political activity was directed exclusively in terms of their own selfish interests. By no definition could they possibly have been qualified as political parties; they had neither platform nor popular following. Further complicating an already difficult situation, few links existed between the central government and the population. From the Emperor down, the officials whom Diem found in nominal authority had long since identified their own interests not with the people but with the colonial administration. The state of Viet-Nam had to be rebuilt from top to bottom.

The most fundamental contradiction was resolved when Diem, despite his long-time dedication to the monarchy as an integral part of the traditional culture, had to recognize that the personality of Bao Dai was too seriously compromised to permit him to remain chief of state. The establishment of the republic in 1955 symbolized the clearing away of the debris of the colonial system, thus paving the way for the creation of a true nationalist regime and insuring the co-operation of all patriotic elements.

Since that time Diem has set about building a regime, step by step, on foundations that go deep into what in the past was legitimate and decent for an Asian country, namely Confucianist ethics. It is also not to be forgotten that two other factors have contributed to the total of Diem's political experience. One is his deep Catholic faith. The other is that, as an exile, he witnessed during a number of years the strengths and weaknesses of Western political democracies. This dual influence is evident in the present Vietnamese state where recourse to the basic Confucianist equations has been accomplished by a special emphasis on the rights of the individual. In this development of a political credo which draws its deepest roots from traditions of which Asia can legitimately be proud, the service rendered by Diem to free Asia may well extend beyond the frontiers of his Republic of Viet-Nam.

Commentary: JOSEPH BUTTINGER *on*
ELLEN J. HAMMER

Miss Hammer convincingly presents several aspects of Vietnamese history which help to explain why the political personality of Ngo Dinh Diem does not fit too neatly into Western frames of reference. However, she does not relate the story of Diem's life, at least to the extent to which it is a political story. The picture that most people have of the Vietnamese President's life is quite wrong. Because so little was known in the West of Diem before he became Prime Minister of Free Viet-Nam in 1954, hostile propaganda was able to present him as a complete novice in politics, whose lack of experience would prove a disaster for his country. Illuminating as Miss Hammer's paper is in other respects, it unfortunately does not correct this picture. This is why a few remarks may contribute to a better understanding of President Diem's unexpected and astounding political success.

In 1933, when Diem was chosen to become the Minister of the Interior, he was, no doubt, a little-known political figure. But he was not chosen at random. One reason for his appointment was his reputation as a competent administrator. Although then only thirty-two, he had already successfully administered a large province for four years. But more important was his reputation as one of the few incorruptible men in the colonial administration, in which the higher Vietnamese officials were largely of the sort that could be bought.

He agreed to become Bao Dai's first minister only after the French promised to permit reforms that would give some political autonomy to Viet-Nam. A Commission of Reforms was appointed, of which he became Secretary, but in less than three months he learned that the reforms he had proposed, although modest in comparison to the demands of other nationalists, would never be introduced as long as the French ruled Viet-Nam. It must have been a profound and shattering experience for him to acquire this momentous insight. He never forgot what he learned in 1933. From then on, he was convinced that collaboration with the French was possible for a true Vietnamese nationalist only for the purpose of liquidating the colonial regime.

As a result of this experience, Diem was said to have retired from the political life of Viet-Nam for the next twenty years. It was even said that his interest in politics ceased. This view was based on his persistent refusal to accept any official position. He even refused office during the Indochina war, when French policy aimed at gaining Vietnamese support against the Communist-led resistance through the establishment of a national government headed again by Bao Dai.

What really happened in the twenty years of Diem's life, during which he was allegedly inactive or even politically indifferent? Little was heard of him between 1933 and 1940. After the failure of his first mission he must have devoted a great deal of time, like all other great leaders in history, to study and introspection. But he always maintained some contacts with nationalist groups, and the name of Ngo Dinh Diem was mentioned again as one of the leading figures of the nationalist movement soon after the occupation of Indochina by the Japanese in 1940. This can only mean that Diem had impressed himself during the preceding years on the minds of his compatriots through some political thought and action. In my opinion, he not only developed his present political philosophy during these years but also communicated it to all important national leaders and, in particular, to the non-Communist spokesmen for unconditional independence.

In 1945, twelve years after Diem's first experience in co-operating with the French, and with little visible evidence of public activity, Diem appeared well established as the most outstanding non-Communist leader of Vietnamese nationalism. On page 48 of *The Struggle for Indochina*, Ellen Hammer says that popular demonstrations, demanding a national government under the leadership of Diem, occurred in Hue in March, 1945. Nobody knows the real story of Diem's relations to the nationalist movement and to the Japanese during the years 1940-45. The Japanese are said to have "protected" Diem against the French Sureté during this time, as they did with some leaders of the sects, but whether they wanted him as Prime Minister in 1945, or, as other witnesses claim, prevented his appointment by Bao Dai, and whether or not he would have been willing to head the government shortly before the Japanese defeat, only he himself or perhaps some secret Japanese documents can reveal.

Most authors on recent Vietnamese history were quite aware of Diem's importance as a national leader long before he became an international figure, although no one seems to be able to explain the reasons for his mysterious political reputation. Philippe Devillers, probably the most competent historian of contemporary Viet-Nam, speaks with unrestrained respect of the man who at the time of his writing was supposedly still quite inactive and politically disinterested. He says that even in 1933 Diem was "known for his perfect integrity, his competence and his intelligence" (*Histoire du Viet-Nam de 1940 à 1952*, page 63), and adds, "His reputation was such that real miracles were expected from him." Paul Mus, another outstanding French author on Viet-Nam, in 1952 called Diem "the most respected and the most influential nationalist leader" (*Viet-Nam: Sociologie d'une guerre,* page 166). Indeed, no governmental combination was discussed between 1945 and 1950 without centering around the name of Ngo Dinh Diem. His refusal to participate in any of the many combines during the "Experiment Bao Dai" has been described as proof of a rigid and essentially unpolitical attitude. It is now easy to see that it was really proof of his unerring political foresight and moral strength.

Diem went into exile in 1950. But who in our age would dare say that a man's going into exile proved his lack of political interest? The Communists apparently always had a better understanding of the true meaning of Diem's political attitude. Jean R. Clementin, a French writer sympathetic to the Viet-Minh, in an article in *Temps Modernes* of January, 1954, recognized Diem as a man with a true sense of power, and by implication admired him for his open aversion to the mere appearance of power. Diem, Clementin said, would rather remain a decisive political power in the background than appear as a mere figurehead in the public eye. Most French leaders experienced in Indochinese affairs know this too. They refused to have any dealings with Diem after 1948, not because they thought him "weak and incompetent," but rather because they were afraid of his political strength and personal determination.

Inasmuch as Diem himself, through his actions as the leader of Free Viet-Nam, has already destroyed the image that was presented of him to the world up to 1954, it may seem unnecessary to attempt to correct it with reference to his long political career.

PART TWO

THE REFUGEE PROBLEM

The evacuation of nearly a million people from Red Viet-Nam, and the resettling of them in Free Viet-Nam, is an important part of Viet-Nam: The First Five Years. *Private and government agencies from several countries co-operated in this humanitarian undertaking. Unfortunately, some phases of the refugee program, including the important work done by the United States Operations Mission (USOM), are covered only indirectly here.*

The refugee program was largely financed with American aid, with France and private organizations providing some additional financial assistance. American aid funds, used to purchase materials and to pay salaries, was frequently channeled through private agencies and contractors and through agencies of the government of Free Viet-Nam.

One such group was the Protestant Evangelical Church of Viet-Nam, which assisted in the caring for refugees upon arrival and later distributed medical supplies and surplus food from the United States. Later, the Church World Service founded a "model" refugee village, which carried on useful experiments in village development.

Other co-operating groups included Operation Brotherhood, organized by the Junior Chamber of Commerce of the Philippines, the International Rescue Committee (IRC), and the CARE program. Operation Brotherhood provided needed medical personnel and equipment to assist the Vietnamese refugees at a critical period and prevented a serious outbreak of contagious diseases in the refugee villages and encampments. IRC, using American aid funds and personnel, provided assistance to the many students included among the refugees. In establishing temporary schools and dormitory facilities, IRC filled an important need quickly and effectively. The CARE program originally made food packages available to refugees from both Red Viet-Nam and the war-torn countryside of Free Viet-Nam. Later, CARE turned to the plight of young people and made tools available which permitted them to work as apprentices in a trade.

The Free World has many reasons to be proud of what was accomplished in meeting the needs of the refugees from Red Viet-Nam. In this vast operation, there was first the problem of assisting those who wished to leave but whose departure the Communists sought to prevent. Second was the problem of providing transportation, and then of caring for the great influx of people in an area that had been in military, political, and economic turmoil for nearly ten years. And, finally, there was the most important job of helping to make these refugees productive units of the Vietnamese economy.

The refugee program was a multisided operation, and the experiences here recounted give a deep insight into such diverse aspects of the program as American government red tape, the historical background of the Vietnamese, agriculture in Viet-Nam, the attitudes of the refugees, standard Communist operation procedures, and the work of the Catholic Church.

More could have been accomplished in handling the refugee problem, and mistakes were made, as these writers point out. These shortcomings serve to point up the difficulties of the program and the degree of success attained.

V. The Role of Friendly Nations

BUI VAN LUONG[16]

SEVERAL FRIENDLY countries of the Free World played an important role in the evacuation of the Vietnamese from Red to Free Viet-Nam. In mid-1954, immediately after the Geneva Agreement, France, one of the principal signers, initially assumed the responsibility of evacuating refugees to the south. All available French ships and planes were put into service, as well as a number of requisitioned civilian planes and ships. However, during the first month the number of refugees surpassed all expectations, and it became obvious that France alone was incapable of evacuating all the refugees. Therefore, President Diem appealed to the United States for assistance. In response, President Eisenhower ordered the 7th Fleet to aid in the program. The British and the Formosa governments also loaned a few of their ships for the operation. It should be noted that aboard the ships of friendly countries, the refugees received the most cordial care and the best treatment.

On the opposite side of the evacuation picture is the part the Polish people played in transporting Vietnamese from Free to Red Viet-Nam. The Polish ship *Kilinski* made four trips between north and south Viet-Nam, with no figures available on the total number of refugees evacuated.

To contrast with the treatment given to refugees transported by the friendly countries here is an account of one refugee who traveled on the *Kilinski:* "The Viet-Minh divided us into three classes: the reactionaries, who were shut up in the bottom of the boat, the lukewarm, and the progressives. We were allowed to go up to the deck twice a day. At every meal, each of us received a small bowl of rice and a tiny bit of salted beef. Several women and children fainted for lack of air. The crew did not take the least care of us. We were forbidden to talk. On the other hand, we had to attend daily propaganda sessions held by the Viet-Minh, who forced us to learn the contents of their leaflets by heart."

A summary of the part played by the friendly and the Communist nations in the evacuation program both from Red and from Free Viet-Nam is given below:[17]

By air:
French planes: 4,280 trips, carrying 213,635 persons

[16] Former General Director of the Refugee Commission of the Government of Viet-Nam and present Le Commissaire Général au Développement Agricole. Translated by Phan Thu Ngoc, a candidate for a Ph.D. degree at Michigan State University.

[17] In regard to these figures given by Bui Van Luong here, see the comments by Bernard B. Fall, pp. 54-58, 61-62, as well as the additional comments by Bui Van Luong, pp. 58-61. (ED.)

By sea:

French ships	388 trips	
American ships	109 trips	
English ships	2 trips	carrying 555,037 persons
Chinese ships	2 trips[18]	
Polish ships	4 trips	

TOTAL: 768,672 persons

Not included, of course, in the above figures is a considerable number of refugees who migrated to the south on their own resources, both before and after the complete withdrawal of French and Vietnamese troops from north of the 17th parallel. Some escaped by crossing the river between the two zones on small boats at night. Others set out on rafts, built with a few bamboo sticks tied together with ropes, and after braving the high seas, succeeded in reaching a southern port. Still others took the Laos route and arrived in the south after several exhausting days of walking through the forests of the Annam mountains. Even now, from time to time, small groups of three or four manage to escape by swimming across the Ben Hai River.

To date, the number who have managed to get away by their own means is more than 109,000 people. The total number of refugees in Free Viet-Nam, who now number 928,152 persons, may be divided as follows:

According to ethnic origin:

Vietnamese living in the delta region	913,358
Nung mountain people	13,306
Muong mountain people	900
Man mountain people	588
	928,152

According to profession:

Farmers	706,026
Fishermen	88,850
Artisans, small businessmen, students, government employees, professionals	133,276
	928,152

According to religion:

Catholics	794,876
Buddhists and Protestants	133,276
	928,152

These figures exclude military and quasi-military personnel, who number approximately 120,000.

[18] It is not known whether the Chinese ships were evacuating refugees from Free or from Red Viet-Nam, or from both zones. (ED.)

In contrast to nearly a million refugees from Red Viet-Nam, only a mere 4,358 persons of both sexes asked to leave Free Viet-Nam to go north. The majority, who had been in the south for many years, had come from the overcrowded provinces of the north to work on the rubber plantations, and most of them were homesick, rather than adherents of the Communist doctrine.

Under the resettlement program, each refugee family was given a house and the food and necessary equipment that would allow its members to exist until they were able to become useful, productive members of the community.

As indicated above, farmers made up about 80 percent of the total. Unable to sell their houses, plow animals, their rice fields, and even their paddy crops, they left Red Viet-Nam penniless.

There was no dearth of land in the south, and it was not difficult to allocate some to these refugees. Besides the cultivated rice fields, there were, and are, huge tracts of land still uncultivated and extremely productive forests as yet unexploited.

In addition to a piece of land or a rice field, each farm family was given a house, not necessarily a comfortable one but at least adequate, as well as work animals, farm implements, seeds, and fertilizers.

Fishermen from the north presented few problems, for they could earn a living along the coastline of Free Viet-Nam which is rich in fish. With the handicrafts virtually undeveloped in the south, the refugee artisans could find opportunities there.

One million refugees seems like an insignificant figure in view of the immense resources of south Viet-Nam. In former times, under the French regime, the lack of man power was a major obstacle to exploitation of these resources. Now that the refugees are there, the problem, therefore, is providentially solved.

The government of Free Viet-Nam has received generous financial aid from the United States. It was American aid (administered in Viet-Nam by United States Operations Mission, or USOM) that supported 97 percent of the refugee aid. Next to the United States, France was the largest contributor of financial aid. Great Britain, Australia, Western Germany, New Zealand, and the Netherlands, as well as numerous welfare organizations such as the National Catholic Welfare Conference (N.C.W.C.), the Junior Chamber of Commerce, CARE, and the United Nations Children's Fund also made contributions, either by sending technicians or by distributing merchandise, foodstuffs, and various other gifts.

The general Commissariat for Refugees, more commonly called COMIGAL, which stands for the abbreviation of the French name, has been in charge of the resettlement program. A knowledge of its operations will help one to understand the many phases of the operation.

COMIGAL's first task was to find areas that were capable of accommodating the refugees according to their professions, and thereby ensure them a relatively adequate future. To accomplish this, prospecting commissions, made up of experts and refugee representatives, were sent to the provinces to find resettlement centers with the necessary requirements: land suitable for cultivation for farmers; favorable points along the coastline for fishermen: and areas near cities or population centers for artisans.

Once the locations were determined, the Planning Office (Direction du Plan) proceeded to set up subprojects in accordance with instructions by the prospecting commissions.

The plans for a subproject first approved by the Commissariat General for Refugees, were then sent to USOM or to the French Technical and Economic Cooperation Bureau for approval and allocation of necessary funds. It seldom took more than two weeks to complete and get approval of a plan. A maximum of nine months was allowed for the completion of a subproject.

Once a subproject was approved, the refugees were carried by truck to the selected site. The number of refugees in each case depended on the potentialities of the site. It varied from 1,000 to 3,000 persons (i.e., from 200 to 600 families, assuming an average family to have five persons). As far as possible, refugees belonging to the same religion or the same village in north Viet-Nam were relocated together. However, frequently Catholics and Buddhists originating from different villages or provinces went to the same village, living there peacefully, too, and understandably so, considering that freedom of religion has long existed in Viet-Nam, and that the Communist danger served to unite people of different faiths and backgrounds.

Upon arrival at the site, the refugees were housed in either American aid tents or hangars, which were built of light-weight material. They immediately proceeded to elect representatives to an administrative committee. These official election returns were submitted to COMIGAL for approval. From then on, the administrative committee worked as an intermediary between the refugees and COMIGAL for everything regarding the resettling operation itself and between the refugees and the local authorities on all matters. Each administrative committee had either three or five members, depending upon the size of the village. In villages of 2,000 population, the committee consisted of a president, a secretary, and a treasurer. In those having more than 2,000 people, there were, in addition, an assistant to the president and a substitute member. Each committee member received a monthly allowance of 750 piasters for nine months, that is for the duration of the subproject. The responsibility for the execution of a particular subproject fell upon these committee members, with their work being supervised by a provincial delegate of COMIGAL. The priest, the bonze, or the minister served as a spiritual guide for the village and adviser to the committee.

Immediately after the proposed subproject was approved, the administrative committee devoted itself to carrying out the project. *A copy of the subproject was posted at the village meeting hall so that everyone could become acquainted with it.*[19] Men, women, and children then set about to build a permanent village. Using the funds allocated for the area, they built their individual houses, public buildings, roads, and bridges. Farmers cleared their land, plowed and sowed their fields. Fishermen built their boats and made nets. Artisans set up their shops, acquiring necessary equipment and tools. And thus the young village grew. Bushes, large trees, and entire sections of virgin forests disappeared to be replaced by a community, with well-built roads, orderly rows of thatched-roof houses, rice or other cultivated fields. Teachers, male nurses, and midwives were put to work. Children resumed their studies, and the sick were cared for. In the meantime, as the farm implements, chemical fertilizers, and plow animals arrived in Viet-Nam, COMIGAL distributed them to the villages. Rice was distributed regularly to feed the refugees until they were ready to provide for themselves.

In theory, each new village had a subproject. However, several villages were sometimes placed side by side, sharing the same subproject. There have been 127 subprojects financed by American aid, amounting to 681,420,784 piasters. French aid has financed five subprojects, at a total cost of 33,525,000 piasters.

A total of 319 resettlement villages had been created as of mid-1957. Of these, 288 were for farmers, 26 for fishermen, and 5 for artisans. These villages are distributed as follows: 207 in south Viet-Nam, 50 in the delta region of central Viet-Nam, and 62 in the mountain region of central Viet-Nam.

Of the almost one million refugees, only a little over 500,000 live in resettlement villages; the others (merchants, government employees, military personnel with their families) prefer to live on their own in the cities and the countryside. Consequently, the resettled refugees are distributed as follows: 394,682 in south Viet-Nam, 52,988 in the delta region of central Viet-Nam, and 64,342 in the mountain region of central Viet-Nam.

To summarize the accomplishments of the subprojects: 92,443 individ-

[19] Italics by editor. For additional information, see the comments by Cardinaux, on pp. 87-92.

ual housing units have been constructed. In the field of education, 317 elementary schools have been built, with 1,636 classrooms and 66,176 pupils in attendance; 18 secondary schools have been started, with 49 classrooms and 1,521 pupils in attendance.

Progress in health and sanitation is indicated by the following construction figures: 2 hospitals, 143 infirmaries, 55 maternity clinics, 105 first-aid posts, and 6,029 wells.

In agriculture, 38,192 hectares have been cleared for cultivation: Plow animals sold on long-term credit include: 5,215 buffaloes and 3,416 oxen. The following small animals have been distributed (except those locally bought by refugees): white Leghorn chicks, 108,800; local breed ducklings, 12,140; and Berkshire and Yorkshire boars, 345. Chemical fertilizers in tons distributed include: ammonium sulfate, 2,461,900; potassium sulfate, 590,700; superphosphates, 698,000; and tricalcium phospates, 2,957,000. Agricultural implements—including plows, harrowteeth, pickaxs, hoes, shovels, spades, hatchets, machetes, scythes, pulverizers, saw blades, rakes—have amounted to 1,897,966 kilograms; and seeds for market gardening have totaled 25,163 kilograms.

In the artisan industries, 1,000 sewing machines and 440 power looms have been sold on long-term credit.

In the fishing industry, 125 boats have been built, and 740 fishing tackle outfits and 877 nets of various types have been made.

Due to the central supervision of COMIGAL and the valuable assistance of USOM, all villages completed their resettlement subprojects. Their living standard has improved, and in most cases is higher than that prevailing in the north.

As soon as the refugees were no longer in need of special assistance they were ready to be integrated into the local communities. In an official ceremony, the Commissioner General handed the refugee village over to the chief of the province. The latter—taking into consideration the geographical position of the village, the size of its population, and its economic potentialities—let it stand as a village or turned it into a hamlet of an existing village. The administrative committee was dissolved; and the refugees elected a communal council to replace it (if the village remained a separate village) or only a representative to be a member of the existing village council (if the village was turned into a hamlet). All expenditures hitherto borne by the subproject's funds from then on devolved upon the province's budget. Integration, which started in April, 1956, came to an end in mid-1957. By that time, all refugee villages had been absorbed into the local administrative structure.

Commentary: BERNARD B. FALL[20] *on*
BUI VAN LUONG

WITH THE deactivation of the *Commissariat Général aux Réfugiés,*—
referred to in Viet-Nam by its French initials as COMIGAL, on December 31, 1957, by decree of President Diem an important phase
in Free Viet-Nam's development ended. To move nearly one million
well-trained soldiers in peacetime is a major feat of transportation and
logistics. To move that number of disorganized civilian refugees on a
"crash" basis in less than one year surely will remain an accomplishment of note for a long time to come.

For purposes of clarity, the refugee problem of Viet-Nam may be
divided into three distinct phases: (1) the movement phase, (2) the
temporary sheltering phase, and (3) the permanent resettlement and
integration phase. All three terms are self-explanatory and roughly
cover a period from June 1, 1954, to the present. In these comments
I shall limit myself to considerations of the movement phase.

The Vietnamese is generally considered to be attached to his rice
field and to the tombs of his ancestors, much as is his "elder brother"
and neighbor, the Chinese. This popular image, however, is contrary
to historical facts: The whole Vietnamese nation has been on the move
for the past two thousand years. The Vietnamese are known to have
moved from China into what is now north Viet-Nam around 400 to
250 B. C., and ever since one generation after another of Vietnamese
has fought its way south, from the Red River Delta to the plains of the
Than Hoa and central Viet-Nam, defeating the Cham and Cambodian
kingdom, which barred its migration to the open plains of the Mekong.
Saigon was first occupied in 1698, and the Vietnamese reached the
Gulf of Siam at Ha Tien in 1714. In other words, century after century, thousands of Vietnamese left the tombs of their ancestors and the
familiar northern countryside for the fertile lands of the south.

Vietnamese tradition abounds with tales of heroic feats accomplished during those migrations. Hence, the movement of one million
northern Vietnamese to south Viet-Nam, while surely a time of physical hardship to the individuals involved, was not something "unnatural"
to the Vietnamese. As will be seen later, and as was the case during the
last fifty years of French administration in Viet-Nam, the south has
been in need of additional man power for its economic development

[20] Associate Professor of International Relations, Howard University, Washington, D.C.

and for the ethnic "Vietnamization" of the vast highland areas, inhabited by lesser developed tribes of Malayo-Indonesian stock.

From the first day of the Indochina war, and particularly from December 19, 1946, until July 21, 1954, large numbers of hapless civilians lost their houses and rice fields during actions of either the Communist or the French Union forces. The state of insecurity prevailing in the open country created a movement of large numbers of homeless refugees toward the urban areas. Even long before 1954, cities such as Saigon and Hanoi had seen their population increase five- to eight-fold in comparison to pre-World War II figures.

Large-scale movements of population, however, began in May, 1954, after the battle of Dien Bien Phu, when it became obvious that the French troops in north Viet-Nam would have to constrict their perimeter in the Red River Delta to the Hanoi-Haiphong life line, thus exposing the largely Catholic areas of Phat Diem, Bui Chui, Nam Dinh, and Thai Binh to Communist occupation. "Operation Auvergne" was the French code name for this withdrawal, which began in the first days of June, 1954. Hundreds of thousands of Catholics began a hundred-mile trek toward the new perimeter. The great exodus of 1954 had begun.

As Bui Van Luong indicates, the Geneva cease-fire agreement of July, 1954, provided for free movement in both directions for a period of three hundred days. His remarks with regard to the part played by France in making the movement of the refugees a success is the first such statement published in the English language, and he should be congratulated for his fairness. American newspapers at the time made it appear as if the refugee evacuation operation had been a wholly American "show." To recapitulate, in the midst of the rainy season, the French Air Force, pressing into service every military plane and all civilian planes available, flew a round-the-clock airlift, whose difficulties and distances made the famous Berlin airlift (flown in central Europe with the full benefit of the most modern airfields and ground control facilities) look like "a walk in the sun." In addition, French naval and commercial vessels made *three* times as many trips from the north to the south than vessels of all other nations combined. According to a personal inquiry with the Chief of Naval Operations, United States Navy, American vessels carried about 310,000 refugees. Aside from the six voyages made by non-French vessels, the French then must be credited with 214,000 airlifted refugees, 270,000 ship-borne civilian refugees, and 120,000 Vietnamese military personnel and their dependents, not to mention about 80,000 French troops and their equipment. It is also known that a good many of the 109,000 refugees who went south by their own means, "hitched rides" on French vessels not assigned to the population movement (aircraft carriers, combat aircraft, etc.). Thus, a conservative estimate, based on COMIGAL's figures, would credit the French with the evacuation of about three fourths of a million people from Red Viet-Nam.

One word on COMIGAL's figures, however. It may be said that, to the best of my knowledge, they are approximate in spite of their attempt to give the number of refugees down to the last numeral. In its English-language report, *The Exodus of the Northern Vietnamese*,[21] COMIGAL states that the total of "regular" refugees "reached 887,931 people." However, in the same report (page 1 of the Appendix) the total number of refugees is given as 810,484, with 77,447 "irregulars" thrown in to arrive at the above-mentioned total of 887,931. A report published by COMIGAL on June 20, 1957, however, shows yet another set of figures: 747,791 "regular," plus 140,712 "irregulars."[22]

It is obvious that such discrepancies should have been reconciled prior to their publication; it also shows that COMIGAL should have abstained from attempting to be overly precise in presenting its statistics, for it is common knowledge that the refugees themselves, for various purposes, sought to avoid proper registration. For example, a certain number of them, having arrived in the south, smuggled themselves aboard empty vessels or aircraft going north, were registered once more as refugees and, upon their arrival in Saigon, received a second (and, in some cases, a third, fourth, and fifth) food and cash allowance. Likewise, in the case of whole villages migrating to the south, the authorities frequently took the statements of the village leaders on faith. The latter, of course, had a certain interest in bloating the figures of refugees under their responsibility. Since 1955 several trials have been held in Saigon of officials who, as in the case of Gia Dinh province late in 1957, had collected the allowances and food gifts for thousands of fictitious "refugees," thus pocketing tens of millions of piasters of funds and gifts.

Surely, considering the magnitude of the task, some of these shortcomings were unavoidable. On the other hand, some could, and should, have been avoided. Funding and the proper control of funds remained a bottleneck which COMIGAL never completely solved.[23] However, such organizational shortcomings were of minor importance during the

[21] COMIGAL, "The Exodus . . . etc.," (mimeo.), 11 pp., Saigon, December, 1956, p. 3.

[22] COMIGAL, "Activités du COMIGAL (Periode de Juillet 1956 à Juillet 1957)" (mimeo.), 24 pp., Saigon, June, 1957, pp. 1-2.

[23] For an evaluation of COMIGAL operations, see the reports on the subject prepared by the Michigan State University Group in Viet-Nam, dated September 20, 1955, and June 29, 1956. In view of their private nature, they cannot be cited here.

movement phase, since the first housing and care of the arriving refugees was handled by French army units, Vietnamese army units, and aid teams of USOM, as well as teams of voluntary organizations such as the Red Cross, the Catholic relief agencies, and the Jaycees.

The last French ship left the beach near Haiphong on May 15, 1955, thus closing the first phase. By coincidence, but fittingly, the ship's name was *Esperance,* or Hope.

Little has been said in the world press and Western sources about the counter evacuation of Viet-Minh fighters and their dependents from areas south of the 17th parallel to north Viet-Nam. They were transported from their assembly areas around Ca Mau and Qui Nhon via Communist and Polish steamers, as well as by French ships going north empty.

While exact figures are unknown, it is generally estimated that about 120,000 Viet-Minh troops and dependents chose to go north—or rather, were ordered to go north. According to available information, the Communist commanders had strict orders as to who was to remain in place and become a civilian; who was to remain behind in hiding as guerrilla fighters or Communist agents; and who was to go north. Generally, the dependents of both of the regular Viet-Minh units and stay-behind guerrillas were evacuated to north Viet-Nam. All well-known Viet-Minh regular units from southern Cambodia, Free Viet-Nam, and the famous "Inter Zone 5" of southern central Viet-Nam were shipped out as a body. Also sent north were many young boys over fifteen years of age, for further indoctrination and training.

In the north, the refugee resettlement problem presented no major difficulties, since particularly the Catholic provinces had been practically deserted by their population. Southern military units remained together, thus no doubt preserving their *esprit de corps.* Apparently strong efforts have been made to avoid any friction between the local population and the evacuees.

The Viet-Minh government particularly tried to profit from the tensions created in the highlands by the influx of lowland Vietnamese, through special broadcasts in the native tongues of the highland tribes (no such broadcasts exist in the south) and by reinfiltrating into the highlands well-trained Viet-Minh cadres. According to a Michigan State University Group report on the situation, nearly 6,000 Rhadé tribesmen left with the Communists to the north, and Vietnamese Communists, dressed as tribesmen, are active among the tribes.

It but remains to ask the question as to why the Vietnamese, of both Communist or non-Communist persuasions, preferred to abandon all their worldly goods rather than to remain under a political regime with which they disagreed. In the case of Viet-Minh returning to the north, the question need not be asked: As was shown, evacuation was a matter of military and party discipline, and rarely left for the individual to decide.

In the case of the non-Communist refugees going to Free Viet-Nam, the question is almost equally clear—they had been in the midst of a long war and now found themselves, at least temporarily, on the losing side. In view of the ensuing Viet-Minh "Mobilization of the Masses" policy, which, between 1954 and 1956, resulted in the death of nearly 50,000 farmers accused of "landlordism" and was only stopped when the population of Nghe An province (northern central Viet-Nam) rose in revolt, their fears were entirely justified.

There is no doubt that a propaganda effort was made in favor of a mass exodus from the north. But it is certain that the methods of the Viet-Minh were well enough known to incite large numbers of people to leave their homes if an opportunity to do so existed.

Too often, however, this distaste of the refugees for communism is taken as proof of their acquiescence in their present fate, no matter how dismal. This may well become a fatal error. Free Viet-Nam will have to do its very best to raise the general standards of living of all its population, refugee and native, lest it lose in the field of economics the fruits of its psychological victory in the struggle for the lasting allegiance of its people.

Commentary: BUI VAN LUONG[24] *on* FALL

IN HIS COMMENTS, Professor Bernard B. Fall seems to disagree with my viewpoint that the Vietnamese are deeply attached to their rice lands and family burial grounds. I wrote this to show that the exodus of a million refugees was mainly motivated by a horror of the northern Communist regime.

Citing the historical movement of the Vietnamese to the south, Professor Fall writes, "In other words, century after century, thousands of Vietnamese left the tombs of their ancestors and the familiar northern countryside for the fertile lands of the south." He further states that "the movement of one million northern Vietnamese to Free Viet-Nam, while surely a time of physical hardship to the individuals involved, was not something 'unnatural' to the Vietnamese." It is certainly true that two thousand years ago, the Vietnamese lived in the regions

[24] Translated by Phan Thu Ngoc.

of Kwansi and Kwantung in China. Later, to avoid extermination by stronger neighbors, they moved toward the south in search of a more favorable land. Settled in the plains of the Red River and the Song Ma (Ma River) for centuries, they never ceased to show their determination to remain there permanently, fighting valiantly, whenever necessary, against all invasion attempts.

In the sixteenth century, the southward emigration of a portion of the Vietnamese people, led by Nguyen Hoang, was attributable solely to a retreat forced upon Nguyen Hoang and his followers by his powerful rival, Lord Trink. Exploiting popular discontent caused by his enemy's cruelties, Nguyen Hoang easily found admirers and quickly gathered in his territory a sizeable population, which enabled him to extend his jurisdiction all the way to the Cape of Ca Mau.

This migration was, therefore, primarily a popular movement inspired by opposition to an odious dictatorial regime, rather than a planned movement toward fertile lands.

Furthermore, Professor Fall seems to be unaware of a particular Vietnamese psychological trait: the Vietnamese of the lowlands, generally speaking, like to spend their old age among family and friends.

During the French Protectorate period, the Labor Migration Bureau resorted to various devices to induce northern Vietnamese to come and work on southern rubber plantations, but the results were disappointing. Only a few poorer laborers came; yet neither material advantages nor disciplinary measures were sufficient to prevent runaways and repatriation requests when contracts expired. This indicates the innate attachment of the Vietnamese to his native land.

In order to distinguish sharply between the diverse phases of the movement of Vietnamese during the period from December 19, 1946, to July 21, 1954, it should be said that two movements in opposite directions took place during the Indochinese war before the withdrawal of French troops from the southern provinces of the delta in north Viet-Nam. The first movement was that of city dwellers to the country, when the towns were to be destroyed in conformity with the Viet-Minh's policy of "burned land." The second movement was that to the cities of rural people who were aware that they had been deceived by the Communists, and left the villages to come and live in zones occupied by French and nationalist troops, especially provincial capitals and large cities. It is this second movement that caused the enormous increase of the population of Hanoi and Saigon.

As to the evacuation of refugees, it is a matter of public knowledge that the French high command in the Far East made maximum efforts in organizing transportation. According to an official communiqué,

French ships and planes carried half (and not three fourths) the number of refugees; the exact figures are 240,000 by air and 237,000 by sea.

However, public opinion viewed this French effort only as the fulfillment of an obligation of France toward Viet-Nam. France, the reasoning went, as a signer of the Geneva Agreement, owed it to itself to take steps to evacuate all voluntary refugees to the south. Confronted with needs which far exceeded provisions, it was forced to declare its inability to assume this burdensome responsibility alone. Therefore, if it had not been for the swift and chivalrous assistance of the United States 7th Fleet, the Free World would have suffered a second Dien Bien Phu. Therefore, it seems natural to the Vietnamese that the American press should have described the refugees' evacuation as a major achievement of the United States government.

Professor Fall devoted special attention to refugee data, and, admittedly, there was some discrepancy in the published data. This was due to the fact that all the relevant files had been destroyed when COMIGAL headquarters was burnt down by the Binh Xuyen in May, 1955. Figures had to be modified whenever a document which appeared relatively trustworthy was found. The data shown in the report of COMIGAL activities, July, 1956-July, 1957 are the most reliable ones, namely 747,791 "regular" evacuees and 140,712 "irregulars."

Incidentally, it should be pointed out that the armed services, French as well as Vietnamese, only took care of the reception of military evacuees and their families who had been taken to Nha Trang or Saigon before August 6, 1954. After this date, the reception of refugees was, in general, wholly in the hands of the Ministry of Social Action and, later, of COMIGAL. The various international welfare agencies such as the Red Cross, the Catholic Relief Service, and Jaycees generously contributed, but only to the extent of distributing medical care or gift merchandise.[25] As for USOM, whose aid was doubtless the most effective, it played its role only in the difficult phase of refugee resettlement.

The question of evacuation of southerners to the north is outside my competence; however, during the resettlement of Vietnamese in the highlands, necessary steps were taken to offset the subversive propaganda directed at the ethnic minorities. This was done through conferences of provincial authorities, talks by COMIGAL's information section, broadcasts in native dialects by Radio-Dalat, etc. As repeatedly stated, nearly a million Vietnamese left the north for the south for the

[25] For a report on the Catholic Relief Services, see the article by the Rt. Rev. Msgr. Joseph J. Harnett, pp. 77-82. (ED.)

sole purpose of escaping the totalitarian regime of the Viet-Minh. The refugees definitely did not leave their homes in order to improve their material conditions.

Complying on the one hand with the provision giving freedom of choice to the population, and on the other hand keeping in mind its budgetary capabilities—which were not sufficient at the time to handle too large a group of refugees—the Vietnamese government did not resort to an aggressive propaganda campaign to invite northerners to come to Free Viet-Nam.

Nonetheless, to those who wanted to come, it did provide maximum aid in helping them start a new life as quickly as possible. The deactivation of COMIGAL on December 31, 1957, is proof that this objective was achieved. Adequate measures are now being taken to make the refugees the legal owners of lands which they have by their labor and perseverance developed and cultivated for two years.

At present all evacuees have been integrated into the general community. Vis-à-vis the nation as a whole, the government of Free Viet-Nam is relentlessly following its policy of national economic reconstruction, which is designed to raise the standard of living of all, refugees as well as natives. The entire population of Free Viet-Nam has the same identical interest and enthusiasm in furthering this effort. Thus, the psychological victory brought about by the exodus of nearly a million northern Vietnamese will have achieved, in the economic field, the results that it was reasonable to expect for the general welfare of the country.

Commentary: FALL on BUI VAN LUONG

BUI VAN LUONG's scholarly description of the Vietnamese population migrations of the past two thousand years merely further emphasizes the point made—the Vietnamese are ready to move (i.e., abandon their rice lands and the tombs of their ancestors) rather than submit to domination by a regime which they hate, be it Chinese or Communist Vietnamese. I was fully aware of the fact that a Vietnamese likes to spend his old age with his family and friends. Hence, when the Vietnamese migrated, they never migrated as individuals but as whole groups, villages, and cities. In fact, Bui Van Luong's own resettlement program respected this psychological trait in resettling the northern refugees, wherever possible, in entire communities, with their habitual village priests and notables.

With regard to labor migration under the French Protectorate, official figures[26] show that about 15,000 plantation laborers a year moved from north Viet-Nam to south Viet-Nam over the period between 1913 and the economic crisis of 1929. The eminent French economist, Charles Robequain, whose book *L'Évolution Économique de l'Indochine* is universally recognized as the best treatise on the subject, states that all explanations about the attachment of the Vietnamese to their native village and ancestors do not detract from the fact that an "amazing expansion" took place.[27] The even more recent migration of Vietnamese into Cambodia, Laos, and even Thailand testifies to this willingness of the Vietnamese to move.

I am grateful to Bui Van Luong for stating the precise figures on refugee migration, which he sets at 747,791 "regular" refugees and 140,712 "irregulars," and stand corrected in my evaluation of the French evacuation effort at 75 percent of the refugees. Since no one knows exactly how the irregular refugees came south, the French effort (474,000 according to Luong) represents exactly 66.6 percent of all regular refugees.

[26] Haut Commissariat de France en Indochine, *Bulletin Économique de l'Indochine,* January-March, 1952, p. 7.

[27] On page 5 of his book Robequain states: ". . . ces explications ne résistent point au fait historique de l'expansion étonnante du peuple qui, ayant franchi la Porte d'Annam au Xe siècle, est arrivé au XVIIe siècle, aux bouche du Mékong."

VI.   The Role of the United States Navy[28]

CHRONOLOGY OF EVENTS

8 August, 1954. The Chief of Naval Operations informed the Commander in Chief of the Pacific Fleet that the United States government intended to participate in the evacuation of Vietnamese civilians from Communist-held northern Indochina. Major General J. W. O'Daniel, Chief Military Assistance Advisory Group (CHMAAG), was designated the over-all military co-ordinator ashore, to be responsible to the American Ambassador to Viet-Nam, Donald R. Heath. Rear Admiral S. Sabin, Commander, Task Force 90 (CTF-90), was designated the commander of the United States sea operations. Elements of the Western Pacific Amphibious Group, augmented by ships of the Military Sea Transportation Service, were made available for employment in this operation, as requested by CFT-90.

Upon agreement between the Commander in Chief of the Pacific and the Commander in Chief of the Far East, Commander Task Force 90 was released from the Far East Command and directed by the Commander of the Naval Forces in the Far East to report to the Commander in Chief of the United States Pacific Fleet for Operational Control.

17 August. Menard (Attack Transport-201[29]) loaded 1,924 refugees and sailed from Haiphong for Saigon.

18 August. Montrose (APA-212), second ship to load refugees, departed from Haiphong, with 2,100 refugees.

19 August. CHMAAG, Indochina, reported that he was attempting to resolve the many problems arising at the embarkation and debarkation sites, such as sanitation, mass feeding, transportation, tents, inoculations, and organization of control teams to act as interpreters and to assist with the care of refugees on board ship during the trip south.

24 August. Commander-in-Chief, Pacific Fleet (CINCPACFLT, joint army, navy, air command), clarified navy policy on evacuation of French and Vietnamese military units. This policy permitted such units to be lifted in U.S. ships at the discretion of CTF-90 and CHMAAG, Indochina, provided that the lift of refugees and Mutual Defense Assistance Program (MDAP) equipment, would at no time be sacrificed to such employment.

[28] Written by the Commander in Chief, U.S. Pacific Fleet. To retain a maximum degree of accuracy and to preserve the feel of a developing situation, the observations, experiences, and accomplishments of the navy in their evacuation operations, from August 8, 1954, to May 18, 1955, are recorded as they were reported and summarized day by day to the Chief of Naval Operations. Only minor alterations in style were made for the convenience of the reader.

[29] In navy communications, attack transports are indicated as APA, followed by the number which indicates a specific attack transport (APA-201). This style is followed hereafter in this report.

27 August. CHMAAG, Indochina, established a refugee debarkation site at Cap St. Jacques, at the entrance of the Saigon River. This relieved congestion in the Saigon camps and decreased navy problems encountered transiting the Saigon River.

30 August. CTF-90 was informed that the pilot fees for traversing the Saigon River amounted to about $750 for each ship per round trip. This was referred to CHMAAG, Indochina, for resolution with French, Vietnamese, and U.S. embassy. CINCPACFLT was informed.

31 August. A typhoon in the vicinity of Haiphong destroyed almost half of the refugee staging area. However, Military Assistance Advisory Group (MAAG) had sufficient tents after the typhoon had passed to increase the camp capacity to 10,000 refugees.

1 September. Camp sites at Haiphong cleared of debris and back in operation.

Ships of Task Group (TG) 90.8 were directed to be alert for possible sabotage aboard evacuation ships.

3 September. MAAG representative in Haiphong reported to CHMAAG, Indochina, that through 1 September approximately 153,000 refugees had been evacuated; 106,000 by French air and navy, balance by the U.S. navy.

The French unofficially made it known that they did not intend to pay pilot fees for ships traversing the Saigon River. CHMAAG, Indochina, recommended that bills be presented to Special Technical Economic Mission (STEM) for U.S. payment if the Vietnamese government refused to pay the bill.

6 September. CHMAAG, Indochina, reported that refugee camps in the Saigon-Cap St. Jacques areas were becoming overcrowded because refugees were arriving at a faster rate than the Vietnamese government was able to relocate the families. As a result, CHMAAG, Indochina, requested that only one ship, with no more than 2,500 passengers per day, arrive in this area during the period 11-25 September.

9 September. CTF-90 was informed that the French were reluctant to make dock space available for U.S. cargo ships. Their reasons were that 21 French cargo ships were under contract for the operation; that limited port facilities were available; and that each U.S. cargo ship employed would displace one French cargo ship with a resultant loss of revenue for the French.

10 September. CTF-90 conferred with MAAG representatives at Haiphong, CTG-90.8, and Foreign Operation Administration (FOA) representative relative to idle U.S. ships in Indochina. Estimates for refugees were approximately 10,000 per week and cargo for Military Sea Transportation Service (MSTS) ships undetermined. CTF-90 recommended to CINCPACFLT that, if after thorough investigation it is still evident that increased loading facilities will not be made available, U.S. shipping should be withdrawn or drastically reduced.

12 September. CTF-90 reported the following reasons for sudden decrease in number of refugees: (1) poor planning and organization at relocation centers in south caused lack of faith in government; (2) Viet-Minh countermeasures, such as false propaganda and forcible detention, were very effective; (3) the approach of the rice harvesting season; (4) many remain to transact business during the Tonkinese festival season. Vietnamese official requested U.S. lift private industrial material. CTF-90 declined, stating it was not possible under the agreement by which U.S. ships were participating.

16 September. United States Naval Attaché (ALUSNA), Saigon, informed CINCPACFLT that Commander Menon, Indian Navy, president of International Control Commission team at Saigon, had informally asked permission for the committee to visit U.S. ships for inspection. CINCPACFLT advised CTF-90 and ALUSNA, Saigon, that no foreigners will be allowed to inspect U.S. naval or merchant ships under PACFLT OpControl without specific authority of the Chief of Naval Operations (CNO).

18 September. Refugees refused to use matting issued them. Matting was too loosely woven and of poor quality. Ships also consider them a fire hazard. It was decided to turn the mats over to the Refugee Commission in Saigon to be used at debarkation centers.

CFT-90 informed the CNO that French had commenced using military personnel as stevedores on the docks at Haiphong to load U.S. ships.

24 September. Flagship *Estes* arrived at Saigon. Ceremony for 100,000th refugee held at Catinat Wharf. Vietnamese and American diplomatic representatives were on hand to greet the 100,000th refugee and his family.

25 September. French reported they had allocated 8-10 ships to lift Viet-Minh to the north. This commitment should be completed by 1 November. French will then have capacity to move all cargo south.

26 September. It is apparent to all that the Viet-Minh have halted the refugee movement at Hanoi. As a result, a downward revision of weekly evacuee rate to 4,000 was made. Cargo loading and discharging was still painfully slow and considered unsatisfactory. CTF-90 continued to urge CHMAAG, Indochina, to exert all possible effort to improve this situation which was resulting in uneconomic use of American shipping.

29 September. CTG-90.8 reported that a Roman Catholic priest, who escaped from Thai Binh, believed that 20,000 people in that district wish to leave, while an estimated 50,000 people desire evacuation from other towns and districts under Viet-Minh control.

CTF-90 informed CNO that the new Vietnamese Minister of Information, Thai, stated that General Hinh, Minister of Defense, is very capable, dynamic, and popular, making him so indispensable that soon a more important post in the government may be offered him. Thai criticized the government for allowing many useless people to arrive (babies and very old women) from the north, while the Viet-Minh retained really productive elements.

French arrested 12 civilians in Saigon for possessing concussion-type hand grenades in the downtown area most frequented by Americans.

30 September. CTG-90.8 visited Hanoi for final equipment and refugee check before 10 October deadline. No additional refugees had arrived within the last 24 hours. Tents at staging line were struck for transportation to Haiphong. French were removing airstrip matting, asphalt, jerry cans, and empty drums from the airfields. The French have relieved the Vietnamese police in the city. Hanoi took on an abandoned look except for white cars of the Truce Commission and armed troops at every intersection.

1 October. Twenty-seven sampans carrying 2,000 refugees arrived at Camp Pagode, Haiphong, after fleeing their parishes about 70 miles south of Haiphong. Fifty more sampans were reported enroute.

5 October. Vietnamese customs officials inspected refugees that arrived Saigon embarked in the *General Black.* They confiscated the U.S. gift packages. The same treatment was given the crew of the *General Black,* whose personal effects were confiscated. U.S. Consul was able to have the crew's personal effects returned prior to the ship's sailing.

6 October. CTF-90 informed CNO that no interference by Vietnamese customs officers or police occurred during the debarkation of refugees on this date.

7 October. CTG-90.9, Commander A. E. Teall, reported that the Chinese refugees transported to Saigon aboard the *General Howze* (T-AP 134) were required to pass through customs inspections upon debarkation. U.S. representatives present were unable to determine what items were confiscated; however, it is believed the customs officials were searching for opium and gold leafs.

16 October. CTG-90.8 reported reasons given by the senior Vietnamese official at Haiphong, Mr. Luat, why many people choose to remain in northern Viet-Nam: (1) to await developments in Hanoi after the Reds take over; (2) to await the outcome of the political dispute in southern Viet-Nam; (3) to await the completion of the rice harvest in mid-November; (4) to hold off the liquidation of business interests until late January.

18 October. CTG-90.8 reported that 150 refugees arrived by sea in two sampans and two rafts under the leadership of an 85-year-old patriarch. They were greeted by the Mayor of Haiphong and then transported to Camp Pagode.

19 October. A Vietnamese nationalist boarded the *Marine Lynx* (T-AP 194) by climbing a mooring line while the ship was at Saigon. Caught in the act of stealing by Vietnamese soldiers, he was severely beaten and turned over to the French authorities. He died a short time later of internal injuries. The French made an investigation of the incident. The U.S. government did not become involved.

CTF-90 discussed the entire evacuation situation individually with the French and Vietnamese officials at Haiphong. The French attitude was one of wholehearted co-operation, unity of purpose, and maximum effort.

20 October. A decision was reached by the French in regard to pilot and port fees at Saigon. The French declared that in recognition of aid so generously extended, all U.S. ships engaged in the Indochina evacuation are exempt from all port and pilot fees.

21 October. Lieutenant General J. W. O'Daniel, CHMAAG, Indochina, spent the night aboard the flagship *Estes.*

24 October. Refugees continued to arrive from the Bui Chu area via French LST, LSM, and the French ship *Pimodon*. The International Control Commission Team at Haiphong interrogated these refugees concerning their escape. It was reported that the refugees were required to pay 15,000 Viet-Minh piasters, which is about 500 Viet-Nam piasters, for their passage in sampans and rafts.

Lieutenant (Junior Grade) T. A. Dooley, Medical Corps, USN, relieved Commander S. O. Britten as CTU 90.8.6, Haiphong.

27 October. Mr. Michael Adler, FOA representative, reported that Haiphong officials are collecting Viet-Minh piasters from refugees and giving receipts for reimbursement in Viet-Nam piasters upon their arrival at Saigon.

French LST arrived at Haiphong, with 1,800 refugees from Van Ly. These refugees were rescued from sampans and bamboo rafts. Many of them reported that they had been detained by the Viet-Minh and in some cases beaten with rifle butts.

29 October. Helicopter dusted the Haiphong refugee camps with Lindane insecticide, with excellent results reported.

General Black (T-AP 135) loaded 5,224 refugees; this being the largest load to date for any one ship.

Cost of Operation for Period 8 August-1 November

A study prepared by CTF-90 indicates that the total over-all cost of the navy participation in the Indochina evacuation operation for the period 8 August-1 November is approximately $16,000,000. This figure was arrived at by using per diem rates (furnished by Commander, Military Sea Transport Service for MSTS shipping and estimated by CTF-90 for PACFLT units) times ship days (from port of deployment to final port after release), and includes the costs of the logistic support group ships, all special materials furnished by supply activities, miscellaneous expenditures by individual ships properly chargeable to the operation and special installations such as hold ladders and augmented sanitary facilities for time-chartered ships. To 1 November the average over-all cost was $71 per passenger and $166 per ton cargo carried.

The above cost figures are, of course, only tentative, since they are based on estimates and incomplete information available to CTF-90 and furthermore are subject to interpretation depending upon the definition of cost as applied to this operation. The CTF-90 study considers the "true" cost from the standpoint of a commercial operation.

1 November. CTG-90.8 reported that two refugees were wounded by the Viet-Minh, while attempting to escape by raft from Bui Chu area. These refugees were treated by Lieutenant (J. G.) Dooley, MC, USN, and Roman Catholic priest (Vietnamese) Father Khue at the hospital in Haiphong. Pictures of the wounds were taken to be presented to the International Control Commission.

3 November. International Control Commission went into session to consider the complaints of the two refugees allegedly wounded by the Viet-Minh. The proceedings, declarations, and results were not made available to U.S. authorities.

8 November. The International Control Commission has heard the case of the two wounded refugees referred to on 1 and 3 November. The files on this case were sent to Hanoi.

10 November. CTF-90 and CTG-90.8 made a courtesy call on Ambassador Donald R. Heath and newly arrived Ambassador J. Lawton Collins. CTF-90 presented a brief resumé of the sea lift situation to Ambassador Collins.

14 November. It was reported that the Viet-Minh would allow refugees to depart via circuitous water routes by Viet-Minh transportation. The first arrivals are expected not earlier than 17 November, 1954. The French plan to embark refugees at the transfer points. Lack of transportation is not anticipated.

Summary of evacuation totals as of this date (U.S. shipping only):

13,657 military passengers
153,807 civilian passengers
5,791 vehicles
27,977 short tons cargo
48 deaths
92 births

Total refugees, Haiphong Camps: 11,127

19 November. LST 1159 released. 430 Phat Diem refugees arrived at Haiphong. Each refugee paid 250 Viet-Nam piasters for transportation to Haiphong via Viet-Minh facilities.

20 November. Two French fishing contractors, acting as spokesmen for fishermen in the Baie d'Along area, arrived at Haiphong seeking American assistance in the emigration of approximately 100 fishing families, with their boats, to the south. They were placed in contact with MAAG and USOM personnel. This was the first notice U.S. authorities had of any desire on the part of the fishermen of Baie d'Along, almost all of whom were Chinese, to move to the south. They conditioned their desire to move on being allowed to bring their boats with them.

Initial plans were discussed by French navy and local Catholic authorities to effect coastal refugee pick-up in the vicinity of Vinh similar to the Bui Chu operation. Vinh operation was scheduled to be last major effort of Catholic authorities who, as of this date, regarded Phat Diem incapable, because of Viet-Minh restraints, of producing more than a token number of refugees. Vinh operation, scheduled to begin about 30 November, 1954, is expected to produce less than 6,000 refugees. Refugees report constant propaganda and intimidation along the circuitous Viet-Minh route. Also difficulty in obtaining Viet-Minh passports and having to pay 7,000 piasters for transportation, which allegedly is free, has effectively hamstrung the effort.

22 November. Workers at a Haiphong acetylene plant struck when French tried to remove equipment. Workers claimed removal of equipment would destroy their jobs. Red-inspired strikes are expected wherever the French attempt to remove machinery from Haiphong plants.

24 November. Long-expected influx of large number refugees from Phat Diem commenced with arrival of 800 via Viet-Minh boat transport to boundary line at Bac Cuu on Song Van Uc. Temporary refugee camp established at Kien An church, 7 miles southwest of Haiphong.

Fishing colony representative stated that solution to fishing boat problem proposed by French navy, which was to sail boats south in company and under escort in April, was unsatisfactory in view of growing Viet-Minh infiltration of fishing communities. CTU-90.8.1 was directed to ascertain state of junks and feasibility of loading them on CIMAVI (hull-type designation of a MSTS ship) type vessels.

Recent refugee arrivals from Phat Diem related Viet-Minh tactics to the Control Commission. They said they received Red lectures on the horrors of Haiphong refugee camps and were told that the young men would be forced into the Viet-Nam army and sent to Morocco.

A refugee Catholic priest told of his torture and degradation, in which Chinese army officers jammed chopsticks in his ears and beat him with bamboo poles after accusing him of telling lies to the people.

25 November. Conversations with late arrived refugees disclose they want to leave Red-dominated Tonkin Delta less for religious reasons than because of hard work without pay, higher taxes, constant marauding and lawlessness, and intense indoctrination in Communist philosophy.

Many refugees now in Haiphong camps gave reasons for not wanting to leave as "they are waiting for families and to exchange Viet-Minh money for Viet-Nam." CHMAAG believes there may be many other significant reasons.

26 November. A Dominican priest at Haiphong has been ordered by his superior to depart the city permanently along with all other Dominicans in the area. Dominicans have played a major role in the evacuation, being especially helpful in refugee camps.

27 November. *Pembina* completed loading and sailed to Saigon with cargo containing miscellaneous equipment of Catholic church authorities in Haiphong. CTG-90.8 protested the character of the cargo to senior MAAG representative Haiphong. Material was mostly junk and did not make for good stowage.

28 November. Slowdown by longshoremen offloading *Fentress* at Tourane required utilization of French army personnel. This proved very satisfactory; however, the 14 days required to offload this ship is excessive.

CTU-90.8.1 visited villages of Baie d'Along fishermen to discuss the problem of moving their fishing boats south. After survey, he concluded it was impossible to lift boats by CIMAVI, but that the fishermen must be evacuated soon, as they fear retribution after May if they do not trade now with the Viet-Minh. Construction and size of boats precludes hoisting or profitable deck or hold stowage. LSD regarded only vessel capable of making lift. CTG-90.8 recommended LSD not be employed because he did not consider the situation warranted the use of such critical type shipping.

29 November. Among yesterday's arrivals at Haiphong was a patriarch of 102 years who traveled 2½ months on foot to bring his family from Thanh Hoa home to Phat Diem and then to freedom. His family numbered 42 and consisted of 5 generations, the 5th represented by a 2-day-old infant.

An attempt by Vietnamese officials to remove government-owned dental and x-ray equipment from the dental clinic of the Haiphong city hospital had to be abandoned. City police broke up a gathering of nurses, technicians, other employees, and hundreds of friends demonstrating against the loss of jobs. This is second known incident of demonstration protesting removal of "capital" goods from area. No question but what Viet-Minh sympathizers are attempting to induce as many demonstrations as possible.

30 November. CTG-90.8 reported that the problem of moving the Viet-

Nam fishing fleet to the south could be practically solved by either or both of two methods listed below:

1. A French fishing contractor had expressed a desire to arrange transportation for about thirty to Tourane where he would establish a badly needed fishing fleet.

2. The French have refused to transport any but have agreed to escort the seaworthy fishing boats south between the monsoons. This would leave an indeterminate number to be lifted. In any event CTG-90.8 recommended the U.S. not transport them because it would set a precedent not hitherto afforded others. He recommended the entire matter be left up to the French and that MAAG carefully follow the negotiations.

1 December. General Cogny announced via press, radio, and bulletin boards that French government will not be responsible for the military security or orderly evacuation of French nationals who choose to remain within Haiphong perimeter after 1 February, 1955.

Evacuation atmosphere is beginning to permeate Haiphong with the closing of many shops.

2 December. Monsieur Compaign, former French delegate to north Viet-Nam, informed MAAG officers of negotiations then in progress between Viet-Minh and French businessmen and officials. M. Compaign stated purpose of negotiations was to attempt to reach a financial settlement that would allow French to salvage some value from business properties falling under Viet-Minh control.

3 December. Refugee influx steadied at 150 per day as backlog of refugees who had congregated at Phat Diem became exhausted. International Control Commission published figures of 10,800 refugees that had been brought from Phat Diem last 10 days through Commission efforts.

9 December. The problem of fishing boats came up again. CHMAAG, Saigon, informed CINCPAC that the owners of about 180 registered vessels at Apowan will not be ready to leave until the end of the April monsoon. He further stated that transporting them aboard ship was not practicable.

16 December. CTG-90.8 reported that if agreements are reached between private Vietnamese and French companies and the Viet-Minh government, there will be a considerable reduction in the amount of civilian equipment to be evacuated.

18 December. Refugee arrivals averaging 500 per day. Vinh operation again postponed because of heavy seas. Most arrivals during this period are utilizing false and reused *laissez passer.*

CHMAAG, Saigon, recommended that since the French government intends charging 400 piasters per square meter to move civilian barges from Haiphong to Saigon, the U.S. should apply similar rates for the use of LSD.

19 December. Arlo Olson completed first load and sailed for Saigon. Load was principally cement. This was second TAK (cargo ship) load of cement moved by U.S. ships.

20 December. The French are attempting to persuade all possible to move prior to Chinese New Year, 25 January.

21 December. First arrivals of refugees from Vinh reached Haiphong. 525 persons picked up off coast by French ship night of 19 December.

23 December. About 100 refugees per day are joining the Vietnamese army and another 200 are re-entering the Viet-Minh zone in search of their families.

Security has noticeably tightened at Haiphong military installations due to rumors of possible Red demonstrations.

24 December. Haiphong streets presented appearance of armed camp. Special military policemen patrolled all downtown area in large groups. Personnel CTU-90.8.1 directed to remain near billets ashore; radio jeep made available to other U.S. personnel ashore for emergency communication with flagship during hours of darkness.

25 December. No Viet-Minh demonstrations developed on 24 or 25 December.

26 December. Vietnamese authorities delayed loading of *General Howze* until 29 December despite urging for earlier loading by U.S. and French authorities. Vietnamese desire to stage special demonstration 28 December for Vinh refugees, most of whom have lived under Communist rule for 8 years.

29 December. Refugees loaded on *General Howze* included about 500 Chinese descent from Hon Gay region and about 800 permanent Haiphong residents. This is first real exodus of these groups, whom French are urging to depart early. Refugees carried numerous large boxes which seriously hampered loading.

French army intelligence sources stated on excellent authority that Viet-Minh have formulated definite policy toward evacuation of capital enterprises from Haiphong enclave. Policy will be to oppose removal, but methods to be used are heavy propaganda, strikes, peaceful demonstrations, but no violence.

30 December. Thorough check of all available French and Vietnamese authorities in Haiphong by the Assistant U.S. Army Attaché indicated that while the potential for civil or military disturbance within the perimeter will continue high, Viet-Minh policy of no violence has been so well established that probability of serious incidents are virtually nonexistent.

2 January, 1955. Last Vinh pick-up ship returned Haiphong with no refugees aboard. Vinh operation considered ended due to effective Viet-Minh restraint.

9 January. The refugees departing the *Howze* on 4 January were an unusually mixed group. In addition to the normal farming families, there were Nungs, trade union members, and merchants (principally Chinese). The trade union members and merchants posed another of the always occurring problems when they made it known they did not feel they should clean their own compartments. The Evacuation Committee has been requested, in the future, to insure full understanding on the part of all refugees that cleaning of compartments is necessary due to large number of refugees carried.

Reports have been received of severe clashes between Viet-Minh troops and several hundred Viet-Nam peasants in Thanh Hoa area the past few days. The peasants had congregated in the area to seek Control Commission assistance in traveling to Haiphong for evacuation, and when the Control Commission team failed to arrive the peasants determined to escape by force.

10 January. French estimate 100,000 refugees remain who wish to be evacuated, but President Diem places the figure at 200,000.

Haiphong police have seized some 20 Viet-Minh agents posing as Buddhist monks and using Buddhist pagoda, containing communications equipment, as headquarters.

13 January. Howze sailing scheduled for today was delayed until to-morrow due to Chinese bringing a great number of large boxes. *Howze* crew working on 24-hour basis in order to secure for sea. Task is difficult due to flimsy construction of boxes, of which there are about 200 long tons.

MAAG and USOM have been requested to again ask the Refugee Committee to instruct refugees that *Howze* is not a cargo ship.

Seven large junks that were proceeding up the Song Ria have been seized by French and returned to Haiphong. Junks were enroute to Viet-Minh and were carrying cement, gasoline, and lube oil loaded at Haiphong. Event considered important because it implicated large number of Chinese merchants and some Vietnamese government officials.

About 300 nine- to fifteen-year-old children of Chinese descent departed Haiphong for Peking. Chinese Reds and Viet-Minh arranged transportation and have promised free education in Peking.

The clash reported 9 January turned out to be between 10,000 peasants and 4,000 Viet-Minh regulars. The peasants armed only with sticks were dispersed, and the Control Commission apparently accepted Viet-Minh version that the incident was one of suppression of illegal up-rising.

French resumed their intermittent air lift of refugees.

16 January. U.S. authorities in Haiphong received their first notice of a letter dated 28 December, 1954, from Charbonnage du Tonkin Company to Commander French Naval Forces, Tonkin, requesting shipment on French naval vessels of approximately 100 pieces of very heavy equipment during March, April, and May. Director of company has stated that the negotiations which continue in Hanoi between French business and government representatives, and the Viet-Minh, carry the stipulation that U.S. funded equipment will be evacuated from the Hon Gay and Campha port regions without incident. All the equipment for which shipping requests have been made is U.S. purchased, but the total list did not include all U.S. purchased equipment at the mines.

19 January. French LSM picked up 4 refugees off Ba Lang coast and brought them to Haiphong. Refugees were participants in the peasant-Viet-Minh troop clash reported earlier. Viet-Minh now have mortars placed along the shore, making further pickups in that area possible.

21 January. French stepped up air lift. Almost 10,000 refugees Haiphong camps despite air lift and two TAP (personnel transport) sailings.

Confirmed reports from several sources indicated an increasing restlessness among civilian population in the Viet-Minh zone. Buddhists are joining Catholics in resistance to new government and desire evacuation.

Sailing of *Marine Serpent* delayed due to refugees continuing to arrive with excessive baggage. Size of bundles has been cut down but quantity has increased accordingly.

23 January. Chinese New Year holiday commenced throughout Viet-Nam. All activities suspended for 4-day period, except offloading of *Marine Serpent.*

28 January. Although there are an estimated 10,373 refugees in Haiphong camps, only 100 appeared to embark in *Howze* on 27 January. Conferences with French and Refugee Committee indicate holidays as prime reason for nonreadiness.

10 February. Approximately 100 military and quasi-military Viet-Minh deserters arrived at Haiphong. A spontaneous demonstration took place at the city hall, highlighted by speeches detailing suffering under Viet-Minh and shouts of praise for the evacuation. Several deserters claimed to have fought in the Viet-Minh army since 1946. All had grievances against the Viet-Minh regime and decided to leave when they learned escape was possible through Haiphong.

General Cogny published in the press an official proclamation stating that French civilians must evacuate Haiphong by 15 April. After that date they will be considered as desirous of staying past 18 May.

24 February. Pfizer pharmaceutical company donated 100,000 magnamycin tablets to Dr. Dooley for use in refugee camps.

3 May. Among 250 refugee arrivals were 90 escapees from Vinh area. All 90 arrived in 2 junks.

8 May. Estimate 3,000 to 4,000 refugees remaining desiring evacuation. Additional ones reluctant to leave because of current unstable situation in the south and rumors in circulation of 3,000 refugees returning north via Communist shipping.

"Committee of Experts," official Viet-Minh vanguard, arrived in Haiphong for indoctrination in operation of public utilities.

Chinese still in Haiphong indicate they intend to remain.

Local merchants manufacturing and displaying Viet-Minh flags.

French sector is deserted and sanitation conditions are deteriorating.

Viet-Minh demonstrations contribute to tension as deadline draws near.

No MDAP or US funded equipment remains on docks or in warehouses.

Local refugee committee terminated formal administrative procedures and most officials departed.

French naval base is completely stripped and closed.

12 May. Lieutenant Dooley, MC, awarded medal "Officer de L'Ordre National de Viet-Nam" by President Diem, for his outstanding work with the refugees the past 10 months.

14 May. Ten refugees, including infant girl, arrived on the *Doson* from Hanoi at 1400H. Refugees had no baggage or personal belongings. Mother of infant girl chose to remain under Viet-Minh and was deserted by husband. Father and child last official refugees to leave north Viet-Nam and were embarked in *General Brewster*.

French stated they had shipping to evacuate any later arrivals.

15 May. Evacuation of *Doson* and north Viet-Nam completed with the embarkation by the French of 707 military passengers and 120 vehicles.

18 May. Special operation terminated, no refugees embarked. CTG-50.1 in *Cook* departed for Sangley Point. *Marine Adder* sailed to Saigon.[30]

. . . .

3. *Problems Encountered and Solutions* . . .

(3) Language barriers. Interpretation usually was a two-step process: Vietnamese to French and French to English, so that interviewing was quite difficult. Practically no Vietnamese-to-English interpreters were available, and very few navy personnel spoke French.

Solution: None, except the obvious one of more interpreters.

MEDICAL
SUMMARY AND RECOMMENDATIONS

. . . .

(2) The problem of civilian evacuee deaths on board U.S. ships was without available known precedent. It was deduced that the cultural mores

[30] During the period August 8, 1954, to May 18, 1955, the United States Navy evacuated from Red Viet-Nam to Free Viet-Nam a total of 310,848 people, 68,757 tons of military cargo, and 8,135 military vehicles.

and religious beliefs of the evacuees would strongly influence acceptable procedures in disposition of remains of the dead.

Solution: On arrival in area, information was quickly determined in this regard and the operation order was modified to cover the indicated factors. The majority of the evacuees were Roman Catholics who, with the most valuable assistance of their priests, generally consented to the committal of their dead to the sea with appropriate religious services. The Buddhists and persons of other Oriental religions, of which there were a small number among the evacuees, required that their dead be buried ashore. It was provided, in all cases, that the desires of the next of kin on board or the next responsible cognizant party be followed with regard to disposition of the remains of the dead. These matters were resolved between the next of kin and the commanding officer of the ship concerned, and prescribed significant details were reported to CTF-90 by message. For those who required that the remains of their dead be retained for burial ashore, a few plain mahogany wood caskets were provided by the Vietnamese on board each ship carrying evacuees. In addition to this, prefabricated, impervious, sealable barrier paper field-type bags for temporary encasement of the dead were secured and distributed to ships for encasement of the dead prior to placement of the body in the casket. The caskets were then stowed in the coolest possible feasible area until debarkation. There were no reported difficulties from the use of this procedure.

(3) The unique situation of numerous foreign civilian national births on board U.S. combat ships was also without known precedent. The deliveries, recording of births, and question of nationality of the newborn infants of foreign nationals aboard U.S. ships in international waters presented a new problem within a combat-type organization.

Solution: The actual deliveries were well handled within ship's medical facilities, and by our medical personnel assisted by the control team physicians, nurses, and midwives. There were no significant complications encountered. Pertinent details of time of birth, geographical location, sex of infant, name, and national locale of origin of parents and condition of mother and infant were reported by message to CTF-90. A written and signed record tabulating similar information was given to the parents of the infant so that they might register the birth ashore on debarkation. On advice from the U.S. Embassy, Saigon, it was directed that the question of citizenship of the infant not be entered into at all on board ship. If this question is raised at a later date by the Vietnamese or French authorities, the matter will be taken up through the proper diplomatic channels.

VII.   The Work of the Roman Catholic Groups

RT. REV. MSGR. JOSEPH J. HARNETT[31]

THREE THOUSAND Vietnamese villagers trudged along a sunbaked, dusty road, lined with rice fields and tiny forests. It was 9:00 A.M., August 15, 1954, and the place was deep in the Viet-Minh zone in the vicariate of Thai Binh.

The midsummer sun was already beating down on the countryside, as Father Vincent Thiet, the sixty-eight-year-old priest of the Christian villages of Thuong Phuc, Khuc Mai, Van Doan, and Bich Du, led this motley group of rice farmers, river fishermen, tailors, barbers, carpenters, and blacksmiths—away from their ancestral villages and Red Viet-Nam. From the slight elevation of the near-by Viet-Minh village, they appeared to be an approaching flood of bobbing, conical, coolie hats.

The human wave had a precise organizational pattern, according to the ancient traditions of the Vietnamese village society. Father Thiet was leading his people out of bondage, as Moses must have led the Hebrews during their many years of wandering through the deserts. The aged priest was shielded from the summer sun by a large black umbrella, held over his head by Mr. Tap, who exercised this honorable function as the chief elder of the Christian village of Khuc Mai. Immediately behind the leaders came the elders of the various villages, several dozen in all, bearing themselves with an unconscious and quiet dignity. Behind them came the family groupings—young men and women clothed in the traditional brown tunics and trousers of the Tonkinese, carrying crude bundles of clothing tied with rope on their backs, from which hung iron or earthenware cooking pots and vessels. Often the women carried newborn or infant babies on their hips, while the older children skipped gleefully around them, occasionally losing the wooden slabs held to their feet by leather thongs across their insteps. Wizened and bent old men and women trudged along with the family groups, sometimes supporting themselves with primitive canes. Occasionally, a young man carried pickaback an older woman too feeble to walk, and barely able to hold herself erect with her arms clasped around his neck. Though the burden of all was great, even greater were the pangs of separation from their native villages. Though they knew they were only at the beginning of their trial, no murmur of complaint was uttered.

During the remainder of 1954 scenes similar to this were re-enacted all over Red Viet-Nam, from the northern mountains on the Chinese border to the 17th parallel. By sheer weight of their masses, large numbers of people were able to force their way through hostile provinces, traverse

[31] Director of Catholic Relief Services in Free Viet-Nam.

the rivers and streams of the delta area, and eventually find their way into the Hanoi-Haiphong corridor. During their long trek they suffered the cold of night and the heat of day. They bathed in the rivers and streams, drank the same waters, and also washed their children and clothes in them. Their hunger was frequently relieved by friendly villagers, whose homes they passed. They were threatened, cajoled, and ridiculed by the Viet-Minh soldiers whom they encountered. They were told horrible stories of the tortures and cruel death that awaited them at the hands of the French and American authorities in Haiphong, and on the ships of these nations that would carry them south: The American sailors of Task Force 90 would eat their babies; only disaster awaited them in the jungles, on the beaches, and in the mountains of Free Viet-Nam, whose shaky republic the Viet-Minh would, at any rate, take over in 1956. It was a harsh journey and a dismal prospect that lay before them; but they were willing to face the unknown, rather than submit to the known dangers to their lives, their families, their faith, and their villages.

The decision to leave had been taken by the village elders, discussed with the villagers, and confirmed by their leaders. They faced the future as family and village units. Following the democratic pattern of their ancient village tradition, they moved into the exodus under the protection of that same pattern of society.

In Free Viet-Nam Prime Minister Diem had established COMIGAL to direct the resettlement of the refugees as they arrived. Led by Mr. Doi and his dynamic assistant, Mr. Vien, who often endeared himself to his American friends by his un-Asiatic display of vociferous reactions, COMIGAL did a marvellous job of receiving, housing, feeding, and eventually liberating Saigon of the hordes of refugees that crammed the city.

Every week COMIGAL held three-hour meetings, attended by officials of the Military Army Advisory Group (MAAG), United States Operations Mission, the French Army, the Catholic Auxiliary Resettlement Committee, and the Catholic Relief Services. Information on new arrivals, new villages, and new movements of refugees was exchanged. Impending disaster situations in individual areas were examined, remedies decided upon, and responsibility for their execution fixed. A thousand and one considerations were discussed and reduced to a formula: where to house new boatloads of people and how to procure and disburse food to keep the occupants of tent-cities and other refugee centers alive; measures to control inflation of food prices; trucks to move 7,000 refugees to a new village site; water sources to keep them from dying of thirst; bamboo and thatch to shelter them.

The Catholic Relief Services set up operations in each ecclesiastical province of Free Viet-Nam. Because of geographical difficulties, it was necessary in some places to set up more than one center for a province. Regional directors of the Catholic Welfare Committees were located in six principal places: (1) Hue; (2) Qui Nhon, with centers in Tourane, Tourcham, and Nha Trang; (3) Kontum; (4) Vinh Long; (5) Hau Giang, with centers at Sadec, Soc Trang, Chau Doc, Can Tho, Rach Gia, Long Xuyen, and Bac Lieu; and (6) Saigon.

The ecclesiastical province of Saigon extended from the South China Sea to the Cambodian border, and from fifty-five miles south of the city to one hundred and five miles north. It had the largest concentration of refugees, with approximately 500,000 resettled within that province. It was also the area of greatest need for the poor of the country, due to the fact that during the eight years of war with the Viet-Minh many hundreds of thousands of persons from the south Vietnamese countryside had abandoned their homes and farms to seek security in the Saigon-Cholon area.

The Catholic group also concerned itself with the problem of an estimated 4,000 homeless children of Saigon, who earned their living as bootblacks or vendors of cigarettes, newspapers, post cards, and with the ricksha boys, who in many cases were old, ill, homeless, and weary men, who slept in their own rickshas under the trees lining the streets of Saigon.

Since it was impossible to carry out the Catholic program in behalf of the hundreds of thousands of refugees in the Saigon ecclesiastical province with voluntary and part-time workers, the program was operated directly by Catholic Relief Services, with the help of the Catholic Auxiliary Resettlement Committee.

When a shipment arrived in Saigon, it was immediately warehoused, and the Catholic Relief Office proceeded to prepare supplies for each of the refugee resettlement villages. These supplies were consigned to representatives of the Catholic relief centers. They were transported and delivered to the resettlement village by trucks supplied by COMIGAL. This operation could normally be carried out in seven to ten days.

In most cases, Buddhist refugees from Red Viet-Nam were resettled in or around Catholic refugees from the same province. However, there were twenty villages organized especially for Buddhist refugees. Delivery orders for these villages were prepared and turned over to the Buddhist representatives in COMIGAL.

Ten percent of all Catholic Relief Services' supplies were held in the Saigon warehouse to meet particular and urgent requests.

Due to the procedures set up for releasing goods from the warehouse, the Services had, at all times, a constant check on goods destined for a specific area. Repeatedly, instructions were sent out to all distribution centers, committees, and welfare groups working on the program, emphasizing the importance of taking the necessary steps to see that all supplies were used personally by the beneficiaries and forbidding their sale, exchange, barter, or any other method that might allow these supplies to enter into commercial channels of the country.

In the first ten months of its operation, Catholic Relief Services was able to bring to the needy and to 860,000 refugees their food, clothing, medicines, and other supplies, valued at $4,571,315.78. This included more than one and a half million dollars worth of clothing. The total weight of supplies amounted to more than 5,000 tons. Thus, during that early period a private organization set up a program that, although supplementary in nature, brought to the Vietnamese a thousand truckloads of supplies.

However spectacular the achievement record, Catholic Relief Services was far from satisfied with its progress. But Monsignor Swanstrom of Catholic Relief Services in New York had to be even more critical of the record: He had to consider what had *not* been accomplished, what still remained to be done, and what more the organization could do. He concluded that, since Catholic Relief Services was then dealing with two hundred resettlement villages, a 5,000-ton program would mean that only five truckloads (of five tons each) could go to each village, which was too little. The program would have to be built up, especially since forty-five percent of the supplies were going to the nonrefugee poor of Free Viet-Nam! From the monetary standpoint, it meant that Catholic Relief Services had brought supplies having a value of $5.30 per person and that forty-five percent of that also went to the nonrefugee poor.

It was true, of course, that all refugees were not in the south from the beginning of the program, and that their villages had been established at different times. It was also true that the most-needed agricultural surplus foods were not available at that time for this program. Likewise, the Viet-Minh had destroyed bridges, railroads, and highways prior to their departure to such an extent that communications were extremely difficult. Even trucks were at a premium. The United States Operations Mission in Saigon had tried consistently to get trucks from the French army, which the United States had given to the French for their war effort, and, for one reason or another, with no success. Either the available trucks were being used to haul refugees or for military purposes, or were being turned over to the new Vietnamese army. Eventually, Catholic Relief Services imported forty-eight trucks to handle a part of its program.

Regardless of the causes, the fact remained that the Catholic Relief Services supply program was too small. Just before Christmas, 1955, this was remedied by President Eisenhower's declaration that grains would be available for use in the underdeveloped countries of the world. Since grains included rice, the news caused unbounded joy throughout the Far East. Unfortunately, the supply of other items, such as butter oil, vegetable oil, and powdered eggs, had, or was soon to become, exhausted.

During 1956 and the first half of 1957 the Catholic Relief Services' program was geared to the moving of a hundred truckloads of supplies every day to the poor of Viet-Nam. The total value of the program in dollars was to increase to $35,000,000 before the end of 1957. As Monsignor Swanstrom expressed it, "We made a real dent in the poverty of Viet-Nam and similar crisis areas around the world."

Due to the snail-like progress of the official program to aid the refugee villages, the Catholic Relief Services took some special steps to offset the danger of the refugees being economically helpless for an additional year. With this in mind, it ordered fifty small tractors and the farming implements that went with them, twenty-five mechanical portable pumps, twenty-five chain saws, twenty-five harness looms, and the forty-eight trucks already mentioned. Consultations with the leaders of the refugee villages indicated that such equipment was very much needed. Since these leaders were alarmed at the delays that had taken place in the execution of the projects that had been drawn up for their villages, and since they were more aware than ever of the immediate needs of the villages, Catholic Relief Services decided to embark on an area development program.

This program was another form of co-operative enterprise between the refugees and the Catholic Relief Services, whereby the latter would supply the necessary resources to a village, and the people would contribute what they could in terms of personal labor. The outstanding problem at the end of 1955, because of the impending rainy season, was that of clearing the land and making it ready for planting. For a refugee village or a group of villages to participate in this plan, the village leader had to present us with a detailed document, showing the names of the families in his village, the total number of persons in each family, the total number of workers as opposed to nonworkers, and the total number of workers in each family who could contribute their services to the job of land clearing and planting. The entire plan was based on the fact that in a refugee family of five persons at least one would be available for farm work. Presumably, one of the workers would have to continue at his regular tasks to earn money for the normal needs of the entire family, whereas the others could contribute their services to the common problem, providing that Catholic Relief Services would supply the family's daily needs of rice, as well as provide other foods and clothing at its disposal, along with a maximum sum of a thousand piasters for each two and a half acres of land cleared and planted by the family unit in this program.

There were extensive tracts of abandoned rice lands near the villages of Hanoi and more than 750 acres of abandoned rice lands near those of Phuoc Ly. The rice lands near Hanoi, whose ten villages numbered more than 50,000 people, lay between the main highway from Saigon and the Donau River. Abandoned for more than ten years, they were overgrown with brush. The rice lands near Phuoc Ly were all adjacent to the villages established there and were largely overgrown with heavy grass, undergrowth, and weeds. The refugees had to be supported, both with food and funds for additional purchases, while they were clearing the land. Many of them had been grubbing a painful living from their work in the forests or on odd jobs. To leave these tasks to clear land—even though it would contribute to their permanent welfare—was equivalent to giving up their meager, but nonetheless immediate, livelihood.

The Village Development Committees in charge of these operations acted speedily to secure the necessary titles to the lands through the land reform offices of the Vietnamese government. The effects of this program were astonishing. The village leaders explained the program in detail to the refugees, insisted that through general co-operation their villages could be made self-sufficient within the year, and assured them that their basic needs would be met by Catholic Relief Services as long as they worked on these projects. For its part, Catholic Relief Services received regular reports from the village leaders on the progress that was being made, conscientiously fulfilled its responsibilities to deliver the necessary food supplies to the Area Development Committees for the families engaged in this work, and made the financial contributions promptly on the basis of reports and actual costs for the clearing of the land.

As soon as the program was under way in the ten villages of Bien Hoa and the eleven villages of Phuoc Ly, the idea spread to other refugee areas, and Catholic Relief Services was besieged with requests to institute similar projects in other refugee resettlement villages. By the end of December, 1956, there were nineteen such projects under way. They were located at the refugee centers of provinces of Gia Dinh, Bien Hoa, Thu Dau Mot, Phat Thiet, and Cholon. There were 7,500 families engaged in work on these projects, and, by the end of 1956, they had cleared approximately 6,080 measures of land. Costs of the program at that point amounted to 366,000 Viet-Nam piasters, or an average of 60 piasters per measure. The total rice supplied to workers amounted to 154 tons, and the harvest in the following February produced 5,450 tons of rice crop, plus some quantities of vegetables. The total work that was done in programs in all areas was an important contribution to the general welfare of the refugees.

VIII. A Critique of the Program for the Economic Integration of the Refugees

RT. REV. MSGR. JOSEPH J. HARNETT

IN EARLY 1955 the planning of USOM and COMIGAL for the permanent resettlement of refugees was far more comprehensive than that of Catholic Relief Services, since it embraced further resettlement, public works, and outside technical help on a large scale. However, it was also less realistic than that of Catholic Relief Services, since it envisioned the construction of a large bureaucracy, made few provisions to eliminate bottlenecks that would obstruct actual operations, and was less firmly based on the efforts of the people themselves for the development of their villages than it was on the work that would be done by the Section for Technical Assistance within COMIGAL.

By mid-1955 USOM cut its program down to a workable size by suggesting a pilot project, consisting of two Japanese fishing experts, from four to six agricultural extension specialists, four to six rural engineers, and four to six village industry experts. The target date for getting these persons into the field was September 1, 1955.

Catholic Relief Services participated in the weekly planning meetings for the resettlement phase of the refugee program until the beginning of August, 1955. Since the future of the refugee villages might well depend on what was done during the following year with the $35,000,000 United States government funds, Catholic Relief Services was preoccupied with the planning trend that was leading to the creation of the highly unwieldy bureaucracy. The refugees had far outdistanced everyone during the first year, and the presumption was that they would do the same during the second year if adequate means were put at their disposal. The whole trend toward the formation of the technical assistance section in COMIGAL seemed to be leading toward a paternalistic approach to the problem that would put a large group of civil servants between the resources that were available and the people who needed them. Catholic Relief Services continually protested against what was being done. On repeated occasions Catholic Relief Services pointed out that the execution of the village resettlement projects would be impossible because of the administrative procedures that were being enacted, and in the beginning of August, 1955, ceased to participate in those meetings.

The USOM program provided for survey teams which were to prepare total-need projects for the refugee villages. These projects had to have the approval of the provincial authorities. Then they were submitted to COMIGAL and to USOM for approval. The funding of the operations envisioned in the approved projects then went in the opposite direction: Dollars were to be released by USOM to the Minister of Finance, and

83

against this currency the Minister of Finance was to release piasters to the Refugee Commissioner; these resources were then to go from the Refugee Commissioner to the province chief, from him to the disbursing officer for a specific refugee area in which the project was located, and from the disbursing officer to the actual village operations.

To make this clumsy system operative, USOM and COMIGAL started with such places as Blao, Gia Kiem, Tay Ninh, and Thu Dau Mot. Of these villages only Thu Dau Mot could not be considered among the best resettlement areas in the country. Despite that, at the end of the eighth month of that budget year, namely, February, 1956, no action whatsoever had taken place at the village level on the execution of the resettlement project for even these selected best few villages.

In addition to the clumsiness of the operation, "a standard operation procedure" had been drawn up by the Refugee Division of USOM and COMIGAL that resulted in projects that were too one-sided. The tendency in the government offices in Saigon was to consider a village as either an agricultural or a fishing village. Little effort was made to understand the complex nature of a village and the variety of ways in which people might earn a living. Even where a village was primarily agricultural, it was important not to ignore other forms of livelihood that existed there.

While Catholic Relief Services was convinced that administrative procedures were strangling the operation, it was just as convinced that the men who were responsible for these procedures in USOM and COMIGAL were as honest in their judgment as they were mistaken. The fault was not entirely theirs. The total-needs projects form of assistance with its multiple and interminable approvals at all levels seemed to have its origin in a healthy respect for, and an unhealthy fear of, the Central Accounting Office of the United States government. At the end of 1955 the Central Accounting Office sent to Viet-Nam, and to other countries in the Far East, a group of auditors, who seemingly lost sight of the remarkable accomplishments, and wrote highly critical reports concerning the details of the program. The specific financial weaknesses pointed to in these reports were not fundamental.

A basic understanding of the financial soundness of the project can be gained by comparing the amount expended by the United States government with the number of refugees assisted. During the 1955 fiscal year a total of $58,000,000 was spent by USOM, including $10,000,000 paid to the United States Navy for transporting the refugees from the north to the south. This meant that for the 650,000 refugees whom USOM regarded as its budgetary responsibility, the Mission spent about $89 per refugee during 1955. That sum brought the refugee from the north, resettled him in a new village in Free Viet-Nam, fed and housed him, and provided schools and medical assistance for him.

It was improper that a program should be strangled because of reports that were concerned with details, while not doing justice to the total picture. These reports left additional scars in the field operations, and administrative procedures were established to offset the possibility of a future unfavorable auditing that might prejudice the reputation of the Mission and the careers of the men involved.

The United States Congress had provided $35,000,000 for the temporary sheltering phase of the refugee program. Due to administrative requirements in Washington, it was many months before those credits were actually put at the disposal of the USOM in Saigon. Eight months after the budget year was started, namely at the end of February, 1956, not a single penny of those funds had reached the actual operations in the refugee villages. Thus, the worst fears of Catholic Relief Services of eight months earlier were realized. No land clearing had taken place in the villages, and the danger of losing the entire dry season during which the fields had to be prepared for planting threatened the operation. A political problem could arise if the refugees were not able to clear their lands and plant their crops within the next four months. They could not do this without outside help. Their confidence in, as well as their patience with, both their own government and the American aid program could be shattered if this assistance was not received. Besides the sufferings of the people inherent in such delays, an additional economic problem would be created by delay because further aid for the maintenance of these people would have to be provided if they were not made economically self-sufficient during the resettlement phase of the program. The situation was grave.

Late one afternoon in early October, 1955, these problems were discussed with a refugee priest who had come to Catholic Relief Services to find out why so many months had passed without government aid of any kind reaching his village. The government maintenance subsidy, which covered the needs of the refugees for two and a half months, had ended ten months earlier. His people were living on the meager resources that they were able to provide for themselves from their gardens and forests, and on the help they received from Catholic Relief Services. Their condition was desperate.

A detailed discussion of the refugee village presented by this priest revealed that he had an intimate knowledge of his people, their resettlement area, their needs, and the potentialities of the region. A detailed and exact total-needs project was prepared for his village, which included full information on: its location, population, place of origin and number of families; primary and secondary occupations of the refugees; land availability; occupational tools, implements, and animals; public institutions and public works already completed, as well as additional ones required; technical personnel and advice available among the refugees and what would be required from outside. All items were studied in detail and drawn up in a total-needs project according to the general provisions of COMIGAL's budget that was intended to provide resources for the development of these villages. The total-needs project that was developed proved one important point: one person who was completely familiar with the way in which the paperwork had to be done, with the general COMIGAL budget provisions that had to be followed, and with the limitations that would be put on the project by the needs of other villages, could work out a total-needs project in *six hours,* provided he planned it with other persons who had an intimate knowledge of a particular village and its people.

Through this proposal, it was possible to break through the first bottleneck that was stymieing the entire refugee program. On October 14, 1955, at a meeting in the Refugee Commissariat with Mr. Cardinaux of USOM and Bui Van Luong, the Refugee Commissioner, it took those present about five minutes to declare that this was exactly the kind of project that was needed for every village. There were 289 villages at that time. Catholic Relief Services offered to prepare the entire 289 village projects if necessary to get the refugee program moving.

Working through the Catholic Auxiliary Resettlement Committee, which was worried about the delays in the program, Catholic Relief Services obtained the services of a staff of thirty village priests. They were given an intense course of instruction, lasting eight hours per day for two weeks. After the first three days of general instructions on how to prepare the total-needs projects, these priests were sent back to their own villages, widely scattered throughout the entire country, to prepare an aid project in conjunction with their own village leaders and technicians who had the intimate and detailed knowledge of requirements and costs of land clearing, boatbuilding, netmaking, and all the other trades, as well as the required information on available man power, public works, and village institutions. Their own people knew all the details and most of the technical problems involved in these matters, and were anxious to be in on the discussions and planning, and were extremely helpful in working out the details of the entire program. When this work was done in their own villages, the priests returned to Saigon for further practical instructions on the particular problems related to each individual village project. The entire group went over one by one the various projects that were brought back, studied the individual COMIGAL provisions, analyzed them for flaws, made necessary changes, and prepared the final drafts of the total-needs projects for the individual villages.

Meanwhile, the Refugee Division of the United States Operations

Mission was busy preparing a Standard Operational Procedure for the preparation of the total-needs projects, and COMIGAL had followed the lead of Catholic Relief Services by giving a similar course of instruction to its own field staff that was to go out into the refugee areas to work with Catholic Relief representatives and the provincial authorities on the preparation of these projects.

The Michigan State University team in Saigon was consulted about this matter and approved the techniques that had been adopted. This group made specific recommendations that the projects be presented, when completed, to the provincial authorities, so that they could get to work at the earliest possible moment on their own job of analyzing and approving the program presented for each refugee village.

In early 1956 the refugee program had been in operation for about eighteen months and the inspiration behind the early sacrifices of almost a million people, although as real as ever, was now more remote and had a less immediate effect on their daily lives. It was the distribution of surplus agricultural products by the Catholic Relief Services that carried the refugees through this period after the early enthusiasm had died and before the cumbersome program was established. The people themselves did not want to receive charity, but it was unrealistic to expect that empty-handed people could be transported a thousand miles, put under roofs in new villages, and integrate themselves immediately into an economy that had been torn apart by eight years of warfare. They needed a little time, and the agricultural surplus program gave them that. It carried them over the trying months until their integration projects were carried out. Catholic Relief Services undertook the burden of that program in Viet-Nam because it realized the great need for it on every side.

Commentary: ALFRED L. CARDINAUX[32] *on*
FATHER HARNETT

IN THE SPRING of 1955 the refugees in Free Viet-Nam were refugees in the real sense of the word. Almost all of them were living in endless rows of houses, stretching for miles along the highways leading north and east from Saigon. There were seemingly interminable chains of villages, many on arid land with little or no resources, and thus without future for their inhabitants. The rich rice fields in the western provinces lay untilled, the vast resources of the high plateaus unexploited, serving only as hideouts to hostile guerrillas. And the 660,000 refugees eligible

[32] Former Chief of Division of Refugee Resettlement, USOM, Saigon.

for assistance were living on government subsistence, in temporary villages within a fifty-mile radius of Saigon.

COMIGAL, with a staff which soon reached the impressive number of over 1,200 functionaries, accomplished what it could in an atmosphere of great urgency, always under the pressure of keeping alive this great mass of people. The majority of the functionaries were clerks and minor officials, many refugees themselves, still bewildered but thankful to have an opportunity to earn a living.

The distribution of American aid funds to hundreds of thousands of people created staggering problems for this government agency, obviously without experience for such an undertaking. With no banks in Viet-Nam, except in Saigon, there was no established system for the movement of funds: Cash had to be carried and distributed to the refugees. Under these circumstances, it was difficult to organize an effective system for the distribution of funds and to establish all the safeguards necessary to insure against their misuse.

In regard to the permanent resettlement and the economic and social integration of the refugees, the administrative machinery of COMIGAL in 1955 was not organized to undertake a project which required meticulous surveys, by qualified agricultural and public works technicians, of existing resources and of the needs of refugees living in several hundred villages—in short, to evaluate and put into concrete form a vast program of economic development for over half a million people. The refugees themselves were a big question mark. Would they be willing to give up subsistence payments for a long-range project of economic development, which meant months of hard work and, in many cases, the abandonment of their present villages in which they had built schools and churches?

Until this time COMIGAL's staff had been concentrated in Saigon, with a few agents in the provinces. In contrast, the resettlement and integration phases of the program required a strong nation-wide field organization. It also required a simple, effective system for the channeling of funds to these village projects. This last requirement soon proved to be a major obstacle in the execution of the projects, for although funds were released by USOM without delay upon approval of the individual village projects, it soon became apparent that they did not reach their destination, but were held up in the winding roads of an antiquated financial procedure dating back to the last century. It seemed that no one was going to assume the responsibility of disbursing funds without a multitude of signatures, checks, and counterchecks, with the end result that the project could not be started.

The first project was approved in November, 1955, providing assistance to 16,000 refugees in seven villages, the same villages which one year later celebrated their integration into the province of Bien Hoa and the achievement of their economic independence. In January, 1956, the number of approved projects had reached seventeen, and by June, 1956, there was no doubt that all the villages would have projects of their own, providing on paper the assistance necessary for their development and eventual economic independence.

By early 1956 the almost complete failure of COMIGAL to get the funds to the villages for the execution of the projects cast a dark shadow over the entire program, which a year earlier had captured everyone's imagination. Unless a drastic change was to occur, the project's future and eventual success would be in serious doubt. This situation, in my opinion, was not the fault of any of the responsible officials. Rather it resulted from the complicated financial procedures, which might well have worked under normal circumstances but were too rigid for this complex project. It seemed as if none of the officials had sufficient authority to introduce the necessary changes.

In the early days of June, 1956, the Ministry of Finance held a meeting, attended by the Finance Minister, the Commissioner General for Refugees, and several representatives from USOM. The purpose of the meeting, like many other previous ones, was to seek a solution to this grave problem. (It may be useful to explain here briefly how counterpart American aid funds[33] were administered: Upon request by USOM, project funds were released by the Treasury to the Commissioner for Refugees, who was responsible for the administration of the funds and for their accounting to the Minister of Finance. All counterpart funds were administered under the laws and regulations of the government of Viet-Nam.)

Each official came to this meeting with an urgent desire to contribute a solution to the problem. There was a general feeling of hesitancy, and no one quite knew where to start. No half measures were possible. No compromise within this complicated and unworkable funding system would bring the desired effect of making the funds flow swiftly to the projects. It took much courage and imagination for the Minister of Finance to say: "Within our present financial procedures and regulations we cannot find the solution to our difficulties. We must approach the problem with new ideas and sweep away the complicated procedures which were inspired only by mistrust and suspicion toward human nature. I believe that we must put the responsibility for the execution of the projects and the administration of the funds into the hands of the people who are the ultimate beneficiaries of the projects, the refugees themselves."

[33] See p. 320 for an explanation of counterpart funds. (ED.)

A simple procedure was finally drafted along the basic principle proposed by the Minister of Finance. About a week later, on June 12, 1956, President Diem signed the decree which made this procedure effective and which was soon to eliminate the bottlenecks and to give the project new impetus. It was a simple document, easy to understand, and provided for elected village councils to administer the funds and carry out the project's execution under the supervision of provincial authorities. The decree, together with details of the budget, was posted in every village. This proved to be most beneficial, because each villager could read on the bulletin board what the government was going to do for him. He now had a direct contact with the local authorities through the village council, which he had helped to elect. Thus, the project's purpose and objective reached down to the people and assured their active participation in its execution. Three months after the signing of the decree, over one hundred projects had received funds and over two hundred villages were booming with new activities which would not subside again. No major obstacle was now to prevent the project's successful conclusion.

Most important of all, the Minister for Land Reform proposed an impressive program for the clearing of 77,000 hectares of rice land that had been lying idle for more than eight years, and the simultaneous resettlement of about 100,000 refugees from villages without economic future and overpopulated areas on the periphery of Saigon. This became the Cai San project.

President Diem directed the Commissioner General and the Minister of Agriculture to tour the villages and to explain to the refugees what they could expect by giving up their present homes. Where refugees were reluctant to move, the President directed the Commissioner General to suspend further help. Critical views about assistance on the part of the refugees were subjected to close scrutiny and no longer accepted at their face value. The Cai San project presented an entirely new approach to the integration problem. Increasing attention was given to technical matters, to economic aspects of the program: The relief provisions still in existence moved more and more into the background. The USOM ordered a hundred tractors for the land-clearing operation, and survey parties departed for Cai San. In March, 1956, over 20,000 refugees moved to Cai San, leaving behind what once had been temporary villages, but nevertheless homes to which they had become attached. These refugees, together with local workers, dug a hundred miles of canals in the staggeringly short time of ninety days. Technicians and representatives of the tractor firms from the United States trained several hundred mechanics, and soon these tractors moved through the man-high grass eighteen hours a day tilling hectare after hectare of land. Seeds were purchased, houses sprang up along the canals, and seven months after the first survey parties had marched through the desolate fields a great new agricultural center had come into existence. The road from Rach Gia to Long Xuyen, which we traveled in December, 1955, under the protection of three armored cars, had become the most-populated road in Viet-Nam, a road from which hostile guerrillas had vanished.

The uncertainty of the early days had also vanished, and new constructive ideas were daily replacing the temporizing hesitancy which had prevailed before. Not only did COMIGAL drastically change its attitude, but also the refugees were caught up by a new will to move ahead. The buffaloes from Thailand and Cambodia, which in a newspaper report a year or so earlier had been called useless because they did not understand Vietnamese, were now appreciated and put to work by the refugee farmers. On the road to Blao, on the site of new villages, a sign in English and Vietnamese proudly announced that twelve gigantic tractors were clearing 300 hectares of virgin forest for cultivation by the refugees, a joint project of the Forest Service of Viet-Nam, COMIGAL, and USOM.

In Saigon the National Investment Fund[34] drew up plans for the establishment of a weaving plant, with 440 looms imported from Japan, which would give employment to over a thousand families, and bring new prosperity to many more. Several hundred irrigation pumps were arriving from Japan, and the refugees were eagerly waiting for survey teams from the Ministry of Agriculture to help them determine what installation would best serve their needs. Because of the shortage of Vietnamese technicians, this, as well as other aspects of the project requiring technical assistance and special surveys, often moved slowly, and in some cases good opportunities were missed. On the other hand, a realistic approach to the problems left no other alternative, lest equipment would be used without a minimum assurance that it would fulfill its purpose and not, in the end, disappoint the refugee. In this, as in other fields of technical assistance, it was difficult to find the middle road.

To what extent were the farmers able to use motors and pumps requiring technical maintenance without proper guidance? How could weavers install and operate mechanical looms, when they had been weaving with looms which had not changed in design for centuries? Perhaps technicians had a tendency to be too cautious, not giving sufficient credit

[34] See pp. 245-54 for a discussion of the National Investment Fund (NIF). (ED.)

to the native intelligence and ability of the people they intended to help.

The project provided for the import of equipment and material, from sewing machines and hand tools to 200,000 baby chicks flown in from Japan, and heavy forest-clearing equipment, sawmill machinery, fishing gear and twine, ten thousand buffaloes and oxen, seeds, and fertilizer totaling over $7,000,000. Whereas in the early days the refugees did not look upon these purchases with much favor, preferring money to items which were only on paper, they now awaited their arrival impatiently. The purchase of many of these items had been executed long ago, but because of time-consuming bid and purchasing procedures the major part of these items arrived in Viet-Nam only toward the end of 1956, some even later. This turned out to be an advantage, because it coincided with the achievement of a great deal of stability in the villages. Agricultural conditions of the villages were well known to COMIGAL, extensive information on the skills and professions of the refugees was readily available, and the imported equipment could by then be put to use according to realistic plans, based on well-known needs.

Commentary: BERNARD B. FALL *on*
FATHER HARNETT

THE SHELTERING and integration phases of which Monsignor Harnett writes proved to be a most arduous task of the refugee program. Much of the Mekong hinterland, the ideal area in which to resettle large numbers of refugees, was in the hands of Hoa Hao and Cao Dai insurrectionist bands. The immediate approaches of the Saigon-Cholon urban area were controlled by the Binh Xuyen, another band in open opposition to the government of President Diem.

By mid-July, 1955, the government of Free Viet-Nam had succeeded in establishing a reasonable measure of security throughout the lowlands, and the fanning-out of the refugees from the immediate reception centers to semipermanent or even permanent resettlement areas began in earnest.

Several means were used to resettle the refugees. The simplest of course, was to make refugee resettlements around existing villages or towns. The second was to keep the refugees in more or less permanent camps. Lastly, COMIGAL built full-fledged villages and communities. However, the first method soon proved unworkable, in view of the numbers involved and the lack of housing and sanitary facilities in the urban areas. The second did not represent a long-range solution. However, a combination of the second and third methods proved workable.

COMIGAL set up the refugee villages in areas where an economic basis of support for such a community (fishing, fallow rice fields, lumber, etc.) existed, and helped the refugees until they were more or less self-supporting. Then the village was transferred to the provincial administration of the area.

It is difficult to estimate the number of refugees still remaining in transient or semitransient camps, awaiting final disposition or resettlement. It is said that, for political reasons—in view of their loyalty to President Diem—a certain number of Catholic refugees have remained close to the Vietnamese capital, where their enthusiasm is often felt at various official occasions.

A secondary transitional movement is at present under way, with settled refugees invited to move into the highlands, which are inhabited by non-Vietnamese aboriginal people. This movement may eventually involve up to 150,000 refugees and lead to the creation of a Vietnamese "beachhead" in the Kontum-Pleiku area.[35] In any case, the resettlement phase of the refugee program was, in large, completed by December 31, 1957.

In the case of the resettlement centers, the Vietnamese government, with the help of USOM and of various private agencies, provided the villages with the necessary administrative structure to permit them to become viable communities. This was easy in the case of villages that moved to the south en bloc—mayor, village priest, city council, and all. In such cases the village frequently retained its name, or added the word "New" to it, just as settlers all over the world do. The integration of such a village was obviously easier than to create a brand-new community out of various elements which had no particular liking for each other.

Religion has played an important factor in the problem of final resettlement. Too often Americans tend to forget that Viet-Nam is essentially a non-Christian country. In fact, only ten percent of the population may be considered Christian, and mostly of the Catholic faith. (There are less than 10,000 Protestants in the country.)

However, the south Vietnamese government, including the devout President Diem, is predominantly Catholic. The preferential treatment of northern Catholic refugees in getting relief, in obtaining government jobs, and in other ways, real or imagined, has at times created tensions

[35] See *Vietnam-Presse* (daily government press bulletin), Saigon, August 19, 1957, evening edition; also MSUG report on the highland area, June, 1957.

that could have been easily avoided. There is evidence that American Catholics acquainted with the Vietnamese situation have warned against precisely such an occurrence as a potential divisive factor of which the Communists might take advantage.

Using the refugees to "Vietnamize" the highlands is another highly controversial measure, whose ultimate success is still in doubt. The aboriginal population complains bitterly about this "intrusion" on its hunting grounds, and Michigan State University teams have found evidence that the measure has given Communist propaganda in the highlands a wider audience than it had before.

In the Mekong lowlands, however, the placement of a dense refugee "belt" in the Hoa Hao and Cao Dai fiefs has certainly greatly contributed to making those areas safe from large-scale guerrilla forces. Nevertheless, there has been an increase of the latter since July, 1957, and the Saigon government has promised to take strong measures against them.

No appraisal of the Vietnamese refugee problem would be complete without at least a passing reference to the vast Cai San project. It is generally hailed as the most conspicuous success of the whole refugee resettlement program. Every foreign dignitary, high or low, is given the opportunity to visit it. With its village-lined canals, its 90,000 inhabitants, its churches, hospital, tractor pool, motor launches, and airstrip, it is certainly one of the most ambitious undertakings of its kind anywhere. But that is precisely its shortcoming. Upon questioning by the writer, the engineers there stated that they doubted that any other area in Free Viet-Nam could meet all the conditions found at Cai San: practically no ownership problem (there were only 1,500 inhabitants when the area was selected), existing major drainage canals, and lavish American support. It is useful per se, in view of its production capabilities and because it absorbs 90,000 refugees, but it cannot be considered as a pilot project for other major resettlement centers.

How successful, then, has Viet-Nam's resettlement of refugees been? If the major objectives were: (1) to move to Free Viet-Nam anyone who wanted to come and (2) to get those refugees off the streets and sidewalks of Saigon, then the project is an unqualified success. Most of the refugees today have food and a roof over their heads, and both those factors constitute major achievements in themselves.

But it is equally undeniable that little has been done by Free Viet-Nam to make the best of this unexpected influx of available man power. The economic morass of the country since 1955 is a constant worry to its friends and allies, and seriously affects the possibilities of gainful employment for the refugees.

The much-hailed land reform[36] has, for all practical purposes, stalled in its tracks. Here again, official government figures are eloquent. As shown before, about eighty percent of all refugees are farmers. Yet, according to figures released in Saigon in July, 1957, about 91,000 acres of land had been cleared by the refugees, with less than 70,000 acres planted with rice. Obviously, most of these refugees were then still living from hand-outs rather than from the fruit of their labor. The long-range deleterious effects of such a situation should not be under-estimated.

Commentary: M. J. CARROLL[37] *on*
FATHER HARNETT

THE CRITIQUE by Monsignor Harnett tends to give an inaccurate picture of the administration of the refugee program, in planning and operations, both of which were carried out under the direction of USOM in Viet-Nam. The phrases "clumsy system" and "strangling the operation," used by the author in relation to the procedures employed, leave the impression of gross inefficiency; whereas, from the results achieved, it is evident that the operation was efficiently administered.

By July 1, 1957, 259 out of 316[38] villages were officially integrated into the Vietnamese provincial economy. It is significant that COMIGAL, through prudent administration of funds, realized an economy of approximately 200 million piasters ($5.5 million) in the total piaster allocation for resettlement for the 1956 fiscal year. This reduction is attributable to the ability and speed with which the refugees became self supporting.

In regard to the project form of assistance ("with its multiple approval at all levels"), the procedure used in Viet-Nam has been in world-wide use since 1955 by the International Cooperation Administration (ICA) and its predecessor. The procedure was devised by the ICA Office of the Controller as a means to provide more effective financial management controls over the funds allotted to the Administrator of ICA.

The references by the author to the Central Accounting Office and to the visit in 1955 are incorrect. He undoubtedly intended to refer to the General Accounting Office (GAO) of the United States govern-

[36] See pp. 200-208 for a discussion of the land reform program. (ED.)
[37] Accountant for International Cooperation Administration.
[38] Bui Van Luong, on p. 52, indicates 319 resettlement villages. (ED.)

ment, and to the visit by GAO auditors to Viet-Nam in October, 1956. As an agent of the United States Congress, the Comptroller General (head of GAO), has been given broad statutory authority to review the activities of government agencies. Auditing on a comprehensive basis was instituted by the Comptroller General in 1949 as a means of more effectively discharging the audit responsibilities placed on him by law.

Stated as simply as possible, the purpose of the comprehensive audit is to determine how well the agency or activity under audit is discharging its financial responsibilities, which include the expenditure of funds and the use of property and personnel in furthering programs or activities in an efficient and economical manner. A necessary corollary to such determinations is the periodic reporting of audit findings, including deficiencies observed and recommendations for improvements where required.

Commentary: JEAN LE PICHON[39] *on*
FATHER HARNETT

A PORTRAIT of the refugees, which explains their behavior and reveals the difficulties arising from their resettlement, enables one to better understand the reasons for past successes and also errors in the refugee program.

Before the exodus from the northern Christian provinces, the village fused into the parish. The basic unit remained the family; the social unit was the parish, whose acknowledged leader was the priest. But the parish was first of all a spiritual organization, the first element of a hierarchical religious society possessing a deep inner life.

The parish was a very simple society, composed of peasants, fishermen, small artisans, a few village dignitaries who were peasants themselves, and the parish priest with his catechists, the Sisters. There was no middle class or no leadership groups. Living in the shade of his church belfry, the priest had to deal with only uncomplicated problems, which did not extend beyond the daily little issues of a stabilized rural society. His life was a quiet one, free from material worry, in a village having well-established traditions. He was, as a rule, ill prepared for the role he was called on to assume in the south.

However, with him rested the responsibility of the initial resettlement of his parish in Free Viet-Nam. For many priests the task was too

[39] Technical expert for COMIGAL, 1955-57; a French civil servant. Translated from the French by Phan Thu Ngoc.

demanding, and Monsignor Harnett, in my opinion, has overestimated their capabilities in this respect. It would have been dangerous to have given the parish priests the full responsibility for the resettling program, including the drawing up of budgets. How many of them, even after the new village location turned out to be poor, wanted to detain their parishioners to complete the building of a brick church? How many eagerly launched unwise co-operatives, which cost a great deal, without being of any practical use?

The parishioners quickly realized the doubtful performance of their priests as administrators; in addition, the church was anxious to limit the priests to a spiritual role. Furthermore, the primitive character of the parish itself had to change its structure as the northern Vietnamese adapted to life in the south: To earn a living, the faithful often had to go outside the parish, beyond the influence of their priest.

Understandably so, the attitudes of the people altered, sometimes drastically, in the new environment, sometimes for the worse and sometimes for the better, sometimes because of the situation into which they were thrown and sometimes in spite of it. The northern peasant, or *nha-quê*, is industrious and persevering, but slow and stubborn, and adjusts poorly to new methods. He did not feel at home in the south. Moreover, in his naivety, he swallowed all the propaganda lines. A few refugees hinted they would go back north, and that until then the government would feed, shelter, and give them a hectare of rice land. A number of refugees developed a permanent "social security" attitude. A few even became specialists in the art of "freeloading" on official or private aid.

The farmers demanded that the promise of "a house, a hectare, a buffalo," made when they left home, be kept. However, when they found good land which they knew would become theirs, adjustment was swift. The same was true for northern fishermen; for example, those who settled in Cap St. Jacques almost immediately achieved a better yield than the natives themselves.

Differences in the northern people themselves, as well as where they settled, have accounted, to some degree, for poor or rapid adjustment. The people from the northern villages of Phat Diem and Bui Chu, more than all others, have the gregarious instinct, having lived close to the church and the priest. They are afraid of the forest, and must have water, plains, and rice lands; it will take them a long time to adjust to the highlands. On the other hand, the Thanh Hoa and Vinh people have more initiative, are not afraid of the wilderness, and are not reluctant to live on isolated farms.

For many northern Vietnamese, the resettlement phase gave them a taste for making discoveries. Many went from camp to camp to get information. A few ventured into personal enterprises outside the administrative village, and settled on small isolated "islands" in the provinces. If successful, these will attract other settlers, and a certain number of them will become villages and, above all, parishes; because whether alone or living in communities, the refugees remain loyal to their faith.

In the early period of the resettlement program, many refugees were settled on lands where they could not earn a living. Obvious blunders, such as settling fishermen in forests, were made.

Due to such mistakes the Commissioner General, in conjunction with the various foreign aid programs, put into effect a more carefully drawn-up resettling plan. The major feature of this plan was the creation in COMIGAL of a Technical Division, made up of commissions of development, study, and control. These commissions were charged with: (1) examining each existing refugee colony, determining its potentialities, and drawing up a budget on a *village* basis that would be sufficient to permit its development; (2) seeking out and studying locations for more refugee colonies in order to relieve the overcrowded ones; and (3) organizing "centers" wherever possible. In theory, the center was to be composed of three groups of from three to four villages, or a total of 20,000 to 30,000 people. At the center, a leader was to be assisted by a Technical Service—which included a doctor with a simple medical organization, a technical agent of the Public Works Department with operators, an agricultural technical agent with farming agents, a head mechanic with the specialized personnel necessary to operate mechanized implements and equipment, whose number and composition would vary from region to region. The center's budget was to be allocated on a *village* basis, and funds for each project were to be managed under a system of independent bookkeeping controls.

After the main features of the plan were determined, there remained the task of recruiting technicians and buying the mechanical and sanitary equipment. Because Viet-Nam could supply only a limited number of technicians, an appeal was made to the Free World for young volunteers, with USOM agreeing to finance the operation. In spite of many responses to a first appeal, it was not until 1957 that USOM was able to obtain Japanese technicians. On this point, Monsignor Harnett is right in that much time was unfortunately lost. In early 1957 the plan for delivery of equipment was changed so that it was channeled to a specialized technical organization. Luckily, the numerous deliveries of trucks, jeeps, furnishings, and other equipment made by the French army proved to be of considerable help. After a hesitant beginning, it was possible, with the aid of the new experience, to formulate "Directives for the Establishment of Center Budgets," which USOM called "the Bible." These directives have generally been put into practice.

The first budgets were accepted by USOM in December, 1955; their execution met with so many difficulties, because of administrative complications and inertia, that at one time it seemed hopeless. The "accounting control" system adopted is, in theory, simple, but its adaptation to rules established for the use of foreign-aid funds and the exaggerated caution of the responsible bureaus and services, which demanded too narrow an application of administrative rules, accounted for the loss of time. Moreover, in 1956 USOM itself had to wait for allocations of funds by Washington, which contributed further to delays.

These delays, which, in theory, prevented the plan from being on schedule had a beneficial psychological effect. After the refugees saw that none of the administrative aid was materializing, they ceased to depend on it and had to make an effort themselves, which liberated many of them from the "social security" complex, a serious obstacle to any resettling program. So the criticisms of delays of equipment and technicians, which Monsignor Harnett deplores, are unjustified. However, one can regret that the initial plan was not applied rationally and smoothly.

It was wise of USOM not to have immediately followed the plans and budget estimates drawn up by the missions created by Monsignor Harnett. The idea behind these commissions appeared to be erroneous, and the studies they proposed were seldom valid for the following reasons: (1) The teams of priests in charge of this work were not technicians. (2) The villagers went along with the views of the parish priest, who permitted himself, often in all good faith, to be blinded by personal considerations, such as a desire to keep his parish together. (3) The priests did not have sufficient authority to limit funds to essentials. As a matter of fact, their outlook was that of a spender of funds. Thus, requests, no matter what the purpose happened to be, were always the highest amounts allowed by "the Bible." As a result, all projects cost the maximum sum, although "the Bible" had provided very large margins, because needs varied from village to village. (4) Finally, these teams dared not go counter to local wishes and so came out in favor of projects that often were not capable of development. This was true in particular of certain villages in Hanoi, which incidentally have since been abandoned.

In the early days certain provinces—Saigon, Cholon, Gia Dinh, and Bien Hoa —received too large a share of the refugees. Moreover, in many instances, refugees lacked land, and there were frightful mistakes made concerning the classification of professions.

Eventually, the government determined to settle provinces from the lowlands to the highlands of the center, and the "planning commissions" have acted in this direction. To this administrative action, fortunately, there was the added personal effort of refugees in many places. Certain villages, having a resourceful priest or dignitaries, sought out new locations, and on their own initiative started a new project. Furthermore, certain local potentialities for settlement turned out to be greater than was expected. There was also the discovery of additional sources of work on plantations, farms, or in enterprises. The first settlements in the west were not as a rule successful, either because of the insecurity prevailing at the time or because of lack of land as in Ben Tre or as a result of mistakes, such as that in the Plaine des Joncs. The opening of the provinces of Rach Gia, Can Tho, and Soc Trang furnished new outlets. In these provinces, it was necessary to have very thoroughly studied projects requiring large mechanical means; such was the case of Cai San, which has been the greatest accomplishment of this kind.

On the other hand, the first settlements in the highlands which had been carefully prepared were highly successful. It was thus normal that they should have received the first funds, since theirs were the first plans to have been completed.

One may say that today the refugee problem has, in the main, been solved. Those aspects of development that require a solution are the ones affecting agricultural problems in the south or handicraft problems.

In spite of all the difficulties encountered and even of the mistakes made, the results have been amazing. In the long and painful history of the world's refugees, there has never been another such successful operation on a comparable scale.

The consequences in all fields are bound to be important. After being a burden, the refugees will be a source of wealth for the country in the economic, moral, and spiritual fields. They represent a Faith, an Ideal, and a Will, the spreading of which will have incalculable benefits for Viet-Nam and also for the whole of Southeast Asia. It is the only solid center of ideological resistance able to stand up to the Communist wave in its Asian form.

Commentary: FATHER HARNETT *on* CARDINAUX, FALL, CARROLL, *and* LE PICHON

THE MEMBERS of this symposium have mentioned the complicated funding procedures, as well as the meticulous surveys of the resources and needs that complicated the resettlement work, in Free Viet-Nam. Cardinaux stated that early in 1955 USOM and the government of Viet-Nam initiated plans for permanent resettlement, and that in June, 1956, a meeting was called that resolved the problem of funding the projects for aid to the refugee villages.

Would it not have been possible to foresee the problem of funding and work it out without letting twelve to eighteen months elapse? As a matter of fact, that problem was foreseen, and I was present when it was discussed in October, 1955. Even at that date the refugees had become very alarmed, and feared that they had been abandoned. The Catholic Relief Services projects teams were an unofficial attempt, approved by the Vietnamese government and by USOM more than tacitly, to forestall those fears.

As for the "meticulous surveys," which Cardinaux admits that COMIGAL was not organized to carry out, those surveys were required for the project form of aid, which Carroll states was devised and imposed by the United States government. My observations were specifically intended to indicate my belief that "world-wide" procedures devised in a government office in one place cannot possibly respond to local conditions everywhere, and where they are made a *sine qua non* of an aid program they are self-defeating. Although it is proper to regard regulations imposed by the Office of the Controller with awe, that does not mean that such regulations are beyond criticism. Carroll gives excellent reasons for the institution of these regulations, but the excellency of motivation does not necessarily prevent the resulting techniques from defeating the purposes of the over-all aid program. And, in this case, defeat was only forestalled by the innate strength of the people who were being assisted.

Le Pichon describes the primitive nature of the northern Vietnamese communities. This is so perhaps, but it must be remembered that, by Paris and Washington standards, two thirds of the world might be considered primitive. As a matter of fact, most of the American economic aid programs are presently being carried out in underdeveloped areas of the world. My criticism of the project form of assistance, as it was applied in the refugee resettlement work in Viet-Nam, is based on the fact that it is too complicated to operate in many underdeveloped areas.

The Catholic Relief Services tried to reduce the burden of administrative responsibility that was thrust upon the clergy, which resulted in their being treated as civic, as well as spiritual, leaders. In this Catholic Relief Services was supported by Bishop Pham Ngoc Chi, who only permitted the priests to shoulder the role of administrators because no others were available and the government agencies had not as yet found a solution to the problem. In the fall of 1954 the Minister of Finance proposed to use the clergy to transmit financial aid to the people. I rejected this proposal, because I recognized that the priests were "ill prepared for the role they were called on to assume in the south." In fact, rare indeed was the refugee who was prepared for that role!

Admitting that few of the people were prepared for their new role, as well as Cardinaux's point that the responsible government agency was also unprepared, my contention is that those whose most vital interests were at stake on a day-to-day basis represented a source of strength and accomplishment which was dangerous to ignore. The success of the exodus phase of the program had repeatedly been attributed to these very people. The proposal of the Minister of Finance that finally broke the deadlock in the funding of the projects recognized that fact and put large amounts of responsibility on the people most concerned. Unfortunately, that proposal came very late in the day.

Although Le Pichon implies it, no one ever suggested giving the clergy the responsibility for drawing up budgets for the unfinished work in the resettled villages. I know of no project that was ever drawn up by a priest.

Cardinaux speaks of the need for meticulous agricultural and public works surveys. Needed also were surveys of river and coastal fishing possibilities and needs, crafts, trades of the villagers, and such things. Cardinaux admits that COMIGAL was not capable of making those surveys. "The very simple society" of the village was what had to be reconstructed. The northern peasants had built fishing boats, woven and mended nets, dug rice paddies and wells, opened cart paths, cut lumber, made furniture, thatched their own houses, and built their village schools. The task of the Catholic Relief Services projects teams was to consult with them in their new villages in accordance with the pattern of society to which they were accustomed, and through their elders to arrive at a knowledge of needs and costs according to the best understanding of the "village technicians." USOM and COMIGAL admitting their inability, what could be more natural? After listening to reports from the field in this matter, Catholic Relief Services simply formulated a proposition that had been made to the clergy by their own people. In effect, they said if technicians cannot get out to the villages to do what is required, it will do it for them and report it to Saigon officials some way or other.

Colonialism as a system failed to develop and respect the powers of individual native leaders. In many cases, those who advanced under the colonial system were pushed forward as tools of the system. Independent thinkers and workers who might create something of value for the "natives," something that might help the social, economic, or political development of the colony, were often discouraged in a patronizing manner, or removed because their thinking did not fit the objectives of colonialism. Blocking such persons did not necessarily mean that the colonialists were guilty of formal repression. It was, in many cases, simply easier and quicker to live by a known system than to risk an upheaval of society by entertaining new attitudes and patterns that might not be effective. To obtain their own ends, persons who were thus blocked often became revolutionaries.

American technicians and administrators frequently have fallen into a parallel erroneous procedure that ignores local personnel resources. Sometimes in thinking of themselves as technicians and advisers they unconsciously assumed a superior attitude over others. Local persons became "nontechnicians," with little or no knowledge of these matters. At other times, they have based their operations on sanctified United States government operation procedures that left little room for considering that these procedures might well be adapted to local needs.

Sadly, at that point American efforts to give financial aid to a government to meet local problems are, to an important extent, nullified in their intended effects. Americans end up by stating, as an operational procedure, that things must be done the American way or not at all. In an article entitled "Foreign Technicians and Local Environment," in the *Times* of Viet-Nam on May 3, 1958, these attitudes were lamented by a Vietnamese writer in the following words: "The most common fault of many foreigners is that they do not try to study the real situation of the country. Too confident of their knowledge, they think they can apply their science blindfolded. And if some Vietnamese counterpart wants to give them advice, they think they know too much to listen." To be successful, a foreign aid program must encourage the people receiving aid to give as much as they can of their own intellectual, physical, and material resources to the resolution of their problems. Though an area may be underdeveloped, every society has its own natural leaders, planners, and even technicians who can and want to contribute to their own welfare.

PART THREE

THE CHINESE
AND OTHER MINORITIES

Free Viet-Nam is an experiment in assimilation. Over and beyond the political and economic assimilation of the Vietnamese refugees from north Viet-Nam, there are problems of integrating important minority groups into the new nation.

The Chinese are economically the most important people, because for centuries they have played an important role in Viet-Nam's commercial life. The tribespeople, who live in the mountain areas, largely north and west of Saigon, constitute a second important group. These people live under conditions that are much inferior to those of the Vietnamese. Still a third group, the Cambodian farmers in the Trans-Bassac area, south of Saigon, constitute no major social or economic problem, because their living standards are about on a par with that of the Vietnamese farmers.

The major question raised is: should the minorities be quickly assimilated into Free Viet-Nam or should they be permitted to live according to their own ancient cultures? The problem is somewhat similar to that which the United States, and to a lesser extent Australia, faced at an earlier date. It is doubtful, however, if either the experiences of the United States or of Australia will be particularly helpful in establishing policy in Viet-Nam. It seems likely, though, that America's experience with universal and nearly uniform education for all children will be a concept that can be used in facing up to the difficulties inherent in the situation.

There is one important general aspect of development, frequently neglected, which this section highlights: Briefly, it is that new and low per capita income nations have a population which is diverse and which consists of a number of distinct language, racial, and cultural groups. Because of this diversity, assimilation or, if you will, the development of a national image, is a major problem.

IX.   The Chinese in Viet-Nam

FATHER RAYMOND J. DE JAEGHER[40]

FREE VIET-NAM has faced an especially grave problem with the Chinese, who for centuries have played an important role in the economic life of the country but yet remained politically apart. The Chinese live in their own communities, their own trade-political organizations establish and enforce "laws" among their people, and until recently, when their citizenship became an issue, still considered themselves as citizens of China.

It is difficult to determine when the Chinese first came to Viet-Nam, but it was at least two thousand years ago. In the second century B.C. a Chinese governor established the kingdom of Nam-Viet. When this kingdom was overthrown in 111 B.C., the land became a province of the Chinese empire, and remained so for a thousand years. Chinese merchants, scholars, and political refugees emigrated southward, particularly in periods of crises in China. It cannot be said that any number of these overseas Chinese became a permanent part of the population. With the Chinese coming and going through the centuries, the Vietnamese accepted the skills and, to some extent the ideas of the Chinese, but they remained an ethnically separate people, resisting assimilation.

The Chinese continued to emigrate southward even after Viet-Nam regained its independence in 939, an independence that was uninterrupted except for a brief period of Chinese rule in the 1400's until the French took over the country in the late 1860's. Sometimes they came in vast numbers, such as the three thousand who came when the Manchu dynasty succeeded that of the Ming. These Chinese, called Ming Huong by the Vietnamese, settled first in Bien Hoa, My Tho, and Bien Tre, and later at a new site called "Great Market," or Cholon, now a twin city of Saigon.

After 1663 the Vietnamese divided the Chinese into two groups: the Ming Huong, who had settled permanently in Viet-Nam, had married Vietnamese women, and had helped to develop the country; and those Chinese who had emigrated under the Manchus, and who were required to pay heavy taxes and could only settle in a few designated cities. Certainly, during the seventeenth and eighteenth centuries, the Ming Huong were the privileged Chinese in Viet-Nam.

After 1841 a "Congregation" of seven Chinese groups, originally from Fukien and Kwantung provinces, organized themselves into a general community called "Chi-Fou-Cong-Souo." The "Congregation," which did not include the Ming Huong, decided the prices of goods sold by Chinese merchants and also resolved conflicts among the Chinese.

When the French took over Viet-Nam, they gave equal rights, at the

[40] Director of Free Pacific Association, Saigon, Viet-Nam.

107

beginning, to both the Chinese and Vietnamese. Later, in 1865, the French organized a council in Cholon, consisting of five Vietnamese, fifteen Chinese, and five Ming Huong. (The latter were considered as "stateless.") In 1867 the French gave the same rights to the Ming Huong as to the Vietnamese.

In 1862 the French, for purposes of taxation and of checking illegal immigration, introduced an identification card system for the Chinese, as well as a head tax each year for every Chinese in the country. Beginning in 1871 every Chinese landing in Viet-Nam had to register into one of the seven "Congregations" of the country. An Immigration Office was opened in 1874, with each Congregation having a representative at the office to register incoming Chinese.

In 1948 the French changed the title of Chinese Congregations to "Chinese Regional Administrative Group," and gave a new law to the Chinese community: The Chinese Regional Administrative Group was to elect a president and a vice president, both to be approved by the French authorities and the Chinese Consul General. In effect, the French gave special legal status to the Chinese, treating them as a separate national group within Viet-Nam.

During the past twenty years there has been a rapid growth of the Chinese population in Viet-Nam. In 1937 there were 217,000 in the country; these were geographically divided as follows: north Viet-Nam, 35,000; central Viet-Nam, 11,000; and south Viet-Nam, 171,000. By 1951 these figures had increased to 52,518, 16,119, and 396,955, respectively. In 1957 the estimated total of Chinese in the country was 800,000.

When Diem came to power, and later founded the republic, the Franco-Chinese arrangements for special legal status for the Chinese were not recognized.[41]

After President Diem had resolved his country's most serious political problems, he turned his attention to the economic plight of the nation. Apart from the integration of the refugees into the economy, there were problems of getting the co-operation of large minority groups, including Chinese, Cambodians, and aborigines.

As mentioned, the Chinese were the most difficult problem. Through hard work and patience, the Chinese had built up a substantial part of the commerce of Viet-Nam.[42] They had been accorded a privileged economic position by the French, which the Vietnamese resented.

Though the Chinese recognized the great political victory that Diem had won and were ready to help him, they also wanted to keep their special

[41] See comment on this point by Bernard B. Fall on pp. 111-17. (ED.)
[42] See "A Survey of Chinese Occupations in Viet-Nam," pp. 118-25. (ED.)

privileges. Too, the rapidity of change in the country, from French colony to free nation, left the Chinese behind in their thinking. Under French rule, they had kept away from political activities, devoting themselves to business and following the middle path between French and Vietnamese.

Suddenly, in the spring of 1956, President Diem requested the Chinese to take a positive role in the economy of the new Viet-Nam. At meetings between Chinese leaders and the President, Diem explained his plans of having the Chinese start industries, and put more emphasis on industry than on commerce. The Chinese, who were merchants and not industrialists, were not ready to co-operate. They had seen so many changes in recent years—French, Japanese, and Communist rule, as well as differing groups of Vietnamese leaders under the French—that they could not recognize the importance of the economic revolution that Diem proposed.

But for Diem, this was *the* revolution. If the Chinese did not comprehend the fact that Viet-Nam's economy must be overhauled, then other moves would be necessary to make them understand.

Without warning, two presidential decrees aimed at the Chinese were announced. On September 6, 1956, a decree announced that *foreigners* were forbidden from the following eleven professions: fishmongering and butchering, general stores, selling of coal and firewood, dealing in petroleum products, dealing in second-hand goods, selling textiles and silks with lengths under 10,000 meters, dealing in scrap metals (iron, copper, and bronze), dealing in cereals, transporting merchandise and passengers by road vehicle, launch, or junk, rice milling, and commission agencies. In effect, the Chinese were to be no longer merchants exclusively. While the measure affected the Chinese in the practice of the specified professions, the situation was tempered somewhat by the fact that many Chinese who were married to Vietnamese women could continue to operate their businesses in the name of their wives.

Another decree, also issued on September 6, 1956, granted Vietnamese nationality to all Chinese born in Viet-Nam. Chinese taking advantage of this decree would have the same rights as Vietnamese citizens.

Through these decrees, the President endeavored to integrate the Chinese into Vietnamese life, politically and economically. The Chinese, he reasoned, should be a close part of the country in which they had their homes and property. As a real part of the nation, they could assist in building a strong, united Viet-Nam to confront the common enemy, communism.

However, the Chinese were psychologically unprepared to accept the decrees, and actively opposed them. Even though the measures would, in principle, assist them, they interpreted them as anti-Chinese in intent. They objected that Vietnamese nationality was given to them without the right to accept or refuse. Thus, the decrees created great unrest in

Chinese communities. The Chinese appealed to the Chinese Consul General[43] from Nationalist China to present their case against the decrees to the government of Free Viet-Nam. When the Vietnamese government rejected the chargé d'affaire's appeal, relations between Nationalist China and Free Viet-Nam became seriously strained, and remained so for about six months.

Taking advantage of this situation, Communists tried to foster trouble and disturbances through class and race struggle. Local Chinese mobs in Saigon wrecked the Chinese Legation, but fortunately no blood was shed. Incidents such as this showed clearly that the Communists wanted an everlasting fight between Chinese and Vietnamese, aimed at the ruin of all Viet-Nam.

In the meantime, Chinese business came to a standstill. The months of July and August, 1957, were crucial months, and even those immediately following did not show any measurable change. The President and Vice President, who was also the Minister of National Economy, understood the seriousness of the economic situation and that a total break with Free China would be a blow not only to Viet-Nam, but also to the Free World. So, a period of appeasement was suggested to allow the Chinese to reconsider the accepting of Vietnamese citizenship. Frequent meetings were held between the Chinese Minister, Chinese Congregation leaders, leaders of the Free Pacific Association, and the Vietnamese Vice President. Through these, leaders of the Chinese community became more aware of the danger of continuing the stalemate.

In the following months more Chinese became citizens. The much-feared break between Nationalist China and Free Viet-Nam never occurred, and the door remained open for Chinese co-operation in the economic life of the country.

The Chinese had learned a hard lesson: Many Chinese companies had closed down; others had gone to Hong Kong, Singapore, or to other places in Southeast Asia to start anew; a few had left for Nationalist China.

The Vietnamese, too, had learned that there was a real danger of national economic suicide in attempting to "go it alone" without the help of the Chinese who had been in Viet-Nam for centuries.

True, some Vietnamese are showing opposition to the Chinese who became citizens. They are attempting a policy of discrimination against them. However, the President will not discriminate against them if the Chinese, as new citizens, co-operate sincerely with all Vietnamese in the

[43] The Chinese had a consul general in Saigon, who became chargé d'affaires after Nationalist China recognized Viet-Nam. Later, at the end of 1956, China sent a Minister to Viet-Nam.

strengthening of the national economy. For their part, the Chinese are slow to act, studying every move carefully, but when they make a decision, it is done seriously and in full faith; they do so with the intention of carrying through decisively and well.

The Sino-Vietnamese co-operation should be of material assistance not only to Viet-Nam but to all Southeast Asia. The internal pattern of co-operation established in Viet-Nam could bring about greater co-operation among all Southeast Asian nations, and especially with Free China, and thus greater promise for the eventual salvation of all this part of Asia.

Commentary: BERNARD B. FALL *on*
FATHER DE JAEGHER

FATHER RAYMOND J. DE JAEGHER'S role as an eminent Sinologist and anti-Communist is well known. He is the founder of the Union Research Institute in Hong Kong—a group of Chinese scholars doing excellent work on developments on the Chinese mainland—and is also Director of the Free Pacific Association. He is also a close adviser of President Diem, and has staunchly supported his cause since Viet-Nam's independence. What Father de Jaegher has to say about the Chinese colony in Viet-Nam, therefore, must not be taken lightly. However, there are points in his paper that must be considered with a great deal of caution, or from another viewpoint.

First of all, Father de Jaegher errs on some aspects of the legislative basis of Sino-Vietnamese relations.[44] The French authorities, in their treatment of the Chinese, were subject to several international treaties, inasmuch as the Chinese in Viet-Nam were citizens of China, with which France maintained diplomatic relations. The first treaty, signed on April 24, 1886, at Tientsin, granted the Chinese free entry into Viet-Nam and the right to establish businesses throughout the country. However, China, as it emerged as a modern power, felt that the assimilation of its citizens with the Vietnamese put them on an "inferior" status in comparison to other foreign nationals (e.g., Indians, French) living in Viet-Nam. A new treaty was negotiated and signed on May, 1930, known as the Nanking convention, which, substantially, granted the Chinese in Viet-Nam a most-favored status. This

---

[44] For an official Vietnamese study on the legal aspects of Sino-Vietnamese relations see *Vietnam in World Affairs*, Vol. I, Nos. 3-4, published by the Secretariat of State for Foreign Affairs, Republic of Viet-Nam, Saigon, December, 1956, pp. 110-26.

change of status, on the other hand, made the Chinese subject to all taxes levied on the other foreigners living in the country.

China's emergence as one of the "Big Five" at the conclusion of World War II put it in an even better bargaining position—the more so as it occupied Indochina down to the 16th parallel between VJ-Day and the return of the French. The latter, in a weak military and diplomatic position, had no choice but to agree to Chinese conditions in order to obtain the evacuation of the Chinese from northern Indochina. A new treaty was signed at Chungking on February 25, 1946, which suppressed all remaining fiscal and juridical inequalities between the Chinese and foreigners of European origin.

The Chinese government itself was against the Congregation system, which tended to favor the development of regional or provincial allegiances among the Chinese instead of an over-all allegiance to the Republic of China. Thus, in furtherance of the provisions of the 1946 Chungking treaty, an exchange of letters took place between the French and Chinese governments—equivalent in terms of American constitutional law to an executive agreement—on August 20, 1948, which provided for the elimination of the Congregations in favor of Regional Chinese Administrative Associations over which the Chinese consular authorities in Viet-Nam have extensive regulatory powers.

Thus, contrary to what Father de Jaegher asserts, the position of the Chinese in Viet-Nam is not based on any French "law" but on a valid international obligation undertaken by the French and Chinese governments. And again, contrary to Father de Jaegher's statement, the government of President Diem has *not,* to anyone's knowledge, canceled its international treaty obligations inherited from the French colonial administration, of which, under international law, it is the successor. There is, therefore, no basis to the assertion that under the republican regime of Free Viet-Nam, "the Franco-Chinese arrangements . . . were not recognized."

Free Viet-Nam, however, acted within its legitimate rights as a sovereign state in barring the Chinese who were noncitizens from certain professions. Practically every country gives its own citizens preferential treatment in political and economic fields. In this sense, Vietnamese legislation has lagged behind the stringent anti-Chinese legislation of neighboring Cambodia and Thailand.

Hence, what caused the resistance of the Chinese against becoming Vietnamese citizens, when the Chinese in other countries complied with similar decrees rather willingly? (In Cambodia, so many Chinese wanted to become nationals that the Khmer government had to make its naturalization regulations stricter to stop the overflow of candidates.) As high officials in Taipei explained to me in 1957, "We did not object to the legislation as such, but to the fact that it left the Chinese no free choice in the matter—in violation of the United Nations Declaration on Human Rights—and for the narrow and petty way in which the legislation was applied."[45]

And there lies, perhaps, Father de Jaegher's greatest flaw of reasoning and one which, as a sincere friend of the Chinese, he should not have overlooked: The Chinese are *people,* with a sense of dignity and honor—and they do not like to be "pushed," and even less to be "pushed around." And this is exactly what happened in Viet-Nam between the spring and fall of 1957.

For example—and all the facts cited here can be confirmed from fully authenticated Vietnamese sources—for months the Vietnamese police simply arrested Chinese citizens, confiscated their alien identification cards and, whether they liked it or not, issued them identification cards attesting their Vietnamese citizenship. In view of the example set by the central authorities in Saigon, local officials in the provinces acted in a like manner. According to the Saigon newspaper *Tin Dien* (The Message) of March 1, 1957, the authorities of Can Tho province were going to levy a fine ranging from 200 to 2,000 piasters ($6 to $60) upon every Chinese not "naturalized" by March 8.

Little wonder that the Chinese colony retaliated in the only way it could—by nearly wrecking the Vietnamese economy during the summer of 1957. Within a few days after the application of the decrees, the Chinese began a run on the banks where they had deposits. Soon, a sum varying between 800 million and 1.5 billion piasters (close to one sixth of the whole currency in circulation in the country) had disappeared from circulation. Commercial transactions came to a near-standstill. The value of Vietnamese currency on the Hong Kong free market tumbled from an official rate of 35 to $1.00 to 90 and 105 (its usual "free rate" being about 75-80).

This writer also notes Father de Jaegher's version of Free Viet-Nam's industrialization plans which apparently seek to shift to foreign investors the burden of building up a sound basis for the country's economy. If this were really the intention of President Diem, Viet-Nam would soon find itself again under extensive foreign economic control—with the Vietnamese owning the groceries and retail shops and the foreigners (be they Chinese, French, or American) owning all the industries. As of May, 1958, it was apparent, however, that this somewhat unsophisticated economic thinking has been superseded by a sounder appraisal of the situation. Present plans still provide for foreign in-

[45] For a full discussion of the problem see Bernard Fall, *The International Position of South Viet-Nam, 1954-58,* New York, Institute of Pacific Relations, 1958, or "Viet-Nam's Chinese Problem," in *Far Eastern Survey,* May, 1958.

vestment in Viet-Nam, but it is understood that 51 percent of the capital of such new corporations will be in Vietnamese hands.

As it turned out, the Chinese were not easily replaceable. While there were nearly enough Vietnamese candidates to take over the 596 Chinese butcher shops in the Saigon area, the 1,013 *chap-pho* (grocery-general stores) vacated by the Chinese as of June 4, 1957, found only 96 Vietnamese takers.[46] The social and economic effects of the whole operation throughout Viet-Nam can be imagined in view of the fact that out of a total of 11,115 *chap-pho* licensed throughout Free Viet-Nam, 4,606 were known to be in Chinese hands.

In addition to this almost insuperable distribution problem, the Vietnamese government apparently underestimated the drastic loss in tax revenue which the anti-Chinese legislation brought in its wake—not to speak of the problem of sudden Chinese unemployment. By mid-July, 1957, the Saigon area had 25,000 new Chinese unemployed. Throughout the countryside, the Chinese rice millers, who had usually helped (at usurious rates, to be sure) the Vietnamese farmers tide over the lean months prior to the harvesting of new crops, failed to come forth with money. The business slump snowballed into the countryside, as Vietnamese farmers complained that their rice was not being collected for milling and that trucks and junks for the transport to the mills were lacking.[47]

What happened thereafter was simply a more or less veiled capitulation of the Vietnamese authorities in the face of the mounting economic crisis, also brought on by other factors for which the Chinese were not responsible. On July 19, 1957, the Prefect (Area Governor) of Saigon-Cholon called in one hundred and fifty Chinese businessmen and told them they could reopen their businesses if they put their shops in the name of Vietnamese "strawmen," took out citizenship, or put their shops in the name of their Vietnamese wives. He threatened them with deportation to Formosa if they refused.[48] Some of the Chinese complied; others argued that they no longer had sufficient funds to reopen their shops, no doubt hoping to improve their bargaining position by hesitating somewhat longer.[49]

In addition to the internal counterpressure which the Chinese began to bring into play, their countrymen in the market places of Singapore and Hong Kong began to boycott Vietnamese products not sold by Chinese. For example, there is evidence that the Chinese of Hong Kong refused to purchase 40,000 tons of Vietnamese rice which had

[46] *Thoi Luan*, Saigon, June 17, 1957.
[47] *Dan Chung*, September 21, 1957.
[48] *Troi-Nam*, July 20, 1957.
[49] *Tin-Dien*, July 24, 1957.

already been contracted for. The rice was then reshipped to Singapore, and likewise boycotted there.

However, political pressure upon Viet-Nam's Chinese colony continued at the highest level, in spite of American advice to President Diem during his May, 1957, visit to the United States not to cause a breach in the Asian anti-Communist alliance by maintaining an intransigent attitude on the subject. It continued almost unabated—with several Chinese newspaper editors being indicted for allegedly collecting a fund in support of Chinese made destitute by the naturalization decrees—until March, 1958, when sound counsel began to prevail in the political field.[50]

Until early in 1958 Free Viet-Nam had likewise remained adamant on the issue of free choice of naturalization or repatriation, the key issue of the whole problem, as far as Nationalist China was concerned. As the Chinese Foreign Minister George K. C. Yeh stated at the Kuomintang weekly memorial meeting of May, 1958:

> Our policy from the very beginning has been to uphold the principle of free choice for those Chinese nationals born in Vietnam. We feel that Vietnam and China, both being democratic nations, should respect the free choice of our nationals in regard to their nationality.

While evacuation to Formosa was little enough of a choice, even this last loophole was plugged by a registration procedure which, to this day, remains somewhat obscure and subject to sudden changes without notice, with the result that exasperated Chinese finally rioted at the Chinese Consulate General in Saigon in May, 1957. There is no basis whatever to Father de Jaegher's statement that "local Chinese mobs" were encouraged by Communists. No Vietnamese or Chinese source has raised this allegation, either privately or officially.

In any case, the total number of applicants for evacuation was never large enough to cause a problem to Viet-Nam; yet, the government showed little willingness to facilitate their departure. According to Chinese official sources in Saigon, a total of 52,144 applications were received when, without prior warning, the Vietnamese authorities declared the list as "closed" on July 19, 1957. At that time only some 3,000 Chinese had completed their documentation for departure. Their evacuation began via a small airlift on August 2, 1957. But even these evacuees were subject to some last-minute harassments (complete listing of every item, as well as limitation on cash currency they could take along), including a 500-piaster "departure tax" collected at the

[50] *New York Times,* October 5, 1957.

airport, when they were authorized to carry only 400 piasters with them.[51]

The Chinese met Vietnamese deadlines for naturalization registration with a vast shrug of indifference. "Final" deadlines were edicted on March 22, June 21, and August 10, 1957. But even by the last date, less than 80,000-100,000 Chinese had complied with the regulations. Now, deadlines are no longer mentioned in the press, and registration continues on an individual basis.[52]

It is easy to imagine what this situation did to relations between the Nationalist Chinese government in Formosa and the government of Free Viet-Nam. Although both governments recognized each other and appointed chiefs of mission to each other's capitals, Free Viet-Nam's minister did not leave for Taipei until March, 1958, after a visit of the Chinese Foreign Minister, George K. C. Yeh, in Saigon, during the same month, which somewhat cleared the air for further negotiations.

The lessening of tension, apparent in Saigon in the spring of 1958, also brought about renewed talks of a possible visit of President Diem to Formosa, in the hope of settling Chinese-Vietnamese differences at the highest level.[53] This lessening of tension is due to several factors. On the Vietnamese side, there has been a definite softening-up of the position on strict application of the naturalization decrees in the economic field. Vietnamese wives and strawmen have stepped in to take over the businesses of Chinese husbands and friends (to the extent, in fact, that Vietnamese butchers now fear that they are again being driven to the wall by Chinese competitors operating under Vietnamese camouflage) and the urgent need of the Vietnamese economy for *any* capital, regardless of nationality. On the Chinese side, the lack of real alternatives—Formosa being only a poor second choice—has led the Chinese colony in Free Viet-Nam to second thoughts; there are strong indications that eventually more and more Chinese in Viet-Nam will take out Vietnamese identification papers.

However, it is doubtful whether the "granting" of citizenship under such conditions will make loyal Vietnamese out of the Chinese. In fact, there are some indications that the Chinese have deeply resented not only the attitude of the Saigon administration in the matter, but have also not failed to note the "hands-off" attitude of the United States and the powerlessness of Formosa in the face of their plight. There have been some grumblings to the effect that "we Chinese

[51] Fall, *op. cit.*, p. 68.
[52] *New York Times,* October 5, 1957.
[53] These problems include sovereignty over the Paracel and Spratley Islands, in the South China Sea, which both China and Viet-Nam claim.

wouldn't be pushed around like that if we had Mao's (i.e., Red Chinese) passports."

This does *not* mean that the Chinese in Viet-Nam have been, or are, an incipient Red Chinese "Fifth Column." But the propaganda value to Red China of any mistreatment—real or fancied—of Chinese in Southeast Asia should not be disregarded as nonexistent.

These are important, perhaps vital, factors in Free Viet-Nam's future development which cannot be simply dismissed with generalities. It is the considered opinion of many observers, including Vietnamese who have worked closely on the problems of Free Viet-Nam's relations with its minorities, that the Vietnamese authorities in Saigon have shown less than full understanding of the difficulties involved in dealing with minorities,[54] and that this attitude may backfire severely upon them in time of stress when a government cannot insure the loyalty of its citizens merely by an extensive police and security system.

[54] See "The Tribesmen," pp. 126-135, concerning tensions in the tribal areas. (ED.)

X. A Survey of Chinese Occupations

TSUNG TO WAY[55]

"THE SOUTHEAST ASIAN countries," wrote John Kerry King in his *Southeast Asia in Perspective*, "lack not only engineers and managers but also businessmen who can mobilize capital for use in initiating commercial and industrial enterprises and agrarian improvements to essential life. Generally speaking the role of the businessmen throughout Southeast Asia has been left to the foreign minority group, primarily the Chinese." There is certainly no doubt that the Chinese play an important role in the economic life of Viet-Nam.

How do the estimated 800,000 Chinese in Viet-Nam earn a living? Unlike French businessmen who make large investments in farming, mining, forestry, plantations, fisheries, industrial and commercial enterprises, the economic activities of the Chinese are mainly in the field of commerce and trade. The list of Chinese occupations (Table 1) indicates their diversification, with practically no business in which the Chinese cannot be found. True, there are not many Chinese firms of substantial capital and size but, because of their numerical superiority, their influence on the economy is unquestionably great.

Under the category of food and kindred products, there are 26 sub-classifications, comprising 653 firms or authorized dealers. Some of these firms, such as rice mills of medium size, may employ capital of over several million piasters. Others, such as the small ones under the sub-classification of confectioneries or soya bean sauce manufacturers, may own only simple manual machinery or even a few simple tools, thus making one doubt whether these firms may be classified as "manufacturers" in the real sense. Among the local industries there is no doubt that rice milling is the most important. There are about seventy rice mills in the Saigon-Cholon area, and seventy-five percent are reputedly owned by Chinese. For the past ten years, due to the lack of rice paddy, most of the big rice mills have not been and are still not in operation.

Besides rice milling, there is practically no Chinese food industry which is of capital importance. Most of the other food firms manufacture products such as fish sauce, bean sauce, rice flour noodles, and soya bean cheese, which are either not available in the foreign market or the imported products do not suit the taste of the Vietnamese. There are also firms that produce less expensive goods which are intended for consumption, such as canned goods, sugar, confectionery, and pastry.

Textile mill products are second in importance, with more than 600 firms engaged in the spinning and weaving business. However, most of these manufacturers are small family enterprises. Despite the keen de-

[55] Manager of the Bank of China, Saigon.

TABLE 1
CLASSIFICATION OF CHINESE OCCUPATIONS IN FREE VIET-NAM

MANUFACTURING	Number of firms or authorized dealers			
	Saigon-Cholon	South Viet-Nam (provinces)	Central Viet-Nam	Total
Food & kindred products	653	329	63	1,045
Tobacco manufacturers	10			10
Textile mill products	625			625
Lumber & timber basic products	160	116		276
Furniture & finished lumber products	71			71
Paper & allied products	59			59
Printing, publishing, & allied industries	98			98
Chemicals & allied products	43			43
Rubber products	35			35
Leather & leather products	198			198
Stone, clay, & glass products	159			159
Iron & steel and their products	8			8
Nonferrous metal & their products	117			117
Machinery (except electrical)	180			180
Transportation equipment (except automobiles)	38			38
Miscellaneous manufacturing	410	77	26	513
Subtotal	2,864	522	89	3,475
NONMANUFACTURING				
Agriculture, forestry, & fisheries	30			30
Contract construction	60			60
Wholesale trade	1,856	3,398	817	6,071
Retail trade	2,123	2,138	461	4,722
Finance, insurance, & real estate	89			89
Transportation	165			165
Service—Hotel & other lodging service	108		29	137
Miscellaneous repair service	39			39
Motion pictures	20			20
Amusement & recreation (except motion pictures)	9			9
Medical & other health services	135	196	45	376
Educational service	32			32
Restaurant, cold drink, & food supply service	920	408	99	1,427
Miscellaneous	636			636
Subtotal	6,222	6,140	1,451	13,813
TOTAL	9,086	6,662	1,540	17,288

mand for textile goods, as evidenced by the amount of imports each year, Free Viet-Nam does not have a single large textile mill.

A brief review of the subclassifications under miscellaneous manufacturing, third in importance, indicates that making of clothes, shirts, hats, and bedding are among the most important ones. As gunny bags are not produced in Viet-Nam, the subclassification under gunny bag includes firms or factories that repair or recondition old gunny bags.

Under the category of leather and leather products, the making of shoes is foremost. The import value of shoes for 1955 amounted to 3,683,000 piasters, which is far from adequate for the demand. It is evident that a large portion of the shoe supply is being manufactured locally. In the making of shoes and boots, no machinery is yet employed; they are all hand-made. (*Bata* has a modern shoe manufacturing unit in Saigon.) Besides shoemaking, the manufacture of bags, suitcases, belts, saddles, and reins and harness is also of considerable importance. Although cattle hides are the principal source of leather, the skins of pigs, tigers, snakes, and crocodiles are also obtainable in the market. There are 48 firms engaged in the tanning and dressing of skins.

Under the category of machinery (except electrical), there are 180 firms, which build simple machinery of all kinds and also make spare parts for the maintenance of existing machines. The small 50-ton capacity rice-milling machines are all made by the local manufacturers. They are simple, but serve the purpose.

The category under lumber and timber basic products and furniture and finished lumber products, as they all deal with lumber, may be discussed together. None of the Chinese-owned sawmills can really be called a "sawmill" in the strictest sense. Their machines are usually primitive. In view of the rich natural resources of lumber and timber in Viet-Nam, the prospect of forest exploitation is bright. It is estimated that the total forest area in Free Viet-Nam is over 1,104,000 hectares. The production of charcoal and its by-products is also important. In 1955 the total production amounted to 14,200 tons. The quality of native woods, such as rosewood, mahogany, and ebony, are all of the best kind; therefore, practically all the demand for household furniture is satisfied by local manufacturers. The use of rattan for furniture making is common among the inhabitants.

Under the category of stone, clay, and glass products, the most common occupation is that of brickmaking and tilemaking. Bricks are used for all ordinary building and construction purposes. With the exception of the very expensive ones, all tiles, whether for roofing or flooring, are made by local firms. Claywares and glasswares, of low quality and simple design, are also obtainable from local Chinese manufacturers.

Under the category of nonferrous metal and their products, there are

117 firms. However, as both aluminum and tin are not really produced in Viet-Nam, supply of which depends on imports, these firms are not manufacturers in the real sense. The use of aluminum has become so extensive that in fact it can be used for all purposes. Aluminum is used for the manufacturing of kitchen utensils, spare parts for cycles, and office supplies. With a view to economizing the use of foreign exchange, the government has been trying to encourage the import of aluminum sheets instead of aluminum finished products. It is estimated that the imported aluminum sheets cost about 40 piasters a kilo, while aluminum finished products cost 105 piasters for the same weight.

The category under printing, publishing, and allied industries and the category under paper and allied products, from the paper usage angle, may be discussed together. According to the *Times* of Viet-Nam, some 60,000 tons of paper are imported each year. Judging from the per capita consumption of paper in the more industrialized countries, the per capita consumption of two kilos of paper in Viet-Nam is too trifling to deserve comparison. Nonetheless, the capacity of local factories is not even able to meet the above demand, and imports are necessary. There are fifteen Chinese paper factories in the Saigon-Cholon area, but, because of their small capacity and the inferior quality of production, they are of little importance. For years to come, Viet-Nam will be depending upon foreign countries for its paper supply. With respect to printing business, there are 65 firms. Some of these are quite up-to-date; they use modern printing machines, and the largest one employs more than 100 workers. However, the technique of the local Chinese printing house is not comparable with that of their compatriots in Hong Kong.

Under the category chemicals and allied products, soap and candle manufacturers may be mentioned, with 24 factories for the former and 12 for the latter. Both products are mainly for consumption in the hinterland.

As far as the local industries are concerned, the production of tobacco is an important one. The French firms have a monopoly of the market. The Chinese firms are engaged in the production of cheap kinds of tobacco for the consumption of a small section of Chinese population.

Among the nonmanufacturing occupations, retail trade is the most important category. It comprises 15 subclassifications, 2,123 firms or authorized dealers. "Authorized dealers" means those persons who are given the "patent" to engage in the kind of business as authorized by the government. The greatest number of firms are grocery stores, which more or less resemble an American drug or dime store, where one buys whatever one wants. Second in importance are the Chinese medicine shops, which supply Chinese raw or prescribed medicines to both the

Chinese and Vietnamese population. Because of the lack of modern medical doctors, the use of Chinese medicines, especially in the interior, is common. Rice shops and secondhand goods stalls, both of which have 200 dealers, rank third. It is interesting to note that the above retail trades comprise more than half of the entire dealers. Furthermore, if an analysis is made of their business activities it may be seen that they bear close relationships with the daily lives of most of the population, especially laborers and workers. The fact that the "shops" of one third of the 2,123 dealers are stalls indicates that retail traders themselves are laborers and workers.

Under the category wholesale, there are 30 subclassifications, comprising 1,856 firms or dealers. Import and export firms, which total 350, head this category. This type of business is, in fact, new to the majority of both the Chinese and Vietnamese. It was not until mid-1955 that the local Chinese and Vietnamese businessmen started to learn to do import and export business. With the exception of a few dozen of the large ones, these are newly established firms. Rarely do they have special lines of their own. They merely import whatever seems profitable. It is said that before the imposition of deposit margin of 350,000 piasters, there were more than 20,000 import and export firms in Saigon and Cholon. Among the wholesalers, it is surprising to find a large number of dealers in copper and iron scrap. The scrap business is mainly in the hands of Fukien people, who buy and collect not only scrap but also whatever else is worth buying. The recent export of 40,000 tons of iron scrap to Japan is a good indication of the importance of this business. Next in number are the dealers under the subclassification bazaar. There is not much distinction between the business activities of bazaar and grocery; both deal with the distribution of all kinds of imported goods. The difference, if any, is that of capital and business volume. Textile business always commands an important place in a retail market, and there are 100 firms in this wholesale business. In this connection, the important activities of Indian firms may be mentioned; a considerable portion of the silk and textile business is in the hands of Indian merchants. The subclassification under native produce is of equal importance. Besides rice and rubber, there are quite a number of items of which Viet-Nam has an exportable surplus. Among them are articles such as green beans, cattle skin, duck feathers, and dried fish. The export of these commodities is handled mostly by Chinese. Under the prevailing exchange system, these commodities, which are considered of secondary importance, are exported to Hong Kong and Singapore under barter arrangements.

Under the category transportation, there are 6 subclassifications, comprising 165 dealers. Although the numbers of dealers in inland and junk and tugboat transport are not numerous, they are very influential. As railway service is only available between Saigon and Dalat and Saigon and Nha Trang, the distribution of imported goods from Saigon to the hinterland, as well as between towns and villages in the interior, are all done by highway. A large portion of native products is also transported by highway to Saigon for export. For decades the transportation of rice from the interior to Saigon has been reserved to junks and tugboats. This river transportation business is also mainly in the hands of Chinese. It is not uncommon to find large Chinese rice merchants who own junks and do the transportation themselves. As regards the subclassification under steamer company, there are several small steamers of around 500 tonnage owned and run by Chinese. Before the partition, these steamers used to run between Saigon and Haiphong, and occasionally Saigon and Tourane. Under subclassification steamship company are firms acting as agents for shipping companies of either Chinese or foreign steamship companies in Hong Kong or Singapore.

Under the category finance, insurance, and real estate, the importance of the part played by the Chinese banks may be cited. In conformity with the instructions of the government, as passed to them through the intermediaries of either the National Bank of Viet-Nam or the Exchange Control Office, these banks render innumerable services to their clients with no distinctions based on nationality. In view of the lack of credit facilities for the small firms or working class people, the part played by pawnshops and moneylenders is also of significance; the role of the Indians is important here, but many Chinese are engaged in the small moneylending business. With the recent formation of small credit facilities by the government, many of these pawnshops and moneylenders may be replaced in the course of time.

Under the category of service, there are 20 subclassifications, comprising altogether 1,899 dealers, with noodle seller stalls, butcheries, and tearooms constituting over half of the total. Among these occupations, perhaps the lowest capital requirement for the management of an independent business is that of noodle seller stalls. An honest, hard-working man can start with capital as low as 10,000 piasters. There are 100 under the subclassification of dentist. These Chinese dentists are not professionally trained, but learn their trade by practice and experience. They are mostly people of Shantung province. Next in the list are barbershops and dry cleaning shops. During the past year a noticeable number of modern barbershops have been established in Saigon and Cholon. Some of them are even air-conditioned. Taking into consideration the hot tropical weather, the dealers in dry cleaning are far less in number than one might expect. A considerable amount of Chinese capital is being invested in hotels and restaurants. The Chinese hotels in Cholon are not modern Western-style hotels, but they meet the requirements of Chinese travelers. For occasions such as birthdays or marriages, Chinese restaurants are still the popular places to hold such celebrations. Chinese motion pictures produced in Hong Kong or Taiwan are enjoyed by local Chinese inhabitants. There are quite a number of modern cinema houses owned by Chinese. Butcheries, formerly a monopoly of the Chinese, have been practically taken over by Vietnamese refugees from the north.

In the interior one finds Chinese grocery stores and medicine shops in the smallest towns (see Table 2). Besides the above two occupations, many Chinese in the interior are engaged in the purchase and collection of native products from the peasants and farmers. In time of need, they often make loans and advances to the peasants. In co-ordination with the business activities of their compatriots in Saigon and Cholon, these Chinese firms in the interior, form an economic structure that has existed for decades and centuries.

TABLE 2

NUMBER OF OVERSEAS CHINESE FIRMS IN PROVINCES
AND CHIEF TOWNS

Provinces and Chief Towns	Number of Firms or Authorized Dealers
FREE VIET-NAM	
Saigon-Cholon	9,086
Gia-Dinh	423
Chau Doc	351
Tra Vinh	352
Rach Gia	431
Ha Tien	118
Sa Dec	253
Ben Tre	339
Long Xuyen	420
Tan An	174
Soc Trang	478
Thu Dau Mot	453
Tay Ninh	339
Bien Hoa	323
My Tho	359
Ba Ria	135
Cholon	225
Vinh Long	253
Go Cong	293
Can Tho	416
Bac Lieu	408
Cap St. Jacques	119
Subtotal	15,748

CENTRAL VIET-NAM

Thua Thien (Hue)	75
Thua Thien (Tourane)	140
Quang Nam (Faifo)	133
Quang Nam (Quang Ngai)	120
Binh Dinh (Qui Nhon)	180
Phu Yen (Tuy Hoa)	85
Khanh Hoa (Ninh Hoa)	100
Khanh Hoa (Nha Trang)	110
Ninh Thuan (Phan Thiet)	170
Quang Tri	28
Subtotal	1,141

PLATEAU REGION

Thuong Don Nai (Djiring)	97
Lam Vien (Dalat)	75
Bar Lac (Ban Me Thuot)	90
Plei Ku	37
Kon Tum	15
Subtotal	314
TOTAL	17,203

XI. The Tribesmen

FREDERIC WICKERT[56]

THE WORLD has heard about the 3,000 primitive tribesmen who, willingly or not, co-operate with the Communists in the highly dramatized struggle that has been going on for so long in the jungles of Malaya. But there has been almost no publicity regarding a tribal problem of far greater magnitude, that of the 500,000 to 700,000 tribesmen of Free Viet-Nam. Also little known are the problems of hundreds of thousands of tribesmen to the north of Free Viet-Nam. Some of these live in Laos and Cambodia, or to the west of Thailand, Burma, and India, while others reside in Red Viet-Nam and even in China itself.

The mountain tribesmen in Free Viet-Nam, along with the Chinese, the large numbers of Cambodians in the Mekong delta, and the near million refugees from the north (perhaps 150,000 of these are Nung tribesmen, fierce fighters from the Viet-Nam-China border) have created problems for the new government of Free Viet-Nam.

The Vietnamese tend to look on the mountain tribesmen as inferior, uncivilized, lazy, and wastefully occupying much good land. They usually refer to a tribesman as *moi*, which means savage. At the same time, the Vietnamese, accustomed to the crowded, flat rice lands and to cities, tend to be a little afraid of the tribesmen and regard the thinly populated mountainous country where they live as inhospitable.

On the other hand, the tribesmen consider the Vietnamese as a force that may lead to their eventual extermination. The Vietnamese are settling on their lands, with the best lands going first, and the tribesmen see themselves starved to death. They feel that the Vietnamese are letting diseases, such as smallpox, kill them off. Too, they feel that the Vietnamese are trying to force them to give up their culture.

The Communists are another group involved in the Vietnamese tribesmen problem. The tribesmen's country merges into that of fellow tribesmen who live north of the 17th parallel, in Red Viet-Nam. There are only paths through the otherwise trackless jungle and mountains where the 17th parallel runs, although some roads are being built. Communist infiltrators could, and have, come down these paths to spread propaganda among the frustrated tribesmen. It has long been conceded that one obvious route of attack on Free Viet-Nam would be through these jungles.

No doubt the Communists estimate that the tribesmen, if not enthusi-

[56] Professor of Psychology, Michigan State University. Historical references have come from French sources, particularly *Bulletin de la Societé des Études Indochinoises*. Other information comes from the personal experiences of the author and his colleagues in the Michigan State University Group and other American organizations in Free Viet-Nam.

astically friendly, would scarcely oppose them. When the Communists were in control of this area up to the time of Geneva, they did try to make friends. Even today Communist agents, largely Vietnamese from both Red and Free Viet-Nam, are said to work among the tribesmen. They do not assume the superior airs that too many Vietnamese public officials in tribesmen country do. Instead, they live as the tribesmen do—wearing the same clothing, eating the same food, learning the tribal languages, sharing the hardships, even having their front teeth knocked out, as many tribesmen do for ritual purposes. The Communists are reported to have taken many of the best-educated tribesmen to Red Viet-Nam, to have available should the Communists choose to attack Free Viet-Nam.

There is still a fourth group involved in the tribesman problem, namely a few people from the Western world. Catholic missionaries, mostly French, have worked with some tribes for a hundred years. American Protestant missionaries are becoming well established in some sections, despite a not always completely friendly Vietnamese government.

Some American advisers of the army of Viet-Nam, a few technical assistants in the United States Operations Mission, and the Michigan State University Group, and persons from other groups are aware of the problems. Many former French officials and former and present French individuals associated with the plantations in tribesman country also are familiar with the situation.

The origins of the mountain tribes are not completely understood. One group of tribes speaks languages of Malayo-Polynesian stock, while another group speaks languages of the Mon-Khmer stock. This suggests some tie-in with the Malays to the south on the one hand, and to the Khmers (who built famed Angkor Wat) and other groups more or less indigenous to the Indochinese peninsula. Still another group are the Chams, who once were strong enough to attack successfully Angkor Wat at its height (twelfth century A.D.,) but who are now defeated and apathetic, and live at about the same level as some of the tribesmen.

As long ago as the third or second century B.C., the Vietnamese came from China and settled in the Red River Valley, in what is now Red Viet-Nam. In the following centuries they consolidated their position there and then gradually pushed south along the east coast of the Indochinese peninsula. As they moved south, they forced the tribesmen and the Chams into the mountains to the west. It was only in comparatively recent times, perhaps the seventeenth century A.D., that the Vietnamese were able to take firm control of what is now south Viet-Nam.

The mountain tribesmen found themselves between strong groups, the Khmers to the west and the Chams, and later the Vietnamese, to the east.

They frequently paid tribute to both groups. However, they were rather diverse groups themselves, and there is evidence of much intertribal warfare. Even today there is no evidence that tribesmen regard themselves as having a great deal in common with each other.

In the past the Vietnamese were not always successful in controlling the tribesmen. In one area, until relatively recent times, tribesmen owned Vietnamese slaves. In another area, even today, tribesmen are supposed to capture a few Vietnamese each year for human sacrificial purposes.

When the French came to Viet-Nam they did not concern themselves with the tribesmen area. But after World War I, when the French needed rubber, plantations spread from the relatively level south to the mountainous region. The tribesmen fiercely resisted this trend until as recently as 1938.

The stories of resistance to French penetration are remarkably similar to those of Indian resistance during the development of the United States. In one case, a French officer or two, at the head of a platoon of Vietnamese soldiers, came to a tribal village to discuss the transfer of more land to the growing rubber plantations. The tribesmen appeared friendly and invited the party into their stockade. They left the stockade gates open and leaned their spears against one wall. Then they asked the French and Vietnamese to stack their weapons against the other wall, to show their friendly intentions. A few minutes after both sides had seated themselves to parley, the remainder of the men of the village, aided by men from another tribe, rushed into the stockade and slaughtered the entire party.

In tribesmen territory, the French did succeed in setting up a cool mountain resort, where they could escape Saigon's heat, as well as a series of military posts and a network of crude roads and bridges. A number of plantations—producing rubber, tea, coffee, and other crops—were well established in a few especially favored areas. Some Frenchmen were sympathetic toward the tribesmen and did a good deal to develop schools, to introduce modern medicine (for example, in the field of malaria control), to preserve tribal forms of justice, and to keep the Vietnamese out. The area was eventually called the Pays Montagnard du Sud (or P.M.S.) by the French. It was officially classified a crown domain, directly under the authority of Emperor Bao Dai. This set the area administratively apart from the rest of Viet-Nam, and made it possible to reserve it exclusively for French economic exploitation.

Toward the end of World War II the Japanese penetrated a little of the area, but the French, under the Vichy regime, retained control of it during most of the war. With the outbreak of fighting with the Communists, tribal troops often remained loyal to the French. In fact, one French-led battalion of tribesmen evidently penetrated far into China,

This exposure of so many to the outside world has subsequently done much to make the many villages, which had one or two soldiers in the battalion, more receptive to the introduction of outside ideas.

Only since about 1955 have the Vietnamese moved in to replace the French, on the political and administrative front, as well as on the economic. Refugees from the north are being moved into the area in large groups.

The majority of the tribespeople live in villages of from twenty-five to occasionally as many as three thousand or more people. Some live in or near the thriving towns growing up around Vietnamese administrative centers.

The houses vary a good deal from tribe to tribe. One branch of the Mnongs, for example, live in huts on the ground. The interiors may be smoky, since there are no chimneys; the beams and other wooden parts are sometimes painted with tribal designs in various colors. Other tribes, the Rhadé for example, live in long houses situated on upright logs. The logs raise the houses off the ground, from as little as two or three feet up to as much as ten feet or more. One Sedang house is more than one hundred yards long, and some others in the same rather wealthy village approach this one in length.

Some tribespeople pride themselves on the symmetrical and functional layout of their villages. They cannot see how the Vietnamese with their huts crowded together, one jammed any old way against the next one, have anything to teach them about living in general and town planning in particular.

Any given tribe may have from a few to many villages. Although tribesmen may vary a good deal from one village to another and tribesmen from different villages may get to know each other well, the villages within a tribe are quite autonomous. There seem to be no tribal chiefs or other tribal organizations.

In some tribes a matrilineal kinship system exists. The females own the house, ceremonial gongs, ceremonial and storage jars, and other family goods. Men own their weapons and bicycles or elephants. After marriage, the man goes to live at the house of his wife. Groupings of lineages form "clans," and it is forbidden to marry within a clan. Clans sometimes seem to cross tribal boundaries.

As a general rule, the tribesmen are animists. Trees, streams, thunder, for example, have spirits which must not be offended. When a Vietnamese soldier washes his truck in a stream, he may be offending the spirit of the stream. The spirit may have to be appeased by making a sacrifice.

Sometimes it was believed that spirits capable of superhuman deeds were incarnated. One such incarnation gave rise to the rumor, during the French rule, that the golden age was imminent. No one would have to work, and the tribes again would gain control of their land. Armed attacks against the French authorities were common for a time. Famine spread among many tribespeople because they did not plant their fields in anticipation of the no-more-work golden age.

As has been indicated, some villages have been converted to Protestantism or Catholicism. Some may be partly Christian and partly pagan. In addition to bringing in religion, missionaries have been active in improving health and sanitation conditions, introducing new crops, and making improvements in living standards.

There are schools in the few provincial capitals, which permit children to go to school perhaps from four to six years, but few children from far-off villages can go to these schools. In some remote villages, however, one sometimes finds schools. As is true also with the Vietnamese themselves, schooling opportunities are haphazardly provided geographically, though in general the tribespeople have far fewer and poorer schools than the Vietnamese.

Through missionary schools or through one or two public schools in the provincial capitals, it is possible to qualify for a university education. However, so far few tribesmen have; and none so far as can be determined has completed the university. The Government's National Institute of Administration in Saigon is training a small number of tribesmen to take over administrative functions in tribal areas. The course given to tribesmen is shorter and not as high a level as that given to Vietnamese because, as National Institute officials explain, tribesmen are not qualified to take higher level academic work.

Some common diseases are malaria, dengue fever, smallpox, leprosy, and elephantiasis. There are hospitals and some first-aid stations and small dispensaries, but these are often inadequate in staff and in their supply of medicines. Even when they are sometimes fairly well supplied, the tribesmen who have been "trained" to take care of them neglect their duties, and the supplies are wasted.

The basic crop is mountain rice. The bottom lands along rivers that will support wet rice culture have long been used for this purpose, but produce a small part of the total rice crop. Generally, the mountain rice is cultivated by the shifting field method: An area of land is partially cleared of heavy growth, and the smaller choppings are burned when they are dry enough. Large logs and branches, half charred, are often left in the field. Such a field will grow a reasonably satisfactory crop for about three years. Then it is permitted to go back to jungle, and a new area is used for growing. After perhaps five to ten years one can cultivate the same field again. Three or four fields are thus cultivated in a continuous cycle by a given village or family of tribespeople. Much rice is turned into a liqueur, an essential for many ceremonies and celebrations.

Manioc, cabbages, oranges, and other foodstuffs are raised. In many areas the tribesmen grow their own tobacco in small patches. Water buffalo, cows, pigs, chickens, and dogs are raised for food. The water buffalo are commonly slaughtered and eaten at ceremonies. In some places, fish are caught in lakes and streams.

The tribespeople sell vegetables and rice in the markets of provincial capitals. There they buy ceremonial gongs, cooking utensils, safety pins, salt, beads, candy, alcohol to drink, bicycles, secondhand warm wool clothing, and so on. Some earn money by working on plantations or on roads or by joining the army. Some villages rather far removed from the provincial capitals are visited by itinerant merchants.

In warm weather, men may wear nothing but a wrap-around G-string. In the towns, a white shirt or, in colder weather, an old wool jacket, usually left over from the army, is added. Especially in the more remote areas, women often wear no clothes above the waist. Ceremonial costumes for both sexes may be quite colorful, but are seldom worn and are probably disappearing.

In general, the tribespeople remember the French with considerable warmth. They seem to have forgotten that the French forced them to work on roads and plantations. Tribesmen who once were former French army soldiers remain particularly loyal. Some of these learned to speak the French language fairly well. The tribespeople were mostly impressed with their memories of how well the French took care of them, especially in contrast to the little attention they sometimes have received from the Vietnamese to date.

Because of wide variations, it is difficult to give a fair description of the relationships between the tribesmen and their new masters, the Vietnamese. Insofar as one can safely generalize, one can do little more than reinforce what has already been said, namely the tribespeople resent the Vietnamese for their superior airs, their attempts to remake them in their own image, their grabbing of land and other private property, and their general unfairness and discrimination. One tribal official, rather responsibly placed in a provincial headquarters, mentioned how upsetting it was to have Vietnamese toddlers in the street point to him and call him a "savage." It is true that some Vietnamese have the interest and welfare of the tribesmen at heart, but these seem to be in the distinct minority.

In the provincial and district capitals, where the army is in evidence and the Vietnamese are found in substantial numbers, it is the tribesmen who are discriminated against. On the other hand, in more remote spots, one or two unarmed Vietnamese, wandering in the jungle, are likely to disappear, never to be heard from again, and it is not wild animals that account for their disappearance.

Missionaries seem to be well liked, respected, and appreciated in many tribal villages. They are often looked on, however, as just another straw to grasp to help them ward off the Vietnamese a bit longer. Other tribesmen indicate that they are tired of being talked to by missionaries in the same old way, time after time. But they are too courteous to strangers not to come to their meetings.

American Protestant missionaries and their families usually try to maintain American living standards, while Catholic missionaries, one or two to a village, usually live in houses only a shade better than the tribesmen's. Where there are several Catholic missionaries together, they have usually established a school and use it as a kind of administrative headquarters. American Protestant missionaries may travel out and reach more villages, but may do it less intensively. There has been no way to determine how these different approaches affect relations with tribespeople, because tribespeople are hospitable to strangers in general as long as they do not consider them a threat to their village.

American military, economic, and technical aid officials are cordially welcomed. But tribesmen, perhaps naively, say: "You give the Vietnamese guns and military equipment. Why don't you give some to us, too, so that we can fight the Vietnamese?" On economic aid, tribespeople claim that they are discriminated against. They say that the Americans give the Vietnamese tractors and seed and fertilizer. "Why don't we get some, too? How can we compete with the Vietnamese, with all the new equipment you have given them, while we must work our fields with nothing but crooked sticks and no fertilizer?" Some Americans might like to distribute aid more equitably, but this is difficult when aid must necessarily and realistically be distributed through Vietnamese channels.

The Vietnamese view the tribesmen problem in a perspective that indicates that they are doing all they can to weld their country into one strong unit so that it will survive in a big-power dominated world. Their official policy toward tribesmen seems to be governed by five rules: (1) Try to convince them with "sweet talk" (and only occasionally with any action) that the tribesmen and the Vietnamese are brothers; (2) spend no more of the country's scarce recources on them than is absolutely necessary; (3) dominate and absorb the tribesmen—force them to stay on the Vietnamese side; (4) ring them around with Vietnamese settlements and separate them from each other in such a way that they cannot unite against the Vietnamese or side with the Communists; and (5) continue to take their land, regardless of tribesmen's feelings, because there is plenty of land for everyone in the tribesmen country, and the tribesmen better get used to moving out of the way when the Vietnamese choose to come.

In implementing the sweet-talk policy, there is an official campaign to call the tribesmen "mountaineers" and not "savages." But Vietnamese feelings of superiority do not disappear overnight. This same phenomenon is seen in America's experience with its own minority problem.

Too, there are a number of situations where large groups of tribesmen, in full regalia, reaffirm their loyalty to President Diem, and he talks to them in a way that shows his interest in their welfare. Some tribesmen confidentially report that they are forced to go to these affairs and that the enthusiasm they show is not wholly sincere. However, it is difficult to determine with any accuracy how widely and intensively various attitudes might be held among the tribesmen.

With respect to Vietnamese spending money on tribesmen programs, there has seemed to be some discrimination against tribesmen. But the Vietnamese point out that they can get little or no tax revenues from tribespeople and that somehow tribespeople must be made to contribute something to the new, struggling Viet-Nam and not expect to have everything handed to them. There is no easy answer to this. The tribesmen do need outside help, but Viet-Nam has many other needs for its scarce resources.

The remaining three policies are so intertwined that they must be mentioned together. Vietnamese administration of the tribesmen has been sometimes astute and has been improving in quality. The chief of each of the three main provinces with large tribal populations is a Vietnamese. It is said that any provincial chief or other Vietnamese official who gets too soft toward tribespeople, surrounded as he is by them, is soon removed.

The tribesmen staff in provincial headquarters must mediate between the demands of the tribesmen on the one hand and the Vietnamese government policy on the other. These men were once looked on as Vietnamese pawns by their fellow tribesmen, but in some cases they are gaining in prestige. The farther north one goes, the stronger the tribesmen and the more influential are prominent tribesmen. Perhaps the Vietnamese will let this relationship stand. District chiefs in tribesmen provinces, the level below provincial chief, are mostly tribesmen. These have been cleverly selected. Many are sons of former chiefs or one-time strong military noncommissioned officers from French army days, or both. Tribesmen graduates of the National Institute of Administration are now found in provincial and district headquarters. Some Vietnamese graduates of the Institute are sent to act as assistants to tribesmen district chiefs, especially to process paperwork for them. This works fine for the district chief and the tribesmen in the area, but the young Vietnamese bureaucrat is apt to feel isolated, forgotten, lonely, and lacking in influence. On the national level, the Vietnamese have permitted the tribesmen to have four seats in the National Assembly. Tribesmen have felt that this number is too small and that the men nominated were, again, no more than pawns of the Vietnamese. There is some evidence that some of them are doing what they can for their constituents, even though the Assembly in general is not too strong as yet.

At the village level and higher, there has been a determined effort to involve village elders and headmen in the administrative process. This is beginning to work, and these men are becoming more loyal to the Vietnamese government. One villager, for example, has been made a kind of part-time judge at district headquarters, twenty to thirty miles from his village over bad roads. Since his appointment his attitude has become much more co-operative. In another case, three prominent tribesmen stood together and got more money for a tribal school.

Roads and better communications are gradually being developed, in part from American military aid. This is having the usual effect on isolated, primitive peoples.

Voting in elections has sometimes been badly handled. Tribesmen were forced to go to the polls and often did not understand what it was all about. Their village in some cases was left undefended when the tribesmen had to leave for another village where the voting was done. These temporarily deserted villages were sometimes robbed. The memory of having been robbed has been stronger than that of having been given the opportunity to cast a ballot.

The Vietnamese have permitted tribal methods of justice and separate tribal courts to remain. These work as long as the dispute is between tribesmen. However, if there is a dispute between a tribesman and a Vietnamese, the tribesman has, in the past, usually lost. The recent convictions of some Vietnamese in such disputes give some hope that this situation may be improving. The Vietnamese, at least unofficially, were permitting the sale of strong alcohol to tribesmen. This practice in other primitive areas has apparently had a deteriorating effect on the primitive people. It is not altogether clear what motives underlie this practice. Even among its own people the Vietnamese government has been frowning on the use of alcohol.

There are areas where a recent influx of Vietnamese seems to be leading to the dying out of the tribesmen. A visit to dying villages can be a distressing sight. The Vietnamese, with their relatively recently formed government land development organization at the national level, show that they mean to push into the tribal area.

Tribespeople in some instances have crude land deeds issued by French authorities, but the Vietnamese do not recognize these as legal. The whole problem of land remains acute. The tribesmen, with their supposedly wasteful land-use, complain that there is no room for more settlers, while the Vietnamese, claiming that there is enough room for all, continue to send them in.

If there is no Communist invasion of Free Viet-Nam, it would look as if the tribespeople will gradually lose more and more land, and more tribal villages will deteriorate and die out. The stronger tribes to the north may be able to hold off the Vietnamese invasion for a while, but in the long run all the tribespeople will have to integrate themselves economically and politically into the larger, more aggressive Vietnamese culture. The total assimilation of the tribespeople is not going to be easy for anyone.

Commentary: BERNARD B. FALL *on* WICKERT

THERE ARE some details that may have escaped Dr. Wickert's attention. His figure of "150,000 Nung fishermen" must be an error. According to official figures released by the *Commissariat Général aux Refugiés* (COMIGAL),[57] a total of less than 15,000 northern tribesmen (including 13,306 Nung) was evacuated to Free Viet-Nam. This figure may be conservative, but it is unlikely that the total will exceed 20,000. Besides the Nung, the other major northern tribal refugee groups resettled in Free Viet-Nam include about 1,000 Muong, 2,000 Tai, and 600 Man. The Nung, who indeed were hardy fishermen—their tribal flag shows a native junk in its center—are now resettled along the coast of southern central Viet-Nam, while the Tai and Man are resettled on the plateau, in and around Thung Nghia village near Dalat, in an environment which closely parallels that of their home territory.[58]

The problem of Free Viet-Nam's minorities, though consistently swept under the rug in Saigon over the past four years, is an extremely complex one, which deserves the utmost attention on the part of the government authorities. To state it simply, out of the total of 127,000 square miles of all Viet-Nam (i.e., north and south of the 17th parallel), nearly *one half* is occupied by ethnic minorities, whose affinities with the Vietnamese are almost nil and whose loyalties to the Vietnamese are at best doubtful. Table 3, based on updated pre-World

[57] It has already been indicated on p. 56 that there are inconsistencies in COMIGAL statistics, but the Nung tribe at home never exceeded 65,000. (ED.)

[58] The writer had the good fortune of visiting the Tai areas of north Viet-Nam before they were overrun by the Communists and also visited Thung Nghia in 1957.

TABLE 3

THE ETHNIC MINORITIES IN VIET-NAM, 1958

Major Areas or Tribal Names	Population	Area (sq. miles)
Chinese		in cities
Free Viet-Nam	950,000	–
Red Viet-Nam	50,000	–
TOTAL	1,000,000	
Northern tribes		
Tai "Meo" Zone	175,000	18,075 (approx.)
Muong	70,000	1,592
Nung	55,000	1,088
"Viet-Bac" Zone	220,000	15,000 (approx.)*
"Lao-Ha-Yen" Zone	75,000	8,500 (approx.)
TOTAL	595,000	44,255
Southern tribes		
Kontum-Pleiku	340,000	
Darlac	100,000	20,520
Dong-Nai	60,000	
Northern refugees	5,000	
TOTAL	505,000	20,520
Others		
Cambodians in Trans-Bassac areas	450,000	2,000
Northern tribal refugees in south central Viet-Nam	15,000	–
TOTAL	465,000	2,000
GRAND TOTALS		
Chinese	1,000,000	–
Northern tribes	595,000	44,255
Southern tribes	505,000	20,520
Cambodians	450,000	2,000
Tribal refugees	15,000	–
TOTAL	2,565,000	66,775

* Some of the area data are approximates because the Viet-Minh reshuffled their boundaries since the cease-fire.

War II French statistics,[59] indicates the problem to some degree.

In other words, the ethnic minorities in Viet-Nam—and not including the smaller groups of French, Eurasian, Indian, and Malay merchants living in the urban areas—include one tenth of the total population. However, the partition of the country has saddled Free Viet-Nam with nearly two million minority inhabitants, who thus make up nearly *one fifth* of the population! As Wickert correctly points out, the treatment which these minority groups receive at the hands of the Vietnamese majority is in no way commensurate with their numerical or strategic importance.

The strategic importance of the plateau tribal area is immediately obvious to anyone looking at a map of Viet-Nam. The tragic days of 1953 and 1954 showed that most of central Viet-Nam became untenable once the plateau area was heavily infiltrated by Communist forces. Heavy battles were fought for the control of Kontum and Pleiku: The famous French Combat Team No. 100, which had fought with distinction in Korea prior to its transfer to Indochina, was completely wiped out in the spring of 1954 in an attempt to regain control of the road leading to An Khe, a fort at the edge of the plateau. Across the plateau stretches "Uncle Ho's Road," the path along which Communist guerrillas have established depots and rest points for their cadres going into Cambodia or deeper into the southern areas of Viet-Nam.

Wickert speaks of the Communist influence on the tribesmen. The hard fact is that the Communists *are* using the tribesmen to their advantage, and the preliminary report prepared by MSUG for the Vietnamese government on the subject of the plateau region mentions examples of that infiltration. Communist agents, some of them Vietnamese but most of them by now well-trained mountaineers from the tribes themselves, are organizing cells among the Rhadé, Bahnar, Jaraï, and Kohö. Relatively well treated by the Viet-Minh, between 5,000 to 6,000 Rhadés followed the Communists north of the 17th parallel after the 1954 cease-fire, and a special Communist training school in Hanoi graduates 120 southern tribesmen every nine months and returns them for further propaganda and infiltration work in their home areas. As this writer could see for himself during a brief stay in 1957 with Vietnamese army units near the 17th parallel, most of the jungle area of the boundary (or about four fifths of its length) is completely unguarded and thus wide open to the infiltrators from the north.

Contrary to what the southern authorities do, the northern authori-

[59] For a study of the whole problem of minority administration in Viet-Nam, see Fall, *The Political Development of Viet-Nam, VJ-Day to the Geneva Cease-Fire,* Vol. II, pp. 334-80.

ties, for obvious reasons, see to it that the mountain tribes at least get the impression of being full equals of the lowland Vietnamese. Tribesmen have even been sent to the Soviet Union for advanced training, while others follow a special institute for minority nationalities in Peking. Also, contrary to what the southern administration does, the Viet-Minh Communists not only let the tribes use their own dialects, but actually have radio broadcasts in Rhadé, Bahnar, and Jaraï. One Rhadé, Y Ngon Niekdam, is known to be a member of the Communist "National Assembly" in Hanoi; he is Moscow-trained and speaks perfect Russian.

Contrary to the highly centralizing approach (unfortunately backed by the Michigan State University team in Saigon) of the southern authorities with regard to the mountain tribes, the northern regime follows the Sino-Soviet pattern of "autonomous" areas for the minority nationalities. This, in fact, insures over-all control by a "divide-and-rule" policy which, on the whole, seems more successful than the forceful cramming-down-the-throat of unitarianism in areas which are hardly suited to it. Indonesia is an example of how such a policy of forced unitarianism may backfire.

Throughout the Indochina war the Viet-Minh[60] had to rely upon the co-operation of the northern mountain tribes for its military operations. Two of the Viet-Minh's crack infantry divisions were recruited almost exclusively from northern mountaineers. A member of the Tho minority, Chu Van Tan, rose to the rank of brigadier general of the "Viet-Nam People's Army" and is now chairman of the "Viet-Bac" Autonomous Area. This dependency of the Viet-Minh upon the northern mountaineers (lest it be forgotten, the decisive battle of the Indochina war, Dien Bien Phu, was fought deep in Tai tribal territory) perhaps made the northern regime more amenable to an apparently more realistic minority policy. In May, 1955, the Tai and Meo (Miao) tribal areas of Red Viet-Nam were given internal autonomy along substantially the same lines under which they had enjoyed it during the French administration.[61] In 1956 the northeastern part of Red Viet-Nam, inhabited by a conglomeration of Tho and other tribes, received a similar statute, and late in 1957, Hanoi announced the creation of a third tribal zone in the provinces of Lao Kay, Ha Giang and Yen Bay, under the name of "Lao-Ha-Yen."

[60] For an examination of Viet-Minh minority policies, see Fall, *The Viet-Minh Regime,* New York: Institute of Pacific Relations, 2nd ed., 1956.
[61] From 1946 to 1949 all mountain areas had given themselves (under French guidance, of course) written constitutions and fairly well-working local administrative bodies.

To be sure, all this is done for the sake of better control rather than real autonomy, but the mountaineers are definitely left with the external appurtenances of "separateness." For example, while the lowland areas had to surrender all silver coins, the mountaineers, who distrust paper money, were authorized to retain their French silver piasters. Collectivization has not yet made its appearance in the mountain areas, and there are no visible signs of Vietnamese migration from the densely inhabited lowland areas into the Tai or Tho areas. While the tribal groups as a whole are not likely to be in a position to make comparisons between the regime granted them in the two zones of Viet-Nam, the fact remains that the southern government does not even pay lip-service to the principle of local self-government. The grave repercussions of this situation are correctly envisioned by Wickert.

The southern tribal groups are, however, in a position to judge for themselves the difference in attitude between the French colonial administration and its Vietnamese successors, and here, according to MSUG reports, the comparison generally is not in favor of the latter.

For reasons similar to those of the Viet-Minh, the French treated the mountaineers well and granted them—as the British did with the Karens in Burma—a great deal more self-government than to the Vietnamese majority in the plains. The *Bataillons Montagnards* of the French colonial forces were renowned for their endurance and combativity, as were the "Burma Rifles," composed of Kachins and Karens.

French Catholic missionaries on the plateaus were among the best in Indochina, and the mountaineer school and public health system, while by no means adequate, was quite good and a great deal better staffed over the past three decades than the system which replaced it. This writer has been assured from several sources that the Viet-Minh has used the favorable impression the French have left as a weapon for its own propaganda: in the Kontum area, Communist leaflets promised the mountaineers the return of a particularly well-liked French administrator in the event of their victory.

In ethnical terms, the Vietnamese have a far higher cultural level than the southern mountaineers and, as Wickert states, despise them accordingly. This is a fact of life which ethnic minorities now face not only in Viet-Nam, but in Burma and Indonesia as well. Burma, however, was the only country of the three which, on paper at least, preferred to solve the problem of its relations with its own minorities through a federal administration. In the other two, the federal idea is still too closely associated with the colonial "divide-and-rule" of yesteryear to be publicly acceptable without some well-meant outside prodding. In this instance, the United States cannot escape a certain measure of responsibility, for apparently no effort has been made by American officials or private advisers to make even a limited measure of local self-government acceptable to Saigon.

On the contrary, extensive support in the economic, as well as administrative, field is given to implement a Vietnamese colonization plan of the plateau area. This plan involves the more or less voluntary migration of about 150,000 Vietnamese into the Pleiku-Kontum area of the plateau region, in the hopes that such an ethnic "island" among the mountaineers will bring the latter to heel. This project has been given vast amounts of scarce supplies and a great deal of advance publicity. However, according to recent reports, the lowland Vietnamese do not acclimate themselves too well to the malaria-infested climate of the plateau. Incidents occur with the local population, and some of the agricultural projects have met with serious difficulties.[62] There are also signs of mountaineer pressure upon Vietnamese army posts along the Dak Sut-Dak To road north of Kontum.

This writer fully shares Wickert's thoughtful conclusion that the solution of Viet-Nam's minority problem through the total assimilation of those minorities "is not going to be easy for anyone." And the question should be asked, by Vietnamese and Americans alike, whether the price of ultimate success will not be economically and politically higher than Free Viet-Nam can afford.

[62] According to *Ngon Luan* (Opinion) of February 10, 1958 (Saigon daily), a severe bovine plague is in the process of destroying much of the cattle provided the new settlers by American and Vietnamese government aid.

PART FOUR

EDUCATION FOR DEVELOPMENT

The Vietnamese have "a sublime faith that if they can only get an education they will be happy and prosperous . . . to a man, the people respect, even revere, education." And yet at the time of independence not more than ten percent of the adults of Viet-Nam were able to read.

Highly academic and rigid in its methods, the Vietnamese educational system has hardly been adequate for a country faced with urgent economic, political, and security problems.

Although the government's program is to provide a school for every village, many children cannot attend school because the nearest one is miles away. The usual elementary class consists of from fifty-five to sixty-five children, crowded into a classroom of nineteen by twenty-five feet. Among these pupils there are three, four, or perhaps five textbooks. The teacher, with only three or four years of schooling himself, "even in charity, cannot be considered adequate to his task." More schools, more classrooms, more textbooks, more teachers, and more adequate training for teachers—these are but a few of the important educational problems at the elementary level.

Like the elementary level, the secondary schools remain highly academic. As Hildreth points out, "the competitive examination for admission and advancement in secondary education has been designed for the elimination of students. . . . of those who started, only approximately one out of 170 actually completed his secondary education . . . Students of vocational or artistic bent . . . must pass the rigid examinations in the classics, or fail. For example, students who might be brilliant in engineering are eliminated because of lack of interest or aptitude in the humanities."

At the university level, fewer than 5,000 students are enrolled in higher education. At the beginning of 1957 there was only one university in Free Viet-Nam; since then two new universities have been opened up. And, as with the lower educational levels, the curriculum has glaring gaps—with no schools of engineering, agriculture, or veterinary science.

In addition to the general educational problems, Viet-Nam is trying to introduce vocational education, to open up normal schools for teacher training, to integrate the Chinese-operated schools into the public school system, to establish more adult literacy classes, and to strengthen the program for training people for high-level government positions at the Dalat School of Administration.

Two nations are doing a great deal to assist Viet-Nam in its educational problems—France and the United States. France is doing a commendable job in secondary education, as well as offering generous faculty assistance at the university level. The United States is assisting at the elementary and secondary levels, as well as with vocational, agricultural, and adult literacy programs.

XII.   The Challenge in Education

ELON E. HILDRETH[63]

"HE WANTED to learn to read, but there was no school in his village. The nearest one was thirty kilometers away, and that was too far to walk or to go by oxcart. Even if he could get there, there was no seat for him because the beginners' class already had sixty-five pupils in it."

This was the plight of Tran Buu Chi, a bright-eyed little Vietnamese boy in one of the provinces of central Viet-Nam. It remains the fate of hundreds of thousands of other little Vietnamese boys and girls. And this in a land where, to a man, the people respect, even revere, education. They have a sublime faith that if they can only get an education they will be happy and prosperous.

The usual class of fifty-five to sixty-five children is crowded into a typical classroom of six by eight meters, or approximately nineteen by twenty-five feet. The lighting is bad, with only one-half foot candle power in the center of the room. At the front of the room is the teacher's desk and a 4 x 6 wooden blackboard which has been painted a shiny black. Among these fifty-five to sixty-five pupils there are three, four, or perhaps five books, with the teacher having one.

The teacher may have had only three or four years of schooling, which means he would not have completed his elementary education: For the educational program in Viet-Nam consists of five years in an elementary school and seven years in a secondary school. Perhaps the teacher has had the advantage of the in-service teacher training program, financed by USOM, but, even in charity, he cannot be considered adequate to his task.

The lesson commences in strict decorum. Few children are better behaved than the Vietnamese. They sit on long benches, close together. Their bright, well-scrubbed faces show an eagerness to learn. From what resources he has, the teacher begins to cite the lesson. Slowly and laboriously he writes a poem on the blackboard and draws a moral. All the children have pen, ink, and a copybook. Each pupil copies what the teacher writes on the board, be he six or sixteen. Within a half to three quarters of an hour the lesson is copied. Next, the children must memorize it.

After the children have been in school for as little as six months, they do a remarkable job of copying. Penmanship in Viet-Nam is good; it should be, for it is practiced so much. What might have been learned in a few minutes has taken hours.

Viet-Nam is not unlike many of the countries of Asia which have carried on highly formal types of education over a period of many cen-

[63] Chief, Education Division, United States Operations Mission, Saigon.

turies. The early educational system of Viet-Nam was built upon the Chinese cultural pattern. It was codified in A.D. 622, but may have existed as early as the first century. The system stressed the memorizing of characters, texts, and classical literature. Proficiency was tested at graduation when large numbers gathered to be examined for civil service positions by mandarin scholars. In the last great examinations in 1876 and 1879 six thousand candidates took examinations in Hanoi, and smaller examinations continued for some years.

By 1890 French schools were beginning to replace the mandarin system. The curricula, following the pattern in France, featured a dual system, one which was highly academic and cultural for those preparing for university studies and the other designed for the common people. However, even under the French, the cite, recite, and examine method prevailed in Vietnamese education. And education still primarily emphasized the classics, literature, poetry, and symbolism. It was hardly adequate for a people whose country faced immediate and urgent economic, political, and security problems.

Since the founding of the republic, United States assistance to the development of adequate schools in Viet-Nam has been offered on a government-to-government basis. Official channels have been carefully maintained because of the sensitive nature of the Vietnamese. In 1956 the nature of the aid program was changed from general releases of funds to releases of specific amounts for specific projects.

The schools of Viet-Nam are directed, supervised, and largely financed through the office of the Department of National Education. Highly centralized and authoritarian in character, the Department has all the strengths and weaknesses of such an organization. A strong line and staff organization is maintained. Heading up the Department is the Secretary of State for National Education, who is appointed by the President of Viet-Nam. The Secretary holds a seat in the President's cabinet and nominates, for the President's appointment, his Director General, who also serves as Director of the Cabinet. He appoints subordinate Ministry officials and school directors throughout the country.

Originally, the Department was organized under the leadership of Nguyen Duong Don, who remained until his appointment as Ambassador to Rome and Madrid in 1957. He was succeeded by the incumbent, Dr. Tran Huu The.

In 1956 Mr. Don and his assistant, Huynh Hoa, concluded that education had reached the point where it needed re-evaluation and reorientation. In consequence, the USOM Division of Education was called to the Ministry, where many hours were spent crystallizing a master plan for the future of Vietnamese schools. It was agreed that education should be free, public, and universal; that it should be extended to every village in the nation; and that a complete system should be established from the elementary schools through the university.

The Director of USOM and the Deputy of ICA for the Far East agreed with Vietnamese educators that the ideal of a "school for every village" was a worthy goal. It was decided that the United States would furnish the building materials and the Vietnamese would furnish the labor for the elementary school building program. The program provided for: (1) the construction and equipment of approximately 400 elementary schools in Viet-Nam, as the first phase of a three-year program to establish 1,200 new elementary schools, with 3,600 classrooms; (2) the construction of and providing equipment and staff for special agricultural rooms in seven rural elementary schools for the introduction of agricultural instruction; (3) the creation within the Department of National Education of a construction department, with adequate personnel to encourage the formation of village committees throughout the country which would co-operate with the Department in building village schools; (4) United States direct aid to provide the technical services of two American specialists to work with the Vietnamese in implementing the project, and for importation of supplies such as cement and unavailable hardware for building construction.

In 1958 United States funds were to be provided to defray the costs up to fifty percent of the construction and equipment of the schools and one half of the teachers' salaries for the first year. Local currency was to be provided by the United States for one hundred percent of the cost of the agricultural rooms. Vietnamese aid was to be provided to defray all the cost of the land, fifty percent of the costs of local construction, and one half of the teachers' salaries for the first year.

The cost of this program to the United States government amounted to $2,030,679, while that to the Vietnamese government is still not determinable. The classrooms cost approximately 50,000 piasters, or $1,400 each.

In addition to the elementary program, consideration has generally been given to the community pilot school in underdeveloped countries. The community pilot schools, designed to help people solve practical problems, have been demonstrated so successfully in countries such as the Philippines and Mexico.

As early as 1953 suggestions were made by educational advisers that the community pilot school would offer distinct advantages for the Vietnamese. Viet-Nam has, to date, built nine community pilot schools. The buildings and equipment have been furnished by the United States government. Assets in this program are: The buildings are new, of hard construction, and are a source of pride to the community; farm tools and equipment for home economics have been made available so that students have access to anvils, forges, hoes, rakes, cultivators, sewing machines, and other equipment.

In most cases, the school principals have had some training in the Philippines, where they have studied the community schools. Unfortunately, the staffs have not yet had the opportunity to become sufficiently imbued with the community school philosophy to achieve the kind of desired results. Three problems continue to limit the achievements of community school education: namely, insufficient numbers of well-trained staff members, lack of full acceptance by the Department of National Education officials and school inspectors of the worthwhileness of the curriculum, and parental fear that this kind of schooling is substandard.

In each community pilot school an effort has been made to broaden the traditional curriculum; no concession has been made by the Department of National Education to eliminate any of the so-called essential subjects required in the traditional schools. The result has been that the courses of the community school have had to be added to the standard curriculum. The same number of hours are spent per week in the seventeen or eighteen required subjects of an academic education. In addition to these, mostly on an after-school basis or through the extension of the daily program, projects in agriculture and home economics have been added. Generally, it has been the principal of the school, or one of the faculty members who has had some training in the Philippines, who has sponsored the added activities.

The schools are beginning to accept their role in community development, and have organized Parent-Teacher Associations. These have yet to develop the best qualities of forum discussion, but are making progress. One of the most remarkable instances in this field has been directed by a man who had had training for community school work in the Philippines and was placed in a refugee high school. This school is not called a community school, but it has some of the best characteristics of one. Almost on his own, this man organized a Parent-Teacher Association of 1,500 members. The members have raised 100,000 piasters and, without outside assistance, have built one building designed for instruction in the daytime and for community use in the evening.

Projects which are undertaken in the community pilot schools include gardening on the school campus, propagation of tilapia in the constructed fishponds, and the raising of chickens, rabbits, pigeons, hogs, and similar animals. These projects have not always succeeded. Funds for the purchase of feed have had to be procured from any source, and are invariably inadequate.

At one community pilot school a tragic incident developed. The principal, fresh from a three-month tour in the Philippines, where he had watched the beginning of hog, cattle, and poultry projects, was highly enthusiastic about projects for his own school. The livestock project had been given fine breeds of poultry, a pair of pigs, and a cow. At the close of his first year he came into the offices of the Education Chief of USOM in Saigon to report some of his experiences.

When asked how the livestock project was doing, he replied: "Not so good. The cow found the climate inconvenient for him and died." From the report of the USOM field representative, it was learned that the cow had starved to death, the sow had littered but she had been so poorly fed that she lost her milk, and the chickens had to be given to the parents of the students because there was no feed. The principal had become so discouraged by that time that he wanted to go back to the standard curriculum, where no feed was required.

Conversation with a Nha Trang principal brought to light another factor which limits the success of projects at community schools. The inspector of education for the province visited the principal and found him spending the time of students and faculty with these "frill" projects. The inspector, as quoted by the principal, said: "Fifty years from now maybe this kind of school will be all right in Viet-Nam, but not now. You must go back to the fundamentals. We will not brook any more of this kind of insubordination." As a result, the principal resigned and moved back to Saigon, where he found employment at a higher salary in a private school.

In spite of all the frustrations, the community pilot school in Viet-Nam is experiencing limited success in most quarters. It is not surprising that the Vietnamese have been unwilling to accept a new and revolutionary institution without enthusiasm; even the people of the United States have resisted changes in educational practice. In Viet-Nam the community pilot schools are beginning to function as the vehicle through which the desires of the villages are made known. They are becoming the social centers, and as such offer some relief to the dull and monotonous life which characterizes too many villages of Viet-Nam.

A survey of secondary schools indicated that most of the larger cities had at least one lycée. However, because approximately half of the secondary schools were in Saigon, there was a great need for additional schools in the outlying provinces.

Due to the fact that money was not available to build additional secondary schools, the curriculum was analyzed. It was found that the secondary curriculum, even more so than that for elementary schools, remains highly academic. Obviously, the competitive examination for admission and advancement in secondary education has been designed for the elimination of students. Approximately seventy percent of the elementary graduates who take qualifying examinations are eliminated each year. This may be necessary, for the schools cannot accept all who could profit from a secondary education. Money is not available for the employment of enough teachers, and well-trained teachers for the upper levels are scarce. Examinations are so difficult that, of the 70,000 students in the public and private secondary schools in 1957, only 747 passed the first baccalaureate and only 422 the second.[64] In other words, of those who started, only approximately one out of 170 actually completed his secondary education. The failure of such large numbers is due to two factors: (1) The examinations are not entirely based upon the subject matter taught; and (2) the curriculum of the school is not designed to serve the innate capacities of many students. Students of vocational or artistic bent, for instance, must pass the rigid examinations in the classics, or fail. For example, students who might be brilliant in engineering are eliminated because of lack of interest or aptitude in the humanities.

There are more private secondary schools than is the case with elementary education. For instance, of the 70,000 students in secondary schools in 1957, more than half, or approximately 40,000, were being educated in private or semiofficial schools.

A substantial portion of the secondary education is financed and carried out by the French Cultural Mission to Viet-Nam, at no expense whatever to the Vietnamese government. During 1957 this Mission contributed approximately $3,000,000 to the educational program in Viet-Nam. The Mission still operates public lycées, in which it pays all the expenses of operation and maintenance, as well as teachers' salaries. The classes are taught in French by French teachers employed in France and sent there as instructors, or by Vietnamese who have been trained in France. Generally speaking, the French schools are well equipped, the students have textbooks which have been printed in France, and the teachers do not lack the essential instructional materials as do those in the public lycées of Viet-Nam. Despite the fact that the French secondary schools are perhaps too academic, with curricula which may be regarded as too theoretical, the French are doing a commendable job in secondary education.

No consideration of education in Viet-Nam would be complete without reference to the School of Agriculture at Blao. This school is not under the Department of National Education, but is managed and financed as an institution of learning by the Ministry of Agriculture. Rather than theory learning, which has characterized too many schools in Viet-Nam, the Blao School stresses the practical "dirt farming" type of learning.

Prior to the partition, the French government had used the Blao School as an experiment in agriculture. The school, as well as the enrollment, was small, and not much money had been invested there. After partition, ambitious plans were made for its development. Located on a site of ap-

[64] Annual report, 1956-1957, Ministry of Education.

proximately a thousand hectares, classrooms, dormitories, dining halls, faculty homes, and outbuildings have been completed, or are in the process of construction. It is expected that the school will house some 400 to 450 students at the end of 1958.

Admission to Blao is based on competitive examination, and approximately 1,000 students took this examination for the 1957-58 school year. The school is co-educational, and approximately one fourth of the students are women.

Because agriculture is the basic industry of Viet-Nam, the Minister of Agriculture attempted at the beginning to make admission to the school as attractive as possible. To that end, scholarships of 1,500 piasters per month were set up. These have been reduced recently to 1,000 piasters per month, but, with living quarters and dining hall available, that sum is quite adequate. In 1957 the enrollment was 170 students, and this was expected to increase to 200 by September, 1958.

Obstacles to the full development of the school do not relate to money, for USOM, through its Agriculture Division, has been generous in its support. The greatest problem is staffing the school with adequate people. Thoroughly trained agricultural teachers are not available in Viet-Nam. In this one sees the persistence of the culture pattern: For generations on end, people have farmed as their parents did, and, as a consequence, few aspire to a career in agriculture. Only recently have the Vietnamese begun to realize that they must learn the science of agriculture if they are to improve their yield.

A second problem has to do with the general orientation of the school itself. Originally, the Ministry of Agriculture conceived of the school only as a place to train inspectors and junior functionaries for the Agriculture Ministry. It is now pretty well understood that this objective must be broadened to include the training of people for careers in private enterprise forms of agriculture.

At present, the courses are of secondary level, general in nature, with little specialization. Agronomy, animal husbandry, and some citriculture are taught, and plans are being made to extend experimentation in plot planting, animal breedings, soil analysis, soil fertilization, and soil conservation and improvement.

Two possible levels of training are contemplated for the future: (1) to continue as a strictly secondary educational effort, which might be comparable with the vocational agricultural classes taught in United States high schools, or (2) to offer university agricultural education. If the level of work for some of the students is to be raised to a higher level, the school will, of course, have to be made a part of the university.

Even at this early date some conclusions may be drawn about the Blao School. It is succeeding in limited fields, and its future holds genuine promise. However, to obtain its full stature it must have a markedly improved faculty, and to achieve this it will have to be raised to university standing. Secondary salaries are so low that talented and well-trained people will not be attracted. Too, because status is such an important factor in Viet-Nam, it will take the entry of a university into the agricultural field to give this occupation the stature it deserves. Finally, to reorient the Vietnamese to the opportunities in agriculture, the school should be shifted from the Ministry of Agriculture to the Ministry of Education. This would make it an institution of higher learning rather than a training station for civil servants.

There is a critical need for the development of industrial techniques in Viet-Nam to prepare the country for its new role in the family of nations. It must become economically strong, and basic industries must be established which will raise the living standards. Unfortunately, only the most rudimentary beginnings in vocational education were begun by 1955.

The French, during their regime, did establish some vocational schools, such as the College Technique de Saigon. These schools have been taken over by the Vietnamese government, with the French continuing to offer both teaching and professional advice. Fewer than 4,000 students were enrolled in vocational schools, in 1957, which indicates that only a few out of the many hundreds of thousands are being given this essential training.

A limited number of vocational schools had been established in Hanoi and Haiphong, and after the partition some were moved from north to south Viet-Nam. One of these was moved to Hue, just below the 17th parallel.

In 1955 American and Vietnamese advisers decided that a vigorous program in vocational education should be started, and USOM in Saigon employed a technical adviser for this phase of the educational program. The 1955 budget of $321,113 was increased to $882,511 for 1956 and to $900,000 for 1957.

In vocational, as with agricultural, education, the question of status arose almost immediately, because of the Vietnamese belief that education should prepare one for a life of ease as an adult. Most people still regard hand labor as improper for educated men.

The first new vocational institution to be established was the Vietnamese Institute of Technology in Phu Tho, a section adjacent to Saigon. This was an all-out effort on the part of the United States to provide an institution of status for the encouragement of trade and technical training, and represents a compromise between the Vietnamese ambitions for an engineering education and the need for vocational skills.

Schools of public works, radio electricity, and marine navigation are already in operation. Training courses in the metal construction, and motor mechanics trades are to be offered.

Students from the lycées and colleges may matriculate directly in that part of the school which will some day be engineering training. Those from College Technique, which is a lower level vocational school, may enter the second part, and from there advance to engineering. Those from the apprentice or polytechnic schools may enter the Institute and prepare for jobs as skilled workers in industry and public works.

The movement to establish polytechnic high schools was based on an effort to engender democratic methods and thinking in the schools. To accomplish this goal, an ideal vehicle would have been to set up comprehensive high schools such as those in the United States. However, the idea of introducing woodworking into the lycée program is repugnant to the Vietnamese. Therefore, it is hoped that academicians and trade trainees will live and learn and work on the same campus of a polytechnic high school, and that this new institution may eventually bring about a comprehensive high school, much as it evolved in the United States. A generation or two ago all large cities in the United States were building polytechnic high schools, with the Los Angeles Polytechnic High School and the San Francisco Polytechnic High School as cases in point. Such schools are no longer being established in the United States, and it is hoped that the Viet-Nam educational development will follow the American pattern.

Higher education in Viet-Nam is a matter of considerable importance to the upper echelon people in government. However, the actual enrollment in universities is not high. At the beginning of 1957 there was only one university, the University of Viet-Nam, located in Saigon.

As of June, 1956, there were five schools in scattered locations throughout Saigon, with 64 professors and *chargés de cours,* plus 24 assistants, the rector, vice rector, and five deans. The total enrollment for 1955-56 was 2,481, distributed as follows: Medicine and Pharmacy, 820; Faculty of Science, 774; Faculty of Law, 661; Faculty of Letters, 187; School of Architecture, 39. The opening convocation was presided over by the present rector of the university, Dr. Nguyen Quang Trinh, and the Secretary of State for National Education, Mr. Don.

At the close of the 1956-57 academic year, there were 3,823 students. Enrollments in the various schools had changed markedly. In one year, the Faculty of Law, with 1,759 students, had climbed from third to first in size. The Faculty of Medicine and Pharmacy had dropped to second in size, with 841 students. The Faculty of Science had 769 students; the Faculty of Architecture, 129; and the Faculty of Letters, only 325.

USOM has never given substantial material assistance to the University. However, the French Cultural Mission is offering generous faculty assistance, and is well equipped to do it. At present the Republic of France pays the full-time salaries of some thirty professors.

Several schools essential to a rapidly developing country are missing. There is no school of engineering, for example, although there is hope that the Vietnamese Institute of Technology may some day become one of the University schools. There are no schools of agriculture or veterinary science, and, in a country which is so largely dependent upon agriculture, the omission of these schools is unfortunate.

In addition, there are some glaring gaps in the curriculum of some of the schools. The higher School of Architecture offers work which is more nearly akin to the fine arts than to modern architecture. The present curriculum concerns itself largely with floor plans, art forms, building façades, landscaping, and similar courses. The basic courses in engineering, essential to modern buildings, are inadequate.

Two new universities have recently been established, the University of Hue and the University of Dalat. The University of Hue, a public school sponsored by the Vietnamese government, opened in 1957 with approximately 500 students. At present it is both a preparatory school and a university, and the curriculum concentrates on the liberal and fine arts. The preparatory sector is included because of the limited number of lycée graduates in Viet-Nam. Currently, three fourths of the students at Hue are of preuniversity level. The faculty is headed by a Catholic priest, Father Cao Van Luan, and there are four priests and one Christian brother on the staff of fifty members. Despite this fact, the school is not a religious institution: Few other men in the area are sufficiently well educated to occupy chairs on the faculty.

The University of Dalat is still in the process of formation. It is located on a mountain plateau, 5,200 feet high, where the climate is mild and conducive to study. It will have room to expand in an area where lands are not so expensive as they are in Saigon.

Because the land and buildings have been supplied by the government, it might be regarded as a semipublic school. The control and the expense of maintenance, operation, and salaries are, however, being supplied by the Catholic Church. When Cardinal Spellman made a trip to Viet-Nam, he gave $25,000 to the University, thus indicating the genuine interest of the Catholics of the United States in this school.

The authorities of the University of Dalat, after considering the role the school may play, have examined the curricula in the sciences and engineering in the United States, and have decided to emphasize science, mathematics, and engineering.

High on the list of priorities in the aid program to education is teacher training. Viet-Nam has some good teachers, but not enough of them. In contrast to the more highly developed countries, teachers do not have access to thousands of professional books on what to teach or how to teach it.

The Higher School of Pedagogy, of the University of Saigon, trains secondary teachers. Generally speaking, this institution has the capacity for turning out secondary school teachers as fast as the government can provide the funds for the building and staffing of new secondary schools.

Elementary teacher training presents another picture. Approximately 200,000 students have been added to public elementary schools alone within the last two years. With United States aid, the Vietnamese government is increasing the number of schools so rapidly that the problem of furnishing enough teachers to provide a teacher for each classroom has become staggering. To meet this problem, USOM provided a completely new normal school, the National Normal School, in 1953.

In many ways the National Normal School offers much promise for the improvement of education. It has many advantages. The physical facilities there are adequate, as they are in almost no other place. As a new school, with a new building, it has been possible to assemble a faculty which was deemed to be ideally suited to the new tasks. Two of the people on the faculty have had a full year in the United States, where they have studied the methods and practices of elementary school education. The school is headed by a dynamic school administrator, who has a burning spirit of patriotism and who believes that good teachers and sound education will do much to advance his country.

Being new, the National Normal School has not become weighted down with traditions. Much remains to be done in improving the curriculum. Discipline in Vietnamese elementary schools has always been very strict. The courses of study have been followed slavishly. Students are regimented through one year after another, preparing for the examination which determines advancement to the next grade. Memory work with little opportunity for creative thinking has been the rule.

At the National Normal School, rigid regimentation is being broken. One who is used to American education, which permits free exchange between student and teacher, and which has as its objective the building of self-direction rather than obedience, may not realize the remarkable advances that have been made at the Normal School.

The faculty at the Normal School is receptive to new ideas. They believe that they are there because of their willingness to keep an open mind and to experiment and search for new methods.

One of the big problems at the school has been the exposure of young people from rural villages to life in Saigon. After becoming accustomed to city living, with its improved sanitation and better living standards and transportation, they seek a job in a city, and either refuse or are most reluctant to go back to the conditions under which they grew up. Yet it is in the villages of Viet-Nam where education is so desperately needed. More children are already in school in the cities of Saigon and Cholon than in the rest of the country put together. On the other hand, only 5,000 of the 10,000 villages have schools, and only 670,000 of the 2,500,000 children of elementary age were in school as of June, 1957. If universal education is to become a reality, thousands of teachers will have to be willing to teach in the rural areas.

The challenge of the two new rural normal schools being built with American aid is that of furnishing schools which will be so attractive, so well equipped, and so well staffed that the young people will want to teach there rather than in a city. The rural normal schools, through their faculties, must instill in their graduates a desire to teach in the most remote areas. The students will have to have a feeling of a mission, so that they will not only be willing to endure hardships, but will seek them out in order to ameliorate the conditions of the back country.

American aid is also being used to assist the Tan An Agricultural Teacher Training Center, which is a joint enterprise of the Vietnamese government and UNESCO. Located some 40 kilometers from Saigon, this school has been in operation for several years. Its special job is to train teachers for community schools, and, toward this end, it places particular emphasis upon acquiring understandings and skills in community development. Some fifty teachers per year are being trained at this Center.

TABLE 4

PROGRESS OF EDUCATION IN VIET-NAM

	1954-55	1955-56	1956-57
Public primary schools			
No. of schools	1,598	2,137	2,766
No. of classes	7,000	9,258	11,471
No. of students	363,160	461,362	571,019
No. of teachers	7,760	9,105	11,203
Private primary, elementary, and special schools			
No. of schools	532	561	707
No. of classes	1,944	1,977	2,799
No. of students	74,925	75,626	100,566
No. of teachers	1,678	1,680	2,320
Public secondary schools			
No. of schools	31	41	48
No. of classes	441	552	624
No. of students	26,082	42,469	39,043
No. of teachers	730	860	1,392

(Table 4 continued)

Private secondary and semi-official schools			
No. of schools	94	132	142
No. of classes	510	820	719
No. of students	21,817	28,127	32,977
No. of teachers	501	1,532	1,828
University of Viet-Nam			
No. of students	2,109	2,841	3,823
No. of teachers	115	125	165
Public primary vocational schools (training workshops)			
No. of schools	7	8	12
No. of classes	—	—	—
No. of students	524	223	823
No. of teachers	17	20	42
Public secondary vocational schools			
No. of schools	—	—	—
No. of classes	—	—	—
No. of students	1,003	1,663	2,031
No. of teachers	65	81	134
Public higher vocational schools			
No. of schools	—	—	—
No. of classes	—	—	—
No. of students	419	408	664
No. of teachers	56	74	116
Public home economics courses			
No. of schools	14	17	18
No. of classes	—	—	—
No. of students	586	1,064	1,014
No. of teachers	42	57	56

In any city of size in Viet-Nam, the Chinese live in their own sector and, by and large, have built and maintained their own educational institutions. The 1957 report of the Department of National Education indicated that there were 45,709 students enrolled in 180 Chinese elementary schools. There are twelve secondary schools for Chinese students in Saigon-Cholon.

These schools are private in character, and are presided over by a board of education elected by members of the Chinese Congregation. A large part of the financial support of the schools comes from tuition, and the balance is contributed by the Chinese community.

The educational program in Chinese schools, which follows that of the

United States more closely than does the Vietnamese, consists of six years in an elementary school, three years in a middle school, and three years in a high school. The upper level of secondary education for the Chinese is called high school, as opposed to the Vietnamese lycée. The two secondary levels are coming to be known as junior and senior high schools.

Along with efforts of the Vietnamese government to integrate the Chinese into the political and economic structure of the country, there have been moves to regulate the schools maintained and operated by the Chinese. In 1957 all Chinese schools were placed under the supervision of the Department of National Education and made subject to inspection by agents of the Department. Chinese schools, which have always taught in the Chinese language, are now required to instruct in Vietnamese.

The reasoning behind the requirements for educational integration of the races is obvious. The program for carrying it out, however, has been, and will be, difficult. Most Chinese teachers are unable to teach in Vietnamese because they do not know how to read and write the language. Even if they knew the language, their pupils would not understand it. The Vietnamese have wanted to insist on this point, but have been unable to do so, for it has become obvious that, even with the best of good will, the Chinese could not have complied. Fortunately, leaders in the Department of National Education have come to realize that the immediate integration of Chinese and Vietnamese students in the same school is both impractical and impossible, and that the requirement for an abrupt switch in the language of instruction is unworkable. Consequently, a new plan will be inaugurated to begin a period of instruction in the Vietnamese language with the lower elementary grades, which will be extended to the upper grades. This policy will undoubtedly bring about a reduction in emotional tension and a more realistic basis for the solution of this difficult interracial problem.

There are indications now of improved Vietnamese-Chinese intercultural relations. It seems likely that, as funds become available, more and more schools will be built by the Vietnamese in the Chinese sectors and, that as tensions lower, the Chinese will choose to enter such schools. It is improbable that the Vietnamese will be able to do without the Chinese schools. Considering their private basis, they are no burden to the Vietnamese educational budget.

A final problem concerning Chinese education has to do with the provision of instructional materials. The Chinese still use the Chinese characters in reading and writing. A proposal has been made in many areas that the Chinese alphabet be romanized, but this would only add to an already difficult situation. The Chinese are a conservative people and take great pride in their formal written and printed characters. This form of printing existed centuries before the Western nations got around to any form of printing.

Whatever form of printing is used, the classes in Chinese schools will continue to need text materials. The Vietnamese are not in a position to produce these materials in the Chinese language. Recently, Free China offered to supply textbooks to the overseas Chinese on a minimum fee basis. In the absence of adequate textbooks there has been a temptation to smuggle in Red Chinese textbooks, which are available just across the border. These textbooks, filled with propaganda, should be resisted at all costs, and the anti-Communist Vietnamese government is on guard against the possibility of their use. To meet this problem, steps should be taken either to allow for the free importation of textbooks developed by Free China or for the production of Chinese books in the United States.

Both Catholic and Protestant churches have contributed to education in Viet-Nam. Long before the conquest of Viet-Nam by France, French Catholic missionaries came to the country. These missionaries were dedicated men. After the formal arrival of the French, a climate favorable to Catholicism was established, and Catholic schools, as well as churches, were instituted. Teaching orders were founded all over the country for the purpose of saving souls on the one hand and for the education of priests on the other. The fine teaching order of the Benedictines in Hue is an excellent example.

Figures and enrollments for the Catholic schools are not available. In the elementary field Catholic schools may be found in almost every Catholic village, and there are Catholic lycées in several of the larger cities. The elementary schools are primarily taught by the Sisters, and the segregated boys' schools are generally taught by the teaching brothers. French priests are still found in the teaching orders, but for the most part the Sisters and teaching brothers are Vietnamese.

The Protestant churches, which numerically do not enjoy the same positions as the Catholic Church, have been working in Viet-Nam for a period of thirty to thirty-five years. Their representatives have carried on missionary work in the finest of Protestant traditions. At the present time, there are mission schools for the mountain people at Ban Me Thuot, Dalat, and Nha Trang. Ministers are taught to read and write in the language of the tribes and, in turn, are expected to go back to the mountain villages to establish Bible schools there. Two hundred and twenty-nine ministers have gone to the villages, and thirty-five schools are reported to have been organized by them, with a current enrollment among the tribespeople of a thousand students.

The law of the land requiring instruction in Vietnamese has presented a problem to the Christian and Missionary Alliance people. The mountain people cannot speak or read Vietnamese, and the Vietnamese are beginning to realize that some concessions will have to be made to allow the tribespeople to continue using their dialects while gradually learning to read and speak the national language.

At the time of independence not more than ten percent of the adults of Viet-Nam were able to read. If the nation is to become strong, the adults as well as the children must become literate.

Every underdeveloped country realizes the great need for popular education. In Communist, as well as in free, countries it is generally accepted that education is the principal tool to bring about that kind of patriotism that can be depended upon in times of crises. It is generally recognized, too, that there is not enough time in tension areas to wait for the slow maturation of this feeling among the growing children. Next month or next year may become the time of crisis when citizens may be called upon to enter the armed forces for the protection of their country.

In Viet-Nam the adult literacy program was begun in March, 1951, through the mass education program of the Special Technical Economic Mission (STEM). At that time, north Viet-Nam was receiving the major portion of the aid. It was reported then that 2,558 classes in adult literacy were being conducted in north Viet-Nam, 151 classes in central Viet-Nam, and 158 classes in south Viet-Nam.[65] With the partitioning of the country in 1954, unfortunately for the Free World, much of the early effort was lost to the Communists. The effort continued, however, in Free Viet-Nam, where there were 385,074 students in 12,869 classes in 1957. These classes were taught by 19,226 teachers, many of them working as volunteers, without salary. The United States invested a total of $355,192 in this program in 1957. In general, the program called for three months' training courses for approximately 500,000 adults per year. American aid provided for the procurement of supplies, such as copybooks, primers, blackboards, and gasoline lamps.

The program is well begun, and it is believed that it has such popular appeal that United States funds, which will always have to be limited, should be spent for other needs. The viewpoint upon which United States aid is established favors withdrawing support for a program as soon as it can stand alone. The adult literacy classes are believed to be well enough established at this time to carry on without United States aid and American assistance. Therefore, this program is being concluded in 1958.

The increased interest in learning English has been amazing. Here are people, educated in the French tradition, who have an indigenous language

[65] Report of Economic Cooperation Administration in Viet-Nam, May, 1950-1953.

but who, for purposes of communication with the outside world, have used French for almost a century. The new spirit of nationalism has moved the authorities to require that all instruction shall be in Viet-namese. There is no second official language in Viet-Nam, though all the learned people speak French, and the rising generation is learning to speak English. French and English are required throughout the lower levels of the public secondary schools, and in the philosophy and litera-ture division both are required for three periods a week. In private Viet-namese secondary schools, French and English are offered on an optional basis. In private French schools—and they still provide the best secondary education in Viet-Nam—the instruction is given in French, and English is offered only as a foreign language. If the Vietnamese were to choose the easy way out, they would choose French, because they are already acquainted with it. Instead, in cases where options are allowed in the secondary schools, there is more interest in English than in French.

Thousands of adults study English at off hours and at night. One Viet-namese commented, "I want to learn English so that I can learn what makes the United States so rich and so powerful." The teaching of English has become almost a racket. If one goes into a garage to get a car fixed, he is told by a mechanic: "I speak English a little bit. I go to English classes at night school." Many of these private enterprise schools are more interested in profit than in good teaching. The racket is lamenta-ble, but the objectives of the students are commendable.

For the past three years USIS has sponsored the Vietnamese-American Association, a bicultural center. The American staff provided by USIS consists of an American director and two assistants, a small staff of Vietnamese, and a large number of American wives. The center is directed by a board of trustees, made up of both the Americans and Vietnamese, and one of its main objectives is to promote the English language. The capacity of the school is 300 students. Unfortunately, limited facilities have required first preference be given to members of the Vietnamese army. These people are placed there for a period of three months of study. At the close of the first three months those whose plans require it, as well as those who have done exceptionally well, are permitted to con-tinue in classes. The time is all too short, but it is remarkable how much they learn working six hours a day for a period of three months.

There is something subtle that comes in the learning of another man's language. To learn the language is to learn the man and his motivations. It may be that the teaching of English represents one of the most potent means of keeping free Viet-Nam within the orbit of the Free World. This is understood by the British and the Australians who are in Viet-Nam working under the Colombo Plan. They, too, are lending their assistance to teaching English, for they are offering four full-time English instructors at the University of Viet-Nam. The French Cultural Mission, aware of the value of language, is offering one full-time instructor in English to the University, as well as many in French.

A number of private groups have been working in Viet-Nam since 1954. Compared to USOM, these groups are small. Yet in some cases their work has been significant. To mention only a few, The Asia Foundation, CARE, International Rescue Committee, and Operation Brotherhood have stayed long enough, sent enough people, and done enough to merit special mention.

Operation Brotherhood, which was developed in the Philippines as a movement of the Filipino people to help a sister nation, has closed its operation. However, during the two years that it was in Viet-Nam, it offered significant assistance in social work, health and sanitation enterprises and rudimentary educational projects.

The *International Rescue Committee* also has closed its operations. Its funds were raised largely in the United States. During the two or three years of its work the committee was headed by an American, who was assisted by several Vietnamese. Along with counseling and guidance among the people generally, the IRC worked especially with the refugee students who had come from north Viet-Nam. Hundreds of the young secondary students who had fled from the north were without parents and would have had to close their formal education if it had not been for the International Rescue Committee, which furnished tuition grants, living subsidies, and, in some cases, even clothing to these needy people.

The Asia Foundation, which is still operating in Viet-Nam, illustrates the flexibility so desirable in times of crises. The University at Hue had been organized after the project agreement on higher education had been drawn up in 1957 by USOM and the government of Viet-Nam. That school had many needs, both in personnel and instructional supplies and equipment. For the year 1957 the Foundation provided a substantial beginning to a very good library for the University, as well as one full-time professor.

The nature of the *CARE* program in Viet-Nam has changed markedly within the last few months. Previously, it was assisting in the feeding program. That has been given up now, and the CARE agency has turned its attention to the plight of needy students, especially in the field of vocational education. The CARE program has supplied tools to students so that they could begin work as an apprentice or as a student in a trade school.

It will be many years before the impact of foreign aid to education in Viet-Nam can be properly appraised. The Vietnamese are beginning to learn that there is a relationship between cause and effect and that the explanation of the success of the American people can be found in their educational institutions. Whereas once they accepted American advice only as a means of getting the money which went with it, they are now beginning to see that, while the money is important, it is the understanding which they need.

The United States effort in education in Viet-Nam has been a big one. Moreover it has been expensive. Within a five-year period it has cost approximately $13,000,000. (See Table 5.) Most of that has been spent within the last two years. It is very likely that it will continue to be expensive both to the Vietnamese government and the United States aid program, if it is to succeed. At the present rate of progress is seems obvious that American assistance to Viet-Nam's educational program will have to continue for many years. Each of the projects currently under way is a continuing one. It is designed for a nation of 12,000,000 people, of whom 2,500,000 are of elementary school age. At the present rate, within the next fifteen years, schools will have to be constructed to handle all these children.

TABLE 5

TOTAL U.S. DOLLARS BUDGETED FOR AID TO
VIETNAMESE EDUCATION

Type of Education	1955	1956	1957	Total
Technical, vocational education	$ 321,113	$ 882,511	$ 900,000	$2,103,624
Primary, secondary lycées	1,807,878	2,500,309	2,681,167	6,989,354
Teacher training	120,000	788,617	1,385,898	2,294,515
Higher education	15,235	106,256	400,000	521,491
Miscellaneous, adult literacy, educational publications, etc.	304,888	361,904	355,192	1,021,984
Annual Total	2,569,114	4,639,597	5,722,257	12,930,968

XIII. The National Institute of Administration
NGHIEM DANG[66]

OVER AND BEYOND general educational problems, Viet-Nam, in 1954, as a new and independent nation, had few people trained to fill high-level government positions. As has been indicated, due to the long period of French rule, during which few links existed between the central government and the people, the government of Viet-Nam had to be rebuilt from top to bottom.

In 1954 there was only one school in Viet-Nam which trained students for civil service positions, the Dalat School of Administration, established by the French at Dalat in January, 1953. However, this school was located far away from governmental activities and was engaged in training only a limited number of civil servants for field positions.

After Viet-Nam gained its independence, the Dalat School underwent a number of changes and reorganizations to make it a more adequate training ground for Vietnamese officials and leaders. French advisers, professors, and instructors were replaced by high-ranking Vietnamese officials. A contract was signed in April, 1955,[67] between the Vietnamese government and Michigan State University which provided that a group of MSU professors and specialists would come to Viet-Nam to assist in improving the school's program.

The school itself was moved from Dalat to Saigon, the nation's capital, in July, 1955, and renamed the National Institute of Administration (NIA). Its objectives were broadened to provide: training for high-ranking government offices, in-service training, research on administrative organization and modernization of operating procedures, documentation and research, and management of a library of administrative science, etc. The level of scholarship, as well as the number of students, was raised, and during the training period vigorous efforts have been made to promote the intellectual, moral, and professional qualities of the students.

General qualifications of applicants for a teaching position, which give consideration to both academic degrees and administrative experience, were established by a Presidential decree of August 9, 1955. The staff, which in 1957 numbered eighteen, with the assistance of the MSU group and several experienced and able high-ranking Vietnamese administrators, was able to meet the added responsibilities created by the new, broadened program of the school.

To increase the effectiveness of its staff, the Institute, in 1956, sent two of its people to the United States to observe and study public administration and teaching methods. In 1957 another staff member went to the United States to study methods in administrative research and subjects

[66] Assistant Director of the National Institute of Administration.
[67] This contract was renewed for another two years on April 19, 1957.

related to organization and method. Similarly, a group went to Korea, Japan, and the Philippines to make on-the-spot observations on problems of comparative administration.

Since 1955 the NIA has had a steady growth, and its structure has become more solid. In seeking improvements and increasing efficiency, the Institute has changed its curriculum three times. As it now stands, the schedule calls for classroom studies, practical exercises, and field training. The goal is to provide students with a high level of scholarship and general knowledge, an all-round familiarity with administrative organization and methods, and a superior skill in solving problems that will enable them to execute the government's policies efficiently.

The program stresses the latest concepts in administration (management, budgeting, planning, organization and methods, human relations). At the same time, it tries to keep the student's attention focused on the political, economic, and financial problems which the government faces at the present time.

In addition, NIA in 1957 prepared an advanced program, then planned to be ready within a year, for the training of high-level specialists. This was to provide a thorough study of doctrines and theories in administration, economics, and finance, and a comparative study of techniques practiced by various underdeveloped countries of East Asia.

An evening program of courses in administration and economics was instituted in December, 1956.

NIA's enrollment figures increased by approximately fifty percent between 1956 and 1957, and this increase is an indication of the success achieved by the Institute. (See Table 6.)

An in-service training program for three levels of government employees—high-level administrators, technical personnel, and clerical personnel—was begun in 1956. High-level administrators are offered courses on administration and leadership. Regular courses on customs and duties, business bookkeeping, budget management, and rules and regulations affecting Treasury operations are provided for various technical people. For clerical personnel, NIA has courses in accounting, stenography, archive keeping, typing instructing, and statistics.

Through the program, government officials have become more aware of the progress that can be made through in-service training methods. NIA, in this program, was really reviving an ancient practice: As far back as the Lê dynasty, high-ranking officials were required to take periodic examinations to prove their continuing fitness to govern.

In accomplishing its objective of modernizing government operating procedures and doing research on administrative organization, NIA has done several things. In 1956 a committee drew up questions and problems

TABLE 6

ENROLLMENTS IN NIA

Day Program	1956	1957
Preparatory section	55	61
PMS (tribal people) section	14	29
Economics and finance		
Second year	25	34
Third year	23	25
General administration		
Second year	10	21
Third year	24	10
Special section	39	38
Graduates in military service	7	54
TOTAL	197	272

Evening Program		
General administration		
Public administration	455	563
Administrative and political		
organization in Viet-Nam	225	276
Administrative law	162	288
Economics and finance		
Political economy	529	489
Financial legislation	228	270
Economic development	166	291
Optional courses		
Accounting	189	449
Administrative problems	122	154
Constitutional law	114	304
Statistics	35	153
Money and banking	163	144
Personnel management	160	159
TOTAL	2,548	3,540

on the civil service, thus providing groundwork for the reform proposals to come from people who had studied civil service bureaus in the United States, Japan, and the Philippines.

Another committee has secured writings on the compilation of recently enacted rules and regulations, or enacted during the French occupation and still applicable. This committee is also studying measures needed to improve the civil service. Sponsored by NIA, a group called "Association for Administrative Studies" was formed in 1956, and by 1957 had one hundred and sixty members. The NIA hopes that the Association can publish a journal, and that this publication, which can reach a greater number more quickly and effectively, will bring about a greater understanding of public administration matters among government circles, as well as among business and cultural groups.

To bring the NIA's program in line with the present governmental structure, the program of the Institute was modified in August, 1957. The adjustments included: (1) a change in the Executive Council which would enable those organizations directly interested in public administration matters to help in setting up the training program for government employees; (2) modifications in the system of practical training, and entrance and final examinations, so that the new training program could be started; (3) the creation of an in-service training branch to deal exclusively with that phase of the program.

The contract with Michigan State University, which expires in 1959, will be renewed and revised so as to define procedures in connection with the spending of American aid money and the participation of the MSU group in research and teaching.

By making the heads of the different NIA services responsible for the courses related to their own fields, the NIA hopes to set up more flexible qualifications for teaching posts. Thus, it could solve the problem of its present small teaching staff, and also secure better qualified teachers for those parts of its program that are closely tied up with the administrative situation.

To meet the needs of the various government agencies, the Civil Service Bureau proposed increasing the enrollment in regular NIA sections. In 1958 NIA expected an increase in the number of scholarship students, and planned a campaign to get more fee-paying students.

Plans are being made to revise and bring the PMS curriculum into line with the special needs of the tribal people, who, generally speaking, do not have the same cultural development as the rest of the country.

In a little more than three years the NIA has developed from a small nucleus to train high-level government officers to a multiprogram school. It now is a training center where high officials can learn the latest concepts in public administration, a clearing house for the exchange of in-service training experiences, and finally a center for the study of various administrative problems. Much still can be done in the latter area. The NIA staff, together with MSU specialists, and in co-operation with the various government ministries, should conduct studies on matters related to public administration, economics, and finance.

The NIA might participate in the work of interministerial commissions set up for study and research, or it might contribute consultants, especially the MSU people, to the different ministeries. An "organization and methods" service, to be run jointly by NIA and the Budget and Foreign Aid Office, could make studies that would increase the efficiency of the various agencies.

Academic participation in and advice to government is a relatively new practice in the Vietnamese structure. The NIA has a dual goal: to promote the value of the individual to the Vietnamese government and to increase the effectiveness of the various government agencies.

Commentary: GUY H. FOX[68] *on* NGHIEM DANG

PROFESSOR DANG has modestly effaced his own significant role and contributions to the National Institute of Administration. To a large extent, the progress of the Institute has resulted from his flexibility of mind, his receptivity to new ideas, and his managerial talents.

That the assumption by the Institute of its present functions marks a revolution in the thinking and practices of the Vietnamese ought to be emphasized. In a sense, it is true that the NIA can be traced to the Dalat School of Administration. But, in another sense, the NIA is something entirely different. The Dalat School trained a limited number of civil servants for field positions. With the creation of the NIA in 1955, this rather narrow function was subsumed into a much broader program, involving also the preparation of civil servants for the higher echelons of central ministries, and including functions relating to in-service training, research, consultation with and advice to government officials, the development of a comprehensive library in administrative and other governmental matters, the conduct of conferences and conventions for the consideration of administrative problems, the sponsorship of a professional society and journal in public administration, and other activities for the betterment of public service. In spirit and vitality, influence and prestige, and scope of activities and accomplishments, there is little resemblance between the former Dalat School and the new Institute.

The new curriculum also represents, in a large measure, the acceptance of fundamental concepts and approaches which are new to Viet-Nam. As could be expected, however, the NIA was not prepared to abandon its traditional concepts and methods, which were based largely on those of the French. As a result, the present curriculum is essentially a compromise between old and new ideas, as influenced by the expressed desire of President Diem that the courses be made "practical."

[68] Former Chief of Michigan State University Advisory Group to the National Institute of Administration.

Several major curriculum problems were faced by the Institute. One was the question as to what extent the legalistic phases of government and administration ought to be de-emphasized and how much attention should be given, first, to the managerial phases of administration and, second, to the study of the social, economic, political, and psychological environment within which civil servants must function.

Although some members of the Michigan State University advisory group were disappointed that the Institute has remained largely in the hands of lawyers, that the study of administration is not yet receiving sufficient attention, and especially that students are not receiving a broad background in the social sciences, they have been impressed by the degree to which the Institute has been willing to depart from traditions and precedents and to accept new ideas and practices. To view any criticisms of the NIA program in true perspective, certain facts must be borne in mind. A majority of the Institute's administration and faculty have their *Licence en Droit,* and have, primarily, a legal interest in administration. The study of the dynamics of administration is a relatively new and unaccepted idea, and there is a lack of qualified staff to teach such courses as budget and fiscal administration, personnel administration, comparative administrations, government planning, organization and methods. Moreover, few of the faculty are broadly trained in the social sciences, with the exception of economics.

NIA also faced the problem as to whether it should emphasize technical, "how to do it" courses, or courses which would give civil servants a fundamental knowledge and understanding of administrative processes and a broad background in the social sciences. Somewhat of a compromise was reached between the two divergent views; the Institute decided, and regrettably so, to emphasize technical courses. The decision was influenced, as already indicated, by President Diem, who declared on several occasions that he wanted Institute graduates to be acquainted with existing laws and ordinances and to be able, upon completion of their training, to step into administrative posts, with the ability to perform the specific tasks to which they were assigned. Michigan State University advisers, whose advice the Institute is, of course, free to accept or reject, have maintained that such technical courses fall more properly within the province of in-service training and that the Institute's degree program, which is aimed at producing effective high-level civil servants, can best accomplish its purpose by insuring that its graduates receive a broad, general training, especially in the social sciences, plus a knowledge of certain tool courses, such as accounting and statistics.

In drawing up the new advanced program, to be introduced in 1958, the Institute gave serious consideration to what kinds of courses would be most appropriate. The advanced program is open to graduates of the Institute or the Faculty of Law, or to selected, experienced functionnaires. It was decided that the advanced curriculum would stress "theoretical" subjects and introduce participants to certain of the social sciences which were not in their undergraduate curriculum. It would have been better to offer all the general introductory courses in the social sciences during the undergraduate period and to reserve the advanced program for narrower, but more penetrating, courses.

Several comments may be made about the "level of scholarship" of students. Students for the regular degree program are selected by competitive examinations from applicants, both in and out of the service, having the baccalaureate diploma. The Institute manages to get a good share of the talented youth of the country. Unfortunately, however, scholastic standards of the Institute could be higher. Failures were virtually nonexistent before 1958, and it was quite possible for a student, while taking a full course load at the Institute, to work several hours a day in an odd job to supplement the income received from the Institute scholarship, and at the same time to complete his law degree at the University of Saigon. However, the NIA faculty may be becoming more concerned with the problem of standards: In the January, 1958, examinations, several first and second year students failed.

The qualifications for staff require both academic degrees and administrative experience, and the Institute is able to draw heavily upon University of Saigon personnel and upon qualified experts in various national government departments.

Because qualified Vietnamese staff were not generally available to teach such newly introduced courses as personnel administration, budget and fiscal administration, comparative administrative systems, and organization and methods, Michigan State University personnel had to assume such courses temporarily, or to work closely with Vietnamese teachers. Michigan State University personnel were also asked to teach several economics courses, emphasizing money and banking, taxation, the principles of economic development, and intermediate economic theory. In the meanwhile, the NIA took steps to prepare qualified Vietnamese faculty. This was done partly by assigning joint responsibility to Vietnamese and Michigan State advisers to courses, by sending present and prospective Vietnamese faculty to the United States and other countries for several months of observation and study, and by establishing seminars and informal discussion sessions between the Vietnamese and Michigan State University staff members. However, these were stop-gap measures. Joint teaching and seminars and discussions sessions in particular did not meet with an unqualified welcome at the NIA, and consequently did not take root. The long-range solution to this problem must await the return from the United States of Vietnamese faculty with graduate training.

Several accomplishments and an indication of significant work in progress may be added to Mr. Dang's account of Institute research. Several issues of the professional journal in public administration have now been published. Several faculty members have written textbooks for at least four courses in economics, and a fifth is now in progress. A book of readings in Vietnamese for the introductory course in public administration has been finished, and a basic textbook is planned. A textbook titled *Money, Banking and Economic Development in Free Viet-Nam* has been published, and mimeographed manuals on "Organization and Methods," "Budgetary Administration," "Statistical Methods," and "Readings in Economic Development" have been prepared. Already completed, also, are studies on governmental revenues and expenditures, and local taxation. Now in preparation are books on public works legislation, as well as the *Modern Political History of Viet-Nam*. An ambitious project, just completed, was the preparation of a Vietnamese government manual, similar to the well-known *United States Government Manual*. Furthermore, the Institute is preparing a trilingual glossary of terminology commonly used in administration.

Despite its research accomplishments, the Institute suffers from a severe shortage of research personnel and has not been able to free staff members from teaching and administrative responsibilities sufficiently to permit them to do much research. Most of the projects listed in the preceding paragraph were carried out by MSU personnel. Professor Dang's extensive and thorough book on public finance in Viet-Nam, soon to be published, will be the first such text to be completed by a NIA faculty member. Until a solution to the staff shortage problem (which is largely a problem of budgetary restrictions) can be found, NIA research will be seriously handicapped.

Closely related to the research functions of the Institute are its responsibilities in consulting with and giving advice to government agencies. It is the inadequately staffed Research Division of the NIA which is charged with this consulting activity. Again, progress will probably be limited until additional qualified personnel joins the NIA faculty. Training and background will be an important question here, for most of the present personnel, with their legal training and approach, do not have a strong interest in the kind of surveys and analyses called for in consulting work.

The library of the Institute deserves mention. It is excellently equipped, and the number of its publications is growing rapidly. At present there are approximately 6,000 books, exclusive of pamphlets and UN documents; approximately fifty percent of the books are in Vietnamese or French. It receives about 150 periodicals; three newspapers are received on microfilm, for which the Institute possesses an up-to-date viewer. It has attempted to obtain all available publications in governmental administration written in the Vietnamese language. Because of its access to a reproduction machine, it is able to make, with assured accuracy, its own copies of many government documents which the departments cannot furnish. However, large gaps exist and progress in developing a collection of Vietnamese government documents has been unavoidably slow.

The aim of the library is to become the center of materials and the headquarters for research in the field of governmental administration. To further this end, the Institute plans eventually, if and when the necessary staff becomes available, to compile a general catalog or master index giving the location of all public administration materials in Viet-Nam, wherever they may be.

There are certain obstacles to effective internal management of NIA. Many decisions on relatively minor and even ministerial matters regarding the Institute must be referred to President Diem. Moreover, even in instances where presidential decision is not legally required, Institute officials have sometimes been reluctant to act before receiving Presidential approval. Within the Institute itself there is also a comparable degree of overcentralization. The resultant bottleneck in the decision-making process has caused delays and inactions and has imposed an undue burden on President Diem and upon top Institute officials. Improvement would undoubtedly result, also, from a reduction and regrouping of the sections into which NIA divisions are divided; the excessive number of sections, especially as they are now constituted, tend to produce rigidity, complexity, and fragmentation which could be lessened by a simpler organization. Greater emphasis on planning by Institute officials is also in order.

Potentially, the in-service training program could be the largest and most significant one of the Institute. In January, 1956, the Institute took the initiative in bringing about the creation of an Inter-Departmental Council on In-Service Training and participated in the Council's deliberations, which were held at the NIA. Before the end of 1956 the Council had recommended a comprehensive program to President Diem and had drafted an *arrêté* which, when signed by the President, would inaugurate the program. Although the President has repeatedly expressed his basic agreement with the program, he has not yet ordered it into effect.

In the meanwhile, the Institute has been active in the field of in-service training. The large evening classes, held at the Institute for over 3,000 students, virtually all of whom are civil servants, may be regarded as an in-service training program. The Institute is also participating in in-service training programs with the Directorate of Budget and Foreign Aid and with the Directorate of Taxation. Programs are soon to be initiated in the Civil Service Directorate, the Viet-Nam Press Agency, and Ba Xuyen province. A second province has requested assistance from the NIA in setting up an in-service training program.

The question has arisen as to whether it might not be better to vest central responsibility for developing and encouraging an in-service training program in the Civil Service Directorate rather than the NIA. To be sure, a logical case can be made that the Civil Service Director-ate should handle the function. Although it is desirable to transfer central in-service training responsibility from the NIA to the Civil Service Directorate, it would be a mistake to do so at this time. For numerous reasons, the Institute is better prepared to handle the activity now and for the foreseeable future. This view is bolstered by the un-fortunate experience of the Philippines, where a promising in-service training program conducted by the Institute of Public Administration of that country was transferred prematurely to the civil service agency, which was not ready for the task. The fact that the in-service training program of the NIA is part of an inseparable, integrated program for improving governmental administration should also be given considera-tion in any contemplated transfer of the function.

It has also been argued that the making of surveys and organization and methods studies of administrative agencies ought to be vested in the Budget agency instead of the Institute. As with the idea of trans-ferring in-service training to the Civil Service Directorate, there is considerable logic to support this view. Nevertheless, for much the same reasons the in-service training program would suffer if moved from the Institute in the near future, it would be a mistake, it is be-lieved, to vest the making of administrative surveys and studies in the Budget agency, at least until after the Budget Division has the necessary personnel, attitudes, and skills to handle the task.

A look into the future of the NIA should include the plans for a new campus and plant equipment. In June, 1956, the United States Operations Mission agreed to furnish American aid funds amounting to 18½ million piasters toward the building and equipping of a new Institute. The government of Viet-Nam, in turn, agreed to furnish the necessary land and to contribute 13½ million piasters, the amount of American aid funds invested in the present premises.

Although progress will undoubtedly be slow, there is every reason to believe that the Institute will continue to realize its goal of becoming a source of leadership and a center for programs designed to improve governmental personnel and administration in Viet-Nam.

PART FIVE

INDUSTRIAL AND
AGRICULTURAL DEVELOPMENT

On the economic side Viet-Nam has faced a dual task of converting a colony into a nation and a wartime economy into a peacetime economy. Three fourths of the Vietnamese people live in agricultural villages, using outmoded methods to work the land. Commerce centers around the romantic but costly Eastern bazaar. Largely devoid of industry, manufacturing in the Western sense in Free Viet-Nam is limited largely to cigarette making and food processing, i.e., nondurable consumer goods. Transportation by ancient oxcart and barge is too disorganized and slow to meet present-day requirements and, where Western equipment is used, the methods are too costly.

As a low per capita income country, Viet-Nam has been faced with two fundamental decisions: Whether limited investment resources should be concentrated on industrial or on agricultural development, and whether the government should largely plan and implement or should only provide the climate for industrial development.

The First Five Year Plan (1957-61), as explained by Frank Rosebery, "looks to a continuing agricultural destiny for Viet-Nam." In agricultural development, Viet-Nam faces the problems of expanding its area under cultivation, diversifying its production, and increasing its yields. "Realization of these possibilities," comments David C. Cole, "will require greater and more efficient application of labor and capital to the available land and amelioration of certain institutions related to agriculture, including land tenure, credit, and taxation." Between World War II and the partition of Viet-Nam, there had been much talk about agrarian reform programs but no action, as Price Gittinger points out. Since independence the government has sought to regularize credit controls and agreements between landlords and tenants, to establish reasonable rental rates, to set up local agrarian reform committees, and to bring more abandoned land into cultivation.

In covering industrial development efforts, Lawrence Morrison points out that the survival of Viet-Nam as a free nation is underwritten by American aid, which maintains an artifically high standard of living by the amount of funds being used to import vast quantities of consumer goods. If the economy of the country is to grow to fill the "aid gap," there must be a balanced development of both the agricultural and industrial sectors, according to Morrison.

Nguyen Phuc Sa writes of the industrial development hopes of the young energetic leaders of Free Viet-Nam, and stresses the achievements of the government to date: raising the low standards of the rural population, restoring the potential of agricultural production, rebuilding the communications network, and developing the educational system—all of which "strengthen the economic framework that will make possible the successful industrialization of Viet-Nam."

H. Robert Slusser presents a case report of efforts to establish a useful industrial development bank in Free Viet-Nam, as well as an evaluation of the achievements of the National Investment Fund up to 1957.

XIV. Economic Setting

DAVID C. COLE[69]

THE TWO political regions of Free Viet-Nam are geographically significant. The central region is a predominantly mountainous area, while the south consists mainly of the broad delta of the Mekong River.

The central region can be divided into three zones—coastline, mountains, and plateau. Most of the population is crowded along the coastline and maintains a relatively poor level of living from intensive, double-crop cultivation of rice. Lying to the west of the coastal mountains is a plateau, which slopes toward the valley of the Mekong in Cambodia. Much of this plateau is covered with heavy forests and jungles. Until recently, it was inhabited only by mountainous tribal peoples. However, within this century a number of plantations have been established by the French, and at present large numbers of Vietnamese are moving into the area.

Like the central region, the south of Free Viet-Nam also consists of three zones. In the northeast there is a rectangular area sloping up from the sea and the delta to the southern extremities of the mountains of the central region. Much of this upland area of dark-red soil, formed by lava flows, is extremely rich and ideally suited for the growing of rubber. In this century, large areas of jungle have been cleared and planted to rubber. The population is sparse because of the plantation form of agriculture. Recently four new provinces have been created in this area; numerous refugees have been settled there, and the jungle is being cleared and planted to dry-land crops.

The second area of the southern region consists of the Mekong delta lying to the north of the Bassac River. It has been settled by the Vietnamese for several centuries. Most of it is planted to rice, and, except in a few small areas around My Tho where double-crop cultivation prevails, only one crop per year is grown. Fruit and coconuts are also important crops along the coast and riverbanks, while maize is grown during the dry season in the western sector. The northern part of the region, along the Cambodian border, has never been cultivated because of the lack of drainage canals. Such canals are currently being dug, and the land opened to exploitation.

The third area, below the Bassac River, has been developed fairly recently. It is barely above sea level and, therefore, subject to inundation by salt water. Many parts, especially along the western coast, are covered with mangrove swamps. Drainage canals and dikes have been built, mainly along the eastern coast and the Bassac River. This land is devoted

[69] Assistant Professor of Economics and Assistant Director of the Graduate Training Program in Economic Development, Vanderbilt University.

almost exclusively to rice, which is grown in large fields, mostly by tenant farmers working for large landowners. Population density is relatively light, and, consequently, the area is the main source for surplus rice production in Viet-Nam.

All of Viet-Nam is subject to a tropical, monsoon climate, with uniformly high temperatures throughout the year except in the high mountains. Most of the country has a six-month rainy season from June to November, followed by a six-month dry season. However, the northern half of the central coastline, because it faces northeastward toward the China Sea, experiences heavy rainfall during the fall and winter months, when northerly winds prevail.

Of the total twelve million population[70] of Free Viet-Nam, more than ten million are Vietnamese, with the Chinese totaling about 700,000 and the tribal people between 600,000 and 700,000.

Estimated population for the southern region is about seven and one half million, with nearly two million in Saigon and the remainder in the provinces.[71] The central region has a little more than four and one half million people, with 500,000 in the highlands and a little over four million in the lowlands.[72]

More than nine million persons, or seventy-five percent of the total population, live in agricultural villages. The urban population is estimated at nearly three million, or about one fourth of the total population. About sixty percent of the urban inhabitants, and nearly fifteen percent of the total population, is in Saigon, the capital and a large commercial center. The remaining urban population is located in the other three prefectures and the provincial capitals, which are also governmental and marketing centers.

In characterizing the Vietnamese economy in broad terms, it can be said that the country is primarily agricultural and that rice is by far the most important crop. Commerce, dominated by the Chinese and French until recently, is the second largest sector of the economy. Free Viet-Nam is largely devoid of industrial production; before the partition most of the limited industry was in the Hanoi area, which is now part of Red Viet-Nam. The only manufacturing establishments of any size in Free Viet-Nam are engaged in cigarette-making and food processing. Income per capita is relatively high in comparison with other countries of South

[70] The figure given by the National Institute of Statistics (*Annuaire Statistique du Viet-Nam*, 1956, pp. 36-43) was 12,261,000. Population figures are not very accurate, since they are based on projections of a prewar (1937) census, as modified by estimates of population shifts, the effects of the war, and some crude censuses. Preparations are now under way for a national census in 1960.

[71] *Ibid.*, p. 36.

[72] *Ibid.*, p. 40.

and Southeast Asia (see Table 7). Income levels in the southern region of the republic are significantly higher than those in the central area, due to the higher ratio of cultivated land to population.

A general view of the Vietnamese economy can be obtained from the national income and product figures. (See Table 8.) The value of domestic production in 1955 was 72 billion piasters, which is equivalent to either one or two billion U.S. dollars, depending upon the exchange rate which is used.[73] Some 61 billion piasters, or 85 percent of the gross domestic product, went for private consumption. The government absorbed nearly 20 percent, and gross capital formation, nearly 5 percent.

TABLE 7

PER CAPITA INCOME OF SOUTH AND SOUTHEAST ASIAN COUNTRIES*

Country	Year	Measure per capita	Amount in U.S. dollars†
Burma	1955	National income	$ 44.7
Ceylon	1955	Gross internal product at factor cost	131.8
China (Taiwan)	1955	National income	121.4
India	1954	" "	55.4
Indonesia	1952	" "	87.5
Japan	1955	" "	215.7
Malaya	1953	Gross national product	246.9
Pakistan	1954	National income	53.1
Philippines	1955	" "	181.6
Thailand	1954	Net internal product at factor cost	64.2
Free Viet-Nam	1955	National income	144.0

* Admittedly, international comparisons of per capita income are difficult to make, especially when they are based on unrealistic exchange rates. For what they are worth, these figures are offered for such comparison. Only Japan and the Philippines have a higher national income per capita than Viet-Nam. The gross national product per capita in Malaya is higher than any of the other per capita figures.

† All U.S. dollar figures are derived by conversion from local currencies at official rate of exchange. Such rates give an upward bias to the figures for both Viet-Nam and the Philippines, since the currencies of these two countries are artificially maintained at overvalued rates. More realistic figures for Viet-Nam and the Philippines would be about $100 and $120 dollars, respectively.

Source: *Bulletin Économique de la Banque National du Viet-Nam,* Supplement No. 2, 1956, "Estimations du Revenue National du Viet-Nam en 1955," p. 24.

[73] The official exchange rate which is applied to most imports is 35 piasters to one U.S. dollar. See the article, "Foreign Exchange," on pp. 288-301. (ED.)

TABLE 8

DOMESTIC PRODUCT OF VIET-NAM, 1955

(*millions of piasters*)

GROSS DOMESTIC PRODUCT		EXPENDITURES FOR PRODUCTS	
Gross domestic product at factor cost	65,726	Private consumption expenditures	61,190
Indirect taxes	6,338	Government purchases on current account	14,059
LESS: Subsidies	−48	Gross internal capital formation	3,369
		Changes in stock	—
		Exports of goods and services	4,283
		LESS: Imports of goods and services	−11,142
		Statistical error	257
Gross domestic product at market price	72,016	Imputed expenditure on gross domestic product	72,016

Source: These national income and product figures are from "Estimations du Revenue National du Viet-Nam en 1955." This was the first time that income and product accounts had been estimated for Free Viet-Nam, and only the second time for north and south Viet-Nam in any form. The general unrest which pervaded the country in 1955 was manifested in the amount and quality of the data on which these estimates were based and in the relationships of the estimated amounts.

This excess of consumption, government expenditure, and investment over current production of some 6.5 billion piasters was met by a large import surplus equal to 10 percent of domestic production. The import surplus was financed by foreign aid. Private and government savings were negative by 1.7 billion and 7.1 billion piasters, respectively. The capital formation and depreciation figures are questionable, but they indicated approximately zero net capital formation.

A study of the breakdown of the gross domestic product (see Table 9) indicates the surprising fact that in 1955 the commercial sector produced as much as agriculture and animal husbandry.[74] The government sector, represented by payment for services, was next, followed by property income, transportation, and fishing. Industry was relatively un-

[74] Part of the explanation of this was the large profits being earned by importers and speculators in 1955. During that year, prices of most consumer goods were high and rising, while imports were being brought into the country at low prices based on the official exchange rate. By the end of 1956 some of these pressures had abated as a result of increased agricultural production, absorption of currency through expanding exports, and the imposition of price controls.

TABLE 9

GROSS DOMESTIC PRODUCT BY SECTOR OF ORIGIN, 1955

(*billions of piasters*)

Sector	Amount	Percent
Commerce	17.1	24
Agriculture and livestock	17.0	24
Government	9.5	13
Rental income	5.7	8
Transportation	4.3	6
Fishing	4.2	6
Clothing and textiles	2.6	3
Food processing	1.3	2
Domestic service	1.3	2
Tobacco	1.1	1
Other	7.9	11
TOTAL	72.0	100

Source: "Estimations du Revenue National du Viet-Nam en 1955," p. 14.

important, accounting for less than 10 percent of total product. Most of the rental income was derived from agricultural land. Part of the income from commerce, transportation, and fishing was earned by the peasantry. The urban population does, however, receive a much higher average income than the rural inhabitants.[75]

Agriculture has been and, in the foreseeable future, will continue to be, the most important sector of the economy. It has experienced great expansion over the past century and, despite recent declines in production as a result of the war, development plans have stressed the importance of continued growth. The possibilities of expanding the area under cultivation, diversifying production, and increasing yields appear to be favorable. Realization of these possibilities will require greater and more efficient application of labor and capital to the available land and amelioration of certain institutions related to agriculture, including land tenure, credit, and taxation.

The principal crop in Viet-Nam is rice, which accounted for some 40

[75] Thus, it should not be concluded that the rural-agrarian population, which comprises some 75 percent of total population, receives only 24 percent of the income. According to a study by the National Institute of Statistics made in 1956, the 9.4 million village inhabitants had a total income of 27.4 billion piasters, which was equal to 44 percent of the 1955 national income of 62 billion piasters. The estimated per capita income, for the village population on the basis of these figures was around 3,000 piasters. Average income per capita for Free Viet-Nam was some 6,000 piasters, and for the urban population, 12,000 piasters. (National Institute of Statistics, *Monthly Bulletin of Statistics*, No. 3, March, 1957, pp. 6-8.)

percent of the total value of agricultural and livestock production in 1956.[76] Rubber was the second most important crop, with an output of around 70,000 tons and a value of over one billion piasters.[77] Other major crops are maize, sugar cane, coconuts, manioc, peanuts, sweet potatoes, tobacco, tea, and coffee. No reliable figures are available on these crops, but together with the raising of animals, especially pigs and fowl, they account for nearly half of agricultural production.[78]

Agricultural output reached its peak in the first years of World War II. Production of most crops gradually declined during the war and, in the ensuing civil war, fell off sharply as the countryside became insecure and many persons moved into the towns and cities. Table 10, which gives

TABLE 10

PADDY PRODUCTION IN THE SOUTH REGION OF VIET-NAM

Year	Area *(millions of hectares)*	Production *(millions of tons)*	Yield *(tons per hectare)*
1935-40 (average)	2.2	2.8	1.3
1942-43	2.3	3.2	1.4
1950-51	1.2	1.6	1.3
1951-52	1.3	1.9	1.5
1952-53	1.3	1.9	1.4
1953-54	1.5	2.0	1.3
1954-55	1.6	2.0	1.3
1955-56	1.7	2.3	1.4
1956-57	2.1	2.8	1.3

Sources: Figures for the years up through 1954-55 are from "Les Perspectives du Développement Économique au Viet-Nam," p. 116. Those for the last two years are from "Évolution de l'Économie du Viet-Nam en 1956," p. 13.

[76] Production in 1956 of 3.5 million tons of paddy at an average farm value of 2,000 piasters per ton gives a total value of 7 billion piasters, or about 40 percent of total agricultural and livestock product value of 17 billion piasters for 1955, and probably about the same in 1956.

[77] "Evolution de l'Économie du Viet-Nam en 1956," pp. 16-18.

[78] A rough estimate can be made of the amount and value of animals slaughtered during 1956. The Veterinary Service is reported to have inspected the following number of slaughtered animals ("Évolution de l'Économie du Viet-Nam en 1956," p. 29): pigs, 890,234; cattle, 47,577; oxen, 15,355. Using only the figure for pigs, it is likely that at least 100,000 pigs were slaughtered without inspection so that probably one million pigs were killed in the year. The average price which a pig buyer in Ben Tre province was paying to farmers for grown pigs in 1956 was about 1,500 piasters. Applying this figure generally, the estimated value of the pigs killed in 1956 would be 1.5 billion piasters. The probable value for all livestock (including fowl) sold by farmers in 1956 might be between 2.5 and 3 billion piasters.

figures for paddy production in the southern region, illustrates this trend. The year from 1953-54 on showed a steady increase in areas planted and in production. The central provinces also increased cultivated area from 423,000 hectares in 1954-55 to 480,000 in 1956-57, and production from 583,000 tons in 1954-55 to 671,000 tons in 1956-57.[79] The expansion of rice production to 3.5 million tons of paddy by 1956-57 was a reflection of improved security and greater stability in the countryside which permitted farmers to return to their fields. Also, the arrival of some 800,000 refugees from the north, most of whom were farmers, provided a mobile labor force which could be moved into the abandoned and uncultivated areas. Several large Vietnamese and American government-sponsored resettlement projects have enabled these refugees to assume productive roles in agriculture.[80]

Rice exports, which had been discontinued in 1956, were resumed by 1957, and 187 thousand tons were exported.[81] Assuming then that domestic consumption of rice amounted to the equivalent of about 3,250 thousand tons of paddy, it appears that only production above that level will be available for export in the next few years.[82]

It is important to note that, while prewar production of 2.8 million tons of paddy in the southern region provided an exportable surplus of from 1 to 1.5 million tons, the same level of production in 1957 permitted export of less than 200,000 tons. Increasing population and consumption levels have absorbed most of the former surplus, and production levels much higher than those of prewar years will be required to attain comparable exports. It appears that to have an exportable surplus of one million tons of rice will require production of 4 million tons of paddy (an increase of 43 percent over the 1956-57 crop), or reduced domestic consumption. Since neither is likely, and since internal needs will rise with an increasing population, it must be concluded that Viet-Nam is not likely to regain its prewar export levels.

Rubber production also declined during the war from 51,000 tons in 1940 to a low of 30,000 tons in 1947,[83] but recovery started earlier than

[79] "Évolution de l'Économie du Viet-Nam en 1956," p. 13.

[80] *USOM Activity Report, 1954-56,* p. 27.

[81] Press Information Office, Embassy of the Republic of Viet-Nam, Washington, D.C., *News from Viet-Nam,* Vol. 4, No. 11, April 4, 1958, p. 12.

[82] The 187,000 tons of rice exported is equivalent to about 280,000 tons of paddy (the reduction ratio is 65 percent). Internal needs of 3,250 thousand tons of paddy correspond to the estimate of the U.N. Mission, which proposed that a population of 12 million consuming an average of 160 kilograms of rice per person would require that amount ("Les Perspectives du Développement Économique au Viet-Nam," p. 118).

[83] United States Department of Agriculture, Office of Foreign Agricultural Relations, "The Agriculture of French Indo-China," Washington: 1950, pp. 31-32.

for rice. By 1952 production was over 50,000 tons and had reached 70,000 tons in 1957.[84] Replacement of old rubber trees had reportedly been neglected during the war years, which is likely to result in some decline or at least less rapid growth in production in the future.[85] These trends in rice and rubber production are probably indicative of the general changes which have occurred in the output of other crops.

Many opportunities for expanding agricultural production still remain. Much of the rice land abandoned during the war was back in cultivation by 1957, but several hundred thousand hectares of land along the Cambodian border (Plaine des Joncs) and at the southern end of the Mekong

TABLE 11

RICE YIELD PER HECTARE FOR ASIAN COUNTRIES

Country	Quintals of paddy per hectare	Country	Quintals of paddy per hectare
Japan	34.3	Burma	14.0
Korea	31.8	Thailand	13.9
Taiwan	25.0	India	13.3
China	24.9	Viet-Nam	13.0
Indonesia	16.9	Philippines	11.0
Pakistan	14.0	Other Asian countries	11.9

Source: "Les Perspectives du Développement Économique au Viet-Nam," p. 110.

Delta (Rach Gia, Ca Mau) can be exploited once drainage canals are dug and dikes built to keep out salt water. There are also possibilities for developing irrigation systems along the several channels of the Mekong, which would permit the growing of two crops.[86] Finally, large areas of the High Plateau, which are currently being opened up with the use of heavy machinery, will offer continuing opportunities for settlement. These undertakings will require capital equipment, and particularly labor, to dig canals, build dikes, and clear the land.

In addition to bringing new land under cultivation, the yield from land currently in use can be increased. Viet-Nam had, in 1953, one of the lowest rates of yield per hectare for rice of all Asian countries (see Table 11). The average yield for all Asia was 17 quintals (1.7 metric tons) per hectare. A thirty percent increase in yield would be necessary to achieve this

[84] "Évolution de l'Économie du Viet-Nam en 1955," p. 17, and "Évolution . . . en 1956," p. 16.
[85] "Les Perspectives du Développement Économique au Viet-Nam," p. 152.
[86] *Ibid.*, p. 71.

level, and to do so would require more careful cultivation, some use of fertilizer, and improved seeds.

Finally, possibilities exist for developing new crops and diversifying production, which would result in higher income and better use of existing land resources. The U.N. Mission has recommended increased production of sugar cane, jute, tobacco, corn, cotton, fruits, oil-producing plants, and vegetables, as well as the introduction of some new crops.[87]

The Vietnamese government has recently summarized its plans for agricultural development as follows:

> In agriculture, emphasis is placed upon the recultivation of abandoned lands, the exploitation of new areas and the intensification and diversification of cultivation in the four main resettlement areas of Cai-san, Baclieu-Camau, the Plaine des Joncs and the Upper Plateaus. Development is also planned in factory crops (sugar cane, mulberry, cotton, castor oil plant, tobacco, rubber) and forestry.[88]

In addition to these plans which are specifically directed at raising the level of agricultural output, various governmental programs for agrarian reform, agricultural credit, and improved marketing facilities may have similar effects or, at least, result in higher incomes for the peasantry.[89]

Commerce is the second most important form of economic activity in Viet-Nam. However, it would be erroneous to interpret this fact as an indication of a high level of economic development, as suggested by Colin Clark.[90] Rather, it is a result of the colonial period and current distortions within the economy. Commercial activity, mainly in the import and export trade, expanded greatly under French domination. Special groups established dominant positions in the commercial sector and were able to exploit them to some degree.

In the past few years, inflationary pressures and the financial arrangements for handling the aid programs (particularly the low exchange rate used for the commercial import program) have offered favorable opportunities for commercial profits, and the entrenched groups have taken advantage of them. This was especially true in 1955 and 1956. As these exceptional conditions are corrected, the income of the commercial sector

[87] *Ibid.*, pp. 57-66.
[88] The Colombo Plan, *Sixth Annual Report of the Consultative Committee* (Saigon: October, 1957), p. 172.
[89] These programs are discussed in the chapter on "Agrarian Reform," on pp. 200-208. (ED.)
[90] Colin Clark, *The Conditions of Economic Progress* (London: Macmillan, 1957), 3rd edition, pp. 492-95.

should recede somewhat in relative importance. However, the inherited commercial system contains certain undesirable characteristics, against which various measures have been and still need to be taken. The most important weaknesses are the preponderant role of foreigners, the prevalence of monopolistic powers in certain sectors and the excessive commitment of resources in commerce.

Commercial activity is carried on at four principal levels in Viet-Nam. At the top are large international trading companies. Next are the internal distributing and collecting businesses. Then come the small retail stores of the cities and towns. Finally, there are the very small, full-, or part-time merchants and peddlers in the market places of the cities, towns, and villages. All, except the lowest level, have been dominated by foreigners, principally French and Chinese. The French have been most interested in foreign trade, particularly the importing of manufactured goods from France. The Chinese have handled most of the internal commerce and also an important share of the exporting of rice and raw materials to neighboring Asian countries.[91]

There was necessarily much co-operation between the French and the Chinese because their interests and areas of activity were complementary.[92] The French were dependent upon the Chinese for moving imported goods out to the retail levels for sale, and also for collecting and bringing to Saigon the goods for export. Through a system of contacts throughout the provinces, the Chinese controlled the movement of goods into Saigon or out to the countryside, and it was difficult for an outsider, especially a non-Chinese, to break into the system.

The center of Chinese activity is in Cholon (now a part of Saigon).[93] This area, not only contains many of the retail outlets of the city, but is also the headquarters for directing the movements of goods within the country. The Chinese firms in Cholon have representatives, or deal with other Chinese, in each of the provinces of the south and center. Usually these representatives or contacts are located at the provincial capitals, and

[91] Prior to the disruption of trade patterns resulting from the depression of the 1930's, Indochina's foreign trade involved mainly the exporting of foods and raw materials to neighboring Asian countries (especially China, Japan, Indonesia), and imports of manufactured goods, especially textiles and metal products, from France. During the 1930's France and the other French colonies were obliged to absorb increased shares of Indochina's exports as sales to the Asian countries declined. (Robequain, *The Economic Development of French Indo-China*, pp. 321-30.) This tended to expand the role of the French and reduce the role of the Chinese exporting firms in Indochina. (*Ibid.,* p. 43.)

[92] *Ibid.,* pp. 36-40.

[93] For a description of the political and economic position of the Chinese in Viet-Nam, see Bernard B. Fall, "Viet-Nam's Chinese Problem," *Far Eastern Survey,* Vol. XXVII, No. 5, May, 1958, pp. 65-72.

they, in turn, have relations with the Chinese shops and dealers in the larger villages of the province.

Throughout the southern countryside at the present time, probably 80 to 90 percent of the established retail businesses outside of the public market are Chinese. These businessmen also act as moneylenders to tenant farmers, landlords, and other businesses. In recent years, the Chinese also have been entering food processing, particularly rice milling.

Goods are transported mostly by water and truck in Viet-Nam. Rail transportation is not important. The excellent network of canals through the Mekong delta makes it possible to reach every provincial capital in that area by boat. Most of the population is located along the waterways, which are frequently the principal lines of communication. The coastal areas of the central region can also be reached by boat, and there is frequent traffic between Saigon, Nha Trang, and Da Nang (Tourane). Trucks are used to reach the highlands, the plantation areas, and some parts of the south. Chinese have had an important role in the development and operation of these various means of transportation.

One of the major objectives of the Vietnamese government since gaining independence has been the "Vietnamization" of their economy, which means primarily replacing the Chinese and other foreigners in the commercial sector. In 1955 a number of French businesses withdrew from the country or reduced their activities in anticipation of difficulties with the new government, but recently they have been returning along with foreign trading representatives from various other countries (e.g., Japan, Germany, and the United States). A large number of small Vietnamese import businesses were spawned under the influence of lucrative profits from imports through the U.S. aid program, and the void left by departing French. Because most of these new Vietnamese importers were neither financially nor technically capable of effective operation, the government, by various means, sought to reduce their number and strengthen their operations.[94] Most such businesses, however, still tend to depend on Chinese or other foreign firms for capital or guidance.

The government's main repressive efforts were directed toward the Chinese wholesale and retail businesses. A recent decree has prohibited foreigners from engaging in eleven types of business, most of which were predominantly conducted by the Chinese. Although the decree is being implemented gradually so as not to unduly disrupt the economy, its complete enforcement will entail a major reorganization of internal commerce. The government is attempting to accomplish this, in part, through establishment of marketing and credit co-operatives. So far these have not been very effective.

[94] For example, the government divided imported goods into 12 categories and required importers to pay 350,000 piasters for a license to import goods in any one category. One firm could only hold three such licenses.

The Vietnamese find it difficult to assume these new commercial responsibilities because they lack experience and capital. Practically the only Vietnamese who have engaged in commerce previously are the peasants (who bring their own produce to market), the very small permanent retailers in the market place, and the peddlers who carry their wares on their backs or squat along the roadsides. There are a great many persons engaged in such small commerce in Viet-Nam, as well as in other parts of the Far East. This superabundance of small merchants parallels and is related to the idle agricultural population. Throughout much of the year the peasants are not occupied with farm work, whether by choice or force of circumstances, and some of their spare time is devoted to "sociable selling."[95]

The market places, in which these sellers are found, are normally covered buildings or sheds located in the center of the towns and larger villages. They are divided into different sections or stalls for permanent or daily occupancy. Also, the sellers of certain kinds of goods are usually grouped in one area. Most of the products are foodstuffs, but textiles and some hardware items are also available. The market places are built by the village or provincial government, and a tax is levied on all persons selling within their limits.

As a consequence of wartime and postwar foreign assistance programs, imported goods have taken on greater importance for all levels of Vietnamese commerce.[96] The predominance of consumer goods in total imports is indicated in Table 12.

On the other hand, exports, especially rice, have declined sharply. This means that the commercial sector which, before the war, was mainly engaged in collecting rice and other raw materials for export, has been turned

[95] One should distinguish between the permanent sellers, who earn most of their income from commerce, and the occasional sellers, mostly peasant women, who bring garden and home produce to the market in order to earn small amounts of cash. The former are more directly affected by changing commercial conditions, taxes, etc., while the latter consider commerce as much a social as an economic activity.

[96] In the period of 1933-37, Indochina's exports exceeded imports by almost 50 percent (exports averaged 154 million piasters and imports 106 million). Robequain, *The Economic Development of French Indo-China*, p. 306. In 1956 imports were nearly five times the exports (7.1 billion vs. 1.5 billion piasters) and equal to ten percent of the gross domestic product, see *Supplement au Bulletin Économique de la Banque National du Viet-Nam*, Revue Trimestrial, No. 1, 1957, pp. 55-67. The increased importance of imports was largely a result of the methods of financing the American aid program. Since the aid was provided primarily to offset the inflationary potential of large government deficits, the aid program consisted mainly of foreign exchange which was sold to importers for local currency that could be used to cover the deficits.

TABLE 12

IMPORTS BY TYPE AS PERCENT OF TOTAL IMPORTS, 1956

(Total value: 7,606.2 million piasters)

Type of Imports	Percentage
Consumer Goods	*82.9*
Textiles	20.0
Food, drinks, and tobacco	19.0
Chemical products	6.5
Petroleum products	6.0
Private transportation equipment	5.0
Rubber and cellulose	3.1
Minerals	2.5
Paper and paper products	1.8
China, glassware, etc.	1.0
All other	18.0
Investment Goods	*17.1*
Machinery	5.0
Electrical equipment	3.1
Metal manufactures	3.0
Metals	3.0
Scientific instruments and meters	1.5
Commercial transportation equipment	1.5
	100.0

Source: USOM, "Annual Report, 1956-57," p. 74, based on Bureau of Customs figures.

around into a distribution system for massive consumer-goods imports. This has occurred concurrently with the government's program to replace the existing Chinese commercial businessmen with Vietnamese. Such changes were bound to create some confusion and difficulties, and there will undoubtedly be further problems in the future as the economy moves toward some sort of equilibrium. This stability will require expansion of the flow of rice and other exports and some diminution of consumer imports. The new Vietnamese commercial firms, which are currently learning the techniques of one pattern of commerce, will in time have to accomodate themselves to a new and different pattern. Also, it is to be hoped that many of the foreign merchants now excluded from numerous forms of commercial activity and also some of the surplus Vietnamese merchants will engage in other forms of productive activity, especially agriculture and industry.

Because of the agricultural basis of the Vietnamese economy, the lack of industrial minerals, and the flow of French manufactured goods into the country, industrial development in Free Viet-Nam has been limited to the processing of agricultural products and the manufacture of some consumer goods which could not easily be imported. North Viet-Nam was better suited for industry and mining.[97]

Most of the industry in Free Viet-Nam is located in the Saigon-Cholon area. A number of large rice mills were established in Cholon during this century to process rice for export. With the lack of a sizeable exportable surplus in recent years, these mills have been idle much of the time.[98] Rice milling has tended to move out to the southern countryside, where a number of small mills now process the rice for local consumption and shipment to Saigon.[99]

The processing of fish is another major industry, which is centered in the coastal cities of Phan Thiet and Da Nang and on the island of Phu Quoc. The principal product is a sauce made from fermented fish.

There are four cigarette factories in Saigon, which use imported and local tobacco. Also there are several breweries and soft drink companies, whose products are distributed throughout the country.[100]

Small-scale weaving has been expanding among refugees from the north. Numerous small lumber mills produce building materials from the large logs of the highland forests. There are also a number of small metal and woodworking shops in the Saigon area, which make bicycle frames, tools, household utensils, and furniture.

Vietnamese officials have repeatedly expressed their desire to expand the industry of the country. President Diem, speaking in September, 1955, stated, "Finally, I would like to emphasize a fundamental point of the economic program of the government: the industrialization of the country."[101] The Vice-President recently declared the government's policy to be one of "gradual industrialization born of the general expansion of the

[97] The existence or lack of industry, however, was not, and is not, an indication of greater wealth or per capita income. Free Viet-Nam is decidedly more prosperous than the Communist zone. To illustrate this, the gross product estimate for all Viet-Nam in 1954 was 119 billion piasters, and in 1955, after partition of the country, it was 72 billion piasters for Free Viet-Nam alone. The population of the republic is slightly lower than that of the Communist zone, but gross product is estimated to be 40 percent higher in the republic.

[98] Even exports of 187,000 tons of rice in 1957 did not provide for more than a month of capacity operation by the big mills.

[99] In the Center, most rice is milled in the homes.

[100] In the smallest and most remote villages, it is possible to obtain cigarettes and soda pop, indicating that the distributing facilities for these products are very effective.

[101] Speech of President Ngo Dinh Diem, September 19, 1955, at the dedication of the Dong Cam dam, in *Major Policy Speeches by President Ngo Dinh Diem,* Press Office, Presidency of the Republic of Viet-Nam (Saigon: 1956), 2nd edition, p. 16.

economy."[102] He went on to note that the government was creating an Industrial Development Center to provide technical and financial assistance to industrial ventures. The occasion of his talk was the inauguration of Viet-Nam's first spinning mill, which has 10,600 spindles.[103] The Vice-President stated that new industrial projects currently under consideration included a glass factory, a paper mill, modernization of a sugar refinery, two additional spinning mills (bringing the total number of installed spindles to 50,000), and some weaving mills.[104]

The government is encouraging private investment, both domestic and foreign, in these industries, and apparently stands ready to offer some financial backing. The new industries are engaging mainly in the production of consumption goods (using both imported and domestic materials) to meet internal needs and to replace goods which are currently imported. The rate of growth of such industry probably will be relatively modest in comparison with the North, for example, but it should reduce dependence on heavy import of consumer goods. Also, gradual industrialization will leave resources available for agricultural development, from which more rapid and higher rates of return can be expected.[105]

Commentary: LINDHOLM *on* COLE

A FEW ADDITIONAL comments might be made to Cole's section on agriculture. During 1955 and 1957 the primary aim of the Vietnamese government and American aid program was to put back into cultivation the some 700,000 hectares of rice land that had been abandoned during the Indochina war, as well as to eliminate the shortage of 80,000 work animals. Although the program has been largely successful, it has not succeeded, as Cole has indicated, in making any great quantity of rice available for export.

Undoubtedly, the failure is partially explained by the higher standard of living in the villages and the increased size of Vietnamese families. Because land rents have been decreased and property taxes are extremely low, the typical Vietnamese family can eat more rice, or they

[102] Quoted in *The Times of Viet-Nam*, Vol. III, No. 6, February 8, 1958, p. 12.

[103] *Ibid.*, p. 4.

[104] *Ibid.*, p. 16.

[105] A study is presently being made by the American engineering consulting firm of Day and Zimmerman, which will give a more detailed report of the industrial potential and the most desirable patterns of industrial development in Viet-Nam.

can feed more of the crop to ducks and pigs and thus improve the family diet, or they can make more alcohol from rice.

Moreover, it is unlikely that Viet-Nam will be able to produce surpluses for export comparable to the prewar period. The improved living conditions on the small subsistence rice farms indicate that the rice production will not greatly exceed the amount needed to feed the people of the Saigon-Cholon and other smaller urban areas.

The Vietnamese government and the American aid group have centered their efforts nearly entirely on improving the productivity of small-scale farming. One effort in this direction was the establishment of twenty rice storage co-operatives. These co-operatives were set up as a part of a consolidated agricultural credit program, which, although it has not yet proved successful, does provide a framework for the development of a system of financing the production and marketing of rice. By thus replacing the monopoly currently held by the Chinese, the government of Viet-Nam could achieve an important political and economic victory.

Other efforts toward increasing agricultural productivity have been the establishment of an agricultural extension service and an agricultural school at Blao.[106] These projects have been financed, in a great part by American aid, and partially staffed with American personnel. Programs such as these are badly needed to introduce more efficient farming methods and to develop greater agricultural diversification. However, progress will be slow, due to the traditional Vietnamese viewpoint that by studying technical subjects one does not get an education.

Activities aimed at the expansion of agricultural diversification have been carried on nearly entirely through the American aid program. Several steps have been taken to make livestock raising more profitable. One has been an extensive program to eradicate the rinderpest; another has been to introduce improved breeding stock in chickens and pigs. One of the most ambitious aspects of the program has been to develop improved varieties and growing methods for sugar cane and long-fiber vegetables. Agriculturists seem to agree that the one way to make Vietnamese agriculture more productive is through greater diversification.

The only important agricultural export today is rubber. At present, production is being expanded by the private French companies which own and manage most of the plantations. Although production of synthetic rubber is expanding in the United States, and to some extent in Western Europe, the future markets for natural rubber seem to be assured by the even more rapid expansion throughout the world of the automobile market and other machinery using rubber.

[106] See pp. 148-50 for a discussion of the Blao School of Agriculture. (ED.)

In addition to rubber, some tea and coffee are raised on plantations, primarily owned by the French. However, some Vietnamese are beginning to enter these agricultural areas and undoubtedly more will as credit and educational developments permit them to do so.

The introduction of machines, and in some cases additional pumping equipment, would make it possible to raise two crops in areas where only one is raised at present. Also, the introduction of commercial fertilizer and the use of improved varieties of seed would increase yields substantially. In large areas of the highlands, now being opened to modern agriculture for the first time, products such as coffee, tea, corn, and fruits, as well as dairy cattle, can be raised economically. Besides having a world market, these can be used to enrich the diets of the Vietnamese and to sharply reduce imports.

Vietnamese and American experts estimate that the agricultural exports of Viet-Nam will reach $80 million in 1960, which would represent a threefold expansion of the present export trade. There is no doubt that the agricultural future of Viet-Nam can be bright, with improvement in farming techniques, controls on land ownership, regulation of credit and marketing, and the development of new land areas.

XV. Experiment in Planning Economic and Social Development, 1956-57

FRANK D. ROSEBERY[107]

To ASSIST in planning a program for balanced economic development, the Vietnamese government in 1955 arranged for a United Nations Mission[108] to undertake an over-all survey of Viet-Nam's economic prospects. It also placed the planning bureau, Direction Générale du Plan, in the office of the Presidency to emphasize the importance of planning. This bureau, guided and assisted by the findings of the United Nations Survey Mission, and in collaboration with Vietnamese ministries and the United Nations advisers, prepared a *First Draft* Five Year Plan (1957–61) for Economic and Social Development,[109] which was submitted to the Presidency in June, 1957.

The Plan Document made an estimate of aggregate resources needed for economic growth during the five-year period. The national wealth of the country was estimated at 250 billion piasters—50,000 piasters per head of working population. This figure was derived by multiplying annual output in Viet-Nam, for which there is an estimate, by the ratio of national wealth to output in other underdeveloped areas. A requirement for new investment of 20 billion piasters was developed, based on maintaining capital stock per head and allowing for an increase in population and a decrease in unemployment. Replacement, estimated at 4 percent of annual output, implied an additional need of 16 billion piasters. Thus, gross investment needs were indicated at 36 billion piasters.

It was only in the final stages of the preparation of the Plan Document that this 36 billion piaster requirement was developed. For new investment, instead of 20 billion piasters, the Plan initially had figured 17.5 billion, and total expenditures of that amount are foreseen in the document. This requirement was based on the following rule-of-thumb approach: Other underdeveloped Asian countries have been requiring an annual net investment injection equal to about 10 percent of output in order to achieve a growth rate of 2½ to 3 percent annually. A comparable investment injection in Viet-Nam would require increasing by some 3.5 billion piasters annually (or by 17.5 billion in all over five years) the recent level of gross investment, equal only to about 5 percent of output and presumptively allowing little net investment.

Ministries which assisted in the drawing up of the Plan received directives and verbal instructions for draft projects. The planning bureau

[107] United Nations Economic Planning Consultant to the government of Free Viet-Nam, 1956-57.
[108] The request was made to the UN in July, 1955, the survey undertaken in Nov.-Feb., 1955-56, and the report submitted in Oct., 1956.
[109] Hereafter called the Plan or the Plan Document.

pointed out the need for insuring consistency of projects, suggested that standards in other Asian planning areas might be considered as guidelines for the size of projects, and emphasized that projects must always be realistic in terms of available material and human resources. Nevertheless, the planning bureau, looking for the suggestion of more projects than could be executed, so as to exercise selectivity, requested the ministries to disregard what they might consider financial limitations. In planning projects, the ministries were called on to distinguish between expenditures on: (1) physical assets and on capital like economic and social services and (2) those creating wealth and those that were financial expenditures (e.g., purchase of an existing building). In addition, they were asked, to make a breakdown between local currency and foreign exchange requirements; compute the impact of projects on future government operating expenditures, on the balance of payments, and on unemployment; and suggest private sector projects (agriculture and industry).

The material drafted by the ministries was then analyzed, verified, screened, and co-ordinated by the planning bureau. As a policy, the bureau sought to give priority to those projects promising quick results at low cost. In reality, this yardstick gave rise to a minimum of pruning. Only the public works sector was significantly reduced.

Of the 17.5 billion piaster expenditure recommended in the Plan, the approximate 80 per cent for the public sector is in the order of magnitude of a five-year projection of the 1957 level of United States economic aid. It represents about 40 percent of the total United States aid, with the balance serving to finance Viet-Nam's military effort. The 1957 economic aid represents an aid: (1) which had just reached new high levels and whose contributions to capital formation presumptively still had pipeline features (i.e., not reflected in recent investment levels); and (2) in which operating expenditures arising from development projects had bulked large at the expense of investments in physical assets and capital like services (training, research). For this double reason, it seems quite possible that the present levels of economic aid, properly *redirected,* might make a substantial contribution toward financing the public sector of the Plan.

Continuation of American aid is admittedly problematical. However, the gradual reduction of aid is the cardinal objective of the Vietnamese government. Extension of aid, at a level roughly equivalent to the public sector expenditures of the Plan, to Viet-Nam, which would maintain its military effort while moving toward economic independence, seems a not unreasonable postulate. The Plan document itself, however, does not examine the problem of resources, domestic or foreign, public or private, which might finance either aggregate or Plan investments.

Most of the 17.5 billion piaster expenditures initially indicated in the Plan are earmarked for investment in physical assets (structures, machinery, equipment). The public sector accounts for about 80 percent of outlay and key private investments absorb the balance. A breakdown of expenditures is as follows:

Public works	31%
Power	12%
Agriculture, including irrigation	22%
Health, education, housing	12%
Industry	9%
Unallocated	14%

The primary emphasis on public works (roads, railways, canals, communications) and power, with a total of 43 percent allocated, indicates the desire to endow the country with sufficient overhead capital to support and stimulate future economic growth. Both the road network and the railway and canal systems are to be restored to their prewar status; roads and bridges are to be widened to accommodate present-size vehicles. The hydroelectric power project of Danhim is scheduled, however, to at least double present capacity, while water supply facilities in Saigon are to be enlarged substantially.

The Plan looks to a continuing agricultural destiny for Viet-Nam, with 22 percent of the funds earmarked for agricultural development. The increase in national income to be derived from rice, as abandoned lands are recultivated, is the highest of any crop—equal to that of all other crops combined. However, the tonnage target has been set below prewar levels because of the questionable outlook for export markets. Sugar cane, silk, tobacco, and oilseeds rank after rice in anticipated contribution to national income. Rubber projects are well supported under the program, but the maturity cycle will prevent an effective contribution to output within the life of the Plan. Cotton production is to be increased, but is only to reach significant proportions after 1961. There are also important livestock, forestry, and fishery programs.

Some of the agricultural projects are devised, in part, to lessen urban and rural unemployment. Overpopulated Saigon and densely populated coastal areas are to supply man power for rice cultivated in the south (Bac Lieu, Ca Mau) and west (Cai San), as well as rubber, tea, and coffee cultivation in the sparsely inhabited, rich plateau regions. These colonization projects are also tied to important over-all agrarian reforms and community-development programs.

Although health, education, and housing programs do not make a very large claim on funds, only 12 percent, this sector looks to the creation of facilities markedly above those prevailing before the war. In the field of education, while the humanities will not be overlooked, there is to be special emphasis on the training of engineers, doctors, agriculturists, veterinarians, and technicians in general, and on the schooling of foremen and specialized workers. In the field of public health, new hospitals are to be constructed and a large-scale antimalarial campaign is scheduled to eradicate malaria in five years. Although the housing projects are mainly located in Saigon, in the interest of relative decentralization, the provinces are to share the new public health and educational facilities with this city.

Development of industry receives considerable recognition in the Plan, even considering that agricultural contribution to the increase in production is nearly three times larger than the planned increment in industrial output. Anthracite coal is to be mined, and domestic lime and clay are to supply a new cement plant. (The cement and coal industries, located in the north where the mineral resources were most favorable, have been lost to Red Viet-Nam.) More particularly, light industry is to be developed (textiles, paper, small tires, light metal rolling), which will process for consumption in the domestic market both agricultural produce (wood, sugar cane, cotton, jute, rubber) and imported semifabricated products (yarns, ingots).

The orientation of the projects indicates Viet-Nam's aspiration, through diversification, to stabilize its economy, by insulating itself somewhat from the injury of a damaged crop, a lost market, or a commodity price collapse inflicted on a two-crop export economy (rice, rubber). It also indicates the conviction that the foreign trade deficit can be more effectively reduced by decreasing imports as well as by increasing exports.

In contrast to plans of other Asian countries, the Plan specifies certain anticipated private investments to be fostered through government loans and other incentives. In agriculture, land will be cleared with machinery owned by the state. However, other improvements will be undertaken by the private sector, notably in rubber, both through loans and other financing. Some of the new industrial enterprises (cement, coal) are to be state-owned. Others (sugar, textiles) will be state-financed for later resale to private interests or financed jointly with private interests. Still others (glass, paper, artisanal weaving) are to be private ventures. Certain quite sizeable private thermic power projects are incorporated in the Plan. Virtually the whole housing program is private, but to be promoted through government loans.

In making a critical assessment of the selected projects, one must remember that the Plan was prepared in a brief six months, which limited consultations with nongovernment sources. Moreover, many of the projects called for long-range research. The government preferred to sacrifice thoroughness in favor of a swift publicizing of a Plan which might serve as a platform for discussion and mobilize public interest in the cause of economic development. Solidity was further handicapped by the lack of basic statistical data, which is common to all underdeveloped areas but particularly acute in Viet-Nam, where war resulted in loss and dispersal of records and where political changes often necessitated difficult adjustment of available data.

Already, some of the projects deserve to be questioned. In the public sector, for instance, the great hydroelectric project at Danhim, and the largest single project in the Plan, appears controversial. It reflects apparently latent aspirations to expand industry to a level not implicit in the projects of the Plan. Danhim appears to provide the country with a power potential beyond absorptive capacity. It may well be that a less ambitious and costly project at another site would better serve the country. The public works sector also includes large outlays for both the road and railway system. The Trans-Indochina Railway, establishing a coastline link between the south and the north of Viet-Nam, was built before the war for administrative and prestige considerations. It is debatable whether it was an economically justifiable project even in those days. The rehabilitation of this railway, paralleling a coastal shipping lane, in the age of the truck and the airplane, is at least open to question. In the agricultural sector, the prospects for the successful execution of the colonization projects, devised largely to reduce urban unemployment, appear dubious. Populations once established in urban areas are not readily induced to resettle in the countryside. While certain social overhead expenditures have been directed to rural areas, Saigon is also generously cared for, especially in respect to housing; and the gravitational pull of the capital city is likely to remain considerable.

The sizeable artisanal hand-loom project, aimed at reducing not only urban but also rural underemployment, adds significantly to output at relatively little cost and makes a substantial foreign exchange saving; however, consumer resistance based on quality and cost of the product is likely to prove a severe obstacle.

Naturally, the first purpose of economic development is to increase production. Planned growth under the specific projects involves directly only a segment of the economy. The relation of return to investment on the specific projects is often high, particularly in certain agricultural sectors where minimal investments will bring large returns, as abandoned lands are again put to use. An estimate in the Plan Document of increase in output, based on the flow from the specific projects combined with estimates for the balance of the economy, shows a growth of 27 percent in agriculture, 70 percent in fisheries, 20 percent in industry, 15 percent in transportation and commerce, and 5 percent for other services—or an average gain of 18.5 percent for the economy as a whole. However, the figure was held as overly optimistic, and, in its discussion of aggregates, the Plan Document foresees over 1957-61 an increase of output of 12 billion piasters, 16 percent in all, or 3 percent annually.

In mid-1957 investment, public or private, was low. There was no public savings, in national accounts terms; and consumption was high, making for a relatively high standard of living in Asian terms. Investment and consumption exceeded domestic production. This excess is supplied by aid. Total aid, in the neighborhood of 8 billion piasters, is supplied to the public sector and is spent largely for national defense but also for economic development purposes. This aid specifically finances a budgetary deficit of about 8 billion piasters, and in point of fact covers approximately a balance of payments deficit of comparable proportions.

The Plan Document suggests that, in 1961, the increase in output, 12 billion piasters over present level, should make a minimal contribution to the economy where it is strong—in consumption—and chiefly serve to fortify the economy where it is weak—in investment and in self-dependence. Thus, the standard of living, already high, is to be frozen at present levels. Allowing for the population increase, this would claim 4.5 billion piasters of the 12 billion increase. Of the balance, 4 billion piasters are allocated to bolstering the low level of investment, 3 billion piasters to reducing the internal (budgetary) and external (balance of payments) deficit, by the same token curtailing aid by about 40 percent; a small residue is directed to increased governmental operating expenditures (civil). The Plan postulates maintenance of military outlays at current levels.

The government did not await publication of the Plan to experiment with measures aimed at creating the climate in which economic growth was to take root and at the curbing of internal and external deficits.

The National Investment Fund and the Industrial Center are institutional instruments recently created. The former is devised to encourage investments in smaller businesses through government loans and participations, and the latter, aid underwritten, aims to bring together skills, data, and funds for industrial expansion.

Both fiscal and monetary policy have been designed to promote growth. A Presidential Declaration of May, 1957, accorded tax incentives to approved new investment undertaken with resources brought in from abroad and with domestic funds, and assured approved new foreign investment of equitable terms for repatriation of principal and interest. The monetary fiscal policy of 1956-57 served to bear down on the long persistent inflation, and its arrest is a prerequisite for sound private investment, by a series of technical measures designed to curb the effective money supply (adoption of a differential exchange rate, increase in the Central Bank's reserve ratio requirements, exaction of a guaranty deposit from importers).

Administrative and structural tax reforms[110] have been initiated, which by increasing revenues will reduce the budgetary deficit and aid. There has been a trend from a multiple stage to a better yielding single stage sales tax. Preliminary tax relief has been accorded beginning domestic production, although eventually a reversal of this policy will be necessary when more vigorous domestic production comes, in part, to replace traditionally dutiable imports.

The curtailment of price inflation is likewise aimed at shrinking the trade deficit. Stable or lower prices are a prerequisite for expanding exports in world markets. Commercial policy was also directed at the trade gap. Multiple exchange rates served to subsidize certain commodity exports, and luxury imports were heavily curtailed through quotas.

The necessity of transforming a colonial economy into a national economy often results in adoption of policies not conducive to capital formation. The entrance into the field of foreign trade of an inflated number of inexperienced, undercapitalized Vietnamese importers, the partial elimination of the Chinese from important sectors of the economy, the absence of a clear policy regarding the prospects in the economy for large French rubber interests were examples of attitudes temporarily harming economic development. In Viet-Nam it is necessary not only to resolve the traditional conflict in underdeveloped areas between diversification and comparative advantages, between full employment and maximum growth, but also the conflict between an experiment in economic growth and in economic nationalism taking place at the same time. The solution of this last conflict may well prove to be the most delicate of the three.

Heavy aid itself, which in the past has been directed largely to consumption, may constitute a drag on development. Viet-Nam has, in a sense, enjoyed the fruits of development without significant investment. This may tend to obscure its need and blunt a sense of national urgency.

It must be remembered that Viet-Nam has faced a dual task of converting a colony into a nation and a wartime economy into a peacetime economy. Therefore, it has greater psychological difficulties to overcome than most other underdeveloped Asian neighbors. It is amply apparent that all Vietnamese administrators charged with acquiring skills in economic planning concepts and methods have made, in a short time, great strides. Actual economic development is a different matter. The best assurances that blueprints will become realities over the period ahead are the unusual vitality and industry of the Vietnamese people.

[110] See article on "Tax Reforms" on pp. 309-311. (ED.)

XVI. Agrarian Reform

PRICE GITTINGER[111]

IN SOME AREAS of Free Viet-Nam, and particularly in the south and west where large landowners have existed from the initial period of development, landlords own large farms, worked by tenant farmers. Through high rents and interest these landlords exacted a major share of the production, and are said to have received from 40 to 70 percent of the total crop in rental income and repayment of loans.

During the period of unrest after World War II, the French and semi-independent Vietnamese government sought an agrarian reform policy which would strengthen the loyalty of rural families. The first indication of such a policy was expressed in the message of Emperor Bao Dai in February, 1951, in which he promised to regularize tenancy agreements and credit controls. However, nothing came of this promise. Two years later President Nguyen Van Tam announced that henceforth the prewar rent of 50 percent of the crop would be reduced to no more than 15 percent. However, it was evident at the time that this decree could not be enforced.

Meanwhile, Vietnamese and American agricultural specialists were urging the promulgation of an effective agrarian reform program. The long-dormant National Committee for Agrarian Reform met in 1953 to draft suitable legislation, and four ordinances were promulgated in June of that year. Again, these ordinances had a propaganda value, but no change in land tenure resulted. The most striking omission was a lack of enforcement measures, and their vague and sometimes contradictory wording made them too complicated to be enforceable or for tenants to understand.

During the fall of 1954 American and French advisers agreed that the immediate goals of land reform could be realized by a rent reduction and tenure security program. They believed that a land transfer program would have to come at some later time, but that the government was not ready to embark upon such a reform.

In 1954 agrarian reform constituted a principal point in the advisory program of General J. Lawton Collins, President Eisenhower's special representative. General Collins called upon President Diem in December to present the American viewpoint, and later, on the same day, the French High Commissioner, General Paul Ely, called to present an identical French position. Within hours, President Diem convened a group of Vietnamese, French, and American agricultural specialists. This group worked quickly, and the President promulgated Ordinance No. 2, regularizing

[111] Specialist in Agrarian Reform with USOM, Saigon, 1955-59.

tenancy and limiting rents, on January 8, 1955, and Ordinance No. 7, governing recultivation of abandoned land, on February 5, 1955.

Ordinance No. 2, which technically amended one of the 1953 ordinances, provided that: (1) all established tenants were to have a written contract, following a prescribed form and registered in their village; (2) rents were to be set at the rate of 15 to 25 percent of the principal crop, depending upon the fertility of the land; (3) annual rent for tools, draft animals, etc., was not to exceed 12 percent of their value, and loans to tenants were not to exceed 12 percent annual interest; (4) contracts were to last for a least five years and to be renewable at the tenants' option; (5) village and district agrarian reform committees were to be formed which, with the provincial committees established by the 1953 legislation, would administer the program, report abandoned lands, and arbitrate disputes; and (6) failure to comply with the ordinances was to be punishable with stipulated penalties.

Ordinance No. 7 provided that: (1) communal councils were to submit to the government a list of arable lands not cultivated the previous season; (2) landowners had to declare their intention either to lease abandoned land or to cultivate it themselves; otherwise, they were to be considered absent; (3) landlords who declared their intention to lease abandoned land had to sign a prescribed contract with new tenants which reduced the normal 15 to 25 percent rental but exempted the landlord from liability for land taxes; and (4) in the case of absentee landlords, abandoned land could be leased to tenants by the communal council, using a prescribed form. Tenants on recultivated land would pay no rent the first year and reduced rent the next two years. The rent collected would be held for the landowner. This ordinance expired on December 31, 1955, and was replaced by Ordinance No. 28, of April 30, 1956, reinstating the same provisions on a permanent basis.

Mandatory contract forms were appended to these ordinances, to aid in the implementation of the decrees. Appended to Ordinance No. 2 for established tenants was the so-called Type A contract. It embodied the terms of the ordinance relating to land rent, annual rent for equipment and animals, interest on loans, and the duration of the contract. Appended to Ordinance No. 7, governing abandoned land, were two different contracts: Type B for use where the landlord was known, and Type C for use by communal councils where the landlord was absent. These, too, embodied the terms of the ordinance relating to tenancy conditions.

In framing these two ordinances, an explicit attempt was made to correct deficiencies and take advantage of the experience in other Asian nations. American technical help proved of particular value here, since United States advisers had had experience in Japan, Taiwan, and the Philippines. Although allowing the rent to vary from 15 to 25 percent was partly a political expedient, since the government was saddled with the unrealistic rate publicized in earlier propaganda efforts, the reform also attempted to relate rent to the productivity of the land. To provide a local administrative unit and to encourage democratic growth, each village was urged to establish a local agrarian reform committee. The general terms of the ordinances were simplified to make administration possible, and the emphasis was narrowed to rent reduction, interest control, and tenure security. The model contract was retained to make the law easier to administer. And, of course, the inclusion of penalties corrected an earlier omission.

To help villagers understand the tenure security program and its operation, the Vietnamese government, with American technical and financial assistance, prepared blank contract forms and publicity materials. Two million contract blanks were printed, each type with a different colored line drawing so that semiliterate peasants could readily distinguish between types. Posters were printed at a ratio of one to every 150 rural people. To identify the explanations with the proper contract forms, posters were color-keyed to match the line drawings. Leaflets were distributed on the basis of one for every three families.

As implementation began in early 1955, an interesting paradox in landlord and tenant attitudes emerged. Much of Free Viet-Nam had either recently been recovered from Communist control, or Viet-Minh forces still retained paramount influence. In these areas, particularly those in south Viet-Nam, landlords had sometimes not collected rent for as long as eight years. Therefore, landlords looked upon the contract program as a means to assure them a rental of at least 25 percent of the crop. On the other hand, tenants in these areas resisted the program, since they had been paying no rent at all (although they had paid heavy Viet-Minh taxes). By July, 1955, however, the increasing stability achieved by the national government had changed the environment, and more orthodox positions were taken by tenants and landlords, with peasants in favor of the rent rates and landlords protesting that they were too low.

Although the agrarian reform program had been foreseen as a partial solution to immediate problems, the impact during the 1955 season was small. Six months after the promulgation of Ordinance No. 7 there were only some 20,000 contracts registered. Of these, 16,200 were Type A for established tenants, and 3,800 Types B and C for abandoned land. As information about the program spread and field agents began to reach tenants, the number of contracts climbed. By the end of 1955, nearly a year after promulgation, there were 276,345 contracts registered, 204,313 for established tenants and 72,032 for abandoned land. Two years later, at the end of 1957, there were 675,075 contracts, 502,989 for established tenants, and 172,086 for abandoned land. These combined figures represent some two thirds of all tenants in Free Viet-Nam, and some 4.5 million acres; just over 3.3 million individuals are directly affected. Approximately one million acres of abandoned land have been recultivated under registered contracts.

Most of this progress has been realized in the south, where in some provinces four fifths of the tenants have contracts. In central Viet-Nam at the end of 1957, there were only 142,194 contracts of all types registered, including 18,716 Types B and C contracts, reflecting the small amount of abandoned land in the crowded center. Other factors have also slowed down progress in central Viet-Nam. The law limits rent to 25 percent of the main crop, which is fitted to conditions in the one-crop south, but is not realistic in the two-crop coastal deltas. In the south landlords have much larger holdings, and do not link themselves closely to the village. In central Viet-Nam, where holdings are small, the landlord is very much a part of communal life, and exerts a strong influence on tenant thinking. In these coastal deltas, tenants are more concerned simply to find land to cultivate than they are in the more spacious south. The tenant who raises the issue of a contract is likely to be evicted, with no alternative holding available.

Throughout the nation, problems of enforcement and administration are still great. Although contracts clearly set the maximum rent at 25 percent of the main crop, in practice most tenants with contracts pay a third or slightly more of each rice crop. Even so, contract holders feel the program has been of distinct benefit to them, and point to neighbors without contracts who, now that stability has been restored, pay 50 percent. The clauses relating to tenure security have proved difficult to enforce. Only about half the villages have agrarian reform committees, and these meet infrequently and have often been irregularly appointed. Even though illegal eviction is a common complaint in the countryside, few disputes have reached formal arbitration. At first the regular courts were unsympathetic to the program, but more recently tenants with contracts have won most of the disputes which they have appealed to the courts. Nevertheless, the high costs of this legal action and the slow judicial process combined to make recourse to the courts all but inaccessible to tenants.

President Diem moved to resolve some of these enforcement problems when he promulgated Decree No. 498 of November 27, 1957, establishing a special agrarian court in each province. These courts are to have original jurisdiction over all disputes arising between landlords and tenants relative to the rent control and tenure security program. (Cases arising over the land transfer program are referred to the National Agrarian Reform Commission.) Each provincial court includes a judge advocate and two assistants, appointed from officers of existing courts and administrative services. The agrarian courts will accept disputes without fee, and peasants may plead their own case. The court is obligated by the decree to render a final decision within forty days after a complaint is lodged. The first court was organized in Saigon in May, 1958, but organization of provincial courts has been delayed.

By the summer of 1956, the government felt that the time was appropriate to undertake a land transfer program. Accordingly, President Diem promulgated Ordinance No. 57 of October 22, 1956, which was aimed at increasing agricultural production, permitting a more equitable distribution of land, and making it possible for tenants to become small landowners. Also, it was to reorient large landowners from agricultural to industrial activities.[112] It provides that no person may own more than 100 hectares of rice land, and all persons holding more than that amount as of the date of the ordinance must sell the excess to the government, which in turn will sell it to cultivators. (A later modification provided that until formal government expropriation takes place, landowners may sell parcels of up to three hectares to established tenants or other individuals not members of their immediate families.) The ordinance applies only to land suitable for rice cultivation, exempting land planted to what are termed "industrial crops," including substantial holdings in rubber (largely owned by French citizens), and areas in forest, sugar cane, tea, coffee, coconuts, fiber crops, fruit, etc. Landowners will be paid 10 percent of the purchase price in cash and the balance in nonnegotiable government bonds bearing 3 percent interest per annum. The bonds are to be redeemed over a period of twelve years.

Cultivators who purchase land from the government pay for it in six equal annual installments with no interest. The landowner receives his last rent payment at the harvest of the crop year in which the transfer is effected, and the new owners begin their payments at the following harvest. The ordinance stipulates that, in addition to the 100-hectare limit, owners may retain up to 15 hectares of land bequeathed to them for private ancestor worship. Established tenants have first priority in the purchase of expropriated land, with local landless laborers and veterans and war victims following in that order.

Other provisions provide for: (1) a National Agrarian Reform Commission to supervise the implementation of the program; (2) special commissions to deal with such unsettled matters as land prices, areas to be retained for ancestor worship, and arbitration of claims arising out of the implementation of the ordinance; and (3) penalties for evading or opposing the implementation of the ordinance. The terms of the ordinance tend to be quite general and an important group of decisions is left to

[112] For comments on this phase of the ordinance, see p. 212. (ED.)

the commissions, which must operate almost without legislative guidelines.

Accurate statistics on the distribution of land ownership in Viet-Nam are not available. The best estimates available are summarized in Table 13, based largely on information more than two decades old.

Landowners were required to declare the land available for transfer by February 28, 1957. Although a few are known to have failed to comply with the regulation and are being searched out and proceedings instituted, to date 2,600 persons owning more than 100 hectares have declared total holdings amounting to 1,075,000 hectares. After following the deduction of the 100-hectare limit, the 15 hectares which may be retained for private ancestor worship, and certain other minor exemptions, the Department of Agrarian Reform estimates some 740,000 hectares will be available for transfer to tenants.

The Vietnamese Institute of Statistics and Economic Studies reports that 1,993,500 hectares of rice land were cultivated in the 1955-56 crop season. Estimates derived from 1934 figures quoted by Peautonnier indicate an additional 457,000 hectares of privately owned land still lie idle as a result of disturbances over the past decade. Thus, out of a total of approximately 2,450,500 hectares of rice land in Free Viet-Nam some 44 percent is held by landowners having more than 100 hectares.

Virtually all land subject to transfer lies in the provinces to the south and west of Saigon. In this area lie a total of some 2,185,588 hectares of rice fields, including almost all the abandoned land. (This total includes the 2,049,928 hectares in 14 major rice-growing provinces tabulated in Table 13 plus an estimated 135,660 hectares in six minor rice-growing provinces.) The current total number of individuals owning land in this area is not known, but the best estimate is that given in Table 13, even allowing for concentration of ownership and for rice landowners in minor provinces. Assuming this total of 255,056 rice landowners in 1934 is still relatively valid, in the area where the transfer is to take place the one percent of the owners holding more than 100 hectares claim title to some 49 percent of the total rice land.

Comparison with the 1934 figures in Table 13 indicates a substantial concentration of ownership has taken place in the last two decades. The area held by individuals owning more than 100 hectares has climbed from 733,800 to 1,076,000 hectares, while the absolute number of such large owners has remained approximately the same. Where one percent of the owners held 36 percent of the total rice land in 1934, they now own 44 percent of the total.

In general, the provinces farther from Saigon are the ones with the higher concentration of cultivator-ownership. The landlord returns indicate that in the minor rice-growing province of Tay Ninh, for instance,

TABLE 13

LAND OWNERSHIP PATTERNS*

Region	Size Classification (hectares)	No. of Landowners	Percent of Landowners in Size Classification	Area Owned (hectares)	Percent of Cultivated Area in Size Classification
CENTRAL VIET-NAM †	Less than .5	450,000	68.7	‡	‡
	.5 to 2.5	165,000	25.2		
	2.5 to 5	31,000	4.7		
	5 to 25	8,500	1.3		
	25 to 50	300	.1		
	Over 50	50	Negl.		
TOTAL		654,850	100.0		
SOUTH VIET-NAM ¶	Less than 1	85,933	33.3	42,966	2.1
	1 to 5	97,060	38.1	194,120	9.5
	5 to 10	37,616	14.8	263,312	12.8
	10 to 50	28,141	11.0	562,820	27.5
	50 to 100	3,613	1.4	252,910	12.3
	100 to 500	2,449	.9	489,800	23.9
	Over 500	244	.1	244,000	11.9
TOTAL		255,056	100.0	2,049,928	100.0

* Adapted from Yves Henry, *L'Économie Agricole de l'Indochine* (Hanoi: Gouvernement Général de l'Indochine, Inspection Générale de l'Agricole de l'Élevage et des Forêts, 1932) and G. Peautonnier, "Contribution a l'étude des conditions de l'exploitation de la rizière en Cochinchine," *L'Information d'Indochine Économique et Financière,* December, 1946.
† Applies chiefly to northern provinces.
‡ Unavailable.
¶ Fourteen major rice-growing provinces.

only 9 percent of the rice land belongs to individuals owning more than 100 hectares. A comparable 1934 figure is not available. Of the major rice-growing provinces for which Peautonnier quotes figures, the lowest concentration in 1934 was 14 percent in Cholon province, adjoining Saigon. By 1957 this had increased to 24 percent. At the other extreme, in the province of Rach Gia, on the coast southwest of Saigon, some 62 percent of the total rice land is in the hands of large landowners, as compared to only 52 percent in 1934.

In the absence of accurate land tenure information, it is difficult to estimate how many tenants will be affected by the land transfer. In the area where most of the transfers will take place, the average tenant holding is approximately two hectares. Since it is likely landlords will choose to retain rice land now under cultivation, the land available for transfer probably will include a substantial proportion of land abandoned during the disturbances of the past decade. It is estimated that about 225,000 hectares of the land available for transfer is not currently cultivated. On the remaining 515,000 hectares, the best estimate of sitting tenants affected by the land transfer is thus about 257,000. To the sitting tenants must be added approximately 55,000 additional farmers who will benefit from development and sale of the abandoned land. These new owners will be largely drawn from refugees from Red Viet-Nam and local landless laborers. Thus, a total of some 312,000 farmers will be benefited by the land transfer program. It must be emphasized, however, that these totals are based on very general estimates and can at best be only indicative.

Approximately 200,000 hectares of the 740,000 hectares of rice land subject to transfer are owned by French citizens. By far the largest part of this land is worked by tenant farmers.

It is not expected that the land transfer program will have an appreciable immediate impact on rice production nor upon the pattern of cultivation, since virtually the whole area affected is now either cultivated by tenants or lies abandoned. Landowners in Viet-Nam provide almost no management function for their tenants, who follow traditional planting dates and cultivation techniques. Little fertilizer is used. Although many large landlords were a primary source of credit for their tenants before World War II, they were less willing to make loans after the war due to Communist guerrilla warfare. Currently, most credit in rural areas comes either from local merchants, or from small or medium landowners who live in villages rather than urban centers and who are thus in a position to collect their loans. The government has undertaken a $10 million national agricultural credit program, which it hopes will replace any credit now coming from large landowners and a substantial portion of that from small landowners and merchants.

In late September, 1957, the government announced a schedule of prices based on productivity at which landowners would be compensated for their holdings, and indicated that tenants would be able to purchase the land at the same price. These prices range from $7 per hectare for remote abandoned land to $428 per hectare for double-crop land in the Saigon region. The administrative costs of the transfer are to be paid from regular government budget sources and from United States counterpart funds. However, no American funds will be used for the purchase of land. The price schedule was established after a series of meetings with representatives of the Ricegrowers Syndicate, a large landowners organization. To initiate payments, the Department of Agrarian Reform has been allocated 200 million piasters ($5.7 million). The Department estimates a total of some 2.4 billion piasters ($68.5 million) in cash and securities will be necessary to complete the land purchase. Since down payments to landowners will amount to only 10 percent of the total purchase price, the government has already made available from regular national budget sources virtually all the cash necessary to complete the land transfer.

An agreement has been worked out between France and Viet-Nam to pay for the 200,000 hectares subject to transfer owned by French citizens. The French government has made available 1,490 million francs for the purchase of this rice land. Owners are given a choice of accepting a price in francs established by a joint Vietnamese and French commission, or accepting the price in piasters as offered by the Vietnamese government to its own citizens.

It is estimated that the administrative costs of the land transfer program may come to some 77 million piasters ($2.2 million) spread over a three-year period, with the heaviest expenditure during 1958. A large proportion of this cost will be supported by counterpart assistance made available by the USOM, and the balance paid for from national budget sources.

Despite a delay in setting prices and making payments to landowners, large-scale transfers began in the latter part of 1957. As of September 27, 1958, a total of 258,969 hectares had been allocated to 97,229 existing tenants. This amounts to slightly more than one thind of the total land to be transferred. Preparation of formal titles is lagging behind the actual allocation of the land, but 55,740 titles were ready for distribution as soon as the prices for specific land parcels had been determined. Local price commissions are working in the wake of survey teams to determine the yield of the parcels in question and thus to establish the price according to the published schedules. President Diem marked the first fully completed transactions when he handed the first title deed to a new owner and the first down-payment check and land bond to an expropriated landlord at a ceremony on May 9, 1958, at Cai Lay, 60 miles south of Saigon.

This procedure of allocating land to tenants before the yields, and thus the prices, have been determined by the local price commissions and before formal titles have been prepared may seem to be undesirable at first. However, in view of the government's desire to indicate its concern about rural levels of living and its pressing need to demonstrate its determination to carry out an effective land transfer program, this procedure seems to be appropriate.

Commentary: DAVID WURFEL[113] *on* GITTINGER

AGRARIAN REFORM in Free Viet-Nam, as Gittinger points out, began with dramatically announced decrees which were never enforced. The political effect of unenforced reforms is, of course, more detrimental to a government than no reform at all. Although efforts to enforce subsequent rent reduction and land transfer legislation have met with some success, there is still a real danger that these efforts may halt far short of the substantial benefits that the tenant has come to expect as his due.

Enforcement of rent reduction and tenure security legislation can be effective only when there is an organized tenantry pressing for enforcement. The Federation of Tenant Farmers' Unions has been such a group, but, though it was among Diem's earliest supporters, its activities in the past two years have frequently suffered from stringent government restrictions, usually initiated at the local level, but condoned by authorities in Saigon. Widespread rent reduction, consistent with the law's provisions, is thereby inhibited.

The ultimate success or failure of the land transfer program will depend on the payment provisions—whether they are realistic and how they interact with the Vietnamese economy. Since prices are to be fixed on the basis of the land's productivity at the time of transfer, tenants who buy rich land in full production may find it difficult to meet payments when due. The punishment for default on payments is eviction and forfeiture of installments paid. In such a case, cultivators would be faced with the necessity of contracting usurious loans. Thus, a more adequate low-interest agricultural credit system is urgently needed.

Although the law prohibits new landowners from renting, mortgaging, or selling their land within ten years after it is allocated to them, experience in other countries has shown that such legal prohibitions are meaningless if strong economic pressures encourage their violation or circumvention. These pressures do exist in Viet-Nam. Large landowners who are forced to sell some of their land may simply reacquire rights from new farmer-owners who are short of cash, if there is no readily available cheap credit for the cultivator or if there are no

---

[113] A student of Far Eastern affairs at Cornell University, who spent a month in late 1956 in Viet-Nam studying the land reform program, immediately following a similar study of one year in the Philippines. His research was made possible by a grant from the Ford Foundation, which is, however, in no way responsible for facts or opinions in this commentary.

attractive investment alternatives for the landlord. Only a few such alternatives have appeared.

In the final analysis, of course, the Vietnamese are responsible for their own economic development, but American officials must, in part, be held accountable for the failure of more new enterprises to be born, since American aid funds make up such a large percentage of the government budget and of available foreign exchange in Viet-Nam. One cause for the delay of industrialization has been United States insistence on development through free enterprise, which is unrealistic in a country where native investment capital and managerial skills are so scarce, and where there is a determination to destroy alien dominance of the economy. Even the Philippines, strongly committed to free enterprise, has found it necessary to resort to government initiation of some industries. Japanese economic history also indicates that conservative governments can and must play an important role in the early stages of rapid industrial development in an agricultural economy.

Partly as a result of American policy, therefore, one of the most commendable provisions in the Land Transfer Ordinance, allowing the use of the "nonnegotiable" bonds held by landlords for subscription to securities in state enterprise, is inoperative. This technique has been used successfully in Taiwan to begin the transfer to private, ex-landlord, ownership of many establishments taken over by the government from the Japanese after the war. But the comparable section in the Vietnamese law also includes a provision for the bonds' redemption in cash at the end of twelve years, thus weakening the incentive to convert them into corporate securities. A generous conversion ratio, as well as careful management, would be required to make private investment in state-initiated enterprise more attractive than cash redemption.

If this technique is not used in Viet-Nam, industrial development will not only be slowed, but it is likely that cash payments to landlords under the reform program, an important segment of the nation's sparse capital accumulation, will either be dissipated in consumption or be reinvested in land. The resulting inflationary pressure might expand luxury imports and cause a depletion of already scarce foreign exchange, but it would probably not have a great enough influence on farm prices to be of any substantial benefit to the new landowner. Substitution of capital for consumer imports in the aid program, one solution already proposed, would itself be inflationary. This effect could only be prevented by a reduction in military forces, the nonproductive beneficiaries of the great majority of the aid. But certainly successful agrarian and industrial development would make as important a contribution to long-range political stability as a division of troops.

If neither a greatly expanded credit program is launched nor new investment opportunities created for bond-holding landlords, the latest dramatic announcement of agrarian reform may also, in the long run, prove of little value to the tenant farmer. The economic and political consequences for Viet-Nam would be most unhappy.

Commentary: LINDHOLM *on* GITTINGER

IN HIS ANALYSIS of Ordinance No. 57, Gittinger does not consider some of the probable economic effects of some of the provisions, nor does he consider whether the action was a wise use of the limited technical and financial resources of Viet-Nam.

Article 3 sets the maximum land holdings at 100 hectares, only 30 of which may be actually exploited by the landowner: This seems to mean that a landlord may not operate a rice farm in excess of 30 hectares. (It is implied that the maximum holding applies only to rice land, but this is not specifically stated in Article 3; however, Article 4 excludes land used to raise industrial crops, which apparently means any crop other than rice.)

There is an unconscious economic assumption in Article 3 that it is more important that the size of the ownership of rice land remain relatively large than that the size of cultivation be large. The basis of this position apparently is that it is more vital that the landlord's income based on rents provide a certain level of income than that rice be cultivated on a rather large scale under one ownership.

If Viet-Nam is to raise the per capita income and still compete on the international rice markets, modern rice cultivation methods may have to be used. Large-scale production might be much more important in achieving efficient methods in rice cultivation than would be the case for a number of other crops, such as coffee, fruit, or tobacco, where the size of a farm is not limited by law. However, under the present law, landowners could only apply modern rice cultivation methods if they used the necessary equipment on a co-operative basis.

Also, it might be desirable to require farmers not raising rice to make an economic sacrifice, which might be accomplished by a tax on agricultural land other than rice land. The rate of this tax could be based on the size of the holding and the value of the land, not upon its actual productivity.[114]

The two most interesting articles to students of economics and finance are 21 and 22, which provide for the method of payment to the owners of the rice land that is expropriated by the government.

[114] See pp. 312-14 for a discussion of land taxation. (ED.)

As Gittinger explained, ten percent of the total payment is to be made in cash and the remainder in "registered non-transferable bonds guaranteed by the state bearing an annual interest of 3 percent and amortized in 12 years." Although these bonds are generally non-negotiable, they may be used to pay "land and inheritance taxes owed on the expropriated lands." In addition, they may be used at par value to pay for a "subscription to securities of any enterprise created by the state in the framework of a program of national economic development.[115] The obvious economic purpose of this provision is to give landlords losing land an opportunity to become industrialists, which is certainly commendable but its implementation may cause economic difficulties.

Article 22 does not mention the way bonds can be used after receipt by a new business, nor does it indicate that they cannot be purchased or discounted by the National Bank. However, the provision that title is nontransferable would certainly seriously restrict the use of these bonds as collateral.

A loophole may be in the first sentence of Article 22, which states, "The aforesaid bonds may be pledged and are legal tender for mortgage debts contracted with the Agricultural Credit Agency." If this route were selected, a landowner could put up the property in his possession as security for a mortgage loan. After the loan was received, he could use his bonds to retire the mortgage. This would leave him with free funds to be used to invest in industry, while the land he owned would again be free. If later additional funds were needed to develop his lands, he could apply for another mortgage loan. This procedure would permit the conversion of bonds into money, within the provisions of Ordinance No. 57, but in so doing would raise several questions: Where would the Agricultural Credit Agency obtain its funds? Would the landlord, under these circumstances, purchase gold or a new automobile instead of placing his new liquid assets into a new industry?

Commentary: A VIETNAMESE OFFICIAL[116] *on* GITTINGER

IN GENERAL, Gittinger's treatment of the agrarian reform problem is accurate. However, a few additional comments will help to clarify the situation.

[115] See Wurfel's comment on this point on p. 210. (ED.)
[116] Name on file with Michigan State University Press.

It is true that, at the beginning, execution of the program was slowed down by internal troubles, especially around April, 1955, by the repression of the Binh Xuyen and the religious sects, the Cao Dai and Hoa Hao. Moreover, the Ministry of Agriculture, which controlled the general direction for agrarian reform, did not have sufficient means to carry out the program.

As to the transfer of lands, some delays were inevitable. It goes without saying that if such a program—a completely new experience for young Viet-Nam—was to be successful, thorough studies were necessary and administrative procedures had to be established. A great part of the delay resulted from a change in leadership of the Department of Agrarian Reform. Almost immediately after Ordinance No. 57 had been promulgated in October, 1956, the government appointed Do Van Cong to replace Nguyen Van Thsi as head of the Department.

The landowners' hostility to the expropriation of their lands is easy to understand. It was only natural for them to try various ways and means to escape being dispossessed. Over and beyond this normal economic reaction, the Vietnamese, more than any other people, are strongly attached to their land, particularly if the land is inherited: The son who sells land given him by his parents dishonors himself and commits a breach of filial piety. This attitude was gradually changed by an intensive propaganda campaign conducted by the Department of Agrarian Reform. Landowners, for the most part, saw the necessity and validity of the government's measure in the face of Communist peril. To protect their interests as far as possible, they did request to take part in all meetings, councils, and commissions to discuss the practical applications of the ordinance.

XVII.   Industrial Development Efforts

LAWRENCE MORRISON[117]

THE GUIDING PRINCIPLES of the French colonial economic system in Viet-Nam were: (1) the exploitation of natural resources for export, and (2) the reservation of the Vietnamese market for manufactured products of France. Every natural resource that could be profitably exported was exploited, and only those industries which supported that exploitation, or which served the local market without infringing on French interests, were privileged to exist. This rigidly channeled development resulted in an almost total absence of local production for satisfying the Vietnamese demand for manufactured goods. Consumer production was confined to those items which were uneconomic to import from France or which were peculiar to the culture and not available elsewhere.

One exception was the manufacture of textiles. There were many weaving factories which, though modest in size, were definitely larger than handicraft and cottage industry. Yarn-spinning capacity was about 100,000 spindles. Textiles were produced in north Viet-Nam in large quantity. Even so, annual textile imports amounted to tens of millions of dollars, and France was almost the sole source of supply. This is but one of many examples of goods imported from France which could have been produced economically in Viet-Nam.

During the Japanese occupation of Viet-Nam in World War II, and the eight years of the Indochina war which followed, Vietnamese industry was seriously affected. In World War II Allied bombing of industrial and mining operations and of transportation facilities were part of the campaign against the occupied territories supplying the Japanese war effort. In the Indochina war the Viet-Minh suppressed, as unproletarian, the traditional handicraft silk industry, next to agriculture the largest native industry, and destroyed, in one area of central Viet-Nam alone, more than two thousand pedal looms, painstakingly carved from wood. This tragic destruction accomplished its purpose by returning the silk producers to the land, where they raised food for their malefactors.

The wrecking of industrial installations is only a part of the story. Industry was further crippled by the destruction of communications and transportation. Highways, bridges, railroads, canals, barges, and tugs, all shared in the devastation.

When the Geneva Agreement divided the country into two areas, the division was a mixed blessing to south Viet-Nam. It cut off Free Viet-Nam from its source of coal and cement—two extremely important factors in an industrial base—and necessitated adding these to the already

---

[117] Chief of Industry Division and Mining, USOM, Saigon, 1955-57.

swollen roster of imports. With the exception of coal, cement, and a minor part of its textile supply, Free Viet-Nam, industrially and commercially speaking, lost little else from the partition. The north had always been an agriculturally deficit area, dependent on the south to augment its food supply.

Under present conditions Viet-Nam is dependent on economic aid for its existence. There is a very real question about the durability of political independence when it is not supported by economic independence, and in the case of Free Viet-Nam the lack of even a bare minimum of economic self-sufficiency makes enduring political independence only an illusion.

The survival of Free Viet-Nam as a sovereign free nation is underwritten by American aid, which is available on a year-to-year basis and is subject to variation according to Congressional reaction to a multitude of influences, many of which are completely divorced from the Vietnamese facts of life. The majority of the aid is used in a manner that maintains an extravagant standard of living, raised to its present level as a result of eleven years of heavy foreign spending in Viet-Nam.

Vietnamese leaders are almost unanimous in their belief that the standard of living cannot be allowed to drop very much if the present hard-won anti-Communist political gains are to be preserved. This contention may or may not be true. However, if it is a fact, it is clear that the United States Congress can exercise a veto on Viet-Nam's independence, and probably its freedom. The nation's dependence on the United States is, or should be, a matter of great embarrassment to both countries. And it is probably a source of propaganda to the Viet-Minh, who can make a strong case that the United States is effectively replacing France as the new master of Free Viet-Nam.

If the nation is to remain free, not only free of communism but also of external aid, it is vital for it to expand its economy. With a predominantly agricultural economy producing two major crops whose export markets are shrinking, Viet-Nam is in a difficult situation. Even if it were to regain its prewar export market potential, which is unlikely, it is doubtful that it could earn enough foreign exchange to support anything resembling its present demand for imported goods. If this demand for manufactured goods must be satisfied as a matter of political survival, then Viet-Nam must develop the industrial capacity to satisfy at least a part of it. The extent to which manufacturing can be developed will determine in large measure how much of the present standard of living can be maintained after foreign aid is reduced or eliminated and Viet-Nam must stand on its own.

An effort to aid Viet-Nam in the fields of industry and mining began in January, 1955, with the establishment of a one-man Industry and Mining Division in the United States Operations Mission to Viet-Nam. Prior to this date another division in USOM was responsible for these fields, but a Vietnamese-French agreement concerning technical aid to Viet-Nam specified that France should be the primary source of such aid. Except for a few instances when it was possible to "bootleg" technical assistance, USOM technical activity was practically nonexistent. Consequently, there had been no external effort to aid industry in Viet-Nam other than that which came about on a chance basis through United States aid to France.

On the Vietnamese side, there was no government action toward industrial development. The one Vietnamese organization concerned with industrial affairs, the Direction General of Mines, Industry, and Handicrafts, in the Ministry of National Economy, numbered perhaps three or four men in its professional ranks. However, these men lacked experience with industry other than their government's control activities; as colonial functionaries, they had little opportunity to develop the initiative, attitude, and professional stature required in their new role as nation builders. The Vietnamese government recognized this deficiency, and a Ministry of Plan was established in early 1955. It was staffed by some of the ablest technicians to be found among the Vietnamese expatriates in France. Shortly afterward the Minister of Plan resigned. The remaining people, most of whom had been recruited by the Minister and were personally loyal to him, became politically suspect and, after the Minister's departure, were leaderless and statureless, both as a group and as individuals. Energetic but understaffed, unfamiliar with conditions in their own country, reduced to a lower status and poorly placed in the government hierarchy, this group suffered one setback after another and never really got started as an effective planning organization. This was the situation of the counterpart organization in early 1955 when the first opportunity presented itself for direct United States aid to Viet-Nam in the industrial field.

The first proposal for American aid came from the Direction General of Mines, Industries, and Handicrafts. It requested a coal deposit survey specifically for the purpose of determining the feasibility and requirements for exploitation by strip-mining methods. The Director General, doubling as Principal Engineer of Mines, was being advised by a French mining engineer employed by the Vietnamese government on loan from the French Overseas Mining and Geological Service. A strip-mining survey project based on the discussions, reports, and other supporting documents submitted by the two mining engineers was approved by the International Cooperation Administration in Washington, D.C. (ICA/W). Preparatory work prerequisite for the survey had been ordered and, during the first weeks of the project, reports from the mine site indicated that everything was proceeding according to plan. The reports raised questions about the mine that neither of the government mining engineers were able to answer. It developed that they had never been to the mine site and that all the information and data concerning the mine had been pieced together from various diaries and reports, some dating back to the last century and obviously obsolete. At USOM request, the Vietnamese government arranged an inspection trip attended by the USOM Industry and Mining Officer and the French Mining Adviser; the Vietnamese Principal Engineer of Mines was unable to attend. The visit showed that the reports of progress were false, and little had been accomplished to prepare for the survey. Further investigation showed that there was not enough known about the deposit to justify a specialized exploitation survey, and the project was canceled.

This minor fiasco exposed the gullibility of the USOM officer and the fallacy of overlooking important details in the interest of getting something done. It exposed the physical laziness and the professional and technical ignorance (for it is hardly fair to consider the event a fraud) of the personnel of the Vietnamese government Mining Section.

Greatly embarrassed by this affair, the government set out to develop the area to the limit of its resources without recourse to American aid. To carry out this work, the government engaged a young Vietnamese mining engineer, recently returned from France after completion of his studies, and a French civilian mining engineer with some twenty years of experience in Vietnamese coal field development and mining. After a period of approximately one year of prospecting and mine development work, the stock of reliable information about the mine was increased and the mine itself put into operation on a limited hand-working basis. At that time the French government assumed the salary obligation of the mining engineer and augmented the Vietnamese government staff by the addition of a mining geologist to study the subsurface in the mine area. The Vietnamese government engaged the services of a Japanese drilling contractor to do the necessary core drilling work in the mine area, and USOM brought in a coal-mining development specialist to conduct a pre-project investigation of the entire deposit to determine the feasibility of a full-scale exploration.

The combined efforts of the Vietnamese, French, and American specialists were as successful as the previous experience was abortive. As a result of the excellent co-operation and co-ordination of the technicians of the two foreign aid groups the work proceeded rapidly with a minimum of overlap. Within a short time, available information indicated that the potential of the area was great. ICA/W approved an aid project for exploration, which started in early 1958. Whether or not the exploration survey leads to a mining development satisfactory to Vietnamese requirements and aspirations, limited operation of the mine has taken place, and its modest production has alleviated a fuel shortage in towns near the mine. This limited operation is a tribute to reawakened Vietnamese initiative, assisted by French technical aid. The large-scale exploration and possible further mine development will have resulted from the type of integrated aid effort which could serve as a model for other situations in which two or more external aid groups are working in the same problem area.

In mid-1955 the second proposal for American aid was submitted by the Direction General of Planning and concerned the reconstruction and expansion of textile production in Binh Dinh province. This proposal was an example of the inspired and comparatively high quality of workmanship performed by the Direction General of Planning early in its existence.

Four provinces of central Viet-Nam—Phu Yen, Binh Dinh, Quang Nam, and Quang Ngai—had comprised the Viet-Minh 5th Interzone, which was one of the areas south of the 17th parallel that had served as a regrouping and embarkation area for Viet-Minh troops under the terms of the Geneva Agreement. This zone had been almost exclusively in Viet-Minh control throughout the Indochina war, with the consequence that its economy had been reduced to subsistence level. The departing Viet-Minh had thoroughly propagandized the people, terrorizing them with tales of the horrors that awaited them under National Government rule and occupation by the National Army. The Vietnamese were assured that the Viet-Minh would be returning as victors of the elections one year later and that the slightest co-operation with the National Government would be judged ruthlessly and bring the harshest punishment to offenders. The government regarded it a matter of primary political and economic necessity that measures be taken to restore the area's shattered economy not only to relieve the suffering of these people and obviate the need of continued relief, but also to win their allegiance to the National Government. The joint Vietnamese-American project for reconstruction of the war-damaged Dong Cam Dam in Phu Yen accomplished these objectives in that province by providing for the irrigation of a large area of parched land which formerly had been highly productive. In the minds of the people, and in reality, the dam, with its canal system, was the key to prosperity in that area; its successful reconstruction in record time was a singularly and dramatically important act which rallied the people to the National Government.

In the province of Binh Dinh the silk industry was the counterpart of Phu Yen's Dong Cam Dam. The majority of the population of this province was in some way associated with sericulture, silk spinning, and weaving. Prior to the Indochina war thousands of hectares were devoted to growing mulberry trees, and tens of thousands of people were engaged in supplying or operating the several thousand handicraft looms and the large French silk mill at Phu Phong. The Viet-Minh destroyed all this— mulberry trees, worms, spinning and weaving equipment—and forced the people back to food production for the Viet-Minh armies. The Vietnamese government planning group, which had done such a magnificent job of planning and co-ordinating the dam project, had prepared a physical and financial plan for reconstructing the Binh Dinh silk industry and for diversifying into cotton and rayon weaving and finishing. The plan was workmanlike in all major respects and was used with little change as a basis for comprehensive planning by the government and USOM.

By this time the earlier mentioned internal difficulties of the government planning group were seriously affecting their ability to perform, and they lost several of their members. At the same time, the chief of the group was given an additional assignment which, because of its immediate importance, demanded the major portion of his time. Thus, the work on the Binh Dinh plan suffered the loss of its principal technician and the administrator of the over-all planning work. Work on the plan proceeded slowly to a consideration of the organization and staffing of the groups which were to carry out the project. Normally, the task of accomplishing projects would fall to the appropriate functional department, in this case the Direction General of Mines, Industry, and Handi crafts of the Ministry of National Economy; however, as has been previously mentioned, this organization lacked personnel with the necessary ability and experience for an undertaking of this character. Because of this, the chief of the planning group wanted his people to carry through on the project implementation as they had done so successfully in the case of the Dong Cam Dam project. However, the weakened planning group had no others of sufficient caliber and experience to head up the job with the exception of the chief himself. It was inconceivable that a project of such magnitude be administered on a part-time basis by a man who, although extremely capable, was already overtaxed by responsibility for two assignments, each of which deserved full attention. Regretfully, the project was set aside until such time as Vietnamese government personnel would become available on a full-time basis.

The Binh Dinh proposal again became the subject of government interest about a year later when economic conditions in that province had left the people in a state of near destitution, resulting in a serious deterioration of the political situation. The people of the province co-operated to the fullest extent when the original field surveys for the proposal had been made. Their hopes had been raised by the promises of help from the National Government. It is not difficult to imagine their disappointment when the government could not follow through on its promises and their dissatisfaction when they were bombarded constantly with propaganda pronouncements glorifying the National Government as their benefactor. The industry and planning staffs of USOM and the government agreed that one part of the original proposal, a cotton textile plant, should be developed as rapidly as possible by the National Investment Fund (NIF), whose chief engineer was the exadministrator of the dam project. Field investigators overcame their distaste of venturing once more among the disgruntled, desperate people of Binh Dinh to collect current data and study various plant sites. NIF negotiated with the provincial government for land acquisition and on the other details concerning the management, ownership, and legal conditions governing the operation of the proposed mill. The negotiations quickly ran afoul of the avarice of the local politicos whose price for co-operation was a controlling equity share of the business.

The demand of the local politicians was extortion, and both NIF and USOM refused to have anything to do with it. Unfortunately, the Binh Dinh proposal—vitally needed and eminently justified—had to be shelved and, to this date, has remained inactive. Why the government allowed gross corruption to interfere with the realization of the project is anyone's guess. The reasons must have been powerful to make the National Government ignore the desperate need of the Binh Dinh people. This affair illustrates one of the truths about the matter of giving aid—it is futile to hope that complete integrity can be maintained and still do the job, because objective merit sometimes plays a minor role.

The case histories of the preceding projects span the period from early 1955 to mid-1956. They represent two of several attempts of the government during this period to take action on the problem of expanding industrial production. Of the others, the only one worthy of mention concerns the establishment of a development financing organization—the National Investment Fund mentioned in connection with the Binh Dinh proposal above.

Those in the government who were responsible for planning the economic reconstruction and development of Viet-Nam realized, after one year of experience with American aid as an independent nation, that one of their most serious deficiencies was the lack of technicians to study and program the use of available resources to the best advantage. The USOM technical staff supposedly filled this need, but in practice these technicians were only available to the Vietnamese government as consultants. USOM personnel were situated in the USOM building rather than with their various counterparts in Vietnamese government offices. As a consequence, contact between the specialist and his counterpart was sporadic. Also, the dual responsibility of American technicians as guardians of the purse strings and as technical advisers made complete objectivity in the latter capacity difficult, if not impossible, to maintain. USOM was not adequately staffed to take on the task of Vietnamese government planning; in fact, it sorely missed personnel to map out its own activities. The government needed and wanted foreign technicians to augment and guide its own planning staff, but in order to be effective they felt that these technicians should work full time on government premises and be solely responsible to them.

The problem of acquiring foreign technicians was discussed with USOM because of the Vietnamese government request that aid funds be used for this purpose. The difficulties of such a scheme were considerable. First, the language barrier would make it necessary to work through skillful technical interpreters, who were not available. One of the governing policies of American aid is that all technicians provided under the program are required to be American citizens. Too few of the Vietnamese staff spoke English with adequate fluency to avoid the use of interpreters, and it would be virtually impossible to find enough French-speaking Americans who could meet the technical specifications of the job. Second, the understaffed government planning group would require a large number of foreign technicians to round out its personnel for a full-scale planning effort. If there were a real lack of Vietnamese technicians, this would be unavoidable, but there were actually many who were misused or unused. As an alternative to a large semipermanent group of foreign technicians, handicapped by language difficulties, it seemed more practical for the government to build up a full complement of Vietnamese technicians, supported by a smaller but adequate group of foreign specialists until the government staff was able to function without external help. This was suggested, with the assurance that an increased government planning group would receive personnel and material assistance from American aid. Months passed, and nothing was done. Action on the suggestion required the agreement and participation of high officials, which the planning chief was apparently unable to get.

In an effort to solve the planning problem and circumvent the difficulties, the chief of planning appealed to the United Nations Technical Assistance Board (UNTAB). He requested that a group of specified technicians be assigned to the Vietnamese government for planning purposes, and, as a result, UNTAB agreed to provide a team to conduct an economic survey. The team arrived some months later and conducted a three-month study, which yielded a massive report covering every important phase of Vietnamese economic activity.

Of the sections concerning industry, mining, and forestry, only that on forestry was an example of professional competence and subsequent usefulness. Taken as a whole, the UNTAB report suffered from a lack of consideration and apparent concern about the problem of accomplishing the measures it recommended. It was conspicuously silent in the matter of financing, without which any consideration of recommendations is academic. The report would have been useful as a frame of reference for a group with responsibility for carrying out its proposals. Lacking this responsibility, the UNTAB group could have served its purpose more effectively by translating its conclusions into meaningful, practical suggestions on how to proceed with the problems it pointed up. Unfortunately for Viet-Nam, the report was only a half-completed job, and, as such, has joined the ranks of numerous similar reports gathering dust on the bookshelves of the world's underdeveloped nations.

For some months prior to the release of the UNTAB report, a Vietnamese businessman had been negotiating with a large United States paper company, hereafter called Papco, on the organization of a joint Vietnamese-American papermaking venture. The idea was to use large stands of Vietnamese pine as a source of pulping material. Papco offered to make a survey, for which the Vietnamese interests would pay a fraction of the cost as evidence of good faith. The report of adequate supplies of pulping material and the rough economic estimates contained in the UNTAB survey quickened Papco interest, and one of its officials went to Viet-Nam for an on-the-spot investigation of the situation.

The talks between Papco and the Vietnamese interests produced a preliminary proposal in which they agreed that Papco would make a comprehensive survey of industrial-scale papermaking in Viet-Nam. If the results justified such a venture, it would be organized along the following lines: (1) Vietnamese private investment would contribute the majority of the total capital required. (2) Papco investment would amount to a small minority of the capital requirement—between ten to twenty percent. This investment would be in U.S. dollars converted to local currency at a rate acceptable to the Vietnamese government. (3) The government would invest the amount necessary to make up the difference between the total capital required and the sum of private Vietnamese and Papco investment. (4) Papco would expect investment security from the government by the usual guarantee covering expropriation, repatriation of capital and profits, and salary transfers. (5) Papco would set up the facilities under a turn-key contract. In other words, it would have complete charge of all phases of the project concerned with the actual construction and operation of the facilities. In turn, Papco would guarantee the performance of the plant. (6) All imports required for building and operating the plant would be acquired through regular Vietnamese import channels, and the joint company would pay in local currency, as would be normal for any Vietnamese company. (7) Papco would, where economically and technically justified, supply pulp and papermaking machinery through its manufacturing affiliates. The balance of the equipment, representing approximately 50 percent of the total equipment value, would be procured on a competitive bid basis. Charges for Papco machinery would be the lowest prices to other buyers of identical equipment under export turn-key job contracts. (8) The joint company would require forest concessions and would request reductions in duties and taxes in order to increase profits up to the minimum required to attract private investment.

In discussion with USOM, Papco stressed the exploratory nature and flexibility of the preliminary proposal. Their representative made it clear from the start that his company's primary interest in the project was to be able to supply the equipment and that their decision to invest would depend on acceptance of that feature of the proposal. Other than that, Papco had no preconceived ideas concerning details of how its investment would be made.

USOM acquainted Papco with the three methods provided by the Vietnamese government for converting foreign currency to Vietnamese currency for investment purposes: (1) Conversion at the legal rate of U.S. $1 to 35 piasters, with unrestricted use of the piaster proceeds. (2) Conversion at the controlled free market rate of approximately U.S. $1 to 75 piasters, with restricted use of the piaster proceeds. (3) Conversion at a rate negotiable by investor and foreign holder of blocked piaster accounts, with government approval and more rigidly restricted use of the piaster proceeds.

Papco was informed that if it converted at any rate in excess of the legal rate, there was a possibility that the joint company would be denied the privilege of importing goods through the Commercial Import Program.

The Commercial Import Program is the U.S.-financed import plan whereby selected Vietnamese imports are paid for with funds supplied by American aid. The Vietnamese importer must, in turn, pay in local currency at the legal rate for each dollar, or equivalent, of the foreign currency cost. This is the process which converts U.S. dollars to Vietnamese money used to pay the local costs of the aid program without causing runaway inflation.

USOM thought that the company might be denied the import privilege because it could be considered that Vietnamese dollars acquired at a premium rate would be used to purchase imported equipment at a lower rate, resulting in a profit on the currency transaction. Papco pointed out that the Vietnamese investment in the project would exceed the total import bill. As a consequence, it might be considered that the Papco investment would not be used for importing. Nevertheless, Papco was completely flexible in this respect. They stated that once it was decided to invest, they would convert at any rate of exchange acceptable to the Vietnamese government. USOM offered to present the details of the proposal to ICA/W and request a ruling on the proposed importing method with respect to existing regulations.

ICA reaction to the proposal was hostile. This came as a shock to USOM, which had received the proposal favorably. The complete arbitrariness of the ICA attitude was surprising. It lacked any basis in violation of regulations. Apparently, the proposal offended the sensibilities of ICA reviewers—but in matters either unfamiliar to them or outside their jurisdiction. Their displeasure was rooted in three particulars of the proposal.

First, it disturbed ICA that Papco might be allowed to convert their cash dollar investment to local currency at a higher rate than the legal rate of exchange. This would result in two evils according to ICA: (1) it would gain Papco a higher equity in the venture than their investment warranted: and (2) the cheap piasters thus obtained would be used by the joint company to import equipment at the legal rate of exchange. The first alleged evil is fanciful nonsense. The legal rate of exchange is a completely unrealistic measure of the value of Vietnamese currency and exists mainly for American aid and monetary control purposes. No Vietnamese, private or government, expects a foreign investor to value his capital at the legal rate; they realize that it would not be fair. But, the annoying thing about ICA in this instance is not its naïvete; it is its interference in a matter which is strictly not ICA business. The amount of equity Papco gets for its investment is a matter for negotiation with other investors in the venture within the limits imposed by Vietnamese law. The second alleged evil can be credited to ICA ignorance of the Vietnamese government regulations governing currency conversion. According to these regulations the proceeds of any foreign investment conversion at a premium rate may not be used for importing through the Commercial Import Program. Furthermore, the proceeds are blocked for uses specified by the government and may not be withdrawn without its approval. This currency conversion plan had been drafted jointly by the Vietnamese government and USOM and had been approved by ICA in Washington. The question need never have been referred to ICA in the first place except for USOM timidity. Nevertheless, having the question before them, ICA might have taken the trouble to review their own files on the subject before taking their position.

Second, ICA contended that, in reality, Papco would merely be investing a portion of its anticipated profits from the sale of equipment to the company, implying that in some vague and unidentified manner they would get that much and more in return and that this would be undesirable.

Two features of this attitude are disquieting: First, ICA could not have had the slightest idea of the magnitude of Papco profit from the sale of equipment, because the equipment to be supplied by Papco was as yet undetermined. The amount of its investment had been estimated originally at approximately $300,000. By the most conservative estimate, Papco would have to enjoy a net profit after taxes equivalent to 25 percent of sales in order to invest that amount out of its profits. This is a rare profit in the heavy machinery business. The second disquieting feature is that, regardless of the lack of validity, there is something sinister about the ICA objection on this basis. Papco was the only foreign firm, in the writer's experience, that proved a willingness to invest and had a concrete proposal for genuine manufacturing operations in Viet-Nam. There were several inquiries concerning pseudomanufacturing operations, such as final assembling. These were devices to circumvent restrictions on imports of finished refrigerators, air conditioners, and automobiles. Others concerned soft drink bottling, milk reconstituting, and similar businesses. From the viewpoint of national benefit and economic importance, they cannot be considered in the same category as the paper project. Papco was ready to back up their evaluation with hard cash. The fact that they might invest only their anticipated profit from the sale of equipment does not cheapen their investment or detract from the risk involved. They would still be gambling to the same extent as other investors. Furthermore, their reputation would be at stake as well as the considerable effort of their staff in developing the project. The main target of ICA in this case seems to be Papco's desire to profit from the venture. But, there was no indication that this profit would be unearned or unreasonable. Perhaps too long an association with "grant" aid programs had dulled the realization that the profit motive is not in itself immoral or irresponsible, and had led some in ICA to the notion that they must *a priori* defend the Vietnamese against the depredations of marauding American businessmen.

The third ICA argument was that the proposed survey might lack complete objectivity because of the conflict of interest considering Papco's position as a potential supplier. This concern was completely valid. However, the measures taken to resolve the problem left much to be desired. ICA insisted that its own team would make a survey, thus obviating the need for a Papco study. Papco felt that surveys conducted by disinterested parties tended to be academic. In any event, it would be necessary for Papco to make its own survey to gather detailed information for a specific proposal and to assure itself that it could guarantee the performance of the plant. The type of investigation intended by ICA would not include this amount of detail. Papco suggested that its report would be available to ICA for review and approval. If ICA found the survey inadequate or biased, it could make one of its own, but if Papco's was accepted, it would save the government needless expense. For some unexplained reason ICA rejected the logic of this idea, insisting that an independent survey would be made. Furthermore, they warned that American aid support for the project would be withheld if the Papco survey preceded theirs. Papco was in a bad spot. It had technicians waiting for final arrangements on the Vietnamese financing. To delay their efforts until ICA recruited and organized a survey team would be costly and disruptive. In fact, there was a good chance that the Vietnamese businessmen, unfamiliar with the difference between the two surveys, would be reluctant to pay. Why pay for something when it could be had free of charge?

Papco made their survey a short time later when the ICA objection had been withdrawn. It showed that a pulp and paper industry could be successful in Viet-Nam if there were proper forest management and if taxes were lowered to reasonable levels. The ICA-sponsored survey which followed took a dim view of the project. Their investigators neglected the possibility that existing conditions could be altered. Papco is now negotiating its proposal with the Vietnamese, and the ICA attitude toward the project has improved.

In the final analysis, Papco's trouble came about as a result of its efforts to deal honestly and openly. Without breach of good conduct, Papco could have avoided contact with United States agencies in Viet-Nam and transacted its business with the parties directly concerned. Many American businessmen have found this to be the wisest procedure. It is evident that ICA anticipated foul play, but there was not a shred of evidence to support that feeling. Local observers of the affair interpreted this fear of being victimized by its own businessmen as United States government resentment to competition from private industry.

By the latter half of 1956 two proposals for industrial projects were submitted to USOM by the Administration of External Aid (AEA), a division of the Vietnamese government that performed the function of controllership over American aid. They concerned the building of plants for processing sugar cane and cotton—both important commodities in Vietnamese life. With the exception of the paper project, and to a lesser extent the NIF affair, the lack of accomplishment in industrial development in Viet-Nam was a result of untimeliness and government inertia and disinterest. The case histories of the sugar and cotton proposals show what happened when the government inertia and disinterest were overcome and the burden of performance was placed squarely on the American aid program.

Prior to the Viet-Minh hostilities, the portion of Viet-Nam south of the 17th parallel had extensive land area in the production of sugar cane. There were three industrial size mills producing semi-refined sugar, which constituted the bulk of the annual demand of approximately 50,000 metric tons. The war resulted in destruction of two of the mills, as well as the canal system and sampan fleet which were the supply arteries of the remaining mill at Hiep Hoa. Loss of these mills and insecurity in the countryside caused farmers to abandon tens of thousands of hectares of sugar fields. The small refining unit from the Hiep Hoa mill was set up in the port of Saigon, and equipment was added to enable the refining of imported raw sugar at a rate of approximately 18,000 tons per year. The Hiep Hoa mill was out of production for several years, but with the cessation of hostilities went back into operation at about 15 percent of capacity.

In mid-1956 the government submitted a proposal for the redevelopment of sugar growing and milling in the Tuy Hoa area of central Viet-Nam. This proposal involved: (1) the reintroduction of sugar cane as a crop in the area where the Dong Cam Dam irrigation system had been rebuilt, and (2) the erection of a 1,000-ton per day mill to replace the one destroyed there during the war. Taken by itself the proposal was a good one, but from an economy-wide point of view, compared to other alternatives, it left much to be desired. The government had defined the problem in terms of one solution—reconstructing and expanding cane culture and milling in central Viet-Nam—while ignoring the existence of the Hiep Hoa mill in south Viet-Nam, which was then operating at a mere 15 percent of capacity.

There were manifold reasons for the Vietnamese government approach. First, the deplorable situation in central Viet-Nam made it extremely desirable for the National Government to revitalize the economy of this area. In fact, political considerations were so overwhelming that there was a split in government thinking on where to re-establish the sugar industry. The Ministry of Agriculture, perhaps with the balance of power in its favor, was insisting on the province of Quang Nam, surely the most destitute in central Viet-Nam, as an ideal location. In opposition, the AEA was urging the Tuy Hoa area of Phu Yen province, which was by far the most ideal location on strictly technical and economic merit.

Second, the government wanted to "Vietnamize" certain French-owned industries, including the Hiep Hoa mill, and delay would work in Viet-Nam's favor. That this was the motive in this case was confirmed by subsequent appeals to American aid to finance Vietnamese equity participation in the Hiep Hoa Company.

Third, it would be extremely awkward and impolitic for the government to take action which would directly benefit a French company to the detriment of Vietnamese private interests. With loss of the means of transporting cane to the Hiep Hoa mill, many farmers changed over from cane to rice culture and others formed co-operatives to build and operate ten- to twenty-ton per day mills. There were enough of these small milling co-operatives for them to be a significant factor in the supply of sugar to the countryside. These outlying areas were on severely reduced rations in times of short supply, which were frequent because of import difficulties and black market operations. The small operators were numerous and remotely located and, therefore, difficult to observe. They took advantage of the situation to violate the government ceiling prices on sugar, often charging as much as 50 percent premium. This enabled them to outbid the price-controlled Hiep Hoa Company for the cane production of the fewer remaining independent farmers, thus making the Hiep Hoa cane supply picture even darker than it otherwise might have been.

On the one hand, it is not difficult to understand the government reluctance to consider the possibilities offered by Hiep Hoa in the solution of the national sugar problem. The alternative of wedding the central Viet-Nam political and economic difficulties to the sugar problem and solving the two problems simultaneously was an easy and attractive way out. On the other hand, USOM felt that it would be a gross error to agree to the use of aid funds for the building of a new plant when existing facilities remained largely unused. The Hiep Hoa interests made repeated proposals, voluntarily and at the request of the Minister of National Economy, for a joint government-Hiep Hoa project to re-establish full-scale production at the existing mill. Company engineers had planned in detail a full program for the reconstruction of the agriculture, the canal system, the canal fleet, and mill modernization and expansion. The company was willing to invest heavily in increased capacity if the government would undertake the dredging of canals, the financing of the canal fleet, and the financing of maintenance and fertilizers for the farmers. In support of this project, the company offered the free services of its technical and field staff which would provide invaluable experience in the complex operations and relationships between the farmers and the mill. In prewar times the Hiep Hoa Company provided the main canal transportation and financed the farmers by providing fertilizers and advancing payments against cane deliveries. But after the war the company felt that its status as a former colonial no longer afforded it adequate legal protection in the event of default by debtor farmers. Consequently, it believed that the government should assume responsibility for financing these services.

USOM succeeded in bringing the government and Hiep Hoa together for discussion on how the problem might be handled, and indicated willingness to consider the financing of an integrated project comprising a simultaneous reconstruction in south and central Viet-Nam. The first proposal to result from the joint discussions suggested that American aid finance a Vietnamese equity participation in the Hiep Hoa operation by paying for mill modernization and expansion. In view of the fact that the Hiep Hoa Company had expressed a willingness to make this investment itself, USOM considered it neither proper nor desirable to use aid funds for that purpose, and the proposal was declined. Further bilateral talks between the government and Hiep Hoa resulted in progress on resolving the differences without sacrificing the obvious advantage of the large private investment. It seemed at this time that an atmosphere of co-operation and mutual understanding had been established by the government and Hiep Hoa, and that USOM could make no further contribution to the achievement of an equitable, practicable agreement between them.

Thereafter, USOM withdrew from active participation in the matter of negotiating a formula and, on the assurance of the Vietnamese government that an agreement would be reached in time, concentrated on the task of designing a project based on the understanding that the Hiep Hoa mill expansion would be financed by private investment.

The diversity of things to be done in the reconstruction of the sugar industry and the interdependence of the various parts of the job made it apparent that all the diverse activities needed integration in a global project under unified authority with complete financing assured from the start. A global plan was designed with a projected government autonomous sugar authority as administrator of the project.

Concurrent with the drafting of the project, USOM provided a survey of the agricultural aspects of sugar cane production in Viet-Nam, conducted by one of the most respected authorities in the field. The report dealt exhaustively with the various aspects of cane production in the several areas of interest and confirmed the pre-eminence of the Tuy Hoa area as a candidate for development in central Viet-Nam. Also the Ministry of Agriculture started on the testing and multiplication of existing and new varieties of sugar cane, a process which would take from three to five years to achieve production in mill quantities.

The sugar development project proposal was submitted to ICA. The reaction was that the global project should be divided along functional and area lines into separate projects. At that time USOM was involved with the heavy load of project submissions for the 1957 fiscal year. There was not time to get the various USOM and Vietnamese government organizations who were functionally interested in the sugar proposal to draft and submit the many individual projects required, and the proposal succumbed under the sheer weight of red tape.

The partition of Viet-Nam deprived the area south of the 17th parallel of a domestic source of cotton yarn and the cotton-weaving facilities which were located in the north. Prior to the final closeout of the city of Haiphong, the Chinese owners of a 12,000-spindle cotton-spinning mill evacuated their equipment and staff to the south, with the intention of either selling out or setting up operations there. After six months of futile endeavor, working through a Vietnamese "front man" of low repute in the business and government circles of the south, the owners decided to move their equipment to Hong Kong or Formosa. USOM urged against this move and brought the owners into contact with the AEA, with the result that the first cotton-spinning company in Free Viet-Nam was formed to buy, erect, and operate the mill, financed with 10 million piasters of private investment and six million piasters of government investment through the NIF. Progress in erecting the mill was remarkable considering the disordered marking, crating, and deterioration of the equipment which resulted from its hasty evacuation from the north and from its improper storage during one year in the south. Completion of erection was, however, held up by delivery time on parts needed to replace those which were unusable.

The economics of cotton spinning are such that units of less than 30,000 spindles are uneconomic in a competitive market. Recent developments in equipment and improved management technique favor minimum size units of 40,000-50,000 spindles. Considering the economic facts and the need for a minimum of 40,000 spindles to satisfy the Vietnamese demand for cotton yarns alone, the government was anxious to expand the capacity of the unfinished mill by 20,000 spindles. It was estimated that 120,000 spindles on a three-shift operation would be required to produce the yarn to replace imports of all common cotton textile at then current rates of consumption. USOM-Viet-Nam negotiations began on a project to increase total capacity by 20,000 spindles, and some months later a cotton-spinning project proposal was drafted.

The cotton-spinning project encompassed all the activities necessary to assure the success of the venture. A projected survey was to study the market and other relevant factors and specify the proper type of equipment, in addition to which it assured expert appraisal of the alternative ways of integrating the new and existing facilities. It supplied complete technical services for engineering, erection, and starting up of operations, and a two-year management contract which would provide training for management and supervisors in all phases of plant operation. All hard currency requirements were to be supplied by a long-term, interest-bearing loan from American aid. The local currency requirements were to be met by a combination of private and government investment, the government holdings to be available for sale to private investors on demand.

At the same time, government discussions with the existing company were in progress on financing, capital structure, new private investment, government controls, and other matters related to the expansion. The company was actively seeking new venture capital with some success, and on the strength of satisfactory progress in the USOM-Viet-Nam project negotiations it had taken options on the purchase of additional land to accommodate the new facilities.

When the project proposal had received all required junior approvals, it was approved by the Vietnamese Secretary of State for National Economy and then was submitted to the Director of USOM for his signature, the final one required for submission to ICA in Washington, where it had already been approved in principle and had been allocated funds. The Director deferred signing the proposal, pending a decision on whether or not to assign the project to a proposed Vietnamese Industrial Development Commission (IDC). The contention was that the IDC should have its work cut out in advance so that there would be no lost motion when it started operating.

There were three reasons why such an action would be ill advised. First, the proposed IDC would require at least nine months, probably longer, to be organized, staffed, and put into operation. It seemed unreasonable and contrary to American and Vietnamese objectives and interests to impose this much delay on a project which was suitable for immediate approval and realization merely for the purpose of allowing the IDC to step into a ready-made situation. Second, a great deal of effort had been expended by the USOM and Vietnamese participants on this proposal and enthusiasm and good will were running high, with the knowledge that at long last, after two years of frustration, an industrial project of magnitude and major importance was on the verge of realization. Delay at this time meant endangering that good will and sacrificing the hard-won enthusiasm to foolish expedience. Third, the effort, good will, and enthusiasm of the various governmental organizations were matched by the private sector of the existing spinning company. They had worked hard at soliciting new investment and had spent scarce funds on additional property acquisition with explicit assurance that the expansion project would go through. Delay would tie up capital for a longer unproductive period than contemplated, sour potential investors on the venture, and reinforce the already too prevalent impression that the United States was vacillating, insincere, and incapable of delivering on promises. Assurances were given that these factors would receive thoughtful consideration. Current information is that the cotton-spinning project has, for the present at least, joined the ranks of sister-industry projects as a casualty of the United States government "know-how" and "efficiency."

Commentary: JOHN M. HUNTER[118] *on* MORRISON

To THE TWO guiding principles of the French colonial economic system, a third one, or perhaps a subprinciple, should be added: To impose an artificial intracolony division of labor on certain products

[118] Acting head, Department of Economics, Michigan State University.

in which Vietnamese businessmen would have found themselves competitors. Copra is a case in point. There may be others which should not be overlooked in considering potential Vietnamese production for domestic consumption or export.

On the need for industrial development, Morrison's remarks require further comment and elaboration. Essentially, he indicates that Viet-Nam cannot truly become independent without economic independence. This means, I take it, independence of the need for gratuitous aid, although self-sufficiency is mentioned. He assumes that the level of consumption (this probably should be explicitly put on a per capita basis) must not fall appreciably if Viet-Nam is to remain free. Further, he assumes that exports cannot be appreciably increased. *Ergo,* to reach the *desideratum* of "full independence" the economy of Viet-Nam must grow to fill the "aid gap," and one gathers that the bulk of this must come from industrialization. Granted that independence is desirable, it does not follow that it is possible or that the wisest policy is to seek this end in the shortest possible time. A "crash program" directed at this end would likely be unsuccessful, and more than likely be wasteful. Further, if Viet-Nam is to follow the pattern of other developing countries, it can expect, over a considerable time, to have a deficit in its balance of payments. Traditionally, this deficit has been filled by the inflow of long-term foreign investment, but no one knows when conditions suitable for large-scale movements of private foreign funds are apt to develop. Thus, the "aid gap" may be approximately synonymous with an "investment gap" for some time to come. It is realistic to recognize this and to devote considerable thought as to how one can operate comfortably under these circumstances with a minimum of infringement of sovereignty, real or imagined.

Morrison dismisses the possibilities of reducing per capita consumption and of increasing exportable production. Certainly, certain consumer luxuries imported in 1955-56 could well have been excluded without materially affecting the standard of living for most Vietnamese. In fact, their import may have actually contributed to political unrest. Further, the Vietnamese people might be willing to forego certain imports temporarily in favor of the importation of capital goods which would shortly result in increased production.

This does not mean that efforts should not be directed toward industrialization or the substitution of domestic production for imported goods. A viable economy is much less likely to be a possibility in anything like the near future that Morrison indicates is possible. An awareness of this will make current policies more realistic. Dealing with the problem as I see it will likely be more fruitful than equal resources devoted to attempting to solve the smaller magnitude problem as outlined by Morrison.

Care must be exercised in industrializing to supplant foreign aid or to cure a balance of payments deficit, as desirable as these objectives may be. Traditional international trade theory has currently fallen into some disrepute, but expensive errors can still be made when the concept of comparative advantage is ignored. The possibilities of expanded trade with other nations through or without such devices as the customs union may hold more promise than the attempt to produce many imported items locally.

Morrison neglected to include the most interesting section of his paper—conclusions. He is more qualified than I to do this, but there are some "lessons" in his accounts.

First, aid programs in underdeveloped countries are constantly faced with the problem of personnel shortage on both sides of the programs. Numbers of capable people are too small, and those available must bear multiple "key" responsibilities. American personnel frequently is not assigned for sufficient periods to accomplish long-run objectives. Inadequate "local" personnel is a part of the larger problem and will be solved only when the central problem is solved; there are possible ways to improve American personnel practices.

Second, oversupervision of aid programs by Washington is chronic. This is attributable, I think, to the zealousness of their opponents in seeking errors and making them *causes célèbres* in Congress and in popular journals. This leads field directors to "clear" every doubtful decision with ICA in Washington, to cover themselves in case of "possible" later criticism. A case in point is the Papco case. Neither the field directors nor ICA are really to blame for this state of affairs. Uninformed members of Congress (in some cases "irresponsible" is a better term), with the mechanism of an antagonistic press to carry their messages, encourage the kinds of bureaucratic controls which are stultifying.

Third, related to the above, aid programs should be considered much as research expenditures are regarded by businesses: There will be failures from which just as much can be learned as from successes. There may be much more to be gained from a project with a 50-50 chance of success than a similar-cost project with a 90-10 chance of success. Under current operating procedures, the selection of the latter is a foregone conclusion. Further, current procedures give a bias in project selection toward those which (1) produce immediate results and (2) produce easily identifiable results. In neither case is the best use of resources guaranteed.

Fourth, the problems dealt with in Viet-Nam by the American

aid program (economic development, securing political stability) are long-term problems. Therefore, long-term commitments and planning of aid expenditures are necessary.

Fifth, simplicity of aid projects and their objectives is crucial for both donors and recipients. Grouping project objectives (Morrison's cotton case is a good example) complicates already complicated problems, leads to delays, confuses the planners regarding basic aims, and leaves aid missions subject to probably legitimate charges of Machiavellianism.

Sixth, relations of private American investors in countries and American aid missions are frought with all sorts of difficulties, some of which are evident in Morrison's account. If this is a general problem, it deserves immediate attention; the problems and risks of foreign investment are great enough without adding the necessity to bicker with United States government agencies abroad. One of the effects of successful aid programs is to create an environment in which foreign investment will participate; the development of this environment will ultimately reduce the need for substantial aid programs.

Commentary: LINDHOLM *on* MORRISON

IN SPEAKING for the industrial development of Viet-Nam, Morrison rests his case on a three-part base. One is that American aid at the present level will not continue indefinitely, and therefore Viet-Nam must begin to produce many of the manufactured products it is now importing or it will suffer a sharp drop in its average income. The second part is that a country cannot be truly independent until it is economically independent, and that this is only possible if Viet-Nam develops industries, thus eliminating (or markedly decreasing) the need for economic aid. The third part, not mentioned but necessarily assumed, is that Viet-Nam, by concentrating on agricultural production, cannot hope to become economically independent or to maintain or increase per capita income, and therefore to maintain and increase the standard of living.

Viet-Nam is fortunate in its possession of an abundance of land, much of which is suitable for raising agricultural and forest products, such as coffee, tea, rice, fruits and nuts, hardwoods, sugar cane, pepper, and cinnamon. It is also strategically situated for intraregional trade. To the west is a giant friendly neighbor, India, and to the east is the populous friendly neighbor, Japan. Both countries possess a considerable industrial development, and are ready and anxious to export nearly all the manufactured imports that Viet-Nam needs. In addition, both must import rather large quantities of foods and other agricultural and forest products, which Viet-Nam can produce so effectively.

The base for intraregional trade is so strong that to neglect its possibilities by failing to use all available capital to modernize Viet-Nam's agriculture and forestry seems to be very bad economics indeed. And, of course, a country emphasizing its agriculture can enjoy a high standard of living. This economic fact need not be proved by resorting to logic or abstract economic analyses, but can be demon-strated by such examples as New Zealand and Denmark.

Commentary: MORRISON *on* HUNTER *and* LINDHOLM

THE COMMENTS by Hunter and Lindholm indicate that there is not such great divergence in our views as appears on the surface. The substantive difference seems to be one of emphasis, and, in the case of Hunter, also a difference of opinion on tactics.

I have repeatedly referred to Vietnamese economic development in deploring what I regard as insufficient improvement for the time and resources spent. True, I did single out industrial development for special notice. But, this was only so because that area of economic activity is my special frame of reference in this book, and it has received less attention and effort than any other area by the Vietnamese government and American aid. However, I neither believe nor intend to convey the idea that concentration on industrial development is a panacea for Viet-Nam's economic ills. On the other hand, un-reasoned concentration on agriculture for export would be an equally poor policy. I favor a balanced development. Indeed, I believe that no other kind is likely to develop unless forced by misguided govern-ment control.

Viet-Nam needs to export agricultural goods, to be sure. There will always be things it requires which are not possible or economic to produce, and for the present, at least, it has no export capability other than for agricultural products. However, there are literally hundreds of items in the Vietnamese market which can be locally and economically processed or manufactured rather than imported. To ignore the possibilities of domestic production of these items would be "very bad economics indeed" for at least three reasons.

First, the resulting Vietnamese economy would be a near carbon copy of the colonial production scheme—lacking only the market preference and price protection which guaranteed its success. Without the buffering effect of industry its consumption would be acutely sensitive to fluctuation of world market prices and demand. In this respect, a diversified agricultural economy is only somewhat better off than a one-crop economy. It is interesting to note that when the Vietnamese economy was this lopsided—when agricultural production and export were at an all-time high—the people had an abysmally low standard of living, not wholly attributable to colonial exploitation. Near starvation was frequent as a result of unemployment.

Second, the essential reason for economic development is to create higher real income, not to close a balance of payments gap, although this is a desirable end in itself. Large numbers of the Vietnamese farm population are chronically underemployed, and there are many thousands of underemployed and unemployed among the urban population. Many of the latter originally came from farms, which they abandoned during the war, and have no desire to return, preferring to eke out a bare subsistence in the cities and towns, which offer some amenities compared to the drudgery and quiet of rural life. These people form a large reservoir of untapped labor which will not contribute to agricultural production unless forced to. They also constitute a potential hotbed of political unrest and dissatisfaction because of their idleness and lack of acceptable opportunity. In addition to being bad economics, it is political folly to allow this waste of human resources which could make an important contribution to the national welfare in the form of a light-industry labor force.

Third, there is not the slightest doubt among knowledgeable people of the existence of industrial opportunities in Viet-Nam. Some are so vastly superior as candidates for investment that channeling development resources into these kinds of production would be eminently justified even at the expense of agriculture. Viet-Nam earned approximately $20 million in exports during 1957. This amount would finance only one half of its annual imports of cotton goods alone. By what omniscience would anyone assert, *a priori,* that it would be good economics or good sense (the two are not mutually inclusive) to reject the possibility of producing cotton goods domestically, and to do this in favor of the roundabout production of agricultural surplus for export to pay for the import of cotton goods?

I am fairly sure that Professors Lindholm and Hunter would agree that the comparative productivity of capital and other resources in various applications is a more sensible measure of where and in what amounts development effort should be expended than any preconceived notions based on trade concepts. Indeed, Hunter recognizes this logic in his comments in support of foreign trade. He does not explicitly recognize that "comparative advantage" is an analytical tool which is equally capable of fashioning support for industrial development where the factors are favorable.

In assessing the market for potential Vietnamese agricultural surplus it seems to me that Lindholm begs the question of serious barriers to such trade, e.g., demand, price, effect of agricultural development in present potential markets, consumption preferences, ability and willingness to pay in hard currencies, and, in the case of rubber, technological obsolescence.

What does the recent history of Vietnamese attempts to market rice and timber indicate? A few years ago when Viet-Nam tried to sell a small surplus of rice it had no takers. The Japanese importers claimed that their people did not like the taste of Vietnamese rice. At about the same time Burma was forced by market conditions to make an extremely bad rice deal with the Russians. These difficulties existed despite the millions of hungry people in India, Pakistan, Japan, and elsewhere. In the case of Burma, it is especially revealing that the Japanese could have driven a hard bargain with development-conscious Burma, which, unaided by the United States, is sorely pressed for foreign credits. Nevertheless, Japan was not in the market and neither was India.

In the matter of forest products for export, for years there have been attempts by efficient French forest operators in Viet Nam to "sell" timber-hungry Japan. These efforts have always come to naught because of price. The cost of timber operations in Viet-Nam is too high, and the required investment in improved private and public facilities is too great to warrant doing anything until there is substantially greater need for and return on such investment.

In my view, rubber will, in the long run, contribute decreasingly to Viet-Nam's export earnings. First, the advent of synthetic rubber and its steady improvement and resulting superiority over natural rubber for many uses has greatly reduced the natural rubber share of the market. Increased efficiencies in manufacturing, which, in turn, will lead to reduced costs, will further the use of synthetics according to experts in this commodity, causing even more grief to natural rubber producers and marketers. Second, rubber growing is a labor-intensive activity which offers little promise for mechanization or other cost-cutting innovations. As the standard of living rises, rubber growers will be forced to raise wages, which will further aggravate the cost situation. As time goes on, it is entirely possible that rubber producers caught in the cost-price squeeze will limit production of natural rubber to the amount required to meet the demand for which synthetics are as yet unacceptable substitutes.

On the matter of agricultural diversification, I am entirely in agreement with Lindholm. More varied diet certainly makes for richer and more exciting material existence, and increased production of fowl and livestock would improve nutrition immensely. However, few of the potential crops mentioned appear to have enough combined export earning power to satisfy the need for import credits.

In my estimation the foregoing reasons and distressing market experiences add up to this conclusion: Exclusive concentration on agriculture for export as a means of importing a better standard of living is a poor choice of action compared with the alternative of hedging agricultural development with an industrial build-up.

In the case of Denmark and New Zealand, cited by Lindholm as agricultural nations which enjoy high standards of living, it is only fair to point out a further truth concerning their economies. Both countries have a considerable industrial establishment. Danish industry contributes 29 percent of the total of Denmark's net domestic product, compared to a 19 percent contribution from agriculture, forestry, and fishing. New Zealand industry accounts for 25 percent of that country's net domestic product as against agriculture's 27 percent (*cf.* 34 percent and 5 percent respectively for the U.S.A.).[119] In this light, it does not seem logical to credit agriculture for the relatively high standard of living in these "agricultural" countries.

Professor Hunter has offered several cogent criticisms, but I would like to clear up some of his misconstruals. Nowhere do I say or assume that Vietnamese exports cannot be appreciably increased. In view of the fact that Viet-Nam is now exporting only 20 percent of its prewar record, it is certainly possible to increase the present amount. But, I do not think that agricultural export alone can maintain and increase the present level of consumption.

Hunter states, "Granted that [economic] independence is desirable, it does not follow that it is possible or that the wisest policy is to seek this end in the shortest possible time." Economic independence is possible for Viet-Nam, and it is illogical to suggest that it is not a wise policy to seek a desirable end in the shortest possible time. Hunter equates "shortest possible time" with wasteful and ineffectual action, i.e., "crash program" in his usage. Nowhere do I advocate a crash program even by implication. I do strongly urge getting on with what will be a long, difficult, and demanding job. This could be considered a crash program in the sense that it is a high priority undertaking which should be executed with dispatch and strength of purpose.

[119] United Nations, *Monthly Bulletin of Statistics,* March, 1957.

He then goes on to say that Viet-Nam will probably have a deficit in its balance of payments for some time to come, and that, unlike the traditional experience of developing countries, foreign aid rather than foreign investment will, for the near future at least, fill this deficit. "Thus the 'aid gap' may be approximately synonymous with an 'investment gap' for some time to come. It is realistic to recognize this and to devote considerable thought as to how one can operate comfortably with these circumstances with a minimum of infringement of sovereignty, real or imagined."

Hunter's analysis is right, but his conclusion is wrong. Since aid is filling the "investment gap" (actually, aid serves a much broader purpose), would it not be sensible and in keeping with the goal of developing Viet-Nam to use a sizable portion of the aid funds as the missing investment funds would be used if they were available? Doing this would certainly have resulted in more economic development than has heretofore taken place. It seems to me that what is required is less concern with "comfort" and more attention to accomplishment.

I fully share Hunter's distaste for infringement of sovereignty. It is best avoided by having clear understanding on the part of *aid-er* and *aid-ed* of the purposes and specific conditions attached to United States assistance. Complete avoidance of infringement, however, is quite impossible unless the aid is given "without strings attached." To do this would be a complete abdication of responsibility to the U.S. taxpayer. The Vietnamese realize this and accept it. The real problems with infringement come about as a result of foggy definition, lax implementation, and subsequent embarrassing differences of opinion regarding responsibilities on both sides.

Hunter thinks "that a viable economy is much less likely to be a possibility in anything like the near future that Morrison indicates is possible." Actually, I do not indicate that it is possible to achieve viability in the near future, but I will say that unless Viet-Nam grasps the opportunity while it can, it will be a lot tougher, maybe impossibly so, later on when gratuitous funds are no longer available.

My account of industrial development in Viet-Nam was intended to be reportorial, and therefore, formal conclusions were omitted. It is difficult, if not impossible, to maintain complete objectivity when one has been as intimately involved as I was in the events which concern this chapter. Nevertheless, it was my intention to present a narrative, with as little editorializing as possible consistent with the need of the reader to understand. In dealing with human events, objective conclusions do not proceed as neatly and surely as they do from simple syllogisms. It is quite possible that I overstepped my self-imposed bounds, but I did give the conclusions which I thought appropriate as the opportunity appeared in the text. If they are not the sweeping type of generalization such as Hunter indicates, I can only plead that my knowledge of aid programs is limited to the one in Viet-Nam during the period mentioned. In any case, I do not wish to present people with ready-made opinions. My aim has been to convey a general impression sufficient to show how things went.

I owe Professor Hunter a debt of gratitude for demonstrating that the intelligent reader is able to draw conclusions from the material, and for acquitting me of responsibility for his conclusions.

XVIII. A General Report on Industrial Development

NGUYEN PHUC SA[120]

IN TRYING to achieve a balanced economic development through the wise use of man power and resources, Viet-Nam had to turn to the creation of light industries which were complementary to agriculture and which could cater to the domestic market.

Generally speaking, industries with the most promising prospects were those processing local agricultural or forestry products (wallboard, sugar, paper, bicycle tires) or local mineral products (Vinh-Hao mineral waters, Nong Son coal, glass, cement).

After the country's partition a large number of foreign enterprises, fearing unfavorable political developments or discriminatory measures, desisted from expanding or reinvesting capital. The clarification of the political situation helped to restore confidence both inside the country and abroad, and, with confidence, came a favorable climate for business activities. Besides, President Ngo Dinh Diem had stated as early as 1955 that he would encourage industrialization as a means to achieve economic independence.

However, there were, and still are, certain major obstacles to a satisfactory development of industry. Industrial production, already low before the Indochina war, declined still further because of destruction of equipment and obsolescence. So, with the serious handicap of insufficient investment capital, there has been the twofold problem of rebuilding old industries and creating new ones. Another obstacle, of course, was the loss, after partition of extractive industries (coal) and of the most important processing industries (cotton, cement, glass).

Excessive production costs are another hindrance to Viet-Nam's industrial development. Obsolete equipment, inordinately large commissions to intermediaries, and high costs of services have inflated manufacturing costs. In addition, there is the discrepancy between low productivity and an artificially high standard of living, made possible by the import of vast quantities of consumer goods bought with foreign aid money.

Another obstacle to industrialization is the lack of technical know-how. Not only does Viet-Nam lack bureaus of industrial statistics and technical studies that are well equipped, but also managers, technicians, and supervisory personnel.

Moreover, certain industrial sectors have run into special difficulties arising from: (1) the absence of industrial quality control programs that would help producers by changing the consumers' attitudes toward local

[120] Director of Technical Assistance; translated from the original French by Phan Thu Ngoc.

241

products (pharmaceuticals); and (2) a low tariff, which at present is not adequate to help domestic products compete with imports.

In the face of these difficulties, what has been done by the Vietnamese government to speed up the development of new industries, and what have been the results?

According to a declaration by President Diem on March 3, 1957, Viet-Nam intended to speed up her economic development according to the following principles:

> Within, free enterprise within the framework of a planning policy in which the State's role consists primarily in orienting, co-ordinating, and giving assistance.
> Through co-operation and increased exchanges with friendly countries.

President Diem thus defined the investment policy of Viet-Nam, and at the same time outlined the projects designed to get development started at as fast a pace as allowed by the available resources. A favorable economic climate was thus created which could attract foreign and domestic capital into the desired channels. The investment-guarantee accord signed by the governments of Viet-Nam and the United States falls within the scope of this policy.

To assist the existing small industries (rice mills, sugar mills, textiles, sawmills, brickmaking factories, hide and leather works, soap factories, plastics, charcoal ovens, etc.) the government, as early as 1955, created the National Investment Fund and has to date loaned, through that agency, over eighty million piasters to industrialists, to enable them to modernize existing plants or to start new industries.

As a result, within three years the capacity of sawmills has risen from 250,000 to 400,000 cubic meters a year, a sufficient increase to fulfill the needs of an intensive reconstruction program. The number of sawmills rose from two hundred to three hundred in 1957. Likewise, the capacity of rice mills has risen until they are now capable of processing the entire rice output of Viet-Nam. Since 1955 four hundred new rice mills have been built, bringing the total to over 1,000. Together, they can handle 3,500,000 tons of paddy annually.

Textiles have made considerable progress. A spinning mill with 7,600 spindles has been assembled and has begun production, which will make possible a saving of $180,000 annually. The number of looms rose from 6,000 in 1955 to 10,200 in 1957, employing more than 10,000 persons and producing 6,000 tons of fabric. Of the 10,200 looms, 3,000 are mechanized, and the remaining are semiautomatic or hand-operated.

The soap factories manufacture all the soap consumed in Viet-Nam.

Capacity rose from 6,000 tons in 1955 to 7,900 tons in 1957. In 1957 industries using aluminum—represented by a single firm, the Delignon concern in 1955—consumed more than 1,500 tons of aluminum annually.

Nailmaking factories, which have increased their production by 200 percent, consumed 3,000 tons of iron and satisfied all Viet-Nam's requirements. The small glassmaking factories, which number about twenty, did not exist before 1955; they have an annual output of roughly 1,000 tons of glass, which represents a saving of $200,000 a year. Three or four pharmaceutical concerns have been established since 1955; the most important of these can produce $500,000 worth of various products each year.

The newly established plastic industries consume raw materials valued at $200,000 annually, and manufacture small articles, toothbrushes, electrical sockets, ashtrays, etc.

Manufactured rubber products have also gained ground. Small industrialists make toys, sandals, rubber nipples, elastic bands, etc. The manufacturing of certain parts for bicycles, motorized bicycles, watches, and clocks has been started, although on a modest scale. The Nong Son coal mines produced 12,000 tons of coal, valued at $200,000 last year.

Besides investments, industrial development requires studies which are often lengthy and detailed. The latter need will be answered, in part, by the newly created Center of Industrial Development. As to investments, the government's support turned out to be indispensable, as is the case with all underdeveloped countries. Investments made by the government will have the effect of a loan for capital formation purposes, which will later be repaid with private savings, as the latter become available. Several companies have been organized or are being organized in this manner. The Sugar Company of Viet-Nam has put the Hiep-Hoa plant, which will have an annual capacity of 20,000 tons, back into operation. And the Vinh-Hao Mineral Waters Company has been operating on a reduced scale, while awaiting the arrival of more up-to-date equipment.

Negotiations for two other firms making wood and glass products are on the point of being successfully concluded. The glassmaking concern will have a yearly output of 15,000 tons and will permit a saving of $2,500,000 a year. A paper mill project, which calls for a 9,000 ton output and a saving of more than one million dollars, is being discussed with foreign investors.

Some people may find the progress made to date rather inadequate. Perhaps they forget the immense task that has been successfully handled by the government in the economic and social fields: raising the low living standards of a portion of the rural population, restoring the potential of agricultural production, rebuilding the communications network, developing the educational system, especially in the technical fields. All these accomplishments strengthen the economic framework that will make possible the successful industrialization of Viet-Nam.

XIX. Early Steps Toward an Industrial Development Bank

H. ROBERT SLUSSER[121]

AFTER JUNE, 1954, Free Viet-Nam had the opportunity, as well as the responsibility, to restore prewar production and to expand its industrial sector as rapidly as possible. The thousands of skilled and semiskilled workers who came as refugees to the south were an especially valuable addition to the labor force. There were plants north of the 17th parallel, chiefly around Hanoi and Haiphong, which could provide machinery and management for new operations; and, with the deadline of May 18, 1955, set by the Geneva Agreement for the evacuation of people and materials from north to south, plant managers were anxious to transfer their establishments before that date, but claimed they were unable to do so without financial help.

Among the "evacuation" projects was a cotton-spinning mill which had provided thread to many of the hand looms and small power looms throughout the country. After direct appeal to the Chief of State, this project was promised six million piasters of government aid, even though no instrumentality existed for putting the promise into effect.

The important commercial banks, which could provide financial assistance, were all foreign owned and previously had not financed industrial activities except through the respective trading or planting corporations with which they were linked. Considering the political situation, they were particularly hesitant about supporting new ventures.

Obviously, there was an urgent need to mobilize all the Vietnamese capital that might exist in unproductive forms as a foundation for the new industrial sector. An industrial development bank, established by the government, seemed to be the answer: It could identify promising investment opportunities, provide various types of technical assistance, and perhaps afford some foreign exchange facility.

During the second half of 1954 Nguyen Van Khai, Director General of Mines, Industry, and Handicrafts, working with a full-time French technical adviser and Vietnamese legal adviser, drew also on the facilities of USOM in an effort to outline the structure of an industrial development bank. Certain aspects of the draft statutes followed the model of PHILCUSA in the Philippines, while other features were adopted from the statutes and documents of development institutions collected in the USOM library. At first the outlines called for a very comprehensive institution, with a full range of financial powers. There was emphasis on equal powers also for fostering and supporting new industrial enterprises technically and administratively. Facilities were included for using ad-

---

[121] Economic analyst, USOM, Saigon, June, 1954, to May, 1957.

visers from United Nations and other foreign aid, as well as for hiring Vietnamese industrial and management experts on short- or long-term contracts.

A little later it was recognized that the creation of such a comprehensive institution required more time and study than could be afforded in the urgent circumstances. It was decided to begin work with a more limited, provisional agency that would have been called COSUDIC, (Superior Committee for the Development of Industry and Commerce) and which would have been supplanted by the more permanent and full-powered development bank at such time as the latter would be established. Each of these plans included a presumption that some operating capital could be obtained from American, and perhaps from French, economic aid. Planning for COSUDIC was supplanted, however, shortly after the end of the year, and before it had received any wide official attention.

The new Minister of Planning and Reconstruction proposed a National Investment Fund. There was no indication that the Fund would be provisional or that further refinements in its structure or its operating field were anticipated. The Fund was not to be limited to loan assistance, but was authorized to become owner or part-owner of the enterprises it would assist. In addition, *subventions* (of which there were two types and only one of which meant outright subsidy) were one of the regular means of financing by the Fund. On the advice of M. Cusin of the expiring French Institute for currency issues in the Associated States, the Minister had included provisions for direct drafts on the central bank. They were to be offered primarily to handicrafts "where losses are certain."

In other respects, the Fund was to have somewhat restricted authority. Technical assistance, training activities, promotion, and other nonfinancial measures for encouraging industrialization did not figure in the statute for the Fund. Further, there was no provision for technicians, whether borrowed from Vietnamese agencies, provided by USOM, or other foreign or international agencies, or engaged temporarily from private industry. In fact, there was little attention to any continuous study of industrial problems and effective means for increasing industrial activity.

The statute for the National Investment Fund encountered less than the usual amount of delay as it moved through all the necessary revisions and clearances by the interested ministries. On January 31, 1955, the statute was signed and issued by the government. The policy board for the fund was a *Conseil d'Administration,* composed of the Ministers of Planning and Reconstruction, Finance, and Economy, and the Administrator General of Foreign Economic Aid.

Staffing the new agency progressed more slowly, due, in part, to budgetary reasons and shortage of qualified personnel. A public works engineer of long government service, became Director of the Fund. His estimates of the capital needed by the Fund were exceedingly high because he visualized operating it as an endowed institution. By his explanation, the Fund would not advance its capital to expansion projects, but would invest in sure—and high—income, as for example in the partially government-owned Air Viet-Nam. This periodic income from such "sure" investments would constitute the funds for financing industrial expansion.

For technical and clerical staff, the NIF was expected to borrow from the interested ministries, although this would create problems of tenure and seniority for the people transferred. Some ministries seemed not to have sufficient interest to be willing to donate, in effect, a part of the Fund's payroll. By March, 1955, the Fund had a director, a chief accountant, a clerk, and a stenographer, but no regularly assigned office space.

Somewhat later, planning and reconstruction was reduced from the status of a ministry to an office without clearly defined status. The Minister returned to France. The small planning staff was held together and guided by a subordinate, who also took a strong interest in the National Investment Fund as the agency to carry out the plans that would be drawn up for the industry sector.

In late spring the Director of the Fund was named Minister of National Economy, leaving the Fund without a director. A new decree on June 4, 1955, recognized that there was no Minister of Planning to sit on the Council of Administration and named as a substitute fourth member, a construction engineer, whose contracting firm had just completed an important part of the rehabilitation of a war-destroyed irrigation system as a USOM project in central Viet-Nam. The decree appointing him was apparently published after some delay. At the same time, he was also being considered for the position of Commissioner of Planning and Reconstruction and Director of the NIF. In conformity with a decree on conflict of interest, he ended his participation in the contracting business, leaving all his time free for such government charges as he would be assigned. In August he became Director of the Fund and began assembling a staff of engineers.

In the beginning the Vietnamese had hoped to begin their development financing with capital contributed by United States aid and French economic aid, while various other sources of capital were being explored and developed. The United States aid mission was unable, however, to make any contribution. Similarly, the French government discussions of aid were protracted and produced no source of capital for the Fund.

Private capital was not considered a promising source. The planning staff estimate in February was that Viet-Nam had only four or five important capitalists, whose total resources would not exceed a billion francs (three million dollars at the official rate of exchange). The only one of them believed to be doing any investing in Viet-Nam was Le Van Vien, leader of the private army that controlled Saigon and the area from there to Cap St. Jacques, who was credited with 350 million francs. The others were believed to have transferred their interests abroad, with no inclination to repatriate under current circumstances.

Since the government was the only remaining source, there were discussions of advances by the Treasury or the Ministry of Finances, or from the National Budget. It was agreed in March that the proceeds (estimated at six million piasters) from 25 million piasters worth of the August tickets of the national lottery would be assigned to the Fund, and tickets for that month bore the "brawn and cog-wheel" theme so generally used throughout the world to symbolize industrial development. The project of the thread mill from Haiphong, with its promised six million piasters of government contribution, was discussed as an opening transaction for the NIF. The Central Bank, whose governor was an observer on the Council of Administration, might possibly be persuaded to make advances, it was felt, against the mortgages which the Fund would take as security for its loans.

By mid-June it was clear that an advance of 200 million piasters could be expected from the National Treasury, but the document covering the advance was signed only on September 7, 1955, by the Director of the NIF and the Minister of Finance. The amounts would be advanced from the Treasury as needed for operations by the Fund, would draw interest only as advanced, and would be repayable over twelve years beginning with the end of 1957.

Planning for industry in the Ministry of Planning and Reconstruction began more or less concurrently with the Fund's review of applications for financing. Survey of rice milling needs and sawmill needs were the first conducted by the planning office. Brick kilns and other industries were to be studied subsequently. Joint effort produced the first tables of projects offered to the NIF Council of Administration at its meeting of March 21, 1955. These tables listed: twenty brick and tile plants asking more than fourteen million piasters; twenty rice hulling mills asking more than eight million piasters; twenty sawmills asking nearly nine million piasters; eleven paint, ice plants, etc., asking nearly six million piasters; one foundry asking fifty million piasters; one jute bag plant asking fifty million piasters; one textile weaver asking thirty million piasters.

The brick plants were marked priority one, the rice mills two, and the sawmills three, while all the others were labeled priority four. Favorable remarks were appended only to five brick plants and one rice mill. Those applications totaled some four million piasters.

Six months later, when the Fund had capital, its first loans were not made to any of the early applicants. The first one million piasters were extended, for five years at eight percent interest, to the Chinese owners of the thread-mill machinery evacuated from Haiphong. Another two million piasters were loaned to the Vietnamese owner of a factory producing toothpaste and plastic articles, including toothbrushes, to enable him to refinance a mortgage previously held by a private bank. Having approved this loan, the Fund began studying ways of financing an expansion of production in the same enterprise. Another loan for approximately three million piasters enabled a Vietnamese management to buy a pharmaceutical plant which the French owners were planning to close and sell piece by piece if a Vietnamese buyer did not appear. Along with this loan, the Fund suggested an extensive rearrangement of machinery in the plant in order to make the production flow more efficient, and recognized that additional borrowing up to one million piasters might be justified for paying a management consultant and buying the missing items for an improved production line. In all three cases, the Fund took mortgages on real estate and other physical property.

In general, all the industrial projects financed were located fairly close to Saigon. Those at any distance seemed to be chiefly rice mills.

In the report of its activity at the end of 1955, the Fund showed the following projects: nine contracts signed, totaling 21,950,000 piasters; two textile projects, 6.1 million piasters; one toothpaste project, 4.8 million piasters; one pharmaceutical project, 6.0 million piasters; one sawmill project, 2.5 million piasters; four rice mill projects, 2.55 million piasters; thirteen contracts in course of "formalities," totaling 8,300,000 piasters; one textile project, 1.0 million; two sawmill projects, 1.75 million; two brick kiln projects, 0.65 million; one fish sauce project, 0.7 million; one sugar project, 0.15 million; five rice mill projects, 2.0 million; one tannery project, 2.0 million; thirty-three contracts in course of drafting, totaling 28,314,000 piasters, comprising textile, ampule, brick, aluminum, and sawmill projects, and seventeen rice mills. Three contracts had been canceled (1.4 million piasters), and there was no indication of projects under discussion with other applicants.

All the Fund's operations thus far stood in direct contrast to the broad powers granted in its statutes. No subsidies or equity participations had been granted. All operations were in the form of amply secured loans. Further, no government enterprise figured among the borrowers; all were privately owned with equities at least equal to the amounts borrowed. Loans were for production, not for commerce. Interest rates of six to ten percent were reasonable, but above subsidy levels. Other policies claimed by the Fund but apparently not strictly followed in some cases were: loans must be for creating new productive facilities, and loans must not finance disinvestment.

The year-end report referred to a sum of 80 million piasters set aside for participations in enterprises, but the form of aid to the thread mill was a normal loan, whereas many officials had assumed from the beginning that the President's promise of six million piasters to this firm would eventually be formalized in a profit-sharing equity for the government. A general decree was promulgated during the year to cover government participation. It gave the government monitor a veto (appealable) over day-to-day operating decisions of the management, and to other government auditors such power to interfere with management, that no enterprise was willing to accept such restraints. If this decree had offered a more workable relationship, it is possible that equity participations might have been taken by the Fund as well as by other government financial agencies.

On numerous occasions in the early months of 1955, Vietnamese pointed out to USOM officers the urgent need for capital for industrial projects, which USOM might help to meet out of counterpart funds. About April the Ministry of Finance presented a written proposal for two credit institutions, one for agricultural projects and the other for nonagricultural projects.

USOM had already set aside for agricultural credit sums which were eventually augmented to about half a billion piasters ($14.3 million). Out of long discussions with the Ministry of Agriculture, agreement on the appropriate institutional arrangements for agricultural credit were tentatively reached only at the end of the following year. However, interim methods of making the credit available to farmers were worked out.

From the large amounts approved by the United States Congress specifically for refugees, 300 million piasters were for development credit. By the nature of the refugee settlements that were established, this was eventually used largely for agricultural credit also.

In order to provide the complement to these programs, and to answer the remainder of the proposal from the Ministry of Finance, USOM drew up a list of the minimum requirements it would like to see in a development bank to which it would contribute capital. Essentially they were: (1) the equivalent of corporate form; (2) financing advances to applicants only in the form of loans; (3) loans only for the establishment of new productive facilities or for otherwise expanding production; (4) loans limited to a safe percentage of the total value of the applicant enterprise; (5) realistic interest rates; (6) operating expenses to be covered out of interest collected (except in the initial months of operation); (7) no loans to agriculture or commerce; (8) the bank should raise capital from private sources; (9) private business and banking should be represented on the bank's board of directors.

Assuming that a bank with these characteristics could be created, USOM offered to contribute 35 to 50 million piasters for its capital, support for operating expenses during the first year of operation, and the continuous availability of the USOM staff of advisers in technical, legal, and financial fields. It was suggested that these advisers could be particularly helpful in the evaluation of projects considered for financing, the drafting of loan agreements, and the follow-up of projects after they were financed. The Mission further advised that the aid project as submitted to ICA in Washington would call for USOM observers to attend the meetings of the proposed bank's board of directors and of its loan committee.

At a meeting with the chief financial officers of the government on June 24, USOM invited the Vietnamese to arrange to discuss all these points informally before their content and their phraseology was finally determined. It was hoped that, through discussion, informal agreement could be reached on a text that could then be sent formally by USOM and quickly accepted by the Vietnamese. Working level representatives of the interested agencies came to one such discussion on June 27, 1955. They expressed no opinions on any of the points, but agreed to deliver the informal paper for consideration in their respective agencies. The meeting enabled USOM to avoid some elliptical phraseology in its draft and to bridge the gap between the United States legal concept of a corporation and those French-Vietnamese legal devices that might perform the same function. No further discussions were deemed necessary by the Vietnamese agencies which considered the draft. USOM proceeded then to draft its final text of the proposal as a letter to the Minister of Finance, replying to the proposal on credit that had been received by USOM several weeks before. An informal French translation was carefully prepared, and the letter and the informal translation were sent to the Ministry on July 13, 1955.

Due to internal messenger difficulties in the Ministry, it was necessary for USOM to deliver new copies of the letter and the informal translation on July 25, and the next day a Finance Ministry official distributed the copies for study by interested agencies. The joint discussions of the formal text which USOM suggested from time to time were not deemed necessary. The formal Vietnamese reply, received by USOM on September 13, 1955, agreed to the idea proposed by USOM. It added, for each of the points in the USOM letter, qualifying or extenuating considerations that were deemed to make each individual USOM proposal impractical at that time.

In a discussion on August 8, 1955, of repayments on the price of a generator supplied by USOM under another project, the Mission proposed to the Minister of Public Works, that the repayments might accrue to the capital of the new development bank which was under review. The Minister received the idea favorably, indicated the great importance of the development bank to the Vietnamese economy, and agreed to propose in writing a basis of repayment to the development bank. This idea, which had been one aspect of Carter de Paul's[122] original aims for a development bank, was again put forward by Mission officers in the remainder of 1955 and later.

Another source of capital for a development bank might have been developed from that part of refugee credit funds which might be allotted to industry and handicrafts. However, refugee credit had to be extended promptly. Since the NIF had neither field staff nor working relations with USOM, and a second development bank was not even an agreed proposal, this was not a feasible device for making refugee credit available.

Still in search of a way to get new capital quickly to deserving projects for expanding nonagricultural production, USOM, through Fred Bruhns, its Field Representative in Dalat, reviewed the work of a regional institution in that town. Viet-Nam Tai-Chanh Cong-Ty had been lending for the expansion of commercial truck gardens, small tea and coffee plantations, and tea processing plants in the plateau region, 150 miles from Saigon. It might have undertaken small industrial operations among the refugees who were settled in the plateau country, as well as older residents. However, USOM could not offer capital, as requested, on the same terms as the original capital of Viet-Nam Tai-Chanh Cong-Ty. That had been a sum of 35 million piasters from the Bao Dai government for the plateau region, drawing no interest and absorbing no losses, but receiving only one fourth of any profits distributed against three fourths of the profits for Viet-Nam Tai-Chanh Cong-Ty's one million piasters of common equity.

In 1956 the National Investment Fund was not able to effect any important new operations. Possibly 25 million piasters were loaned to an unspecified number of borrowers, but clear information about the Fund's activities was not made public. Among the many explanations suggested from all sides for the loss of momentum, some referred to the anti-Chinese policy of the government, others to the NIF demand for excessive collateral, or to political or "squeeze" considerations, or to a supposed lack of native capital to provide collateral, and still others to an averred lack of Vietnamese interest in being manager of an industrial enterprise. Quite evidently, none of these factors could be shown to be the true cause for stagnation, and furthermore only one of them could be eliminated if identified as the cause.

[122] Acting Deputy Director until December, 1954.

One explanation put forward by the NIF staff for the lack of activity by the Fund was the difficulty of calling meetings of the Council of Administration to approve recommended projects. At one time there was an interval of several months between Council meetings.

Far more important than such negative elements was the absence of the all-important positive factors. No government policy toward industry or toward private investment, either native or foreign, was made known. No plan for industry, or schedule of priorities, was established. No training courses were offered; no help on government forms and procedures was made available; no one demonstrated what provinces and local authorities could do to encourage industry before calling on the national government. If the NIF was supposed to be the chief government office open to industrial entrepreneurs, it was largely unknown even by name throughout the country outside Saigon. The idea of industrial promotion as a government activity simply was not grasped. One negative factor truly inhibiting industrial expansion was probably the long, unpredictable, and unexplained delay or outright refusal in connection with import licenses and foreign exchange facilities for new industrial equipment.

In pursuit of aids to new and expanding industries, the USOM Industry Officer encouraged the founding of a professional association of engineers and technicians, and urged that it establish a technical advisory and consulting service for industry. An important start toward a technical library could have been donated by USOM, and some help might have been afforded toward the initial cost of the consulting staff. The professional association was set up in a building donated by the government in the last half of 1956. No library or consulting service was established.

Two interesting ventures were established during the year independently of government aid. Under a young Vietnamese manager, an enterprise began assembling Lambretta motor scooters, in what was described by a visiting industrial consultant as a model factory for Viet-Nam. Once in operation, the manager relied on only two engineering advisers from the parent plant. Plans were to produce locally an increasing number of the parts needed for the assembly.

USOM Trade Division helped to obtain the establishment of a factory to assemble watches from parts supplied by a French factory. In this instance, too, an increasing number of parts were to be produced locally.

Early in 1956 Viet-Nam became a member of the International Bank and the Monetary Fund. One of the delegates to the annual meeting in Washington in September went on after the meetings to Puerto Rico to observe the development program there. From USOM in Saigon, personal contacts were used to assure that he would be shown the full program, including the promotion and the ancillary services to industry that contribute as much as the financing to the program's success. He visited other development programs along his route home; in all his visits he was particularly impressed by the freedom of action of the operating staff in contrast to the NIF's long waits for Administrative Council decision on recommended projects.

Accordingly, after his return to Viet-Nam he drew up revised statutes for a *Credit Industrie* to replace more effectively the National Investment Fund. USOM's growing library of development bank documents served again as reference material. The new draft did not receive encouragement from the financial officers of the government until early 1957, when a new draft was asked for. In the meantime, the original draft was reviewed at USOM on an unofficial basis, and extensive suggestions were made for clarifying the proposed organization and stratifying responsibility, in order to encourage dynamic action by the operating staff within the policy limits established for it. The suggestion was also made that different levels of financing, from short-term loans through subsidies, should be departmentalized to assure that funds were used on substantially the same financial terms as they were obtained.

On the occasion of supplying new development bank documents for use in Viet-Nam, Nathan Rafler in ICA in Washington suggested that USOM arrange for the same Vietnamese to study the industrial development program in the Philippines, where many ancillary services to industry are combined with straight-loan financing, with the aid of the USOM in that country. He suggested also that an adviser on industrial development could give valuable help to Viet-Nam in improving its development bank. USOM did not act on those suggestions.

Early in 1957 USOM Directors from Saigon who were in the Philippines paid particular attention to the Industrial Development Center set up there over an extended period by the government and the USOM. The program was discussed with Industry officers from ICA in Washington who passed through Manila and Saigon.

At the end of April USOM proposed to ICA in Washington a comprehensive project that would create an Industrial Development Center in Viet-Nam, with a banking agency as well as the supplementary technical and advisory services. The project would again staff the currently inactive USOM Industry Division. Also included in the project was a comprehensive industry survey by a team of a dozen specialists from the United States. The relation of the project to the National Investment Fund had not been worked out at midyear, when the third anniversary of the French announcement of Vietnamese independence passed.

Commentary: NGUYEN DUY XUAN[123] *on* SLUSSER

IT IS PERFECTLY understandable that Slusser chose to omit the delicate and somewhat thorny problem of evaluating the achievements of the NIF up to 1957; however, in so doing, he has avoided entering into discussion of the real and deep causes of the stagnation of the NIF which made itself felt at the end of 1956. It may be true that the "negative elements" which were supposed to be responsible for the loss of momentum of the NIF activities were reinforced by the "absence of all important positive factors." (One of the "negative elements" is labeled as the "anti-Chinese policy of the government." This is a strong and rather misleading qualification of the policy adopted in 1957 by the government of Viet-Nam vis-à-vis the Chinese community, namely the problem of nationality of the Chinese born in Viet-Nam. The imperative reasons for this policy lie deep at the roots of the long-term security problems of a wider geographical area than Viet-Nam itself, and it is not motivated by any kind of xenophobia whatsoever.) The points at issue here are: Why there was such an absence of positive factors? and why apparently was nothing done to neutralize or counteract the effects of the negative elements mentioned by Slusser? The answer seems to lie in the political situation of the difficult years of 1954 and 1955.

Of course, no long-term enterprise of any kind can be achieved without political stability, and in 1955 Viet-Nam was hardly out of the transitory political chaos which followed the Geneva Agreement. The government had literally to fight for its dangerously undermined existence, which had been unbearably threatened by many subversive politico-religious groups. Therefore, government activities had been mostly concentrated on crucial problems, such as that of security (which was in addition to the major problem of refugee rehabilitation) and of providing Viet-Nam with a firm and legal constitutional framework. Obviously, the kind of events in Viet-Nam in 1955 did more than to merely discourage all sorts of economic enterprises, they also failed to provide a favorable climate for sound investment. This was the period when rumors of flight of capital were very much in the air.

Amidst these difficulties, it is no easy task to conceive a positive long-term development program, the prerequisite of which would be political stability and confidence of the people in the regime. Economic development, of which industrial development is a component, must be looked

[123] Former adviser to the Secretary of State of National Economy, Viet-Nam.

at as an evolutionary historical process. Noneconomic factors for economic development such as improvement in education, technical knowledge, changes in social attitudes conducive to entrepreneurial activities, recognition of a national discipline and a certain set of "rules of the games," and, above all, political stability must come into existence in balance with economic factors. In other words, a harmoniously balanced evolution of economic and noneconomic factors is necessary, if not indispensable, to economic development progress. In this light, the loss of momentum of the NIF may be attributed to the unfortunate delay in the evolution of the environmental noneconomic factors.

The stagnation of the NIF in 1956 should not be allowed to dim its merits, since it has played, by trial and error, its historical part as the pioneer in the finance of some industrial projects in a country which has just recovered its sovereignty; also, despite its limited activities, the NIF has launched and increased the "industrial development" consciousness among business circles in Viet-Nam.

Slusser has referred briefly to the unnecessary delays in the granting of import licenses and foreign exchange. Unfortunately, these delays were not confined to the field mentioned. Serious and continuing efforts have been made by the government to correct the unnecessary formalities, and these efforts have been largely successful. On the USOM side, there is also this kind of delaying administrative formalities relating to the clearing and subsequent approval of certain types of industrial projects or applications for import of capital equipment. A considerable amount of time would be gained, for the sake of industrial development, if administrative procedures were to be reviewed and, if possible, reduced to a necessary minimum. It would have been more helpful if Slusser had suggested some realistic measures to curtail the delaying effects of administrative procedures and particularly to indicate when contacts between USOM and various Vietnamese organizations will become more frequent, at the operational level, particularly in the execution of the First Five Year plan, and in finding operation opportunities for the Center for Industrial Development.

PART SIX

ASPECTS OF
VIETNAMESE FINANCE

There are many differences in the economic role of foreign exchange and banking in Free Viet-Nam than, for example, in New Zealand, another primarily agricultural country that must import a large portion of its manufactured goods. A few examples will show how fundamental these differences are.

In Viet-Nam most agricultural production goes to meet the consumption requirements of those producing the food, whereas in New Zealand most agricultural goods are produced to be sold in the world and domestic markets. Therefore, a change in the terms of trade or in the domestic currency price of agricultural products has much less of an economic impact in Viet-Nam than in New Zealand.

In Viet-Nam money is largely held as currency outside the banks, and the monetary holdings are usually concentrated in the hands of a small portion of the population, while in New Zealand monetary balances are largely in the banks and the ownership of these balances is widely distributed. This situation reduces the possible effectiveness of central bank policy in Viet-Nam and also reduces substantially the role of commercial banks as allocators of investment funds.

Foreign banking firms predominate in Viet-Nam, and the government cannot effectively control these banks. Actually, they are export-import banks, and are interested only in financing the end product that is to be exported or goods that are to be imported. This situation exists to a much less degree, of course, in New Zealand.

In addition the foreign exchange and banking situation of Viet-Nam is different from that of New Zealand and most other countries, for, since independence, its banking and monetary institutions must digest large quantities of American aid supplied to meet operating budget deficits.

Frank W. Schiff, Huyn Van Lang, and Richard W. Lindholm, who contributed articles on "Monetary Reorganization and Emergence of Central Banking," "The Foreign Exchange Policy of Viet-Nam," and "American Aid and Its Financial Impact," have worked closely with the monetary and banking plans and actions of Viet-Nam since 1954. Some of the discussions are sharply critical, and all attempt to present a background necessary to understanding fundamental financial policy issues related to foreign exchange, banking, and American aid.

Vu Thien Vinh considers Viet-Nam's problems in developing a modern system of public revenues.

XX. Monetary Reorganization and the Emergence of Central Banking

FRANK W. SCHIFF[124]

IN DECEMBER, 1954, France, Free Viet-Nam, Cambodia, and Laos signed a series of agreements in Paris which provided for the breakup of the monetary and customs union that until then had linked the three "Associated States" of Indochina. The various French-dominated "quadripartite" institutions in Saigon which had administered this union—notably the Institute of Issue and the Indochinese Foreign Exchange Control Office—were liquidated, and each state in principle was now free to issue and control its own money, fix its own rate of exchange, and develop independent monetary, exchange, and commercial policies.

To be sure, not all ties that had linked the members of the monetary union were to be dissolved immediately. It was recognized that the existing common currency would continue to circulate in the three states until preparations for creating separate currencies had been completed; each state, moreover, remained in the franc currency area, with Viet-Nam committed to membership for at least a year. In effect, however, the agreements meant that France was relinquishing most of the formal mechanisms through which it had exercised control over the monetary system of the Associated States. The impact of the agreements was reinforced when the United States announced that it would initiate a program of direct aid to these states beginning January 1, 1955, rather than channeling the great bulk of its massive aid to Indochina through France, as previously. On the same date, each of the states established an independent central bank (with a National Exchange Control Office as a department)—a development that symbolized the transfer of primary responsibility for each country's monetary affairs to truly national institutions.

Viet-Nam's monetary and financial system is still relatively underdeveloped, particularly outside of Saigon-Cholon and other urban centers. There are no capital or organized money markets in the true sense of

[124] Senior Economist, Federal Reserve Bank of New York. Schiff was banking and foreign exchange adviser to USOM in Saigon from March-September, 1955, and returned to Viet-Nam in May-June, 1957, to serve as adviser to the National Bank of Viet-Nam. He wishes to give special acknowledgment to Professor Arthur I. Bloomfield of the University of Pennsylvania, Mr. Buu Hoan, Manager of the Research Department of the National Bank of Viet-Nam, and Mr. Alan Holmes, Manager of the Research Department of the Federal Reserve Bank of New York, for their very helpful suggestions and criticisms; the opinions expressed here, of course, do not necessarily represent either their views or those of the Federal Reserve Bank of New York.

the term. Currency rather than bank deposits constitutes the larger part of the money supply; at the end of 1957, for example, currency in circulation totaled 7.6 billion piasters, while demand deposits amounted to only 3.7 billion piasters.[125]

Commercial banking facilities are almost entirely concentrated in Saigon-Cholon; at the beginning of 1958 there were only two other cities where a banking office could be found (Cantho and Tourane), and these offices handled only a small volume of transactions.[126] Nearly all the banks are foreign-owned and operated. When the new central bank started operation in 1955, there were ten commercial banks (or branches of foreign banks) in Saigon. Three of these were French, two British, three Chinese, or Chinese-managed, and only two—the smallest ones— were Vietnamese. Among these banks, the French Banque de l'Indochine had a dominant position, for it not only held more than half of the country's total bank deposits but had also gained enormous influence over economic activities through its extensive and widely diversified investment activities built up over a long period of years.[127] When this bank terminated its commercial banking operations in the fall of 1955, its tasks were partly taken over by a newly created state commercial bank (the Credit Commerciale du Viet-Nam) and partly by a French successor bank (the Banque Française de l'Asie). The latter, while much smaller than the Banque de l'Indochine, is still the largest of the private banks operating in Saigon today.

The activities of the commercial banks have been predominantly oriented toward foreign trade and foreign exchange transactions. While a precise breakdown of loans by major purposes is unfortunately not

[125] These figures are derived from the money supply table published by the National Bank of Viet-Nam. They do not include so-called "deposits" of individuals and corporations at the Treasury which, as far as can be determined, are of relatively small magnitude. (The figure shown in the *Bulletin Économique* for "demand deposits" at the Treasury takes in certain public deposits which should really be excluded in a calculation of the money supply.) Currency in circulation as shown here included cash holdings of provincial Treasury offices.

[126] The Banque de l'Indochine maintained a number of branches outside of Saigon until the fall of 1955, when its commercial banking operations in Viet-Nam were terminated. The banking operations carried out by these branches were limited, however; to a large extent these branches were merely used to assist the Treasury in its tasks of collecting and disbursing funds. Only the Tourane branch has thus far been reopened as a commercial bank branch, under new auspices.

[127] Prior to the establishment of the Institute of Issue in 1952, the Banque de l'Indochine had been the bank of issue for the various Indochinese states; Banque de l'Indochine notes still formed part of the common currency of these states at the beginning of 1955.

yet available, it is clear that the banks (with the partial exception of the Chinese and Vietnamese ones) have focused almost exclusively on financing foreign trade and have done relatively little in agriculture, small-scale industries, and internal distribution. Moreover, at least until recently, there were only a few specialized governmental or private institutions designed to facilitate financing of this type, and their scale of operations was relatively limited. The task of providing credit for such purposes has thus, to a large extent, remained in the hands of wholesalers and local moneylenders, who are mainly Chinese but include some Indians (Chettiars) and a few Vietnamese. Interest rates charged by these lenders tend to be extremely high; thus, while larger firms may be able to secure credit to cover foreign trade transactions from the Saigon banks at rates ranging upward from six percent per annum, interest charges of five percent per month or more for consumption loans, or of three percent a month or more for the financing of a crop or of retail inventories are not uncommon. Another source of credit is the numerous co-operative "credit clubs." These usually consist of about a dozen members who, in line with an ancient custom, pool their savings and then lend them out to a member of the club selected by lot. But while the activities of these clubs are not unimportant, they have generally fallen short of meeting the credit needs even of club members.

An unusual feature of Viet-Nam's financial system is the fact that the national Treasury also performs certain banking functions. The Treasury's offices, which are spread throughout the country, not only make payments and take in funds for the government (all on a cash basis), but also accept "demand deposits" from civil servants, business firms (mainly government suppliers), and banks. In the past several years, interest of up to one percent per annum has been paid on such deposits. At the same time, the Treasury performs rather rudimentary transfer functions for its depositors, in limited volume. The operations of this Treasury "banking" system cannot be considered a true substitute for commercial banking facilities, however. Treasury offices do not make loans to the public and their deposit and transfer facilities for individuals and business firms are, in general, incidental to the collection and disbursement of government funds; thus, a civil servant in a provincial post may make a deposit when he receives his pay in cash and wishes to keep his funds in safe custody or to effect a transfer to an account in Saigon on which his family can draw; the government, in fact, usually requires that a part of a civil servant's pay must initially go into a Treasury deposit account. "Deposits" by banks—which reached large proportions in 1955 and 1956—represent an investment of idle funds in an interest-bearing government asset and are similar to bank purchases of government securities of high liquidity; their popularity was in part explainable by the large excess reserves then held by the banking system and the fact that no Vietnamese government securities were in existence. From the viewpoint of the government, the Treasury "deposit" system has provided a convenient source for temporary borrowing, at times of an inflationary nature.

There are relatively few institutional savings facilities in Viet-Nam, and, at least until recently, neither the government nor private institutions were making serious efforts to encourage savings habits. Only one savings bank is in existence; this institution, which is governmentally owned, has no office outside of Saigon; its deposits, which amounted to only about 100 million piasters at the end of 1957 have shown no significant variation for some time. Similarly, the volume of time deposits held by the commercial banks has been quite small. While the over-all annual rate of private savings in Viet-Nam is probably quite low —though perhaps not quite so low as is widely believed—it would appear that present institutional devices have made only a limited start toward tapping such savings as are currently taking place.

Prior to 1955, the activities of commercial banks in Viet-Nam were subject to almost no governmental controls. The Institute of Issue had no authority to supervise or to examine banks, and it had virtually no power to control commercial bank credit. It was permitted to make short-term advances to the banks but only against the security of government bonds or export and import paper, and the volume of such advances (almost all against government bonds) remained at trifling levels. In deciding whether to accommodate particular requests for advances, moreover, the Institute tended to be guided almost entirely by the quality of the collateral offered rather than by more general economic considerations. Thus, the Institute could not be regarded as a true central bank—i.e., an institution concerned with the management of the country's money supply in accordance with broad economic objectives. Its main functions, rather, were similar to those of a Currency Board: to issue local currency against acquisitions of foreign exchange (i.e., French francs) and to assure the convertibility of local currency into francs for approved purposes.

In view of the virtual absence of formal monetary control powers under this system, it is rather remarkable that a fair degree of monetary and price stability existed in the period just prior to the establishment of the central bank—a period which encompassed the final months of the war against the Viet-Minh. In considerable measure this stability seems to have been attributable to the fact that the piaster payments in support of the local-currency expenditures of French and national armies in Viet-Nam—which constituted the main source of the wartime expansion in incomes—were directly financed by France and yielded the Institute of Issue an equivalent amount of French francs. Given the relative freedom of trade and payments within the franc area, the incomes so generated, and the francs so acquired, tended to be quickly drained away through heavy merchandise imports from the franc zone and financial remittances to that zone.

The tasks which confronted the Vietnamese government when it assumed responsibility for managing the country's monetary affairs at the beginning of 1955, were, broadly speaking, of two kinds.

First, it was necessary to assure that services essential to the proper functioning of the monetary system and the maintenance of a reasonable degree of monetary and price stability which had previously been carried out by quadripartite institutions would now be provided with equal or greater efficiency on a national basis and under Vietnamese management. This meant, for example, that there had to be adequate facilities for the issuance and handling of currency and that preparations had to be made for the replacement of Institute of Issue notes (and of other "Indochinese" notes then circulating in Viet-Nam) with a distinctive national currency. It meant, too, that every effort had to be exerted to assure that the system of international payments would continue to work relatively smoothly during the sudden shift to direct American aid, thus permitting a steady flow of imports and financial transfers. This was of vital importance if inflation were to be avoided, for it was clear that commodity imports— which were largely financed by foreign aid—and remittances and other financial transfers would, for some time to come, have to remain the main instrument for absorbing the excess purchasing power created by the local currency expenditures incurred in supporting the military forces.

But the mere continuation of the type of monetary and credit arrangements which had existed while Viet-Nam was under French control was clearly not sufficient to serve the country's needs and aspirations once it had gained independence and at a time when its economy faced major structural adjustments. The second range of tasks which faced Viet-Nam's new monetary authorities, therefore, arose from the need—and the government's strong desire—to develop more positive methods for promoting monetary stability and economic growth. Thus, a set of mechanisms had to be created through which banking and credit institutions could, for the first time, be effectively supervised and controlled in accordance with a national monetary policy. A major effort, moreover, was required to expand existing credit and savings facilities and to achieve a more balanced distribution of credit among the various regions and sectors of the economy.

The problems which faced Vietnamese authorities as they prepared to cope with these various tasks were formidable. New administrative organizations had to be created overnight (or existing ones reorganized) and had to be largely staffed with Vietnamese personnel—an exceedingly difficult assignment in view of the critical shortage of administrators and technicians with training and experience in finance. The transition to the new monetary system had to be effected at a time when the government did not yet possess full administrative control over the country and when a major share of its attention had to be devoted to problems of political and military survival. The economy, moreover, was only just beginning to recover from the damages wrought by many years of war and civil unrest; it was still largely dependent on foreign aid, which paid for more than three fourths of the imports and over half of the domestic budgetary expenditures; and it faced many special adjustments as a result of the territorial changes decreed by the Geneva Agreement, the massive influx of refugees from the Communist north, and the extensive structural changes in the private business community that were likely to occur as French influence diminished and Vietnamese firms—often with little or no prior experience—sought to enter business fields previously pre-empted by foreign concerns.

Furthermore, the breakup of the monetary and customs union in Indochina and the change-over to direct American aid were in themselves bound to result in important shifts in existing trade and payments relationships that could be expected to produce various temporary economic dislocations and created the possibility that a sizeable "inflationary" gap might suddenly emerge. To be sure, the main purpose of the American aid program was to provide sufficient support to Viet-Nam's internal budget so that military and other essential expenditures in excess of those which could be financed from Viet-Nam's own resources would *not* give rise to inflation; foreign aid, it was hoped, would continue to be "neutral" in its direct impact on the monetary and price situation. The "usual" American aid program,[128] moreover, is intended to provide automatic safeguards against inflation: aid-financed commercial imports are first sold for piasters on local markets (or more precisely, to importers planning to resell the goods); the piasters so generated are then deposited in a "counterpart fund" and budget support is provided only when the U.S. consents to the release of such funds to the Vietnamese government. Thus, the injection of new purchasing power into the economy was in effect to be *preceded* (or at least paralleled) by the withdrawal of a fully equiva-

[128] Under this procedure, known as the procurement authorization system, no foreign exchange is directly made available to the government of the country receiving aid; rather, imports are secured through commercial channels on the basis of procurement authorizations issued by ICA, and foreign suppliers (or their banks) are paid directly by ICA.

lent amount of piasters from the spending stream.[129] But sole reliance on this procedure at the beginning of 1955 was impractical, since the need to provide local currency support to the Vietnamese budget was immediate, while some time necessarily had to elapse until the arrival of the first large-scale shipments of American aid goods. Consequently, it was clear that in the initial stages of the expanded American aid program, the United States would have to make direct purchases, with dollars, of large sums of piasters from Viet-Nam's new National Bank and to make these piasters available to the Vietnamese Treasury as soon as they were needed for disbursement to the national army.[130] Under this procedure, however, there was no immediate offset to inflationary expansion of incomes through the expenditure of the newly created local currency, for it took time until the dollar exchange that had simultaneously accrued to the National Bank could in turn be spent on imports and absorb local currency.

Some delays in the use of newly acquired dollar exchange, of course, were inevitable because of the normal interval between applications for import licenses and final payments for imported goods to foreign suppliers. But there were many additional factors, directly or indirectly connected with the change-over to the new system, which were likely to add

[129] Even in the case postulated here, in which piaster withdrawals under the American aid program equal piaster disbursals, it is not entirely correct to say that the over-all impact of American aid operations on the country's spending stream and price system would necessarily be "neutral." The program could have either an expansionary or a contractionary impact in the case under discussion if there were significant differences between the savings propensities of the groups from whom incomes are withdrawn and those to whom new incomes are disbursed; these differences, as well as other factors, would have to be considered in any complete analysis that would take account of various secondary effects entailed both by the absorption and disbursement of piaster funds. To some extent, the problems encountered here are analogous to those involved in the study of the economic effects of balanced budgets. But in the absence of any detailed knowledge of Vietnamese savings and spending patterns in early 1955, it was reasonable to start out with the initial assumption that the situation described would leave over-all spending approximately unchanged.

[130] It should be noted that this procedure for procuring imports, known as the cash grant or direct dollar procedure, is not necessarily more inflationary than the procurement authorization procedure once the import "pipelines" have been filled and receipts of dollar exchange by the foreign government are approximately balanced by use of such exchange to finance imports. In some ways, the direct dollar procedure has advantages over the procurement authorization procedure, since it is more in line with the customary method by which governments provide exchange to importers and also because it permits speedier adaptation of the import flow to changes in import demand. On the other hand, the direct dollar procedure may not permit as close a check on the use of United States aid funds as the procurement authorization system.

to these delays. Under American aid rules, for one thing, most imports had to be procured on the world-wide competitive basis rather than from the franc currency zone only; while this change promised to bring substantial benefits to Viet-Nam, it initially posed major problems for importers who had to find new sources of supply. Moreover, the rules regarding the types of products which could be imported tended to be more stringent under the American aid system, and temporary bottlenecks in import licensing procedures were almost inevitable since most government officials and businessmen had to adapt their operations to new and unfamiliar operations. Finally, and in sharp contrast to the system that had existed when aid was primarily channeled through France, the foreign exchange which Viet-Nam obtained under the United States aid program could generally not be used for the financing of profit remittances or other financial transfers. [131] All these factors added to the danger that the change to national monetary management and direct United States aid would cause a serious disruption in the balance of payments mechanism through which excess purchasing power had until then been more or less automatically siphoned off.

The difficulties in the way of successful introduction of monetary controls and improvements in the country's credit structure were, if anything, even greater than those directly connected with the breakup of the monetary union and the change-over to direct American aid. These tasks, by their very nature, were almost entirely unfamiliar to the new monetary administrators, who had had at least some previous operational experience with currency and international payments problems. There were almost no monetary and banking statistics that could serve as a guide to the monetary authorities, and the widely varying accounting procedures employed by the different banks greatly complicated the tasks of training bank examiners and initiating an effective system of bank supervision. As in other underdeveloped countries, many of the more traditional credit control instruments could not be used in Viet-Nam—or initially seemed likely to prove of only very modest effectiveness—because of such factors as the limited use of discountable credit instruments (which were subject to frequently prohibitive stamp and registration taxes); the absence of any marketable government securities; and the highly liquid position of the commercial banks. Legal and customary inhibitions against the use of credit instruments, of course, also presented a major impediment to a broadening of credit facilities, as did the virtual absence of a system

---

[131] This stricture applied not only to "direct dollars" but also to so-called "triangular francs" and other "third currencies" generated through U. S. surplus commodity sales abroad and made available to Viet-Nam under the U. S. aid program, with economic effects broadly paralleling those of "direct dollar" grants.

for interchanging credit information. And continued military insecurity as well as personnel shortages seemed to rule out almost entirely any immediate chances for progress in establishing better credit facilities in the more remote rural areas. All in all, it was clear that success in developing effective credit controls and achieving a better balance in the distribution of credit would have to come gradually and would require much experimentation and education.

A major share of the responsibility for carrying out the various new tasks which national monetary independence brought to Viet-Nam was assigned to the National Bank of Viet-Nam, established at the beginning of 1955. It was recognized, of course, that the bank's policies had to complement appropriate policies governing fiscal and trade matters, and that there would be many problems in the credit field—particularly those relating to the improvement of credit facilities—which could not be solved by the National Bank alone. The statute of the bank was drafted with the assistance of Dr. Arthur I. Bloomfield, then Senior Economist of the Federal Reserve Bank of New York, who had had extensive experience in the monetary problems of less-developed countries and was the main author of the central banking legislation for Korea.

To allow a smooth adaptation to the new monetary system, the provisions of the bank's statute were carefully geared to fit the special needs and customs of the country and to endow the bank with wide flexibility in meeting the numerous contingencies that might arise as the economy experienced far-reaching structural changes. Some of the more novel provisions of the statute, furthermore, were to become effective only after specified periods in order to permit proper preparation for the administration of these provisions. The language of the statute was purposely kept simple; rather than attempting to anticipate all possible problems that might arise in the future, it was felt that it might be better to revise the statute at some later date if experience proved this to be necessary.

In part, the new National Bank can simply be regarded as a successor organization—for Viet-Nam only—to the former Indochinese Institute of Issue. It inherited most of the Institute's "service" functions, particularly those connected with the note issue, and took over much of the Institute's Vietnamese personnel, as well as most of its physical facilities. The organizational structure of the National Bank, moreover, was largely modeled on that of the Institute of Issue. Thus, the bank is wholly owned by the government, and its top executive officers are a governor and a deputy governor,[132] who are assisted by a director general and a controller general. The statute entrusts the formulation of the bank's general policies

[132] While a deputy governor was originally appointed, the post has recently been vacant.

and over-all administrative supervision to a board of directors. This board was to consist, in addition to the governor and deputy governor, of five members appointed for three-year terms, two to be taken from the field of banking and economics, and three from commerce, industry, and agriculture; such a board, however, has as yet not been appointed. The Exchange Control Office, which had been independent of the Institute of Issue under the quadripartite arrangements, became a department of the National Bank headed by a director, but has in fact retained considerable autonomy.

It is in terms of its potential ability to affect the country's monetary and credit system that the new National Bank differs fundamentally from the Institute of Issue. Unlike the Institute, the National Bank is equipped with a wide range of central banking powers to influence the volume of bank reserves and of bank credit and to help promote a more adequate distribution of credit. The commercial banks, moreover, were required to furnish the National Bank with any relevant information, and their accounts were made subject to periodic examination by the National Bank.[133]

The statute equipped the new central bank with three principal credit control instruments, two of which were designed to enable the bank to exert an indirect influence over the volume of commercial bank reserves, while the third permitted the imposition, if need be, of direct limitations on bank loan expansion.[134]

The first instrument was a reserve requirement against commercial bank deposits, which was to become effective three months after the enactment of the statute and was initially set at 10 percent. Six months after the enactment of the statute, the National Bank was authorized to vary the minimum legal reserve ratio, provided this ratio was not fixed at less than 10 percent or more than 35 percent.

The second instrument was broad authority to discount, rediscount, buy, or sell credit instruments held by the commercial banks—or to make ad-

[133] The statutory provision calling for initiation of a system of bank examinations, however, was permissive rather than obligatory and was, in any case, not to become effective until at least six months after the date of the statute's enactment. This reflected the fact that virtually no trained examiners were then available to carry out such inspections. The National Bank was also given various other powers relating to the supervision of banking activities; thus, its approval was required before new banks or bank branches could be opened, or the capitalization of existing banks could be changed. The standards to be applied in connection with bank examinations were to be promulgated by the Bank's board of directors and require presidential approval.

[134] The statute did not grant the bank explicit authority to engage in "open market" operations, apparently because it was felt that such a power would for some time to come have little or no meaning, given the undeveloped state of the money market and the difficulties of creating a market in government securities.

vances to these banks against the collateral of such instruments, or of government bonds—as well as full discretion to vary the terms of the conditions attaching to these discounts and advances and to fix the amounts involved. If desirable in terms of the over-all monetary situation, moreover, the bank has complete authority to refuse requests for credit altogether. Credit instruments eligible for discount or as collateral for advances were not restricted to those arising from export and import transactions, or to government securities (as had been the case under the Institute of Issue), but could originate in a wide variety of specified domestic commercial or productive activities; in an emergency, moreover, the National Bank was authorized to grant advances to commercial banks against any collateral that it deemed acceptable. Maximum maturities on credit operations with commercial banks were set at 120 days in the case of transactions associated with commercial activities or storage of nonperishable goods and at 240 days for most transactions based on domestic productive activities.

Finally, the third credit control instrument was the power to impose direct ceilings on the rate of increase in commercial bank loans, either in the aggregate or by categories. This power was granted to meet a situation in which controls over the volume of reserves proved inadequate to prevent a rapid expansion of commercial bank credit. It was, however, only to be applied in case of a severe inflationary crisis, and requires the approval of the President.

To help promote a better distribution of credit, the bank was not only given wide scope in its credit transactions with commercial banks but was also authorized to make advances of up to 365 days against the promissory notes of credit institutions (existing or yet to be established) which specialize in loans to agriculture, the handicraft trades, and industry. Moreover, the bank was enjoined to make a continuing study of needed improvements in the existing system of credit to the domestic sector of the economy.

The statute carefully defined the National Bank's relation to the government. Like the Institute of Issue, the bank is to act as fiscal agent and banker for the government (which may, however, continue to deposit its funds in other banking institutions) and serve as "adviser" to the government on a wide range of problems, including the issuance of government securities. The bank's ability to lend to the government was explicitly limited to making temporary advances for periods up to six months, and the total amount of such advances outstanding at any one time was not permitted to exceed 25 percent of the government's budgetary receipts for the previous year.

The powers of the bank's National Exchange Control Office[135] were

[135] See pp. 288-301, on "The Foreign Exchange Policy of Viet-Nam." (ED.)

defined in the broadest possible terms to enable it to deal with any possible contingencies and provide flexibility for devising new foreign exchange arrangements suitable to Viet-Nam's needs. Provisions concerning cover for the note issue, similarly, were flexible. This partly reflected a general trend in recent central banking legislation but was also made necessary by the uncertain prospects as to Viet-Nam's future exchange availabilities—which, in any case, would for some time have to be largely based on foreign aid receipts. The statute merely indicated that the bank should progressively build up, and eventually maintain, a reserve of 33 percent in gold and foreign exchange against its note issue and deposit liabilities.

While the National Bank, as noted, can make loans to banks and other credit institutions, it was not authorized to lend directly to the public. The task of expanding and improving domestic credit facilities, therefore, involved redirection of the activities of the commercial banks or the creation of new credit institutions. A number of such institutions have been set up in the past several years.

The most important of these institutions, at least in terms of its current volume of operations, is the state commercial bank (Credit Commercial du Viet-Nam). Established at the end of 1955, this bank took over most of the physical assets and part of the business of the Banque de l'Indochine. Since its primary initial task was to help fill the gap in credit facilities created by the termination of the Bank of Indochina's operations in Viet-Nam, its lending activities could at first be expected to focus on foreign trade transactions and to differ little from those of its predecessor or of the other commercial banks in Saigon, except that they were likely to place greater emphasis on filling the credit needs of Vietnamese nationals. It was intended, however, that Credit Commercial would give growing attention to the financing of domestic commercial and productive activities and would, in particular, establish branch operations in various parts of the country as soon as possible. While the Credit Commercial is legally separate from the central bank, the two institutions occupy the same building and the statutes of the former provide that its board of directors be headed by the governor of the National Bank.

The decision to create a separate state commercial bank—rather than set up a commercial department in the central bank—was taken only after careful consideration. There were, in fact, a number of appealing arguments for permitting the central bank to lend directly to the public. Those who favored this approach argued that it would not only allow the most efficient use of the limited number of technicians with training in banking and finance but that it would also enable the National Bank to exert a more direct and powerful influence on the country's banking operations than was otherwise possible. The fact that this approach was rejected was, in the main, based on the fear—borne out in the experience of many other countries—that a mixing of central banking and commercial banking activities would be likely to divert the central bank's attention from its primary responsibilities as a regulator of the country's monetary and credit system, and in effect cause its policies to be dominated by a "commercial banking" approach that would be concerned with profit making and would lead to strong temptations to expand credit in an overly liberal fashion. Moreover, a central bank that engages in direct banking operations with the public is placed in the paradoxical role of being both a regulator and a competitor of the private commercial banks; this may seriously impair its ability to supervise these banks fairly and to gain their confidence. Finally, it was believed that the "economies" in the use of personnel which inclusion of a commercial banking department in the central bank could produce would not nearly be so great as was claimed by advocates of such an arrangement.

Among other official credit institutions created in recent years are several that specialize in the financing of agriculture or industry. In 1955 and 1956 various arrangements of a rather makeshift kind were used for extending agricultural credit, mainly to refugees or in connection with the land reform program. To combine and improve the existing agricultural credit and development institutions, a National Agricultural Credit Office was set up in April, 1957, with the help of both budgetary and foreign aid counterpart funds. This organization is authorized to make low interest loans to individuals and to agricultural co-operatives, to distribute needed fertilizers and farming equipment, and to provide various technical services. A National Investment Fund, financed entirely by the government, was established in September, 1955, to provide both short- and longer-term loans for small and medium-sized industrial projects and handicraft operations, and to help finance government participation in industrial enterprises. The Fund was given little autonomy, however, and no role in mobilizing private capital, as would be true of a development bank. In October, 1957, an industrial development center was created, which is to be partly financed with American aid funds. The Center is expected to engage not only in medium- and longer-term lending activities and in a broad program of technical assistance and advice to new industrial enterprises, but will also serve as an information center and catalyst through which potential investors and managers can be put in touch with investment opportunities.[136]

---

[136] This list of new credit institutions or arrangements is by no means exhaustive. Other recently created financing facilities include: The Caisses de Credit Populaire, set up in 1955 as a kind of government pawnshop system providing credit to individuals at more reasonable terms than private moneylenders; and a special loan fund to small retail and wholesale firms created in late 1956.

To co-ordinate government policies with respect to financial and economic problems, the President of Viet-Nam in June, 1955, created a Supreme Monetary and Credit Council. This council, which meets at frequent intervals, is headed by the President and includes the ministers of Finance and of Economy, the governor of the central bank, and several other key cabinet members.

The difficulties encountered in the actual transition to national monetary management and in shifting from indirect to direct American aid were in many ways even more formidable than had been anticipated at the end of 1954. Civil unrest and the armed uprising of the sects in the early months of 1955 not only greatly complicated the mechanical tasks of shifting to the new system but vastly increased the many hazards and uncertainties which already faced the business community. As a result, many foreign enterprises sought to reduce or terminate current operations and a substantial number of foreign residents left the country abruptly;[137] pressures to withdraw capital increased sharply just as the available exchange for financial remittances and transfers dwindled drastically, since dollars or "triangular francs" made available under the American aid program could in general not be used to finance such transactions;[138] and there was a large and potentially inflationary accumulation of idle balances at the commercial banks, representing funds deposited in connection with applications for transfers. The burden placed on imports as the principal device for containing inflationary pressures was thus further increased, especially since, under the conditions then prevailing, immediate resort to restrictive fiscal or monetary measures was almost entirely out of the question. But import risks also mounted sharply, so that many importers hesitated to place new orders and bankers frequently refused to grant new import credits. Added to bottlenecks in import licensing procedures and other transitional difficulties, these factors for a time brought an almost complete stoppage in the issuance of new import letters of credit.

The reluctance of importers to enter into new commitments, which persisted until the fall of 1955, was, of course, based partly on the possibility of war damages and broad fears regarding the ability of Viet-Nam to survive as an independent nation. It also rested on the feeling, however, that a possible exchange rate adjustment might involve importers

[137] This exodus involved mainly civil servants and persons who had been engaged in commercial activities; foreign-owned plantations and industrial enterprises generally continued operations. Many of the more important trading firms cut their staffs sharply during this period but did not close shop entirely.

[138] Almost half of foreign exchange allocations in 1954 had been for profit remittances and capital transfers. In 1955 such allocations had to be cut to about one fifth of the 1954 volume.

in heavy losses (or smaller gains than anticipated),[139] and on the difficulty of assessing future import demand in a period when the structure of internal demand was rapidly changing as the exodus of foreign civilians (and, as the year progressed, of the French Expeditionary Corps) gained momentum. To complicate matters further, there was a relative glut of merchandise in Viet-Nam during the early months of 1955, because of a heavy volume of import orders placed in late 1954 before the new (and much stricter) exchange licensing procedures went into effect. In a sense this proved a blessing since it provided a "cushion" of accumulated inventories in succeeding months when import volume dropped sharply because of delays in the arrival of goods financed under the American aid program. But it also materially contributed to these delays: the momentary difficulties in disposing of imported goods at customary profit margins (and fears that firms stocked with goods purchased in the franc area would suffer serious losses if there were an early influx of more competitively priced "American aid" goods) were major factors in deterring new import orders and in causing banks to restrict import credit severely.[140]

Under these circumstances, it was inevitable that a major share of the initial efforts of the central bank had to be devoted to various "mechanical" aspects of the change-over to the new monetary and aid arrangements, particularly those relating to the handling of United States cash grants and the initiation of the American aid import program. Thus, a great deal of the time of the new bank's officials in the early months of 1955 was spent in setting up procedures under which the National Bank bought and sold dollars on behalf of the government, acted as custodian of the American aid counterpart fund, established official banking connections abroad, and validated exchange applications and financing arrangements covering American aid imports. The National Bank, of course, was only one of a number of governmental organizations concerned with the functioning of the import mechanism. The enormous burden of administering import allocations and licensing largely fell on the National Import Committee, and the American Aid authorities were concerned with almost every phase of the import process.

However, it is noteworthy that the National Bank's role in connection

---

[139] The possibility of "loss" existed in the case of imports ordered prior to a (hypothetical) devaluation, but which arrived after the devaluation. In such an event, the local currency payments that had to be made into the counterpart funds upon arrival of the goods would have exceeded the amount anticipated when the importer made his cost calculation.

[140] The necessity to provide exchange cover for the exceptionally large volume of import arrivals from the franc area in the early months of 1955 also cut down sharply on franc reserves available as cover for remittances and financial transfers. See *Rapport Annuel* of the National Bank of Viet-Nam for 1955, p. 22.

with the import program was not confined to the development of "banking" procedures and foreign exchange transactions. The Bank also actively explored the possibilities for reducing importers' risks and for improving import credit facilities. A major step taken in this connection was the establishment, in mid-1955, of a system of exchange guarantee contracts between the National Bank and the commercial banks (and concurrently, between the banks and importers) which insured imports against the risk of devaluation. This almost certainly tended to facilitate the resumption of import ordering on a larger scale.

Despite the energies and personnel resources which were thrown into efforts to prevent a disruption of the import process, the difficulties encountered were so great that delays in the placement of import orders remained a serious problem until late 1955. Bottlenecks in licensing procedures persisted throughout 1955 and, to a somewhat lesser extent, through 1956. The physical volume of imports consequently declined sharply by late 1955 and had fallen to less than half of the 1954 level by mid-1956. However, problems relating to financing procedures under the American aid import program had, to a large extent, been resolved by the summer of 1955.

These problems, it may be noted, in general came under the jurisdiction of the American Aid Department of the National Bank rather than of the National Exchange Control Office. The latter, however, had a wide range of responsibilities in connection with the granting of authorizations covering the use of foreign exchange not provided through the United States aid and did concern itself with some phases of the United States program after the spring of 1955 when it was given authority to handle the allocation of "triangular francs." When Viet-Nam decided to terminate its membership in the franc area at the end of 1955, the National Exchange Control Office and the Foreign Department of the National Bank assumed major additional responsibilities; these included, in particular, the creation of an official foreign exchange market in Saigon.

Another major preoccupation of the National Bank during its first years of existence was the preparation of the currency conversion. Preparatory talks with the new central banks of Cambodia and Laos relating to such a conversion were begun early in 1955. The actual currency exchange took place in November, 1955, and, on the whole, was carried out successfully. While this conversion operation gave Viet-Nam an independent currency, not all the notes in circulation were withdrawn; Institute of Issue notes with a "Vietnamese face"[141] were allowed to

[141] Institute of Issue notes of specified denominations had identical "backs" but different "faces" which showed, respectively, representative pictures of Cambodia, Laos, or Viet-Nam.

continue to circulate (they were withdrawn from circulation in Cambodia and Laos) and were replaced with distinctive new national notes only about a year later.

Despite the new National Bank's initial concentration on the administrative aspects of the transition to a national monetary system, a number of steps were also taken during 1955 and the first half of 1956 to initiate central bank controls and to begin to reduce the excessive liquidity of the commercial banks. As provided in the central bank's statute, a minimum reserve requirement against commercial bank deposits was established in the spring of 1955,[142] the requirement initially being set at 10 percent. Since the actual reserves of the banks exceeded 50 percent of deposit liabilities, on the average, the reserve requirement could not be expected to exert any immediate influence on the banks' policies. It did, however, give the commercial banks their first acquaintance with central bank controls, particularly since they were also required to submit regular statistical reports. No immediate move was made to introduce central bank credit facilities (for which there appeared little need at the time because of the banks' high liquidity). At the suggestion of the central bank, however, various stamp taxes that inhibited the use of credit instruments were repealed toward the end of the year, thus preparing the way for the subsequent establishment of a system of rediscounting or of central bank advances against the collateral of such instruments.

Measures affecting bank liquidity, it may be noted, were not confined to the establishment of reserve requirements. Perhaps equally important was the institution, in mid-1955, of a predeposit requirement in connection with exchange guarantee contracts, which amounted to at least 25 percent (and in most instances, 100 percent) of the value of import letters of credit. A third major step that tended to reduce bank liquidity was the establishment, in July, 1956, of the limited access "free" foreign exchange market, which permitted a sharply accelerated rate of profit remittances and capital transfers, though at an exchange rate of about 75 piasters to the dollar rather than at the official rate of 35.

How effective were the various efforts of Viet-Nam's new monetary, trade, exchange control, and fiscal authorities (as well as of the American aid mission) in preventing the emergence of a serious monetary and price inflation during the first eighteen months of the transition period? An examination of the available data on Viet-Nam's money supply (which are admittedly not entirely satisfactory) indicates that the money supply[143] expanded by approximately 12 percent between January and October,

[142] While the statute had provided that such a requirement was to be instituted on April 1, it actually took effect on April 15, 1955.

[143] Defined here simply as currency in circulation plus private demand deposits at the commercial banks, see above. (ED.)

1955. By the summer of 1956, however, it had receded to about the level prevailing at the beginning of 1955. The initial increase in the money supply, moreover, entirely reflected a 44 percent expansion in bank deposits; since many of these deposits were made in anticipation of profit remittances or capital transfers, they were in effect blocked and, while potentially inflationary, probably did not exert an immediate upward pressure on the price structure. In 1956 the volume of deposits started to contract as financial transfers were speeded up (particularly after the establishment of the free market in July). Currency in circulation actually showed some contraction during the eighteen-month period (though the currency conversion makes interpretation of the data for late 1955 and early 1956 especially difficult).

Thus, there was relatively little evidence of monetary inflation except during part of 1955. Such monetary expansion as did occur was largely associated with the rapid build-up of foreign exchange reserves in the first half of 1955 as a result of large American "cash grants," although government deficit spending (over and above the deficit covered by United States aid) also seems to have played a significant part; these deficits were apparently financed by drawings on balances which the commercial banks had deposited at the Treasury and did not entail borrowing from the central bank.[144] Expansionary influences on the money supply were partly offset, however, by a contraction of private bank credit, a build-up of the counterpart fund, and accumulations of exchange guarantee deposits. The leveling off and contraction in the money supply during early 1956, on the other hand, were partly explained by an improved budgetary position, a stabilization in the level of foreign exchange reserves, and further growth in exchange guarantee deposits—influences which were, by and large, sufficient to offset the expansionary effects of substantial reductions in the counterpart fund and of increased bank lending to private firms.

In contrast to the relative stability of the money supply, prices showed pronounced upward movements between the beginning of 1955 and mid-1956. True, they showed little change during the first seven months of 1955—a remarkable record in view of the civil disturbances during this period—but both living costs and wholesale prices of domestic goods in Saigon rose sharply in the fall of the year. In the first half of 1956, retail and wholesale prices of domestically produced items receded somewhat but wholesale prices of imported goods began a gradual upturn. In the summer, both wholesale and retail prices registered sharp new increases, and by August, the wholesale price level in Saigon was 20 percent higher

---

[144] Unfortunately, no adequate assessment of the role of the government sector will be possible until more detailed and accurate information with respect to Treasury operations becomes available.

than in January, 1955, while living costs of Vietnamese workers' families had risen by 25 percent.

What accounted for this rather rapid advance in price levels while total money supply, on balance, remained virtually unchanged? To some extent, the increase in money supply during part of the period undoubtedly created upward price pressures, though with a time lag. But it seems likely that much of the explanation of price trends can be found in temporary shortages of commodity supplies (both domestic and imported), in shifts in the distribution of money holdings between groups with varying spending propensities, and in changes in over-all spending propensities as the political and economic climate underwent significant variations. As noted earlier, the relative price stability during early 1955 (when money supply was rising) was probably mainly attributable to the existence of large inventories and the fact that the additions to money supply consisted chiefly of idle bank deposits. The sharp price increases in the fall were, to an important extent, connected with a short rice crop and temporary distribution difficulties because of the revolt of the "sects"; illegal purchases of rice by Viet-Minh agents for use in north Viet-Nam and some commodity speculation just prior to the currency conversion may also have been factors. Increases in import prices during 1956 appear to have been closely correlated with declines in the rate of import arrivals; during the same period, restoration of internal security facilitated the reopening of markets and may have tended to lead to more active use of the counterpart funds disbursed to the military and to refugees.[145] In retrospect, the renewed upward spurt in prices in July and August, 1956, would seem to have been largely due to temporary supply shortages of both imported products and of domestic foodstuffs rather than the emergence of a "spiraling" inflation based on monetary expansion; bank credit to the private sector of the economy, in fact, did not expand until later in the year when import volume also rose.

The rapidity of the upward price movement in the summer of 1956, nevertheless, caused widespread concern, and led to a series of energetic measures designed to curb the inflationary trend. Stringent price, profit, and inventory controls were introduced in the fall which were reflected in sharp declines in published price indexes after the month of August. In September the National Bank raised the reserve requirement against commercial bank deposits from 10 to 20 percent. To break the serious

---

[145] It would have been logical to expect more commodity purchases and less currency hoarding during the period of civil war, particularly in view of the impending currency conversion. It is my impression, however, that currency hoarding actually increased during this period (though, as mentioned, there was some dishoarding just prior to the currency conversion).

licensing bottlenecks which were still impeding the import process, the import control authorities took vigorous action to simplify procedures and imposed high cash bond requirements on importers in connection with the filing of license applications; the latter step was designed to discourage import applications by firms that had no serious intention or ability to complete import transactions but whose activities enormously increased the work-load of the licensing authorities. Various measures were also taken to improve the government's fiscal position; perhaps most important were the tax reforms carried out in the spring of 1957,[146] which raised taxes on many imported as well as locally produced items and facilitated more vigorous tax collection. The Customs Office, moreover, sharply reduced the volume of customs "credits" which had permitted importers to defer payments of customs duties for considerable periods of time.

By the spring and summer of 1957, these various measures had resulted in a dramatic reversal of the inflationary trend. By March, 1957, the official indexes of consumer and of wholesale prices had fallen 13 percent below their August, 1956, levels; open market prices, moreover, in many cases seem to have declined even more sharply than the official indexes. The money supply declined continuously after January, 1957, falling 5 percent below the December, 1956 level by July, 1957; the decline continued through October, moreover, when it totaled 7 percent.[147] Profits of many trading firms, particularly of importers, were severely squeezed, and there was a rapid accumulation of unsold inventories of imported goods. The liquidity of the commercial banks, finally, was drastically reduced from the very high levels that had prevailed a year earlier. Thus, bank reserves in March, 1957, amounted, on the average, to 30 percent of deposit liabilities as against double this amount a year earlier; since the banks in many cases had no secondary reserves and since the liquidity position of some of the individual banks was substantially below the general average, many of the banks found themselves in a relatively tight position, a situation which was reflected in a rise of interest rates paid on deposits as well as in higher interest charges to most classes of borrowers.

The most important factor accounting for this reversal in the balance of economic forces was a sudden increase in the rate of import arrivals following the successful elimination of licensing bottlenecks in late 1956, an increase that was intensified by a "bunching" in the arrivals of ship-

---

[146] See pp. 309-11, on "Tax Reforms in Viet-Nam." (ED.)

[147] The 13 percent decline from the end of January, 1957, through the end of October was even more abrupt; because of the "Tet" or New Year celebrations in January; however, a pronounced seasonal rise in money supply during that month is normally expected.

ments that had earlier been delayed by the closing of the Suez Canal. By the third quarter of 1957, the physical volume of imports was nearly 50 percent above the level recorded a year earlier. The deflationary impact of this development was strongly reinforced by the fact that the various restrictive measures taken in the fiscal and monetary fields began to take hold just as import arrivals assumed massive proportions; government cash balances, for example, appear to have risen sharply during this period. The situation was further complicated by the consequences of measures affecting Chinese nationals which had been taken in the fall of 1956. These measures initially resulted in a brief panic and in a rapid withdrawal of currency from the banks; by early 1957, they had led to a virtual "strike" of Chinese distributors and moneylenders, and a consequent disruption in important internal distribution mechanisms. This greatly compounded the difficulties of importers, who were in many cases unable to move their commodities into the interior of the country. At the same time, special problems were created for the banks, which not only faced greatly increased import credit demands and growing risks as the volume of importations was stepped up but were also called upon to extend loans to carry retail inventories and to extend other types of credit accommodation to the domestic sector which had until then largely been provided by Chinese wholesalers and moneylenders (who frequently kept their funds in currency hoards).

In many ways, the deflationary trend could be regarded as a healthy development. It performed a necessary corrective function by exposing to more competitive conditions those trading firms which had earned excessively high profits during years of wartime boom and a high degree of protection; thus, profits tended to be reduced to more reasonable levels and there was a weeding out of marginal firms. Nevertheless, the sudden force of the reversal of the inflationary trend created the possibility that deflationary tendencies might go too far, and the government soon recognized the need for some alleviating action. It is noteworthy that the remedial measures which were taken formed part of a co-ordinated program formulated by the Supreme Monetary and Credit Council.

Among the first "anti-recessionary" measures were a reduction in the amount of cash bonds required of importers and a modification of regulations relating to the deferment of customs payments—steps that were of direct assistance in easing the cash position of importers. In April the National Bank initiated a system of advances to commercial banks in line with the provisions of the central bank statute, extending such credit against the collateral of foreign government securities and of export or import documents. By the end of May, the outstanding volume of central bank credit to the commercial banks had reached 120 million piasters, equivalent to about 10 percent of required reserves. While the availability of central bank credit facilities helped to alleviate the liquidity problems of the commercial banks to some extent, it was probably of least benefit to the smaller Vietnamese banks whose liquidity had been most severely squeezed. These banks could not offer foreign government securities as collateral, and also found it difficult to submit the necessary trade documents in connection with loan applications. In June, therefore, the National Bank took the further step of reducing the reserve requirement to 15 percent; in addition, regulations governing the central bank credit system were liberalized, and the discount rate was cut by one half percent. In July, a new type of exchange guarantee contract was introduced under which predeposits in connection with import transactions were no longer required.

While these measures tended to alleviate some of the most critical problems of trading firms and of commercial banks, the "commercial crisis" continued to be a source of serious concern as long as the volume of imports was still rising and internal distribution remained disrupted. As the year progressed, therefore, it became increasingly clear that additional measures needed to be taken that would improve internal distribution and credit mechanisms and that would stimulate domestic production and exports. Some of the more restrictive price and inventory controls which had served as a deterrent to the entry of new firms into the distribution field were modified, and special credit facilities were made available to distributors, though on a rather limited scale. Toward the year end, as already noted, the government began to take a much more active interest in the encouragement of investment than had been the case previously. In the latter months of the year, some of the remedial measures taken earlier began to show some effects, government expenditures were accelerated, and progress was apparently made in reducing excess inventories as the rate of import arrivals returned to more normal levels; reductions in American aid allocations for imports, in fact, created the possibility that import volume would decline further. The money supply stabilized after October, and wholesale prices showed a significant (though partly seasonal) rise, reflecting a relatively small rice crop and the lower rate of imports as well as the impact of adjustments in the effective exchange rate structure (including new surtaxes on certain imports).

In the light of experience of the past several years, can it be said that the basic approach which was taken in dealing with the tasks posed by national monetary independence has been a sound one? The answer must clearly be in the affirmative. Some observers, it is true, have suggested that such steps as the creation of a separate central bank and of a state commercial bank located in Saigon were unnecessary and have merely tended to divert scarce personnel resources from more important tasks in the field of credit, such as the expansion of banking facilities to the interior of the country. But these criticisms fail to take account of the realities and needs that existed at the time the new institutions were created. The fact, is, as noted, that the end of the quadripartite system and the change-over to direct American aid at the beginning of 1955 created a critical need for an institution that would immediately be able to act as a banker and a fiscal agent for the Vietnamese government. The type of institution that was actually established—a National Bank that was able to take over much of the administrative machinery and personnel of the agency which had handled similar tasks previously— was almost certainly better equipped to handle these tasks than any other government organization. Moreover, the Vietnamese government at the beginning of 1955 was strongly determined to create a mechanism that would enable it to exert independent and positive controls over the country's monetary system, and it seems likely that such an objective could be properly implemented only through a separate institution equipped with real central banking powers rather than through a subordinate bureau in some existing governmental agency. The decision to establish a state commercial bank, finally, was directly linked to the termination of the Banque de l'Indochine's operations in Viet-Nam, and to the fact that there appeared to be no practical alternative for filling the wide and sudden gap in credit facilities that had thus been created.

The performance of these new institutions in dealing with the more pressing initial tasks, moreover, has to a large extent justified or even exceeded the hopes held at the time of their establishment. Considering the extraordinary difficulties entailed by the transition to a national monetary system and new foreign aid and international payments arrangements during a period of armed rebellion, it would seem fair to say that the shift was, on the whole, accomplished remarkably smoothly. The inflation that did emerge was relatively mild and was rather quickly reversed. While this could to a considerable extent be attributed to foreign aid imports and to fiscal measures, the development of central bank credit controls also played a significant role; in fact, the effectiveness of these controls in reducing bank liquidity and helping to curb inflationary pressures at such an early stage of the central bank's existence was probably greater than most observers would have expected on the basis of experience with new central banks in many other countries. And in its Saigon operations, the Credit Commercial (which, as expected, has so far operated along lines similar to those of other commercial banks in the capital city) has not only acquired an excellent reputation for competence but is making notable strides in training new personnel.

Progress in coping with many of the other tasks in the monetary and credit field which were outlined earlier—particularly those related to the country's long-term development—has been less marked, at least until recently. Thus, at the end of 1957, little had yet been done to improve credit facilities for internal distribution, or to extend banking services and savings facilities to areas outside of Saigon. A program concerned with over-all agricultural credit needs—as distinguished from the special needs of refugees and farmers affected by land reform measures—had just gotten under way.[148] The National Investment Fund provided equity or loan funds to a number of firms (including textile mills, paper producers, sugar refiners, and various handicraft establishments), but its operations remained on a relatively small scale. No formal system of bank examinations had yet been established, although the statistics regularly submitted by the commercial banks did permit some informal checks; the available statistics themselves, moreover, while a great improvement from early 1955 when almost no banking and credit data were available, still remain far from adequate as a guide to the country's credit situation and needs.[149]

To a considerable extent, the delays in achieving progress in these various fields were to have been expected. During the first year or two of national monetary independence, as noted earlier, such delays were in many cases almost inevitable because of the lack of internal security and the preoccupation of the relatively few Vietnamese administrators and technicians with training in finance with the urgent transitional tasks described previously, including the establishment of the new Credit Commercial in Saigon.[150] In addition, there also existed a genuine concern on

[148] Considerable progress in expanding agricultural credit facilities seems to have been made since the National Agricultural Credit Office was established in early 1957. More local offices have been set up and over a hundred agricultural credit "teams" have been trained and sent into the field. Priority in credit allocation has been given to co-operatives and to loans for replanting idle land; while rice farmers have received a substantial portion of the total credits granted, an effort has also been made to encourage crop diversification.

[149] Money supply and banking data for Viet-Nam are now regularly published by the National Bank of Viet-Nam and the International Monetary Fund. The National Bank has also pioneered in developing the first national income statistics for Viet-Nam, covering 1954 and 1955, and prepares annual balance of payments data.

[150] It has been suggested that the personnel of the local Treasury offices could have been used to institute new banking and credit facilities. While there may be scope for using Treasury agents to perform such functions in some areas, I consider it doubtful that they could have played a really effective role in setting up banking services and credit facilities at a time when their ordinary duties were already heavy and when an intensive effort was required not only to improve the system of tax collections but also the very cumbersome and time-consuming disbursement procedures. In addition, of course, there are serious

the part of many Vietnamese officials that overly hasty action to channel more credit to the domestic sector might merely provide a basis for inflation or for purely wasteful expenditures rather than assist in sound economic development—a concern which is indicative of the conservative attitude in financial matters characteristic of many Vietnamese.

Nevertheless, it seems clear that since many of the "emergency" problems of the transition have by this time been solved and since progress has also been made in training additional personnel, Viet-Nam's financial policies should now place more stress on the achievement of longer-term goals. Thus, more energetic measures are needed to expand existing banking and savings facilities and to achieve a better distribution of credit. At the same time, much can be done to increase the efficiency of monetary controls through closer supervision of banking activities and through other measures. Recent economic developments have served to dramatize both these needs: The crisis in internal distribution and the growing awareness of the importance of more rapid industrial development have highlighted the magnitude of existing gaps in the availability of both short- and longer-term credit; and the realization that monetary controls, in conjunction with import policies and fiscal and foreign exchange measures, have been of considerable importance in reversing the recent upward trend in prices, has brought an increased interest in discovering the precise impact of these control instruments and in improving their effectiveness.

In the recent past, several important measures have been taken to provide more adequate credit and banking facilities. Early in 1958 it was announced, for example, that a postal checking and transfer system is being instituted; this should presumably reach most of the areas where banking facilities are now unavailable. Perhaps an even more promising step is the establishment of the Industrial Development Center, largely financed with American aid funds. As noted earlier, this organization will be far better equipped to deal with the encouragement and financing of industrial development than the National Investment Fund. (The Fund was merged with the new Center in early 1958.) The Industrial Development Center, it may be noted, need not confine its financial operations to direct lending or to purchases of equity shares; in fact, it is likely that much of its effort will be devoted to the creation of mechanisms that will give the existing commercial banks sufficient incentives for engaging in longer-term credit operations or in equity participations. Thus, it may

---

questions whether most of these agents are qualified, by training and outlook, to take on commercial banking tasks. As indicated below, however, there is much to be said for trying various approaches in setting up new banking and credit institutions, and the possibility of assigning such tasks to the local Treasury personnel should not be ignored.

284 VIET-NAM: THE FIRST FIVE YEARS

prove possible to have industrial lending largely carried out by established institutions with staffs that are already experienced in financial matters.

The task of operating the new industrial and agricultural credit institutions successfully should clearly have high priority in the months and years ahead. Other important tasks in the monetary, credit, and foreign exchange fields involving institutional changes or improvements include the following:

First, a more intensive effort is required to extend commercial banking facilities. This will, at first, entail primarily the opening of branches of the State commercial bank, or of the existing private banks, in various parts of the country; it might also involve other institutional arrangements adapted to local needs.

Second, more systematic efforts are required to encourage the use of credit instruments and to explore the possibilities for developing new types of instruments adapted to Viet-Nam's special needs. This means that legal provisions which may still tend to discourage the use of such instruments need to be reviewed and, if possible, eliminated, and that considerable effort should be devoted to perfecting a system for interchange of credit information (*centrale des risques*); further experimentation is also required with respect to discounts of credit instruments by the commercial banks or by specialized credit institutions and for expanding rediscount facilities at the central bank. In some cases, it may be useful to set up devices for insuring all or part of certain types of loans, although considerable care will have to be taken to avert misuse of such an arrangement.

Third, a system of regular bank examinations should be instituted as soon as possible. It is encouraging to note that preparations for initiating such a system and for training Vietnamese examiners are now well under way. Before an effective inspection system can be begun, however, enactment of a general banking law may be advisable which would define the rules governing bank operations and supervision in greater detail than the central banking statute was able to at the time of its passage. It is important, of course, that any law establishing standards for bank examination, or any new supervisory authority set up to enforce such standards, does not in any way interfere with the credit control powers of the central bank; for this reason, it would probably be best to continue to assign the powers of bank examination to the central bank itself.

Fourth, a great deal needs to be done to improve savings facilities, to actively encourage voluntary saving both on the part of business firms and individuals, and to promote an increased use of savings for long-term development projects. Again, these efforts could take a variety of forms and will probably require a good deal of experimentation. It seems possible, for example, that either the Treasury or the postal system could perform important functions in connection with efforts to stimulate the savings habit. A plan designed to mobilize small savings through a system of savings stamps has already been worked out in principle, and prompt implementation would seem highly desirable.

Fifth, a major review of the Treasury's "banking functions" would seem advisable, both in order to integrate the Treasury's activities more directly with other efforts to improve credit, transfer, and savings facilities, and to allow a more accurate assessment of the Treasury's role in over-all credit and monetary trends. Much can be said for terminating the practice under which banks may make deposits at the Treasury and for issuing instead government securities which banks and others may purchase; this would permit closer scrutiny of government debt operations and provide the basis for establishment of a government securities market. The solution to be adopted, of course, will require thorough study, and care will have to be taken that institutional arrangements which have been worked out over a long period of time and have performed important services are not disrupted unnecessarily.

Sixth, various improvements are needed in the present system of banking and credit statistics. In particular, it is most important to develop money supply data that take precise account of the operations of the Treasury and to obtain more reliable and detailed information on the volume and types of loans extended by banks and other credit institutions. Improved statistical information will be of major importance in enabling the central bank to use its credit control powers effectively and in assisting it in its assigned task of exploring methods for improving the country's credit system.

Seventh, there is a need for a continuing review of the exchange system. To be sure, considerable progress has been made toward improving and simplifying the exchange rate structure. Thus, fiscal, monetary, and exchange control measures adopted during the past several years have in various ways tended to absorb importers' windfall profits and have permitted more competitive pricing of exports. Important steps have also been taken to simplify the exchange rate structure, in recognition of the fact that excessive complexity of an exchange rate system can be a serious deterrent to proper business planning and optimum resource allocation. Careful attention should, however, be paid to the possibilities for further improvements in the exchange system in line with the requirements of a sound development program.

Improvements in the monetary, credit, and foreign exchange systems along the lines suggested here can, of course, constitute only part of a broader program designed to encourage more rapid economic growth within a framework of monetary stability, and progressively to reduce abnormal dependence on foreign aid. It is outside the scope of this article to discuss in detail the wide range of other measures that are required to implement this program, such as the establishment of over-all priorities for a balanced development effort; introduction of more efficient methods of production; the improvement of labor skills; development of a larger and more effective class of private entrepreneurs as well as of a better climate for the investment of both domestic and foreign capital; and further reforms in the fiscal system, particularly in the tax structure and also in budgetary management and controls.[151]

In the monetary area, as such, continued progress will, of course, depend not only on further improvement in the international structure, but also on the ability of the monetary authorities to make accurate assessments of the country's financial situation and needs and to devise policies that will fit these needs. Before concluding, therefore, it may be useful to note some of the broader analytical and policy issues that will require attention in the immediate future: How rapidly can the promotion of industrial and other types of development be pushed without creating renewed inflationary excesses? What are the limits to the projected expansion of credit to the domestic sector of the economy in this connection? To what extent is it possible to reduce over-all reliance on foreign aid, or to allow further shifts in the "product-mix" of the import program in the direction of relatively more investment goods imports, without causing sharp increases in prices and the money supply? These questions, in turn, suggest the need for a much more searching analysis than has thus far been possible of the factors making for inflation and deflation.

In view of the relative success of anti-inflationary measures in Viet-

[151] Viet-Nam appears to have inherited many of the defects of the French tax system—almost 90 percent of the taxes collected are indirect—and there would seem to be considerable scope both for exploring new sources of tax revenue and for improving the yield on existing taxes through improved administration. According to the national income estimates of the National Bank, tax revenues in 1955 amounted to 11.4 percent of the national income, which was higher than the average for Southeast Asian countries. Since a large share of these taxes was levied on import items and to a considerable extent merely helped to compensate for the subsidy implied by an overvalued official exchange rate, the 11.4 percent figure tends to overstate the real tax "burden." While the tax reforms discussed earlier have helped considerably in increasing government revenues since 1955, much of the improvement is based on increased taxation of imported items brought in under the American aid program. As American aid is reduced and imports are increasingly replaced by domestic production, government tax revenues would also diminish under present tax rates that fall relatively lightly on internal output. Thus, there is a particular need for increased taxation of domestic production (or of greater use of direct taxation); at the same time, it is important that tax measures do not undermine the incentives for increased output or new investment, and are not pushed so far as to endanger the country's political stability.

Nam to date and the prospect for continued improvements in the monetary and fiscal system, the "financial setting" is today relatively favorable for a step-up in the pace of development activities without a resurgence of inflation. As the development program gains momentum, however, and as planned reductions in the foreign aid program are carried out, inflationary tendencies may again mount. The monetary authorities will thus have a particular responsibility for alerting the country against the dangers of excessive expansion, and for acting promptly and skillfully to help prevent a renewed upsurge in prices, if the over-all volume of added investment should begin to exceed levels that are matched by increased budgetary resources or private saving. On the basis of the record to date, the prospect would seem good that these tasks will be faced with intelligence and courage.

The Foreign Exchange Policy of Viet-Nam
HUYN VAN LANG[152]

THE FOREIGN exchange policy of Viet-Nam took shape gradually, and was the product of circumstances far more than of intellectual design. Moreover, it was evolved and implemented by young people whose schooldays were only a few years behind them. They had zeal, foresight, and intelligence, but lacked experience. This is hardly surprising: For the French government controlled the Exchange Office until the last moment, relinquishing it in January, 1955, after the Geneva Agreement, and then so suddenly that some people likened its handing over to another Dien Bien Phu, in the sense that it was an economic and monetary defeat for the colonialists.

Thus, a Vietnamese foreign exchange policy did not exist before 1955. Prior to that, the Indo-Chinese Exchange Office (OIC) was merely a branch of the Foreign Exchange Office in Paris—in other words, an executive body.

A foreign exchange policy must obviously form an integral part of a government's general economic and monetary policy. However, the Vietnamese policy has not corresponded in full to the over-all government program. To understand how circumstances shaped Viet-Nam's foreign exchange policy, one must go back to the Indochina war.

In Viet-Nam's wartime economy there was an almost complete absence of local production, as well as a profound upheaval in the distribution of population and markets. The Vietnamese economy was largely dependent on the French Expeditionary Force, which in consuming many of the goods and, above all, the services provided the country with foreign currency, which was used to buy French commodities (see Table 14). Such purchases became more and more numerous, and ranged from fabrics and pharmaceutical products to perfumes and precious stones.

Besides making possible the purchase of French goods, the surplus of foreign exchange during the war years allowed a number of French and Chinese companies to profit heavily and to transfer capital freely to France, Switzerland, Hong Kong, and even to the United States. In a country at war a clique always gathers to draw large profits from the war, but behind the transfer there unobtrusively flows a stream of disinvestment.

This flight of capital became extremely pronounced after Dien Bien Phu. It occurred at the same time as the heavy migration of refugees. Some of these refugees had liquidated their assets in north Viet-Nam to

[152] Director of the Exchange Office, Viet-Nam; article translated from the French by Mary de Zouche. The statistical data in this study have been extracted from economic bulletins of the National Bank of Viet-Nam.

TABLE 14

EXPENDITURES BY THE FRENCH GOVERNMENT IN VIET-NAM
(in millions of francs)

1953	....	163,254*
1954	....	215,749
1955	....	40,300
1956	....	310 (1st 6 months)

* This is the inclusive figure for Viet-Nam, Cambodia, and Laos, but the proportion for Viet-Nam is certainly at least 70 percent of the total.

bring money to the south. Almost all well-to-do people had transferred their assets to the south and, among their number, foreign nationals had dispatched most of their property. Moreover, rich people, Vietnamese or foreign, were convinced that Saigon was only a stage in their retreat, and that they were only halting there to await the opportunity to leave and take their property abroad.

In short, the political exigencies of war referred to above created extremely difficult monetary problems for Free Viet-Nam. Inflation, monetary or in the form of excess demand, which had formerly been brewing over the whole of Viet-Nam, settled in the south and exploded, creating an acute demand for foreign bills for the purchase of commodities and services, for expenditure abroad, and also for rapid transfers of capital (see Table 15).

TABLE 15

VOLUMES OF CURRENCY*
(in millions of piasters)

1954	....	15,459
1955	....	17,349
1956	....	17,579
1957†	....	16,630

* At the end of the year.
† As of September 30, 1957.

Other noteworthy points are: both before and after Dien Bien Phu, jurisdiction over exchange remained with France until 1955, 90 percent of the exporters of capital were French, and 75 percent of Viet-Nam's imports were from France (see Table 16). During the last months of 1954 the Indo-Chinese Exchange Office authorized the flow of capital in any form, because all the resulting profit returned to France and its nationals. Moreover, after Dien Bien Phu French families who had lived in Viet-Nam for several generations hastened to leave as quickly as the

TABLE 16

VIET-NAM'S IMPORTS AND EXPORTS

(in millions of piasters)

Year	Imports (1)	Percentage of French Imports	Exports (2)	Percentage of French Exports	Percentage of (2) to (1)
1954	11,429.928	75.5	2,011.282	36.6	18
1955	9,211.626	52.4	2,415.400	37.4	26
1956	7,374.000	24.7	1,471.000	67.5	20
1957*	4,686.895	27.2	1,249.981	60	20

* First six months of year.

French Expeditionary Force. These 30,000 to 40,000 people owned a considerable proportion of Viet-Nam's assets.

After Geneva, the French Expeditionary Force was repatriated rapidly, and the effect on Viet-Nam's economy and currency was considerable. The Expeditionary Force began to increase the pace of its departure when France handed over the *Institut d'Emission,* through which currency had previously been issued, and the Exchange Office, to Viet-Nam. Thus, on the one hand, to guarantee the value of the Vietnamese piaster, the French government bestirred itself to spend rapidly the foreign exchange brought by the Expeditionary Force. On the other hand, for a political reason, the source of foreign exchange dwindled gradually to nothing.

Briefly, then, because of war and the exchange policy and political course followed by France, during the last months of 1954 the general economic, as well as social, situation of Viet-Nam was like a tide from the north battering the frail dikes of the south, or like a force-pump compressing its charge of water into the tiny area of the south. Free Viet-Nam had to meet the problems of exchange created by a large-scale flight of capital and too high a demand for the conversion of Vietnamese currency into foreign money, all at the moment when the tempo of the country's production and export was at its lowest (see Table 17).

At the time, the function of a dam or reservoir belonged to the Indo-Chinese Exchange Office, whose organization, from the administrative and technical aspects, was inadequate. The staff of this office, was responsible to the French Exchange Office, for the regulation of the exchange was French. The policy followed by the OIC was meant to protect, as far as possible, the remaining French economic and financial interests in Viet-Nam. It is not surprising, therefore, that the Vietnamese government's proposal in the middle of 1954 for a scheme to train Vietnamese replacement officers was rejected. The result was that when Viet-Nam took over from OIC the corps of administrators had had no

TABLE 17

IMPORTS, EXPORTS, INVISIBLE TRANSFERS, AND TRANSFERS
OF CAPITAL SINCE 1954

(in millions of piasters)

Year	Exports	Imports	Invisible Transfers*	Transfers of Capital
1954	2,011	11,429	12,617	844
1955	2,415	9,211	2,330	218
1956	1,471	7,374	1,747	178
1957†	1,978	7,491	1,394	3

* This embraces widely differing forms of transfers, which have not been
separately recorded.
† First nine months of year.

opportunity to train, even hastily. The group of eager but inexperienced
young people who took charge of the Exchange Office, and hold it today,
may have made mistakes, but no one can question their integrity.

From 1954 to this day, the official value of the Vietnamese piaster has
been fixed at 35 piasters to the U.S. dollar or to 10 French francs, and
98 piasters to one British pound. During hostilities, the official value of
the piaster was influenced by the franc. In other words, during the artificial situation created by war, there was a large quantity of convertible
foreign exchange. Thus, the valuation of the piaster at the above rate did
not seem exaggerated. But when hostilities ceased and the source of
foreign currency, which the French Expeditionary Force had represented,
dried up—that is, from the moment that the Vietnamese economy fell
back to its proper level—the overvaluation of the piaster became more
obvious from day to day, transfers of capital and demands for foreign
currency for the purchase of goods and peacetime services increased, and
the gap between the official value of the piaster and its actual value on
the parallel, or black, market widened.

With the gradual return to peacetime conditions, the transfers of capital continued, and the general consumer demand for goods and services
became, basically as well as superficially, greater every day. A furious
desire to spend, created by war or previously held in check by it, burst
out chaotically. Acting on the principle that what the country did not
produce could be obtained from abroad, the people seemed to vie with
each other in spending and buying. There were varied reasons why they
did so: because they wanted to make up for wartime deprivations, they
did not know what to do with the money they had, or they believed that
they could not invest in Viet-Nam at the time.

It is certain that the Vietnamese government, by itself, could not have checked the flow of transfers, or this furious spending. Under numerous and considerable conditions and formalities, American aid (see Table 18) was put at Viet-Nam's direct disposal from 1954 onward. However, American aid was only a partial answer, providing for the demand for commodities. But Viet-Nam had to deal both with the flow of transfers and the demand for services, and, with limited resources, it could only partially solve these problems.

The currency provided by American aid does not come under the control of the Exchange Office, but that of another organization, the National Imports Committee, subordinate to the *Direction du Commerce* and under the supervision of the American government. Although American aid has been substantial in comparison with Viet-Nam's own currency resources there is, owing to the excessive demand for goods and the overvaluation of the piaster, a strong tendency toward overspending on imported goods. This may represent good marketing opportunities for

TABLE 18

AMERICAN AID

(in U.S. dollars)

1953-54	$ 40,000,000
1954-55	300,180,768
1955-56	203,149,155
1956-57	262,811,799

foreign economies, but it is bad for the Vietnamese economy. Thus, with 35 piasters to the U.S. dollar, foreign-made goods were so cheap that Vietnamese producers could not hope to compete. Not until 1957, under a new fiscal system, which placed higher taxes on imported goods, was it possible to curb to some extent the demand for foreign goods. The new fiscal system, which was established too late to be entirely beneficial, seems to have accentuated the deflation that Vietnamese foreign exchange measures had caused. (Later, this new fiscal system will be discussed, insofar as it affects the exchange rate of the Vietnamese piaster, that is, to the extent it is actually bound up with Vietnamese foreign exchange policy.)

In a case of a difficult economic period such as this, where demand increases steadily and steeply while the piaster is fixed at too high a rate, a structure of multiple and complicated exchange rates develops. Between the time when France transferred authority over exchange to Viet-Nam in 1955 and the end of 1957, two measures (which will be described presently) were taken to combat the complexity of exchange rates. These measures were: (1) the creation of the limited access free market on

June 30, 1956, and (2) the introduction of the "35 percent system" for imports and exports on October 1, 1957. Otherwise nothing has been done to correct the multiplicity of exchange rates inherited from the French.

From the beginning of 1955 until June 30, 1956, there was an official market carried out by the National Bank, by the Exchange Office, and by the banks of Viet-Nam, with 35 piasters equal to the U.S. dollar or 10 French francs. Side by side with this official market, in a street near the National Bank, there existed a black market, for transfer and the purchase of goods or services. What were the factors governing the exchange rate on this black market? First and foremost, the exchange rate was determined by transfers of capital abroad, by the expenses of transit, and above all, by the import "without currency"[153] of goods scarce in Viet-Nam, including fresh and canned foods, pharmaceutical products, and even stones and precious metals.

Individuals paid for these imports with money which they made from fraudulent foreign exchange transactions. The black market was entirely controlled by the Chinese, who took advantage of loopholes in and lax enforcement of the foreign exchange laws. This profitable operation had existed for a number of years. It was permitted to exist by the French, so that by the time hostilities ceased it had become a multiform, powerful monster. Its existence was not at all surprising, for a black market comes into being as soon as a system of exchange control is established and transfers on the official market for the purchase of goods and services or for invisible transactions are subject to quota allocations and official supervision. What was surprising was the market's prosperity and importance and the fact that it assumed a dominant role in Viet-Nam's economy. It is not possible to determine the amount of business transacted through it, but the average weekly figures of Vietnamese piasters offered on the free market of Hong Kong, with which it is closely related, give some idea (see Table 19).

Outside the two markets mentioned above, there also exists the partly official, partly unofficial EFAC.[154] EFAC is currency which the exporter has the right to sell freely to the importer for the importation of goods or the payment of small services. It is official in that the government allows the exporter this right, but semiofficial because in the sale of the currency, the rate of exchange is freely arranged between the parties concerned, without any official supervision. Owing to the market's official aspect, especially the freedom allowed in the use of EFAC currency to import goods not authorized for official market transactions, the value

[153] So called because such importation is carried out without the government allocating currency, i.e., by means of currency bought in the black market.
[154] Export-Frais-Accessoires.

TABLE 19

VIETNAMESE PIASTERS OFFERED ON THE FREE MARKET
OF HONG KONG

(Average in millions of piasters)

Month	1954	1955	1956	1957
January	–	–	8.5	12.3
February	8.8	–	5.8	11.5
March	–	7.2	11.8	11.4
April	10.4	8.3	11.0	9.8
May	13.3	12.8	10.5	11.4
June	14.5	9.8	9.8	10.3
July	16.8	9.0	11.3	11.6
August	10.5	10.8	8.3	10.7
September	9.1	10.9	14.0	8.7
October	10.0	8.6	14.3	8.0
November	7.9	9.3	16.0	–
December	7.5	9.3	13.3	–

of the piaster in this market is lower than its value in the black market. Thus, the price of foreign exchange in EFAC transactions is very high, owing to the demand and also to EFAC's artificial and exclusive character, so that it apparently does not correspond to the free market value of the piaster (see Table 20).

The EFAC system and "compensated trade" are the main causes of the multiplicity of exchange rates in Viet-Nam. They existed before 1955, and have only recently been supplanted—but in the case of compensated trade not, for numerous reasons, completely replaced—by the "35 percent system."

These two systems are, in effect, simply a form of devaluation of the piaster, which favors exporters. The minimum form of devaluation is represented by such exports as rubber and rice, where 15 percent of the foreign exchange earned can be sold on the EFAC market.[155] At the other end of scale, the maximum form of devaluation arises in compen-

TABLE 20

RATE OF THE VIETNAMESE PIASTER ON THE EFAC MARKET
(compared with U.S. $1)

Year	Maximum Rate	Minimum Rate	Average Rate
1955	100	80	90
1956	150	100	125
1957	130	100	115

[155] Another name for this procedure is compensated trade.

sated trade, where 100 percent of the foreign exchange earned can be sold on the EFAC market. Between these two extremes, the foreign exchange earned on other exports such as duck feathers may benefit from the EFAC market by 30 percent, tea 50 percent, and salt 75 percent. The system does not become unbearably complicated because Viet-Nam has few exportable products: From the viewpoint of both volume and monetary value, rubber, rice, and duck feathers amount to almost 90 percent of the exports. Nevertheless, the problem of the diversity of exchange rates remains very complicated, and it has not been even partially solved. Furthermore, a system of direct aid to exports has also recently been created for certain products, such as fish and timber. This aid, although it only applies to certain products, is, in effect, simply another form of devaluation of the piaster, and it makes the problem of the diversity of exchange rates still more complex.

At the beginning of 1957 a production tax imposed a levy of 15, 25, or 35 percent taxes on imports in addition to customs duties. This production tax is a tax on exchange, which lowers the value of the piaster and has just as marked an effect on its purchasing power as any straight devaluation of the piaster of 15, 25, or 35 percent on import transactions would have.

During the first stage, from 1955 to July, 1956, all invisible or visible transfers had to be conducted on the official market. But owing to the discrepancy between the supply of and demand for foreign currency, and to the shortage of foreign currency at the government's disposal, all transfers were subject to quota allocations, whether it was a question of capital transfers or commercial transactions. At this stage of restriction, the Exchange Office was not content simply to institute quota systems, but felt that it must also revise the regulations, train its own staff, and reorganize its structure, so that it was equipped to meet its new responsibilities and the new situation. Besides that, it had to study the market and the exchange system diligently to decide what were the appropriate measures to apply next.

During this same period, the Exchange Office preached a doctrine of the most rational use of Viet-Nam's liquid assets, in order to cover, and also to keep within reasonable limits, expenditures on those goods and services which were most necessary to the country's economy. Owing to the shortage of government assets on the one hand and, on the other, to the ever-increasing urgent demands relating to government expenditure abroad, to the costs of education, or to the savings of the foreign technicians taken out of the country, or expenses of transport, etc., the Exchange Office proposed a policy of central distribution of foreign aid, for which it had to contend with demands it did not know how to meet, funds from American aid were being only partly used. Theoretically, all payments for services and goods allowable under American aid were submitted to the group administering American aid in preference to being settled with Viet-Nam's foreign exchange. But, in practice, American aid only provided foreign exchange for the purchase of commodities, not services. (There is a category of foreign exchange which American aid permits to be used in payment for services, but this consists of francs owned by the Vietnamese government and on deposit in France.)

The proportion of demands met by the Exchange Office at that time was one to ten, so, understandably, the exchange rate on the black market soared and, on top of that, interference by individual traders in currency made the muddle even worse.

This disorderly state of affairs arising from the excessive gap between the supply of and demand for currency forced the Exchange Office to search for a formula for reabsorbing the huge surplus of piasters offered on the market. Shortly after September, 1955, the Exchange Office contemplated and proposed the imposition of a tax on exchange, but no attention was paid to this proposal by anyone except an interministerial group of technicians, who flatly turned it down.

Then, in October, 1955, a scheme was put forward and discussed before a Committee on Exchange, consisting of Vietnamese and foreign technicians, from whose deliberations three main ideas emerged. The foreign technicians, no doubt more from fear of harming the interests of foreign residents than for technical reasons, disliked the idea of establishing a free market, and suggested the creation of a system of classification and quota allocations. Certain Vietnamese technicians were openly opposed to the free market on the grounds that it would open wide the door to devaluation. Others recommended the free market, provided that it govern Vietnamese exchange, which would have meant the official market becoming a marginal one. The Exchange Office then proposed the creation of a free exchange market to which access would be controlled, and which would be considered simply as an auxiliary to the official one. Numerous difficulties delayed the actual setting up of the free market for six months.

The Exchange Office's proposals for a free market of limited access, after being examined by the Committee on Exchange and criticized by the foreign technicians, were approved by the Vietnamese government in terms of the June 30, 1956, decree.

Several motives led the Exchange Office to advocate it. First, but not the most important motive, was that the Exchange Office could use the free market to reabsorb the surplus of piasters offered, by using the same quantity of foreign exchange as before, but at a different rate of exchange, which would allow the absorption of two or three times the volume of piasters and an immediate settlement of the demands still outstanding at the Exchange Office. The second motive lay in the fact that the nearer the free market's rate approximated that of the black market, the more the usual clients of the black market would be drawn to the free one, taking there the bulk of such business as could be transacted through it, so that it would be possible progressively to lessen the importance of the black market and reduce it to the marginal character it should possess. The third objective was that, by and after reabsorbing the mass of Vietnamese piasters lying fallow while awaiting transfer abroad—that mass which puts pressure on the market and the exchange rate of Vietnamese money—the free market should ensure the progressive raising of the value of the piaster.

The free market has been organized as follows. Offers of and demands for foreign currency are made through banking channels, but demand is partly controlled—hence, the description "of limited access," being "limited" only in regard to demand. And although we speak of limitation, it must be noted that the authorization given by the Exchange Office is very generous and quick. It depends on the motive for the demand for currency, for the free market is not a gateway for the free outflow of capital, nor a field for speculation. Authority for transactions on this free market are not granted where, say, they concern war profits or demands of a nonessential character such as the expenses of tourist travel. The principle is that only transfers with an essential purpose may benefit from the official market (1/35)—such as those relating to governmental expenses, costs of education, savings of foreign technicians, and transfers for payment for services such as insurance or transport, and for certain goods; everything else is to be done through this free market of limited access.

The exchange rate was fixed unilaterally at the beginning on the basis of the black market rate, and since then, it has varied daily according to supply and demand. But in all circumstances, this rate has been higher than that offered on the black market. For example, when the U.S. dollar was equal to 80 piasters on the black market, its value on the free market was 75 piasters.

Today, the free market has been functioning for a year and a half and has produced the hoped-for results. That is, it has absorbed nearly three billion piasters, made it possible to honor all the demands held up for two or three years, annexed some of the clients of the black market, and considerably reduced the importance of that market which it now dominates; and, on the other hand, it has raised the value of the piaster from 75 to 70 on the U.S. dollar on the free market, and from 100 to 80 piasters on the black market. With a given amount of foreign currency, the Exchange Office has solved the problem of transfers, which was formerly unmanageable. On the psychological level, this solution has calmed mass hysteria, reduced the pressure on the market, and channeled the circulation of money toward the free market. However, only national productivity and the over-all economic policy can have a deep and conclusive effect on the nation's money and the problem of foreign exchange; there, the exchange policy only plays a subsidiary role.

TABLE 21

RATE OF EXCHANGE OF THE VIETNAMESE PIASTER ON THE
BLACK MARKET

(At the end of each month, and in relation to the U.S. $1)

Month	1954	1955	1956	1957
January	76	55	80.5	97.5
February	78	58.5	74.5	93
March	84	61.5	84	92
April	81	63	84	90
May	75	68.5	86	91.5
June	76	74	87	86.5
July	69	69.5	91.5	85
August	63	66.4	90.5	84.5
September	56	72.8	93.5	83.5
October	57	74.5	97.5	80.5
November	58	78	102	–
December	50	85	95	–

Other points are worth bearing in mind: Due to the beneficial rate of exchange, certain capital which had previously escaped, and new capital desiring to invest in Viet-Nam, have been brought in through the channel of the free market. The quantity is not large, but promising.

The amount of intervention by the National Bank has been reduced, and the supply of foreign exchange has increased. If this trend continues, it will become a force for strengthening the value of the piaster. The second point is that in a year and a half of operation, the free market has created a reserve fund for the government out of profits on the exchange which, in case of need, will help Viet-Nam enormously, if not to expand her production, at least to maintain the level of productivity of the export industries.

As mentioned, EFAC and compensated trade brought about a growing multiplicity of exchange rates before October, 1957. Where export was concerned, there were not only the EFAC and compensated trade systems, where numerous percentages were applied, but also systems of direct aid, so that in the long run, a special rate of exchange might well have been applied to each category of commodity exported. Diversity in exchange rates was, moreover, also present in imports on EFAC accounts or the compensated trade system, since foreign exchange was sold at very changeable rates and, in addition, the purchasing power fluctuated after the sale, for rather obscure reasons.

The 35 percent system was developed to replace all systems such as EFAC and compensated trade and, to a large extent, if not completely, to avoid diversity in exchange rates. Since, as mentioned, the exchange rate of the piaster seems to have been depressed below its real value, another purpose of the 35 percent system is to progressively restore the value of Vietnamese money. Inherent in it also is the hope of completely destroying the black market by operating where the free market has not been able to reach, that is, in the field of imports without official foreign exchange.

The 35 percent system has been established as follows: Where export is concerned, 100 percent of the foreign currency earned will, in the future, have to be brought home and reassigned to the government, 65 percent of it at the official market rate, i.e., on the basis of 35 piasters to the U.S. dollar, the remaining 35 percent at the free market rate, on the approximate basis of the dollar equals 70 piasters, which the Exchange Office will pay for by making use of the reserve fund from profits on the sale of foreign exchange on the free market. Thus, the exporter will no longer have at his free disposal any percentage of the foreign exchange his exports earn. The currency brought home by exporters will be assigned to the importer by the government at the official rate plus a stabilization tax, fixed by the Exchange Office, initially in relation to the exchange rates on the free market and that of EFAC. Thus, the Exchange Office grants importers the U.S. dollar at the price of 35 piasters, plus a stabilization tax equal to $110-35=75$ piasters—assuming that on the EFAC market the U.S. dollar is rated at 110 piasters. The Exchange Office insists on applying a higher assignment rate than the price operating on the free market for the following two reasons: (1) There are still many EFAC bills of exchange in Viet-Nam, and it would be unfair to apply too low an assignment price and thus harm the present holders of EFAC bills; and (2) some imports are done on EFAC accounts, so that the fixing of a different price by the Exchange Office would cause disparity in the market prices of the commodities. An additional reason lies in the fact that sundry products cannot be exported by the straightforward application of the 35 percent system, but require some direct supplementary aid in piasters. That is why, on the basis of the 70 piaster rate, on the free market, when a U.S. dollar is sold at 110 piasters, the Exchange Office only retains 70 piasters for the Exchange Compensation Reserve, the remaining 40 piasters being put at the disposal of the Department of State for Economic Affairs, which uses it for direct aid to exporters who could not export without this aid.

It is certain that the 35 percent system will immediately simplify the problem of the exchange rates to a considerable degree. But what must be done to strengthen the value of the Vietnamese piaster and wipe out the black market? The 35 percent system will try to achieve those ends by literally authorizing the import of numerous commodities difficult to obtain in Viet-Nam. Furthermore, the Exchange Office knows that import transactions on EFAC accounts or the compensated trade system have amounted up to now to an annual total of around 300 million piasters, while the demand was double or triple this amount. With the 35 percent system, the Exchange Office will have about 800 million piasters at its disposal, if a liberal import policy is followed; it is thus certain that the exchange rate of the piaster will improve by comparison with those operating in EFAC or compensated trade. In short, the Exhange Office will offer a larger quantity of foreign exchange and, in the present period of deflation, this offer will have a tremendous influence on the value of the piaster. As for the black market, the area of invisible operations has, as pointed out, been invaded by the free market and almost completely passed under its control; and as far as visible operations are concerned, that is, importations (official or illicit) of commodities without the official assignment of bills—the foreign exchange used being bought on the black market—the 35 percent system will attack the problem until it completely controls it. Thus, even if the exchange rate on this market has been fixed at its maximum of 110 piasters to the U.S. dollar, the aim is to bring it back to the basis of 80 piasters to the dollar, or to the black market rate. By progressing toward this rate of exchange along the official pathway of the 35 percent system, the blackmarket rate will inevitably be forced down and the rate of 80 piasters to the dollar may be attained. Thus, the black market will have no further attractions, since its rates will have to fluctuate between 70 and 75 piasters. Then, clutched in the vise of the 35 percent and free markets, the black market will be completely under control and will lose its old customers. When it is possible to obtain one U.S. dollar with 80 piasters, import transactions "without currency" will disappear from the black market and be absorbed in the 35 percent system.

At the end of 1957 the 35 percent system had only been in force for three months, and it was impossible to predict its ultimate effect on the exchange rate. Nevertheless, its direct result must be to reduce considerably the multiplicity of exchange rates operating principally in exports, but also in imports. This system will influence the value of the piaster, provided it is not obstructed (especially in the case of compensated trade, which puts currency on the market that competes with that assigned by the Exchange Office and thus destroys the over-all exchange policy). The Exchange Office hopes for a great deal from the 35 percent system, although up to now its currency purchases have been far higher than its assignments. But when the old EFAC bills have run out and there is no more compensated trade, that is, when the forces competing with the Exchange Office have disappeared, the Exchange Office's efforts to raise the exchange rate of the piaster will quickly bear fruit.

Between the two extreme exchange rates of 35 to 110 piasters for the U.S. dollar, there is certainly a realistic rate which can be used as a stable rate of exchange. But no one can say with complete certainty whether this rate is 50, 70, or 80 piasters for the dollar. The exchange policy is, therefore, aimed at determining what it is. The purpose of the quest is not, however, to apply the rate immediately after it has been determined; for, as everyone knows, devaluation, whether official or not, entails extremely dangerous consequences. However, this search for a basic exchange rate in order to reduce the gap between the two extremes operating, and thus reduce the multiplicity of exchange rates, is a necessary task. Step by step, the rate of the free market is nearing that of the official market, and the 35 percent system will carry the rate from 110 to 90 to 80 piasters, that is, toward the black market rate (1/80) or that of the free market of limited access (1/70); and that means the raising of the value of the piaster. If, during this time, the fiscal policy—above all, the production tax of 15, 25 and 35 percent—causes the piaster to be carried progressively from 35 to 40 to 50 on the U.S. dollar toward the free market rate, then it is clear that the present fiscal policy and that of the exchange policy are but two parts of one policy aimed at finding the true exchange rate of the piaster. However, productivity and new economic measures, far more than any monetary or fiscal measure, are the principal means of raising the piaster's value.

Some critics will probably ask, "What will you do after the exchange rate is simplified?" The Vietnamese answer will be, "When the utmost simplification has been achieved, it will not matter whether or not we do one thing more to devaluate the piaster. We can stop there, for a simplified exchange structure can be maintained as the foundation of a sound and healthy economic development."

Commentary: JOHN M. HUNTER *on* HUYN VAN LANG

LITTLE MENTION is made of the fundamental problems of which foreign exchange difficulties are symptomatic. In the past, the supply of foreign exchange in Viet-Nam has been earned through the sale of rubber and rice in the world markets and through funds spent by the colonial government and more recently by the United States government. The rubber and rice markets have changed drastically since Viet-Nam last participated in them in any "normal" year (1939?). Among other things, synthetic rubber has undercut the previously firm base of the rubber market, and former rice importers have decided to attain self-sufficiency (even the United States has become a net exporter in these years). Continued years of war after most of the rest of the world returned to peace left Viet-Nam with a disorganized productive system, and the repatriation of foreign nationals destroyed many of the conventional trading arrangements. Further, political and economic amputation from the north destroyed a major market for rice and source of supply for manufactured imports, principally textiles. Political independence should indicate that no long-range expectation of large intergovernmental transfers is in order.

It is not possible to analyze here even briefly Viet-Nam's balance of payment problems and possibilities; the future is not assured and great effort should be applied to seeking remedies to this basic situation. Likewise, it is impossible to estimate the possible share of the less promising world rice and rubber markets Viet-Nam may be able to capture. Perhaps copra can become a substantial export; other potentials are not obvious and must be explored. Export possibilities depend in part on the exchange rate and its relation to internal prices and costs, so the problem becomes not only one for the Exchange Office but also a problem of monetary and fiscal policy in its broader senses.

The structure of imports, too, must undergo scrutiny and revision. Imports, and too much in the direction of consumer goods, have been oriented excessively in the direction of the European community. Some economic substitution of domestically produced goods (e.g., sugar, textiles) for imports may be possible over a period, although demonstrating physical possibilities will not guarantee success or even indicate desirability.

There is no easy answer to this problem, yet one must be found. It will lie in the direction of increasing exports (perhaps partially through currency depreciation), decreasing imports, and improving selection, through the development of policies which will encourage both foreign and domestic investment in production of import-substitute goods, and in general policies to control price and cost inflation, which will assist in keeping pressures off the exchanges. There may be merit in a Southern Asia customs union. International agreement in rice and rubber marketing has also been suggested; however, there is little help for Viet-Nam in the latter.

Great skill, courage, and *time* will be required in reaching a solution to this set of interrelated problems. Preoccupation with the position of foreign nationals and policies designed to destroy them is not facing up to the really fundamental *economic* problems.

The following are a series of comments related specifically to some of Lang's observations and which have not been commented on before:

First, perhaps Lang overestimates the desirability of a single and stable exchange rate. There is, of course, much to be said for both, but it is doubtful that either can be achieved by an Exchange Office operating *in vacuo*. If a single, stable rate is desired, the government's economic policies should be directed toward the development of economic conditions which will make this possible. Exchange problems are the symptom rather than the disease; only rarely does one have success in treating the symptoms although, of course, symptomatic treatment can make the patient more comfortable.

Second, perhaps the diversity of rates under EFAC was really undesirable. An interim solution might better have been sought along the lines of sensible multiple rates on both sides of the market. Several Latin American countries have lived long and relatively well with multiple rates designed to have particular desired effects during periods of exchange difficulties.

Third, Lang interprets the reasons for the "foreign technicians" opposing the establishment of a free rate in order to protect the interests of foreign residents. I interpret it otherwise. Basically, opposition probably was registered because of the fear of domestic inflation. The free market was felt to be a *de facto* depreciation of the piaster. Depreciation creates a tendency to internal price inflation. The national government did not have the power (or inclination?) at this time to control domestic inflation, a real and major threat to the peace and security of the country. Ergo, policies should be opposed which might contribute more to the internal inflation. There is question concerning the truth of the premise that the establishment of a free market did represent a *de facto* depreciation.

Commentary: PIERRE HUNT[156] *on* HUYN VAN LANG

LANG'S ARTICLE gives the unfortunate impression that France retained control of the Exchange Office until the last moment to allow exploitation of Viet-Nam's resources by French Nationals. As a matter of fact, until December 31, 1954, Viet-Nam, together with Cambodia and Laos, was a member of the franc zone, or the Indochinese Office

[156] Financial Adviser to the French Economic Mission, 1954-56. Translated from the original French by Phan Thu Ngoc.

of Exchange. This monetary bloc, characterized by pooling of exchange resources, had power, delegated to it by the French Office, to apply the set of regulations common to the French Union.

True, its services could have been merged into the four-country Institut d'Émission, created in 1952; however, control of its operations was retained by France until the Geneva Agreement, whose execution brought about the gradual withdrawal of the French Expeditionary Corps. Until then, France had kept the Exchange Office because of important interests it was responsible for as long as the war continued.

Viet-Nam, as well as Cambodia and Laos, was associated with France in a monetary and customs union, whose principal operating agencies were quadripartite. The management of these agencies was a fairly delicate matter and it did not seem desirable to extend prematurely the same principle to the intricate field of exchange control. The end of military operations and of quadripartism in the last months of 1954 automatically meant turning exchange control over to the Indochinese states.

Lang rightly mentions the climate of speculation prevailing in countries at war. But far from giving the idea that the Exchange Office tried, with all available means, to put an end to speculation and financial combinations, he seems to indicate it was actually instrumental in carrying out these transactions. If the office's policy was subject to criticism, as are all administrative agencies which have to handle an exceptional situation without any rules to go by, it does not at all deserve the condemnation leveled at it.

In regard to the franc-piaster relationship and resulting consequences, Lang feels that the one to ten francs parity was valid on account of the considerable expenditures of the French armed forces. Actually, this parity, as the preceding one of seventeen francs to one piaster, was purely artificial. When France returned to Indochina in 1945, the country's economic situation had seemed satisfactory, in spite of the Japanese occupation. Sizeable stocks of rubber were available for export. Failing to foresee the crumbling of Viet-Nam's economic position, due to Communist subversion and war, France had deemed fit to set a piaster parity which would be commensurate with Viet-Nam's potentialities. Unfortunately, this act of faith turned out to be unfounded. Trade terms were quickly thrown off balance, and only extraordinary war receipts averted a serious exchange shortage. Since 1946 the deterioration of Viet-Nam's economy and the insecure political future had led to speculative operations, which did great harm to the piaster and which were not stopped by the 1953 devaluation (from seventeen piasters to one franc, to ten piasters to one franc). The piaster became a fluctuating currency, whose value on the black market was always much lower than the official rate. No valid economic weapon was available to stabilize rates at a certain level.

In these circumstances, the Exchange Office was forced, contrary to an essential policy of the Indochinese Exchange Office, to establish quotas for franc requests. Two alternatives were available: to limit commercial operations in order to free franc holdings needed for capital transfers by French Nationals living in Viet-Nam, or to leave commercial operations as they were but limit "invisible transfers."

It is this latter solution which the office finally adopted. It may be said that this choice was beneficial to Viet-Nam, for it enabled it to meet its needs in consumer goods in a normal way, and thus maintain the population's standard of living even while the fighting was raging throughout the country. True, French businesses were able to transfer profits; and private individuals, a part of their income. But neither the one nor the other was allowed to make capital transfers. Thus, investments necessary to Viet-Nam's economic life were kept in active service, willy-nilly. This policy was forced upon those businesses and persons who might have wished to take their capital to a safer place. The French government, incidentally, is at present being besieged with a number of appeals based on the practical impossibility of making capital transfers from a country which belonged to the franc zone. Finally, the only disinvestment operations allowed have been carried out within the framework of the Franco-Vietnamese Convention of December 30, 1954, regarding piaster purchases by the French Expeditionary Corps. It was the Vietnamese office which handled the execution of this agreement by making available to French Nationals, wishing to make transfers, a portion (20 percent) of the franc assets turned over by the French Expeditionary Corps in 1955. Such transactions did not exceed four billion francs, and the main beneficiaries were individuals or small businesses whose activities were no longer adapted to changes in the political situation.

The preceding explanations are sufficient to justify France's attitude in the particular area discussed by Lang; at the same time, they serve as answers to those objections of a nontechnical character contained in the article.

Concerning the work done since 1955, Lang gives a fair account of the difficulties encountered and recognizes the positive actions taken to improve and strengthen the Saigon Foreign Exchange market. The establishment of a free market of limited access was certainly a bold innovation and a kind of wager on the future of Viet-Nam. A few foreign technicians may have been in disagreement because of the huge piaster holdings whose pressure could have hastened the collapse of the piaster.

As a matter of fact, the caution with which this market was gradually enlarged, the guaranties it gave to foreign companies threatened with asphyxia, enabled it to obtain excellent results. The abolition of EFAC accounts (see p. 299) and the repurchase, at the free market rate, of some of the exchange earned by exporters, greatly contributed to giving the piaster a realistic character, which must be the basis of every exchange policy.

The economic recovery of Viet-Nam should be the goal of all technicians engaged in economic work. In this respect, Lang has not, perhaps, stressed sufficiently the artificial character of the Vietnamese economy. If, until 1954, the war had enabled Viet-Nam to have resources far exceeding the revenue derived from its own economic activities, American aid since 1955 has been giving to the Vietnamese economy that artificial respiration which would allow it to await the return of health. But much remains to be done. The trade balance stays extremely unfavorable. Exports in 1957 covered only 26 percent of imports, and the deficit had to be made up with foreign aid. New investments are insufficient. Production is stagnant.

Confidence in its money will be one of the essential ingredients in promoting the economic and social development of Viet-Nam. The flexibility and effectiveness of the exchange policy followed during the last three years are promising signs. All efforts undertaken toward a more realistic valuation of the piaster and simplification of exchange regulations are evidence of an understanding of economic mechanisms which is a credit to the Vietnamese leaders.

Commentary: HUYN VAN LANG *on* HUNT

THERE ARE several points raised by Hunt with which I take issue. Hunt indicates that France did not retain control of the Exchange Office in order to allow exploitation of Viet-Nam's exchange resources by French Nationals. I do not question the sincerity of Mr. Hunt, but what does he think of the removal to Paris of all papers of the Financial Section of the Indochinese Exchange Office before Viet-Nam took over?

This situation has caused embarrassment whenever there has been a transfer request. However, gradually, after expending considerable labor and effort, Vietnamese officials have been able to reconstruct a large number of the lost documents.

In speaking of the piaster-franc parity, Hunt acknowledges the purely artificial nature of that parity of ten or even seventeen francs to one piaster. Why, then, did French authorities try to maintain this artificial rate? Hunt replies that France mistakenly put too much faith in the potential wealth of Viet-Nam without considering Communist subversion and wartime destruction. There may be some truth in all this but, in my estimation, the real reason is that some people wanted to maintain that state of affairs as long as possible for their own benefit.

Hence, arose the "piaster traffic," whose eloquent indictment was made by a French writer to arouse French public opinion. At that time the massive capital transfers to France were comparable to an internal hemorrhage which threatened to paralyze the dying patient that was Viet-Nam.

Thus, unpleasant memories of this unfortunate phase in Viet-Nam's history will be difficult to forget. Besides, there is the debt borne by the Vietnamese nation and carried in the accounts of the National Bank of Viet-Nam under a harmless-sounding name: Advances to the former Indochinese Treasury—8,331,187,174.46 piasters. There is no justification for the action of the French authorities in Indochina which, under pretext of fighting for the welfare of the Vietnamese people, benefited in the extreme a few big colonists, while leaving the Vietnamese with a staggering debt which is difficult to liquidate in the near future.

Finally, as for being overly preoccupied with politics in a technical study, I acknowledge the validity of the criticism. However, it is also true that everything should be viewed in its proper social and political context. If I seem to emphasize this specter of colonialism, it is precisely to remind the readers that its evil consequences are far from gone.

Commentary: HUNT[157] *on* HUYN VAN LANG

CONCERNING the role of the Indochinese Office of Exchange when it was under French management, undoubtedly abuses were committed but they did not take on the generalized aspect of the "piaster traffic." These abuses, unfortunately, were the inevitable corollary of an uncertain political situation and of an unrealistic piaster-franc exchange rate. To say that the French government deliberately maintained conditions favorable to speculative transactions in order to enrich "colonists" amounts to an unfounded accusation. It is enough to recall the violent Vietnamese reactions at the time of the piaster's devaluation in 1953 to realize that any tampering with the value of the Vietnamese

[157] Translated by Phan Thu Ngoc.

currency brought about economic and political risks which are difficult to evaluate in wartime.

Elsewhere Lang mentioned the advance made by the Institut d'Émission to the former Indochinese Treasury. It is true that important sums for the financing of the war were obtained in that fashion, but such contributions by the Associated States are much smaller than those of the French taxpayers up to 1954. It was only proper that the Indochinese States partially bear the burden of military expenditure, incurred in the fight against communism.

After all, the struggle conducted by France with the help of numerous local forces and that of the United States made it possible to arrest Communist expansion in the Indochinese peninsula. The sacrifices that were made were not wasted because nationalist Viet-Nam, although mutilated, has been able to survive.

On a purely technical level, the advances made to the former Indochinese Treasury cannot be said to be a heavy burden on Viet-Nam. It is only a matter of bookkeeping. At most, Viet-Nam could retroactively worry about the inflationary consequences of the mechanism of advances. But do not present conditions in Viet-Nam show deflationary tendencies which actually slow down the economic expansion currently being sought? Is it not reasonable to think that the increase in piasters without any reserve backing has long been absorbed and that it does not, therefore, constitute a pressure on the Vietnamese currency?

XXII.   Tax Reforms in Viet-Nam

VU THIEN VINH[158]

UNTIL FAIRLY RECENTLY the Vietnamese tax system was patterned after that of France prior to the French reforms of December, 1948. It was based upon the traditional distinction between the levying and allocation of revenues from direct and indirect taxes, which were assessed and collected differently. Direct taxes were reserved for the exclusive use of the regional governments of Tonkin, Annam, Cochinchina, Cambodia, and Laos, and indirect taxes were reserved for the central government of the Union of French Indochina.

Direct taxes consist mainly of income taxes, which evolved from a former head tax, taxes on land and buildings, and the "patente," a sort of license duty imposed on every business. Direct taxes have the following characteristics: They are annually assessed by tax officers by means of formal tax rolls, or registers listing the names of taxpayers and their liabilities, and they are collected by the Treasury, an agency entirely independent from the tax office. When income taxes were not yet highly developed, the yield from direct taxes was relatively small, and their administration was unpopular because of their direct assessment. For these reasons they were left to the regional governments.

The government of the Union of French Indochina had the exclusive use of indirect taxes administered by two agencies: first, the Office of Customs and Excise, which levied import and export duties as well as excise duties on home products such as alcohol, tobacco, salt; and second, the Office of Registration, which levied duties on sales of property, stamp duties, inheritance duties, and a withholding income tax on corporate dividends. These indirect taxes are good revenue raisers, more easily administered because not subject to formal assessment and separate collection. Most of them are hidden levies, not directly resented by taxpayers who pay in the price of goods. They are also powerful tools for economic policy. These reasons explain why they were jealously kept under the direct authority of the French rulers of the Indochinese Union.

In addition to these particular features, the whole system, in the past as, to some extent, at present, could be characterized by: (1) the relatively small proportion—usually not exceeding ten percent—of the national income raised by the government through taxation, (2) the predominance of indirect taxes, which accounted for more than eighty percent of the total revenue, (3) a legalistic approach to taxation, and especially to direct taxes which were developed into a formal system in which little account was given to economic consideration, and (4) discretionary administrative assessment in contrast to self-assessment method such as

---

[158] Deputy Director General, General Directorate of Taxes, Viet-Nam.

practiced in more advanced countries (for example, in the United States and Canada).

Four major changes have been made recently in the Vietnamese tax system, the first two in 1947 and 1953 were dictated somewhat by circumstances, while those undertaken by the present government in 1955 and 1957 were more definite steps toward the modernization of the fiscal structure.

In 1947 a general sales tax was introduced in Cochinchina. It was a multiple-stage turnover tax, levied on transactions performed at the level of producers, as well as on wholesalers and retailers. The change was a remarkable departure from the traditional distinction between direct and indirect taxation. For the first time, an indirect levy was allocated to a regional government. Its political implication was clear: The government of Cochinchina, headed by Nguyen Van Thinh, intended to secede from Viet-Nam. This move ended with the suicide of its promoter, Nguyen Van Thinh; however, the turnover tax survived, and was later extended to north and central Viet-Nam.

The 1953 tax reforms were officially designed to bring about a national codification of four laws—the land taxes, patente duties, indirect taxes, and income taxes, previously enacted by regional governments. Actually, the reforms aimed at providing the Nguyen Van Tam government, then hard pressed by war costs, with a share of the regional revenues. However, the regional governments strongly resisted the move; as a result, only income taxes, whose yield at that time was negligible, were given up to the central government, with the regional authorities retaining control of the more lucrative turnover tax. This change in the allocation of direct taxes on income, which reversed once again the traditional criterion of distinction, indicates the utter confusion which prevailed during this period.

In 1955 the Ngo Dinh Diem government created the General Directorate of Taxes, thus foretelling the dissolution a year later of the regional administrations. The new agency, which is, in smaller scale, the Vietnamese counterpart of the United States Internal Revenue Service, is entrusted with the administration of all kinds of taxes except customs duties and a few minor local levies. These taxes are usually grouped under two categories: the "old contributions," such as the land tax, the patente, the registration duties; and the "modern taxes," such as income taxes, indirect taxes, and the sales tax. Regional levies are thus brought under national control and the distinction between direct and indirect taxes remains no longer in their allocation but only in the method of their assessment and collection. Even this distinction is being questioned, and the problem has to be solved, along with the future reforms.

It took nearly two years for the General Directorate of Taxes to reorganize efficiently the administrative network of its offices throughout the country. And in 1957 a reform of a more fiscal nature came up when the production tax replaced the turnover tax. This was a greatly needed change. The turnover tax was levied, with few exemptions, at a flat rate of four percent on sales, made at every level from producer to consumer. Its administration was cumbersome, and its effects were regressive. The production tax is collected only once on home products and imported goods. It is levied at four different rates and, with many exemptions designed to lighten the burden of the tax on necessities and to encourage home production. This change, made possible by the installation of the General Directorate of Taxes, is likely to have far-reaching effects on the economy of the country.

Changes on the same large scale as the 1957 reform are expected to follow at a faster rate, and official and semiofficial blueprints have been submitted concerning the next phases.

Future reforms, it is commonly agreed, must aim at a greater efficiency of the tax structure. This objective could be achieved, for example, by elimination of nuisance taxes and procedural laws such as most registration duties, by simplification of assessment and collection of direct taxes which should be centralized under the tax department, and by implementation of the pay-as-you-earn principle of income taxation.

As a primarily agricultural country, Viet-Nam, within the next two or three decades, will undoubtedly have to depend on agricultural taxation, and particularly the land tax, for one of its main sources of revenue. This economic determinism must be accepted with all its consequences, and the agricultural land tax must be greatly improved in legislation, as well as in enforcement.

The Vietnamese people will be called on in ever-increasing numbers to pay taxes for the costs of public services. The citizens should be educated in their fiscal rights and duties and encouraged to participate more actively in the making of tax laws and regulations, not only through their representatives in the National Assembly, but also by means of free public hearings, such as is the rule in the United States.

Also, local taxation should not be overlooked. And now that the provincial administrations have been reorganized, an appropriate type of basic contribution at the commune level, of the type of the British general rate, for example, should be devised so that the voting citizens may be trained in public affairs and true democracy.

Commentary: RICHARD W. LINDHOLM *on*
VU THIEN VINH

ONE MUST consider the five general principles of agricultural taxation which are particularly applicable to a fiscal situation such as that in Viet-Nam: (1) Taxation should induce farmers to produce more for the market. (2) It should result in increased production and more efficient use of land now being cultivated, and should, in addition, bring new lands into cultivation. (3) It should not be considered as the equivalent of rent but as a purchase of certain things through the state rather than through family or individual purchase. (4) It should be assessed according to ability to pay. (5) The administrative procedures should be simple, and there should be few enforcement problems.

There are two types of agricultural taxes: one is a tax on the land, based on the actual production of each farm; the revenue from this tax goes to the national government; the other is a tax on products sold in markets; some of the revenue from this goes to the national government and some to the provincial government. The total revenue for the national government from the agricultural sector of the population is probably less than one percent of total tax collections.

To understand the weaknesses of the market tax and why it should not be used as the prototype for increased agricultural taxation, let us consider the effects of this type of taxation, on the basis of the five general principles of agricultural taxation.

The tax induces farmers to produce less, not more, for the market; for the tax is levied on any product taken to market; whereas, no tax payment can be collected on products consumed, bartered, or fed to animals at home.

It creates no pressure to bring unused land into cultivation nor does it increase production on cultivated lands. If the tax were collected on only one item, say rice, it would, to some degree, stimulate the production of other products, and to the extent that this resulted in diversification it could be considered to have a desirable impact. However, pressure toward diversification would be undesirable if, for example, the goal was to increase foreign exchange earnings through an increase in rice production.

The tax can stimulate land use only indirectly. This might be the situation, for example, if the producer considered a certain size of cash income desirable: By reducing cash income below that customarily received, the tax would stimulate a more intensive use of the land.

This type of tax is difficult to associate with the agricultural production of a particular village. The products of quite separate areas are likely to become intermingled before they reach the markets, thus making the taxes collected on the produce coming from individual villages difficult to calculate. In addition, the produce of a single village may be taken to different marketing points.

In spite of these shortcomings, it would be still possible to allocate collections, in a general way, to the areas where production took place. However, even if this were done, the market tax, unless the movement of produce from each village were controlled, would possess the basic shortcomings of not permitting different rates of tax on the produce of different villages.

The tax cannot have rates which vary with the quantity marketed by different producers, and therefore cannot correspond with ability to pay. Variation of the tax burden in accordance with ability to pay would be limited to the difference between the portion of products marketed by large and small producers, with the latter having a greater opportunity to avoid the tax. The ability to pay could also be destroyed by a low tax on livestock or on the types of products requiring considerable technical knowledge and equipment.

The tax can be enforced, but as is true of all taxes, the higher the rate the greater the enforcement problem. In addition, as economic development continues and additional market centers and travel routes are used, the enforcement problem is likely to become greater.

There is another way to tax the agricultural sector other than the market tax or the land tax on actual production: That is a tax based on the production potential of land, with the tax rates increasing with the size of the holding. This tax would be primarily on the capitalized value of the indestructible qualities of the land, such as location, rainfall, altitude, temperature, and basic soil characteristics.

Such a tax would stimulate efficient land use, because the tax liability on unused land would be the same as for land efficiently utilized. In fact, a landowner, not effectively utilizing his land would be in danger of losing it, i.e., the land on which taxes were unpaid could be confiscated: At present this cannot be done. As a tax on property, the difficulty of associating agricultural production with a particular village, as exists with the market tax, would be eliminated.

With graduated rates, according to the size of the holdings, this tax has an ability-to-pay basis. The first two or four hectares of total land holdings of an individual family, association, or corporation could be exempted from taxation. The base rate could be applied to the next four hectares of holdings, with an increase of ten percent on each additional ten hectares.

This tax could be enforced, and the enforcement problem would decrease as commercial farming increased. Initially, the most convenient base to be used in determining value would be rents paid.

The taxation of land at relatively high rates, and the use of such funds for the general welfare, is an important aspect of a democratic state. Land taxation, and particularly the taxation of underutilized land, is also important to the most efficient use of land resources. On the other hand, the taxation of land improvements has the repressive impact on economic development that is characteristic of all tax collections which increase with the intensity of economic endeavor.

The taxation of land, and the spending of the funds collected in a democratic fashion, does much more than provide noninflationary government revenues. It also: (1) assures that the whole nation will benefit from the expansion of productivity and wealth; (2) stimulates efficient use of land; (3) largely prevents taxes from becoming a cost of production; (4) destroys the possibility of a society organized along feudal lines; (5) brings about land reform through the use of the impersonal forces of the market.

Commentary: DAVID C. COLE *on* VU THIEN VINH

IN ADDITION to expanding revenues, developing a fiscal system compatible with economic growth, and improving tax administration, cited by Vu Thien Vinh, one of the most difficult problems facing the Vietnamese people and their government is the attitude to be taken toward taxation. As H. B. Morse said fifty years ago in the opening sentences of his chapter on Chinese public finance,[159] "China is an Asiatic country. It seems absurd to re-state this truism, but in nothing is the fact more clearly marked than in its system of taxation and its methods of providing for the expenses of administration."

This statement applies equally well to present-day Viet-Nam. In essence, Morse was suggesting the difference between systematic and discretionary government. Vague and ambiguous laws require individual interpretation by their administrators. Clear and specific laws are supposed to eliminate, or at least reduce, such administrative discretion, although, as has recently become evident, extensive specificity may cause such complexity as to increase discretionary decision making

[159] Hosea Ballou Morse, *The Trade and Administration of the Chinese Empire* (London: Longmans, Green and Co., 1908), p. 80.

(e.g., the U.S. income tax). Viet-Nam has traditionally had a government by man, or a government by negotiation. Laws have been written in general terms, leaving the practical questions of application to the administrators. This pattern was reinforced by the French administration, and still prevails. Tax assessments are made primarily on the basis of discussions between the taxpayer and the assessor, and the law only provides a general framework within which these negotiations take place.

An outstanding example of this is the business license tax law, adopted from France, which sets very broad limits for the annual levy on specific types of business, with no indications or instructions as to determining where an individual taxpayer should fall within that range. A lawyer, for example, may be taxed from 600 to 10,000 piasters per year, while a bank or credit establishment may have to pay from 3,000 to 100,000 piasters. The actual charge is fixed by local assessment officers. Undoubtedly, within their own areas, assessors try to graduate the tax according to ability to pay, but they have no defined criteria and are not informed as to what rates are being applied to comparable businesses in other areas. The law was worded in an indefinite manner to permit local officials, who were most aware of the affairs of local businesses, to assess the tax in an equitable manner. This may result in equity within an area, but assessments in different areas are, in many cases, very inequitable.

Another example of discretionary tax administration is the market tax. This is a daily charge of provincial and village governments on small merchants who sell food, clothing, etc., in the village market place or along the streets. The rate schedules under which this tax is assessed are so complicated and confused that it would be exceedingly expensive, if not impossible, to make the assessments prescribed in the regulations. Therefore, the taxpayers and collectors negotiate a fixed daily rate, and this is maintained until some reason arises for re-negotiation (e.g., the taxpayer expands his business, or the collector tries to increase charges to all sellers).

In the past, provincial governments, without tax departments or tax officials, were poorly equipped to collect the market tax. Therefore, they farmed out or auctioned off the rights of collection to private persons, who, in turn, paid the government a fixed monthly sum. Although the private collector system, a traditional method of the French, can result in a considerable loss of revenue, most government officials are reluctant to assume the responsibilities, and temptations, involved in the direct collection of this tax.

The problem of discretionary administration of tax laws cannot be solved overnight. However, the choice should be made between vague or specific tax laws. Whichever path is chosen, improvements could, and should, be made. If much official discretion is to be retained, steps should be taken to assure a more equitable application of the tax in various areas.

If, on the other hand, the choice is for stricter tax laws, both the people and the officials must be made aware of the significance and ramifications of this decision. The laws must be revised to contain realistic rates and provisions for the desired amount of equity so that it will no longer be necessary for officials to assume much responsibility for adjustments at the administrative level. As Mr. Vinh states, greater awareness of the benefits of government will make the people more responsible toward their fiscal duties, and thus toward safeguarding their government.

XXIII. American Aid and Its Financial Impact

RICHARD W. LINDHOLM

AMERICAN AID to Viet-Nam has been aimed at developing a politically and economically viable nation that would be able to meet the needs and aspirations of both the illiterate farmer and the graduate of a great French university. To accomplish these aims, law and order had to be established and the possibility of a Communist invasion had to be reduced.

In its allocations, the United States Congress has recognized, if not overrecognized, the military support phase of the aid program. This is apparent in Table 22, which shows total aid granted for three major

TABLE 22

AMERICAN AID, 1954-58*

(in thousands of dollars)

Fiscal Year	Military Support	Refugee Aid	Economic and Technical Assistance	Total
1957-58*	$155,000	—	$ 29,000	$184,000
1956-57	173,000	—	82,900	255,900
1955-56	109,000	$37,000	50,500	196,500
1954-55	234,800	55,785	29,715	320,300
TOTAL	$671,800	$92,785	$192,115	$956,700
Percent of Total	69	9	22	100

Source: Viet-Nam Desk, ICA, Washington.

* Totals for 1958 are tentative. A $25 million loan was also extended which would be added to the economic and technical assistance total of $50 million. In 1957-58 about 50 percent of the economic and technical assistance total was allocated to the construction of a modern highway between Saigon and Bien Hoa.

categories—military support, refugee aid, and economic and technical assistance—during the three fiscal years, 1954-55, 1955-56, and 1956-57, along with estimates for 1957-58.

As Table 22 indicates, two thirds of total American aid has been used to finance the redevelopment of the military forces. In addition, according to Table 23, which provides details of the 1956-57 American aid program, some eight percent of the total allocated for economic and technical assistance was used to develop the police forces ($5,786,640 + $1,000,000 of the allocation for the National Institute of Administration). The amount has been large, but the task has also been formidable.

Refugee aid amounted to 10 percent of the total, which was for the

317

first two-year periods under consideration. Of the total allocated for economic and technical assistance in 1956-57, $10 million (see Table 23), or about 12 percent, was used to support rural resettlement which was largely a refugee-related program.

TABLE 23

ECONOMIC AND TECHNICAL ASSISTANCE
WITH ESTIMATED EXPENDITURE, FISCAL YEAR 1956-57
(in thousands of dollars)

AGRICULTURE AND NATURAL RESOURCES

Small water control systems	$ 1,374
Administration of agrarian reform	607
Land development (rural resettlement)	10,034
General livestock development	1,169
Development of marine fisheries	430
Agricultural extension and information	351
National Agricultural College and general training	687
Research in diversified crops	337
Agricultural credit and co-operatives	190
Agricultural economics and statistics	111
TOTAL	$15,290

INDUSTRY AND MINING

Nong Son coal exploration survey	$ 56
Telecommunication development	719
Electric power development	843
Paper industry survey	25
Sugar industry survey	36
Industrial Development Center	10,000
General industrial survey	804
Rural water supply development	417
Saigon-Cholon water system survey	122
Handicraft development	99
TOTAL	$13,121

TRANSPORTATION

Highways and bridges	$20,694
Viet-Nam railway system	4,413
Saigon port loan	229
Waterways of Viet-Nam	298
Improvement and expansion of aeronautical ground facilities	3,006
TOTAL	$28,639

LABOR

Labor school	$ 200
Labor ministry organization	40
TOTAL	$ 240

(Table 23 *Continued*)

HEALTH AND SANITATION

Malaria eradication program	$ 1,231
Medical and allied education	3,554
Health services development	1,410
TOTAL	$ 6,195

EDUCATION

Technical vocational education	$ 883
Elementary education	1,002
Secondary education	480
Teacher training and higher education	1,450
Adult literacy training	350
Textbook development and special services	204
TOTAL	$ 4,369

PUBLIC ADMINISTRATION

Civil police administration	$ 5,787
Training civil tax expert	8
Fellowship on taxation and public finance	150
National Institute of Statistics	214
National Institute of Administration and MSU administrative support	2,037
Travel costs for Vietnamese scholarship students to and from Viet-Nam	100
TOTAL	$ 8,295

GENERAL AND MISCELLANEOUS

Development of government information facilities	$ 779
National radio network	889
General program administration	5,072
TOTAL	$ 6,740
Grand Total for 1956-57 Program	$82,887

Economic and technical assistance received 22 percent of total American aid during the period under consideration. The amount to be used for this purpose has steadily increased, while the allocations for refugees has dropped sharply; however, the amount spent for military assistance has shown little tendency to decrease.

The average annual total of American aid during this period has been $236.9 million. A large portion of this has been used to finance the purchase of consumer products from other countries. Viet-Nam's negative trade balance of about nine billion piasters is brought into approximate balance by dollars made available by the American aid program.

Viet-Nam's imports for 1956 were concentrated in the consumer area, with about 40 percent consisting of textiles, food, drink, and tobacco. The Bureau of Customs shows that about 17 percent of the 1956 imports were classified as investment goods. If this classification presents an accurate picture, then 83 percent of the imports are consumer-type imports or are used up in the productive process—for example, imports such as coal and oil.

These quantities of imports and approximately these types of imports are necessary to permit the Vietnamese government to spend considerably more than it collects in taxes, while avoiding conditions very likely to cause disruptive inflation. The procedure used in extending aid was developed in Western Europe during the days of the Marshall Plan and was transferred to Asia as an appropriate administrative device. The device has not worked particularly well, primarily because the governments that have received aid have not been able to balance their normal operating budgets and, therefore, the aid is operating budget support, rather than investment support, as was the situation in Western Europe.

One important reason why Viet-Nam in its operating budget relies on American aid counterpart funds (piasters arising from the sale of imports financed with American aid dollars) to directly supply 50 percent of its revenues, and indirectly another 25 to 30 percent, is that the Vietnamese government is carrying on activities that are far above its fiscal capability.[160] The largest of these expenditures is the budgeted amounts for the armed forces. In addition to this expenditure, which is equal to about 50 percent of the total national budgeted expenditures, there are those expenditures related to administration and operation of all the various projects listed in Table 23. Each of these, with the exception of $150,000 listed under public administration, is at least directly a government revenue spending program. The increase of the money value of the productivity likely to arise from these projects is uncertain, and the ability of the government to tap this increased productivity, if and when it does arise, is even less certain. The end result of an American aid program of this type is quite different from that undertaken in Western Europe.

In Viet-Nam the abandonment or reduction of American aid would leave behind an inflated government budget, with some expansion of productivity and skills, instead of largely modern production facilities, as was the case in Western Europe. Vietnamese leaders often speak of the desirability of the type of impact which American aid had in France, or perhaps of the end result of Russian and Chinese aid in Red Viet-Nam,

[160] Somewhat more than 50 percent of the tax revenues of the national government arise from custom duties applied to imports financed with American aid dollars.

and contrast this with the impact of American aid in Free Viet-Nam. An impact similar to that realized by American aid to Europe could be enjoyed under present conditions *if* the economic and technical aid were concentrated in only a few areas, such as land and power development, *if* the military personnel were to consist largely of part-time soldiers, *if* these military savings were funneled into economic and technical assistance, *if* the government of Viet-Nam developed an effective individual savings program, and *if* a tax program were developed which brought in 11 to 15 percent of Viet-Nam's gross national product, instead of 6 to 8 percent as is presently the situation.[161] This sort of program makes a lot of sense, and many persons of good-will in Viet-Nam and the United States favor a development of the American aid program along these lines.

As to the financial impact of American aid, it is the large portion of funds used to pay the Vietnamese army and other military costs that has been frequently misunderstood by correspondents in Viet-Nam. This misunderstanding has led to statements such as: American aid should be used to finance industrial machinery, and not so many new cars; it should be used to produce producer goods, and not consumer goods.

To understand why things have worked out as they have, one can consider, as an example, what happens when the Vietnamese army needs 35 million piasters to pay its troops. To provide budgetary support for this expenditure, the American government has made a credit of one million dollars available to the National Bank of Viet-Nam in the form of a deposit in a commercial bank in the United States. (One dollar at the official rate of exchange equals 35 piasters.)

In exchange for this increase of its dollar holdings, the National Bank credits the account of American aid (ICA in Saigon) for 35 million piasters. A check for this amount is then presented to the Secretary of State for Finance by American aid officials in Saigon, and he deposits it in the Vietnamese Treasury, thereby increasing the balance of the national government by 35 million piasters.

Because soldiers are paid with currency, and not by check, the Treasury generally demands currency in exchange for the check. The National Bank provides this currency either from currency it has received from commercial banks in exchange for deposit credits, from currency it has received from the sale of foreign exchange, or with new currency (coins and paper money) which it issues. After the Treasury receives this currency, it makes it available to army paymasters as needed, and, as it is paid out, the National government's balance at the Treasury decreases

[161] Taken from tax studies of the State Secretary of Finance of Viet-Nam.

accordingly. And the currency in the hands of the army paymasters, and later of the soldiers, increases by a like amount.

The soldiers and the suppliers for the army spend a considerable portion for food, drink, and clothing, and, in addition, purchase trinkets, cigarettes, and transportation. The providers of these goods and services replenish their stocks by purchasing new supplies from domestic and foreign sources: For example, they purchase tea from wholesalers who buy from domestic producers, and canned milk from wholesalers who buy from foreign producers.

The wholesaler can use piasters to make his tea purchases; but, to buy his canned milk supply he must first exchange his piasters for dollars, francs, or some other foreign exchange. If he wishes to purchase a supply of canned milk costing $1,000, he must pay 35,000 piasters to his commercial bank. Eventually, the commercial bank must transfer 35,000 piasters to the National Bank for the $1,000 needed by its wholesaler customer.

When the wholesaler begins to make arrangements to import more canned milk, he prevents a decrease in the quantity of goods that will be available for sale in Viet-Nam: He is making certain that there will be canned milk to meet the demands and, in doing this, he performs the first step in seeing that there will be goods on the market to meet the piasters offered in the market in exchange for goods.

When the wholesaler makes his piaster payment for the dollar exchange, he gives up a considerable portion of the piasters he has received from various customers for canned milk. The economic want for canned milk has been satisfied, and the piasters searching for goods have been reduced by this amount. When the commercial bank makes the payment to the National Bank, the cycle of this flow of piasters is complete. The piasters were put into, and taken out of, circulation by the National Bank.

The types of goods which wholesalers, and also manufacturers, import are restricted somewhat by the regulations set by the Vietnamese government, but basically the types of *goods which they import are items that can be sold*.

Therefore, the use of American aid is determined by how the Vietnamese use their incomes and their savings. The fact that a large portion of the Vietnamese imports financed with American aid are either consumer goods or raw materials used rather directly to meet consumer demands is an indication that the Vietnamese people desire these goods, for they have shown their desire by their willingness to use their piasters to purchase them.

Should the situation change in Viet-Nam so that wholesalers find it difficult to sell radios or gasoline but easy to sell sugar-refining equipment or road-building machinery, they would, of course, request permits to import these products: Should this new situation arise, the piaster supply, which was increased when the Treasury presented the ICA check to the National Bank would be decreased to its former level when the National Bank received piasters spent by the Vietnamese to increase the productive capacity of their country rather than to meet their demands for consumer goods.

If the people of Viet-Nam do not voluntarily refrain from spending their current income or former accumulations on consumer goods which must be imported, or if the government does not reduce its ability to do this through tax collections and a restrictive monetary policy, American aid is not available to acquire producer goods: That is, American aid is not available to acquire producer goods unless the government of Viet-Nam wishes to increase drastically all the problems associated with economic controls and a deterioration of its currency. As a matter of fact, the latter alternative is really not available, for American taxpayers are providing the dollars which ICA/Washington deposits in a U.S. commercial bank in order to prevent inflation in Viet-Nam during this critical period of reconstruction.

Commentary: DAVID HOTHAM[162] *on* LINDHOLM

No DEGREE of industry can ever be introduced into Viet-Nam as long as the only goods that are imported are ones that can be resold. What importer, as Lindholm implies, is going to order equipment for a textile factory or a steel plant, and who, in a nation whose population is 80 percent peasants, is going to buy such equipment?

If one depends simply on the normal working of supply and demand, industry in Viet-Nam, virtually nonexistent at present, can never be developed. Even in the United States, where this method did work and where there was an almost unlimited supply of private capital, it took fifty or more years for industry to develop. Rapid industrialization, however, is urgently needed in Free Viet-Nam because of the Communist menace to the north. How, then, can this new nation, lacking private capital, develop an industrial sector, and do so rapidly?

Far the best and quickest way to introduce some industry is to create state-owned industries. There are many difficulties to doing this, such as the fact that most of the existing industry in the south is owned by the French or Chinese; however, this amounts to nothing more than a few cigarette factories, breweries, and rice mills.

[162] Former correspondent for the *London Times* and *Economist* in the Far East, now stationed in Ankara, Turkey.

If there could be a large influx of private capital invested in Viet-Nam, it might be possible to create industry without infringing on the principle of private enterprise. But there are two factors which render this extremely difficult. First, foreign investors, despite the law encouraging investment, have not hastened to put their money into a country whose political future is so uncertain. (It is significant that there has been almost no private American investment in Free Viet-Nam.) Secondly, the Vietnamese are not in any hurry to repeat a pattern whereby their industries are foreign-owned in the future.

American aid has financed many excellent and well-conceived programs in Viet-Nam: the resettlement of refugees, the anti-malaria and anti-trachoma work, the agricultural improvements, the supplying of thousands of buffaloes, the restocking of fishponds, the reclaiming of waste land, the research on the high plateau of the interior, the invaluable long-term work on statistics, taxation, and other fields, and the training in administration and the introduction of American methods and ideas carried out by Michigan State University. Also, it cannot be denied that the counterpart fund system of aid has helped to avert inflation, which was so fatal in Koumintang China.

It is not the details, but the main lines, of the aid program which are wrong, because they negate the effect of the excellent activities enumerated. If Viet-Nam were a country such as Iceland, isolated and with no serious Communist danger, all would be well. However, Viet-Nam is in intimate competition with Communists next door: It is co-existence at the very closest quarters. Unless the main lines of American aid program are right, democracy shall not win the Vietnamese. The exaggerated overemphasis on the army, the lack of housing in a country where there is terrible poverty and misery (particularly in Saigon where one fourth of the population lives), the quasi-paralysis which afflicts the land reform program, the failure to do anything effective about chronic unemployment and underemployment, and the failure to introduce industry—these are the big things which count in the small cold war north and south of the 17th parallel, in which propaganda counts as much as anything. The best propaganda will be facts which the Vietnamese can see. The vast majority of the population of Free Viet-Nam, seeing 250 million dollars or so pouring into their little country every year, naturally ask where all this money is spent. And the Communists help them to speculate.

Why are Americans so reluctant to help undeveloped countries to industrialize? Is there some fear that the creation of industrial proletariats will encourage communism? Or is it that Americans do not want the countries in question to become economically independent too quickly? Granted that hasty and ill-considered industrialization in any country is a serious mistake, one might still ask has the extra-ordinarily rapid industrialization of Puerto Rico, for example, been wrong?

In the case of Free Viet-Nam, many eminent and hardheaded American businessmen have reported on the good prospects for a varied selection of light industries. The aid program should be adapted to financing such industries and the other things which need doing. Why should economic aid not be given in the form of factories, with American technicians to set them up? If there is some good economic or political reason for not doing so, Americans should know what it is.

Commentary: TRAN VAN KIEN[163] *on* LINDHOLM

OF ALL the aid programs given to Viet-Nam by the Free World (UN assistance, Colombo Plan, etc.), the American program is by far the most important. It would not be difficult, therefore, to draw a balance sheet of results achieved by the latter.

The procedure followed in Viet-Nam was the same as that of the Marshall Plan in Europe; that is why a comparison of the two programs is invariably made whenever an evaluation of results in Viet-Nam is attempted. The outcome of such a comparison is necessarily unfavorable.

While the Marshall Plan brought about Europe's economic recovery, the Vietnamese economy remains, after eight years of assistance, entirely dependent upon American aid. This difference in results is not caused so much, as has been contended, by the fact that the Vietnamese government used the aid as "budget support" instead of "investment support" but rather by differences in the structures of the two economies and also by the political situation in Viet-Nam.

In Europe it was the commercialized-aid formula that successfully cured the dollar shortage caused by Europe's efforts to rebuild its productive facilities which had been ravaged by the war. Thus, European producers were able to use national currencies to pay for equipment needed to put existing plants and factories back into operation; the proceeds in local currencies were then turned over to European governments, which used them to finance their investment programs. This combined effort by private business and governments enabled Europe to become economically independent within a short time. American aid had provided exactly what European producers needed.

[163] Assistant Professor of Economics, National Institute of Administration. Translated from the original French by Phan Thu Ngoc.

The case of Viet-Nam is different. It is true that few investment efforts were made because of budget deficits, as has been demonstrated; but nothing has been done by businessmen either. The Vietnamese economy is not at all comparable to that of Europe which already had a productive apparatus tested and proven by several decades of industrialization, and which also had businessmen and industrialists who knew what their needs were. Furthermore, the political and military situation which prevailed at the time in Viet-Nam was not favorable to any reconstruction efforts. The Vietnamese government was too busily engaged in fighting a war to think of encouraging businessmen in productive investments that would be useful to the country's economy. In addition, the necessity of maintaining a certain level of living standard among the population, in order "to defeat Communism with prosperity," demanded immediate results, which long-term investment programs could not provide.

For these reasons, American aid dollars were not used for investment purposes but to finance imports of consumer goods. In this respect, American aid achieved notable results, enabling the Vietnamese government successfully to deal with problems of the hour. The aid contributed greatly to the preservation of a suitable standard of living for the population and, thus, it is well to stress, to the care and improvement of that form of capital of vital importance for economic development: human capital.

But once the military and political phase has been left behind, the time has come to place the nation's economy on a healthier and more stable basis. The problem is the efficient use of American funds, within the framework of present procedures, which would be difficult to change, so that the economy would remain viable when that aid is discontinued.

Toward this end, Viet-Nam should have a productive apparatus suitable to its needs and capabilities. Concentrated efforts in a few limited fields—agriculture and power—should be only a first phase soon to be succeeded by the gradual establishment of a few industries. It is true the country's partition, which means the loss of the greater part of its natural resources, has greatly diminished its industrial potential but a purely agricultural economy would be subjected to too much instability and would not have the means for absorbing surplus man power resulting from the mechanization of agriculture and population growth. Priority should be given to those industrial sectors producing for the domestic market and using local resources instead of imported raw materials.

To do this, considerable investment efforts would have to be made by the government, as well as private persons. It would, however, be useless, even dangerous, to reduce military expenditures too far as long as the Communist threat persists. The main effort must then come from individuals. The government, on the other hand, would have to develop, as has been suggested, a private savings program and at the same time take suitable measures to encourage and induce the productive effort, particularly imports of capital goods using aid funds. These measures would be all the more necessary because businessmen are inclined to import consumer goods which will bring them profits rather than capital goods. There is the added reason that a fall in imports would mean a decrease in counterpart funds used to finance government operations, as these funds come from payments made by importers. Of all these measures, only one might be mentioned— toward private foreign investments, which has already been considered by the government and deserves to be carried out more thoroughly. Foreign capital flowing into certain well-defined sectors would be a useful addition to the available pool of domestic savings, which is small, as is always the case with a low per capita income economy. Foreign capital would serve as the needed initial impulse to raise national income and, therefore, savings. On the other hand, foreign capital would free a portion of national income which becomes available for consumer goods imports and thus circumvent the necessity of subjecting the people to too severe an austerity program as the one prevailing in the Communist zone. Finally, in the form of long-term investments, foreign capital would provide substitutes for American aid when the latter stops.

Thus, to the extent that it can give Viet-Nam economic independence within the interdependence of the Free World, American aid will have achieved its goal.

Commentary: JOHN M. HUNTER on LINDHOLM

FOREIGN AID should be viewed by its top administrators and the United States Congress much as a corporation views its research expenditures: These expenditures are a necessary, integral part of development. Boards of corporations appropriate sums for such activity, knowing full well that the returns may be nebulous. Researchers, especially in any given period of time, may produce nothing of direct value. They may produce harmful results (e.g., patents that must be "buried"), or they may produce small or great immediate benefits or future benefits whose values are not immediately estimable. They may produce nothing but negative results, but these, too, can be extremely valuable.

In many ways, aid programs are analogous; the same philosophy is applicable, if not necessary. The objectives of foreign aid are more or less clearly defined in the broad objectives of United States foreign policy, but aid on as broad a scale as Americans know it (and as it is apt to develop in the present political and economic world) is something shockingly new to them. Americans have not even a long history of colonial administration (not the same problem, but experience here would be helpful) to assist them. Under these programs, they literally project thousands of United States citizens into parts of the world about whose geography they knew little ten to twenty years ago. Foreign cultures, social structures, economic organization, and values were, and are, an even greater enigma to them. Individually and collectively, the people are improperly prepared to carry out the tasks the world situation assigns to them. "Learning by doing" is the essence of the physical scientists' laboratory; much of the American operation in the field of technical asistance is essentially the same.

Not only are they relative newcomers to the foreign scene, but there is no great body of knowledge to which they can turn for guidance even in their own culture. Basically, aid programs and technical assistance are designed to manipulate governments and something glibly called "public opinion" in nation after nation as if Americans really understood these things.[164]

Like it or not, much of foreign aid will be of an experimental nature. Recognizing this explicitly would be wise administration. Making this a part of the aid philosophy, and effectively incorporating it into operating administration, would contribute substantially to the aid program. First of all, failures of particular projects would not be regarded necessarily as personal failures of their advocates or administrators, but rather as one of the expected costs of experimentation. Honest reporting of the failures, and the reasons therefor, could contribute much to the working paraphernalia of aid administrators who will be on the scene a long time. Failures in experimentation are frequently as valuable as successes and are sometimes necessary forerunners.

Further, more imaginative projects can, and will be, proposed. By removing some of the personal onus of failures, more imaginative projects can be undertaken—perhaps offering much greater returns

---

[164] Perhaps this could be put more palatably, but aid programs *are* a part of U.S. foreign policy which *must* have geopolitical objectives. Even the more physically oriented projects (e.g., improving egg production of chickens) are a part of the "battle for the minds of men."

but not now ventured because of risks of failure. Recognition of imaginative projects should do much to improve morale of personnel in the field and to attract more competent personnel.[165]

A genuine acceptance of this philosophy would free field personnel of many of the frustrations attendant on the bureaucratic processes and avoid the necessity for multiple clearances, multiple project justifications, multiple audits, etc., which so slow the processes that individuals, *who ultimately carry out projects,* are apt to lose enthusiasm or have their periods of assignment run out, or both. It is valuable training for the individual to discover that a technique will fail; it is also valuable to give responsibility and confidence to an individual (or a group) and let him work out his own salvation. Too much time is now spent in getting multiple approvals on everything in order to share responsibility in case of ultimate failure.

Accepting such a philosophy asks a great deal in a political democracy, because it asks Congress to appropriate money with the confidence that wise people will spend wisely, and asks Congress to keep its "second guessing" to a minimum or to what is really more restrictive, an informed and responsible basis. Ultimately, then, the same is asked of the voters.

Presumably, this appeal could be made for nearly any governmental operation, but aid programs present a special case. Their unique elements are the immeasurability of results and the tremendous variations in economies, societies, and cultures in which they must operate — both of which make supervision from afar or on a part-time basis extraordinarily difficult, if not senseless.

Some increase in graft and diversion might occur and perhaps some foolish things would be undertaken, but the program as a whole would become more vibrant and dynamic and the gains would probably far outweigh the costs. The ship of state *can* run areef, while all the crew is busy looking for minor leaks in the hold.

In evaluating foreign aid programs, the basic difficulty lies in the esoteric nature of the underlying objectives and the consequent difficulty of identifying results (output) for comparison with inputs. How *do* you *measure* successes and failures in the battles for men's minds?

Current evaluations lead to unfortunate biases in the selection of projects, and once projects are undertaken may give peculiar and un-

---

[165] For example, a report and recommendations were censured by USOM in Saigon on the grounds that a proposal was "unorthodox." Whether the proposal was good or bad is not at issue; it was never considered *because* of the label affixed to it. Insistence on "orthodox" policy in "unorthodox" situations can be very expensive. An administrative philosophy effectively incorporating the idea of an experimental basis would permit field administrators room to operate outside the shackles of "orthodoxy."

desirable slants to them. Favored projects are those whose results are concrete and can be pointed to, seen, and counted. The numbers of students in schools, the number of plows distributed, the numbers of people seeing United States-sponsored shows, etc., *are* measures of *something* and can be enumerated by an agency in reporting its activities. In so doing, the means and the ends may be confused. Nor may these projects be the most productive in attaining the ultimate objectives. It may be much more important for an American technician to implant the seeds of "research-mindedness" in the mind of one Vietnamese than for the technician to produce five research jobs on his own. It is certainly of greater importance to convince one official of the necessity for widespread education than to seat one hundred youngsters in a new school. Yet, in the kinds of evaluations that now exist, the second project in each case above appears to be the better record.

One of the major contributors to this tendency is American unwillingness to seek long-run objectives on anything but short-run budgeting and planning. The kinds of things that foreign policy seeks to do through aid programs will not be done in a year; no appreciable progress may even be "visible" in that period of time.

If foreign aid programs are to be successful and efficient operations, Americans must stop trying to run them as if they were highway construction programs. They do not know as much about how to achieve desired results in the former as they do about laying concrete over various types of terrain. And they cannot conceivably lay "x" miles of foreign aid *per year* and expect to get sensible programs.

PART SEVEN

SOME EVALUATIONS
OF THE VIET-NAM EXPERIMENT

President Diem's decision to develop an administratively united state and carrying this out through methods that cannot be considered democratic in the British or American sense brings forth a great difference of opinion among expert observers.

R. G. Casey, the Minister for External Affairs, Commonwealth of Australia, sees the use of rather undemocratic steps as perhaps being a necessary early approach: "Some sacrifices of individual liberty are at times necessary in order that a community, as a whole, may eventually enjoy liberty in the true sense." William Henderson, the Assistant Executive Director of the Council on Foreign Relations, Inc., and a Far Eastern specialist, agrees that at the early stages some relaxation of democratic practices may have been desirable and necessary. However, Henderson believes the dictatorship has lasted long enough: "After four years there has been little moderation of the grim dictatorship which Diem has exerted from the beginning . . . Has the time not come to set in motion a progressive liberalization of government and politics, however cautiously the necessary steps may be taken?"

David Hotham, who was correspondent for the London Times and Economist in Southeast Asia and particularly in Free Viet-Nam during the crucial 1955-57 period, agrees with Henderson that President Diem has not offered sufficient opportunity for the development of democratic processes. He labels the government of President Diem a "reactionary police state," which does not even possess the advantage usually attributed to police states of bringing forth an effectively administered nation. "Instead of uniting it, Diem has divided the south."

John M. Mecklin, a correspondent for Life-Time, and Peggy Durdin of the New York Times feel that President Diem's personal courage and honesty plus the programs he has developed have been responsible for making a very bad situation much better. Also, Mecklin believes that "Democracy is an utter impossibility, a contradiction in terms, in a country that is 90 percent or even 50 percent illiterate." Therefore, he argues strongly for the continuation of a government in Free Viet-Nam along the lines of President Diem's and considers appeals to democracy by the Communists in a country such as Free Viet-Nam "one of the most cynical, vicious evils of communism. . . ."

XXIV.   A Summary of Viet-Nam's Political and Economic Progress

R. G. CASEY[166]

WHAT POLITICAL progress has Free Viet-Nam made since its ties with France were severed, and it became fully independent? First, it must be remembered that Viet-Nam, in common with the United States, refused to be a party to the Geneva Agreement, but undertook not to use force to oppose its execution. Because of this refusal, the Vietnamese government has declined to accept formally from France the obligations the latter agreed to in the Geneva Agreement relating to the maintenance of the cease-fire and support for the International Supervisory Commission. Since the withdrawal of the French Union High Command in 1956, Viet-Nam has, however, accepted a large measure of the practical responsibility borne by the French. However, the government of the Republic of Viet-Nam has consistently refused to consult with the Viet-Minh on nation-wide elections, on the ground that conditions permitting really free elections do not exist in the north.

By insisting when he assumed power on complete independence for his country, President Ngo Dinh Diem has won the support of many nationalists who had criticized previous governments as being too much under French domination. When the politico-religious sects (the Cao Dai and Hoa Hao) and the Binh Xuyen, which in south Viet-Nam had been permitted to maintain their own armed forces independently of the Vietnamese national army, resisted attempts by the government to establish its authority over the territories and forces they controlled, Diem succeeded, with the help of the national army, in crushing their political and military power.

This decision to destroy the sects and private armies was crucial. Many of Diem's best friends abroad felt that he was taking on too much and that, faced with the external threat from the north, Viet-Nam could not afford to have fighting between the non-Communists. However, seen in retrospect, the elimination of the sects was essential if the state was to survive: The supremacy of the government meant that there were law and order, a continuity and direction of policy, and the means of eliminating corruption.

In the conditions of peace brought about by the Geneva Agreement, Diem has been able to establish an administration which is firmly anti-Communist. He has taken energetic action to restore internal security and, at the same time, has provided a firm basis for the establishment of representative institutions of government.

[166] Minister for External Affairs, Commonwealth of Australia.

The Vietnamese Constitution, promulgated in October, 1956, in essence, follows the United States model, incorporating features from other countries as well. The presidential system was adopted because Viet-Nam must, in its present circumstances, have a strong executive. To permit party strife to paralyze the executive would be a national disaster. It is important that Viet-Nam should not halt on the road to full democracy as practiced in other countries, but the Vietnamese must make their own judgment as to how fast they must move. Democracy is not something that can be granted or imposed: It must evolve naturally from a spread of political consciousness and a sense of responsibility in a population.

Throughout Viet-Nam's history, the village, with a large measure of autonomy, has been the basic unit of government. In dealing with their own affairs at the village level, the Vietnamese have learned the basic habits of democracy. Moreover, their national temper is conducive to an individualistic approach. But to extend this village democracy into a parliamentary democracy, with the necessary checks and balances, will not be a rapid process, and some widely accepted habits of thought will need to be changed.

During the long period of nationalist agitation against foreign rule, the Vietnamese came to look on government not as a necessary guarantee of social order, but as an enemy to which disobedience was a virtue. Now that a truly independent Vietnamese government has been established, the Vietnamese are beginning to learn to shed the habits of anarchy and to take on the habits of social discipline. They are beginning to realize that *the* government is now *their* government and that they must support it if Viet-Nam is to survive and progress.

Viet-Nam's struggle to gain and preserve its independence and to build an effective democracy is earning increasing moral support for Viet-Nam among newly independent Asian states. South Korea, Malaya, Burma, and many other countries have shown the havoc and disruption that can be caused by Communist or non-Communist insurgents, by destroying or sabotaging industries, by interrupting communications, and by making farmers afraid to go out into the fields to work. And whenever the long-term outlook for a country is uncertain, investment is frightened away. President Diem laid the essential foundation for economic development and prosperity by restoring law and order and giving his own people, as well as the outside world, the assurance that his government was firmly based.

American aid, of course, has done much to give this firm base to Viet-Nam, both in the political and economic fields. A great deal of the criticism leveled at the American assistance program has arisen from a lack of knowledge of how United States aid works, of the priorities which have to be determined in choosing its objectives, and of the problems and difficulties which it has had to face. United States aid has not been granted to Viet-Nam primarily to provide capital equipment and technical advice for a less-developed country in Asia, nor simply to cover a temporary disequilibrium in the country's balance of payments. The first and major objective was to rescue Viet-Nam from a breakdown of the economic structure, which would have helped to open the way to communism. The progressive growth of security and political stability over the past three years could not have occurred if the Vietnamese government had not had the resources to carry out its task. Plans for the systematic restoration and development of the economy had to take second place to the overriding political necessity requiring a "crash" program to make an immediate impact on the many problems and to serve as conspicuous evidence of United States interest and support. However, now the point has been reached where long-term plans can replace what was essentially a rescue operation.

What were the immediate economic needs of Viet-Nam in 1955? The first requirements were: to finance and make possible the heavy military budget—an essential to the re-establishment of internal security—to provide local currency for refugee resettlement, to ensure an adequate flow of imports to reduce the inflationary pressure and to meet the needs of the population in south Viet-Nam, which in a few months had increased by about ten percent. To do all these things, it was decided that United States aid should be channeled as far as possible through the normal processes of import trade and that local currency from the sale of imports should be paid into a counterpart fund on which the Vietnamese government could draw to meet its day-to-day requirements. However, at the beginning of this operation, it became clear that local currency had to be provided far more quickly than the comparatively slow machinery of importation and local sale could supply it. For this reason, the expedient resorted to was the direct purchase of local currency for dollars, taking a calculated risk of inflation. To use up this rapidly increasing volume of local currency and to give impetus to the generation of counterpart funds, the range of goods granted import permits was made much more extensive.

This initial phase of the aid program has been misunderstood, since to outside observers it often seemed incongruous and even pointless that so many nonessential goods were imported. But if an uncontrollable inflationary spiral was to be averted, it was imperative to take local currency out of the economy as fast as the government was putting it in. This could only be done quickly and effectively by importing some goods which met consumer demand and which would sell effectively.

The difficulties of this operation were intensified by the simultaneous need to change the traditional trade pattern with France and to find new sources of supply under the world-wide procurement system of ICA. Another difficulty was that almost all the aid received had to be spent on imports, and little was left to pay for even the most essential transfers of funds to other countries. Growing bank deposits constituted an inflationary threat to the economy and a constant invitation to black market currency dealings. These risks had to be accepted.

The expedient of allowing imports of some nonessential goods to use up spending power is certainly not an attractive method of coping with inflation, but was any short-run alternative really available? The government and the traditions of the country, it must be remembered, did not favor an effective taxation system.

This "crash" operation, and the urgent imposition of new systems of exchange and import control, would have tested the capacity of any administration. Under such conditions, the Vietnamese government and the United States aid administration made a remarkable achievement in limiting economic and commercial dislocation and in attaining the vital, immediate objective of supporting the Vietnamese budget and covering current expenses, in particular those involved in security and the maintenance of the refugees.

For the greater part of 1955 and 1956, the bulk of the United States aid program was for budget support, a large portion going to the military budget and much of the remainder to the refugee program. From a theoretical standpoint, it might be argued that a greater share of this local currency expenditure should have been raised from Viet-Nam's own resources, leaving more United States funds for long-term development projects. This argument disregards the fact that political conditions during the first two years of independence were such that Viet-Nam's resources could not be exploited. In a circle of circumstances where the national income could not be raised until conditions of security allowed rehabilitation of the economy and the large-scale production of the main cash crops, and where generation of counterpart funds could not be slowed down until more revenue could be earned, the restoration of physical security throughout south Viet-Nam was clearly imperative to any planning for future economic development.

Within the limits imposed by necessity, the commercial aid program, nevertheless, did support the importation of worth-while quantities of capital equipment and machinery. These commodities, together with raw materials for local industry, totaled, as early as 1955, some 50 percent of all imports. A further 40 percent was absorbed in badly needed pharmaceuticals and textiles; this proportion could not have been devoted to capital goods without serious hardship to the population and increasing inflationary risks to a degree which could have undermined the whole object of the operation.

The record of United States aid to long-range development schemes, despite their secondary priority, is impressive. Large sums have been spent on land reclamation, drainage, rebuilding, dredging, and irrigation works, and in setting up a national Agricultural College. One outstanding achievement has been the Cai San refugee resettlement project, where over 100,000 acres are now producing rice. This and, for example, the Tuy Hoa irrigation scheme, which cost $2,500,000, have contributed directly to the fact that in 1957 Viet-Nam was again able to export rice. Another big effort is being made in the field of transportation. Saigon airport is being developed and dredged, and work has started on a major scheme for development of the road network. Further large sums are being spent on training administrators and technicians in all areas, on a health and sanitation program, and in the development of local industries.

It would appear that a substantial reduction in the total of United States aid at the present time would cause serious difficulties. However, the successful completion of the refugee aid program has reduced a significant claim on the government's resources. The Vietnamese government has taken steps to increase its own revenues, and the 1957 budget provided for taxation increases, particularly on luxury goods and imports.

Viet-Nam's long-term prospects for economic development are good, as evidenced by the long and detailed report drawn up by the United Nations Economic Survey Mission, which worked in Viet-Nam from November, 1955, to February, 1956. The Vietnamese government has been taking the United Nations Mission's recommendations into account in drawing up its first Five Year Plan. This Plan envisages a 12 percent increase in national income, about half of which would be contributed by agriculture and one fourth by industry, and a 5 percent increase in per capita national income. The plan is based on the assumption that foreign aid will continue at its present level and takes as an axiom that Viet-Nam must depend on that aid and on foreign loans and investment for the bulk of its capital formation.

In March, 1957, the Vietnamese government announced the general lines of a policy designed to attract foreign private investment. Priority has been given to agriculture over industry, since in that field progress will benefit the greatest number of people. Less capital investment is required, and there is a more immediate prospect of increasing production. Short-term projects are the recultivation of some one and a quarter million acres of abandoned rice lands in the Mekong delta and the development of the High Plateau regions by the creation of agricultural settlements, based on maize, sweet potato, and tobacco cultivation, grazing, and forestry. Medium-term projects include an increase in sugar production sufficient to supply all local needs and the encouragement of silk, cotton, and jute cultivation. Long-term projects include the planting of coffee, tea, and rubber, and where necessary to provide better yielding varieties of young trees.

In industry, plans are limited to the processing of agricultural products and the manufacture of articles for everyday use (sugar, paper, cotton, silk and jute thread, tools, cement, glass, ice, and leather) and to increase the production of coal, marble, and phosphates.

As this development program is carried out, there would be, in some cases, an increase in exports; in others, the importation of capital goods would replace consumer goods, and, in even more cases, local products would replace imports.

In the short space of two years, American assistance has put the Republic of Viet-Nam on its feet: The rescue operation is over. United States aid and advice will continue to support the Vietnamese economy, but the need for this assistance will, from now on, tend to decrease, and the Vietnamese themselves will continue to take an increasing responsibility for their own recovery.

Outside of American aid, Viet-Nam has also received some assistance from the Colombo Plan, which it joined, along with Cambodia and Laos, in February, 1951. Not a great deal of aid flowed to Viet-Nam in the early days of the Colombo Plan, but since the real struggle of Free Viet-Nam began, more and more aid has been channeled there.

The total external aid from donor countries to all Colombo Plan countries of South and Southeast Asia since the beginning of the Plan in 1950 until mid-1957 has been about $3,500,000,000. Viet-Nam's share of this total has amounted to about $881,000,000. The vastly predominant position of the United States in the field of economic and technical assistance to Viet-Nam is reflected by the fact that, of this amount, nearly $880 million has been provided by the United States.

Colombo Plan aid by Australia has amounted to about $800,000. Of this amount, some $580,000 has been spent to provide heavy equipment for roads, refugee resettlement areas, irrigation, communications, and agriculture. The remainder has been spent on providing technical assistance—some fifty trainees, six experts, and a variety of technical equipment and livestock. Australia has sought to increase the number of Vietnamese students to its universities, but there has been a language difficulty, which it is presently trying to overcome by sending a number of Australian teachers of English to Saigon.

Assistance from other Colombo Plan donor countries include about $120,000 from Canada in the form of training facilities for over fifty

Vietnamese, about $140,000 from the United Kingdom for technical trainees, and about $25,000 from other countries.

From these figures, it is clear that the key role of external assistance from Colombo Plan countries is mainly the United States. President Diem recognized this fact during his opening speech at the ninth meeting of the Consultative Committee of the Colombo Plan in Saigon, when he said, "American aid, so generously given, will, we hope, continue to play its invaluable role." The annual report of this committee, produced by the Saigon conference, notes, "Viet-Nam has depended heavily on foreign aid in pursuance of the economic rehabilitation of the country."

Commentary: HOYT PRICE[167] *on* CASEY

IN ANY DISCUSSION of economic problems or conditions in Viet-Nam, one can easily find individuals who are extremely optimistic, as well as those who are extremely pessimistic. In fact, the same individual may show signs of both tendencies, depending upon whether he is looking backward or forward. Looking backward he may be optimistic; looking forward he may be inclined to be more pessimistic.

Looking backward there has been tremendous progress since 1954. When Diem returned to Viet-Nam in 1954 as Prime Minister, he had a paper stating that he had full authority in both military and civil matters. In reality, he had practically no powers. The military forces were controlled by a group unfriendly to him, and determined to replace him. The police power had been sold to a gang of ex-river pirates, whose other principal income at the time came from the operation of vice dens in and around Saigon and Cholon. Control of the countryside was in the hands of various semireligious sects and the Viet-Minh. The private sector of the Vietnamese economy was largely controlled by two groups of foreigners, whose support of any truly national Vietnamese government would be halfhearted, to say the least. An agency of a foreign government controlled the financial and economic policy of Viet-Nam through its control of Vietnamese foreign exchange. Control of half of the country was in the process of being turned over to the Viet-Minh regime.

How, then, could Diem's government be expected to endure as an effective government without control of the economic life of the country? As it turned out, Diem possessed only a determination to make a reality out of the cruel mockery of the paper nominally giving him full powers.

[167] United States Foreign Service Officer.

In the economic field, Diem had the assistance of a group of dedicated, hard-working, intelligent young men. These men were few in number—almost too few to meet the enormous problems they faced. Yet they faced the challenges, met the emergencies, and have helped carry Viet-Nam through its first few years of economic independence. After having waited so long to secure effective control and direction of their own economic affairs, they have seemed to want to prove that they are ready and able to exercise that control. An outside observer of this scene can only admire their courage and devotion.

Yet, even considering the progress made by Viet-Nam, one has an uneasy feeling of loss of momentum. Many times success leads to a slackening of efforts, not to a determination to press onward to greater achievements. One looks back and congratulates oneself at what has been done, and does not consider what has yet to be done. If one begins at five and proceeds to twenty-five, the progress seems to be enormous. Yet if the goal is one hundred, the amount remaining to be done is even greater. Lest there be some misunderstanding, the above is not a criticism of the Vietnamese alone, since many of them also feel that there has been some tendency among the Vietnamese and foreign friends to overestimate what has been done, and underestimate what remains to be done.

In the post-Geneva period, one often heard that the first task would be internal military security; the second, political consolidation; and the third, economic progress. It was envisaged that these would occur in 1955, 1956, and 1957, respectively. According to this schedule, 1957 was to mark the beginning of economic development in a broader sense, based on native resources and foreign aid. This economic growth was intended to start building an economic base capable of maintaining the living standards of the population without massive foreign aid. Measured by these standards, the economic record of 1957 has been disappointing.

As a matter of fact, various segments of the life of a nation cannot be bound up in separate compartments, with progress and activity in one and lack of progress and lack of activity in the others. Of necessity, economic problems had to be faced and solved. Of necessity, economic decisions had to be made. At the same time, there has been a reluctance, if not a failure, to face up to some of the necessary basic economic decisions, and minor remedial action has had no measurable effect. It is evident that lack of adequate progress in the economic field is having adverse effects on internal security and political life.

Economic development requires capital, and Viet-Nam is woefully short of capital. It is evident that there is much reconstruction, replacement, and expansion of the basic public works facilities that will have to be done, and that this is principally the function of both the Vietnamese government and foreign aid. Private enterprise, both domestic and foreign, should be looked to for the greater share of economic development, since the resources available from governmental sources will be limited. However, the amount of foreign private capital that will probably be available will be limited, even if the Vietnamese government implements its announced intention of making the country attractive to such investors. This leads to the conclusion that the main source of capital will be Vietnamese residents. The government must see that this source is tapped more effectively, and overcome the tradition of commercial use of idle funds, with high profit and fast turnover, which is one of the principal obstacles to investment in production enterprises. There is apt to be, by foreigners especially, an overly casual dismissal of private holdings of Vietnamese residents as a source of capital investment. While the number of people holding large cash accounts or who have a real savings income is probably a small percentage of the population, the total of such idle resources probably could contribute a sizeable investment sum.

Foreign aid represents approximately one half of total Vietnamese government expenditures. This is not a healthy situation, for either the donor or the recipient—although a lesser evil than the deterioration of the economic situation if the aid were suddenly ended. It would be disastrous if this crutch of foreign aid were pulled away too quickly. And it would be demoralizing if the crutch were depended on too long. Most studies of the Vietnamese economy underestimate the ability of the economy to adjust to changes in external aid—underestimate the resiliency of the Vietnamese economy. (Economics has been called the "dismal" science; it might also sometimes be called the "pessimistic" science.) Tax collections in Viet-Nam are now approximately eight percent of gross national product, whereas experience in many countries with the same degree of economic development indicates taxes should equal at least fifteen percent of gross national product.

The ability of Viet-Nam to achieve true economic independence will depend on the success of the Vietnamese in expanding economic activity and the supply of capital in their country, and in the recapture in taxes of some portion of the total national product. The manner in which Casey poses his questions, plus the actual questions posed, indicates an optimism for the future of Viet-Nam. I share that optimism. The Vietnamese people are hard-working, they have a great capacity to learn, and they seem eager to assume the new role that history is now offering them.

Commentary: WILLIAM HENDERSON[168] *on* CASEY

IN RETROSPECT, the survival of Ngo Dinh Diem's anti-Communist government and the effective consolidation of its power throughout most of Free Viet-Nam in the first two years following the Geneva Agreement constitute a political miracle of the first magnitude. After Geneva, Free Viet-Nam seemed close to chaos. For all practical purposes, Diem's authority was confined to Saigon and a few other urban centers. A "sect" of adventurers known as the Binh Xuyen, banded together for mutual profit and plunder, dominated the capital itself. Much of Cochinchina was in the hands of two other politico-religious sects, the Cao Dai and the Hoa Hao, while the Communists also controlled large stretches of the countryside.

Diem's elimination of the sects as separate centers of political and military power was, as Mr. Casey points out, a turning point in his tenacious struggle to extend his authority throughout the country. But even this would have been impossible without control over the national army, and the army remained a doubtful quantity until after the enforced withdrawal of General Nguyen Van Hinh in the fall of 1954. Only then could Diem move against the sects. His strategy was to divide them first and then destroy them piecemeal. By the summer of 1956 the military potential of the sects had been reduced to mere nuisance proportions. They still could and did cause trouble, especially when operating in league with the Communists, but they no longer constituted a serious threat to internal security.

The sects were not the only dissident force with which the Saigon government had to contend. Despite Geneva, the Viet-Minh left behind a powerful underground organization in Free Viet-Nam. Even after their ostensible withdrawal, Communist cadres continued to dominate many rural districts. The Communists had also extensively infiltrated the army, police, and civil administration. As rapidly as circumstances permitted, Diem set about the difficult task of uprooting and destroying them. An impressive array of political and psychological warfare techniques was employed in this effort, as well as all-out "pacification" campaigns against the main pockets of Communist strength. It was difficult to give an accurate assessment of the results, since the Communists in Free Viet-Nam—apparently in keeping with world-wide shifts in revolutionary strategy—remained comparatively inactive since

[168] Assistant Executive Director of the Council on Foreign Relations, Inc., New York, and Far Eastern Specialist on the Council's permanent staff.

Geneva. But by mid-1956 most observers had concluded that the Communists, whatever their original potential, could no longer endanger the Diem regime without outside support. This was all the more true since Diem had systematically reorganized and greatly strengthened the army and police services. While still not strong enough to hold out indefinitely against an attack from the Communist north, the forces at Diem's disposal seemed adequate for the maintenance of domestic security.

In spite of the many other significant milestones in the two years following Geneva—such as withdrawal of the French army, dissolution of the Associated States, inauguration of independent relations with the outside world, creation of national financial institutions— there was a dark side to the picture. From the beginning Diem ran his government along the lines of a police state. Most manifestations of political opposition, whether Communist or otherwise, were vigorously suppressed. Civil liberties remained an unfulfilled ideal. Elections were far from free, and many of the devices used to stimulate popular support for the regime bore the familiar stamp of modern totalitarian practice. No doubt these moves could be justified, at least to some extent, in terms of the overwhelming problems confronting Diem during his first two years in office, and also the inexperience of Free Viet-Nam's people with the forms and substance of democracy. But, by the middle of 1956, after two years of power, Diem had still to prove that his professed devotion to the democratic cause represented anything more than a façade to disguise the increasingly plain reality of stern dictatorship.

Commentary: CASEY on HENDERSON

PROBABLY NO ONE—not even President Ngo Dinh Diem himself— would deny that the organization of Viet-Nam as a state and its administration still fall short of the democratic ideal in some respects. The fact that Diem in his public and private statements of his philosophy gives a primary place to the role of the individual is important. It should be recognized that no one can quickly achieve everything that he would like. The question to ask is: what are the standards that Viet-Nam itself is setting for its goal? Here may be found some reassurance. Democratic observers in Viet-Nam judge the country's performance by the same standards and goals as they would judge the United States, Australia, or Western European countries. These are the standards Viet-Nam itself professes to aim at. What a difference this is from

Communist countries, which not merely do not accord with democratic standards but do not even recognize that those standards exist!

The situation in Viet-Nam, as seen by its government, is one which need not be perpetuated, but which should rather serve as a stepping-stone to something better. Some sacrifices of individual liberty are at times necessary in order that a community, as a whole, may eventually enjoy liberty in the true sense. This has been demonstrated in other countries—including Australia—during periods of great national stress when individual interests, doubts, or desires have had to be abandoned for a time in the interest of defeating an enemy.

Two facts should be remembered in any criticism of Viet-Nam's administration. First, Viet-Nam is in the front line of the cold war—and only lately out of actual armed conflict. Its government cannot afford to leave openings which its opponents could exploit. This would be fatal not only to Viet-Nam, but most detrimental to the interests of freedom in Southeast Asia. Second, the exercise of democracy on a national scale is a totally new concept in Viet-Nam and, it will take time for institutions, traditions, and habits to be developed which will enable democratic rights to be exercised in a constructive and responsible way. Political consciousness in a people is not necessarily a slow growth, but it has to grow deep as well as wide if it is to be sound. Even the concept of loyalty to the state and to their government is a novel one to the Vietnamese.

Those who accept loyalties to their country and government without question might do well to reflect on earlier periods in their history before the concept of nationhood was firmly fixed, or when the relationship between the people and the government or the state may have been somewhat different from what it now is. Taking into account the state of Vietnamese society and the particular phase of development through which Viet-Nam is passing, most observers can help by discussing the problems and making suggestions, but refraining from hasty judgment.

True, it is important for the government of Viet-Nam to make the right choice among the many political pressures now exerting themselves in that country. However, the means of accomplishing this task must be found by the Vietnamese and the Vietnamese alone.

Commentary: HENDERSON on CASEY

THERE ARE persuasive reasons why strict adherence to democratic principles in the processes of Vietnamese government, and in the normal political life of the country, must be held in abeyance for the indefinite future.

However, four years have passed since President Diem first assumed power in Free Viet-Nam. Surely, during this period there might have been greater experimentation with democracy than has in fact been attempted, some toleration of a non-Communist political opposition, some relaxation of controls on press criticism. Unhappily, the lid is still clamped on tightly. After four years there has been little moderation of the grim dictatorship which Diem has exerted from the beginning.

One result has been the growing alienation of the intelligentsia, never enthusiastically pro-Diem but nonetheless the country's only reservoir of trained man power. Another has been the renewal of armed dissidence in the south. Security has noticeably deteriorated in the last two years. There is a growing separation between Diem and the sorely tried Vietnamese people. So far these developments do not constitute a serious threat to Diem's rule, but they are an ominous sign. Has the time not come to set in motion a progressive liberalization of government and politics, however cautiously the necessary steps may be taken? In the absence of such progress, one can only look to a steady worsening of the political climate in Free Viet-Nam, culminating in unforeseen disasters.

XXV. General Consideration of American Programs

DAVID HOTHAM

IT IS WORTH putting Free Viet-Nam under a microscope, not only to examine the chances of winning the battle against communism in this part of Southeast Asia, but also to try to deduce something useful about Western aid to so-called "underdeveloped" countries. An average of two hundred and fifty million dollars a year of American aid alone flows into Free Viet-Nam, a nation about the same size as the state of Washington, and which has a population of twelve million. It is interesting to observe, from a purely scientific point of view, the impact of so vast an influx of money on this country which only recently ceased to be a colony of France.

The picture that has gone out almost unchallenged to the world is that Free Viet-Nam is the sure and solid point among the shifting sands of communism and neutralism in Southeast Asia. The phrase constantly repeated by those whose business it is to purvey this story is that Viet-Nam is "the bastion of the Free World against communism in Southeast Asia." In so far as this description causes uninformed people to believe that Viet-Nam is the one point in Asia that they need NOT worry about, the "bastion" concept is completely false.

When the Viet-Minh defeated the French army at Dien Bien Phu in May, 1954, the West made the best of a bad situation, by partitioning Viet-Nam and keeping the southern half of the country out of Communist clutches. At that time most people in Saigon and elsewhere pessimistically felt that it was only a matter of months, or even weeks, before Free Viet-Nam would fall to communism.

But it did not; and it still has not today. Hence, the idea of the "bastion" has held. A reasonable concept, one might say. So why worry?

The mere fact that a bastion exists, of course, is not sufficient in itself. There is no way of telling whether it will continue to hold except by examining the situation inside the bastion and weighing its chances. It is always rash to prognosticate political events, especially in Asia, but one must be realistic. In trying to be so, one should scrutinize the facts in Free Viet-Nam to see whether they fully accord with the complacent assumption that the bastion is solid and will continue to remain so indefinitely.

The history of the last three years in this country has been, broadly speaking, the consolidation of Ngo Dinh Diem's power. In 1955 Diem challenged and defeated the "sects" and then proceeded to eliminate his other enemies from the political scene. In 1955 Saigon was the scene of chaos and bloodshed, but for the next three years it was as calm and orderly as any city of the Western world.

346

It was the popular referendum in which Diem was elected first President of the Republic of Viet-Nam that misled the world in believing in the "bastion" concept, by giving the mistaken impression that the regime was a popular and democratic one. The outside world was misled because it made the mistake of assuming that a referendum in an Asian country, or at least in this particular Asian country, resembled a similar event in the United States or Western Europe. Anyone who was there knows full well that the methods used in this referendum had nothing whatever to do with Western democracy. An intense and completely one-sided press campaign has its effect on a largely illiterate people inured to centuries of autocracy. Backed by a large and efficient police force, it is even more effective. These methods are not by any means exceptional for Asia, and a moral condemnation should not be implied. However, it would be well to destroy the myth that Diem's regime was ever a popular one. No one who was in Saigon in October, 1955, unless blind to realities, would dispute this.

Several things follow from this fact. First, the idea that the "bastion" is secure because its government has the massive support of the population is simply not true. Second, the West is backing, with its eyes open, not a democratic regime on a Western model, but a reactionary police state. This is not to say that such a regime, as a regime, may not be the best defense against communism: The West is maintaining a considerable number of reactionary police states all over the "free world." What needs emphasis is that the Asians are intelligent people, and well able to contrast the declarations of principles of the Western powers, especially the United States, with the facts of the regime under which they live. No intelligent Vietnamese can fail to be cynical when he hears American professors lecturing on political freedom in one province, while Diem's army and police are imprisoning thousands of suspected Communists without trial in another.

Here someone might interject, and reasonably, "Diem's regime may be repressive, but it is far better than Russian or Chinese communism." He will be right. That, after all, is the justification of Western aid to rulers such as Franco and even Tito. One is caught in a perfectly comprehensible dilemma here. In the interests of freedom generally, up to what point can one support a dictatorial regime against one's own declared principles? If the answer to this conundrum is based on power politics, and not on principles, one might say that it is worth while backing a strong dictatorial regime, but not worth backing a weak one. It is hardly untrue to say that some dictatorships are representative of their peoples. What is never worth doing is to prop up a weak and unpopular regime. In doing so, one has the worst of both worlds—both the world of power and the world of principle. But this is exactly what the West is doing in Free Viet-Nam.

The chief hope of defending the south from the communism which threatened it at the time of Dien Bien Phu, and which still threatens it today (for the battle is, not won, but hardly begun), was that somebody should succeed in uniting all the genuinely anti-Communist nationalist elements into a regime which would have the confidence of the southern people. Had that been done, the bastion would indeed have been strong. But this is precisely what has not been done. Instead of uniting it, Diem has divided the south. Instead of merely crushing his legitimate enemies, the Communists, he has crushed all opposition of every kind, however anti-Communist it might be. In so doing, he has destroyed the very basis on which his regime should be founded. He has been able to do this, simply and solely because of the massive dollar aid he has had from across the Pacific, which kept in power a man who, by all the laws of human and political affairs, would long ago have fallen. Diem's main supporters are to be found in North America, not in Free Viet-Nam. This is an unnatural situation, and unnatural situations do not last long.

Diem's first and most acclaimed victory was over the sects. At first, the defeat of the sects seemed both inevitable and salutary, but further study of the situation has led to questioning, if not to altering, that judgment. The argument that Diem was justified in fighting the sects is based on the assumption that no negotiated agreement could be arrived at with them. During the Indochina war, the sects were the most ferocious enemies of the Viet-Minh, and it may be conceded that it would have been better, if humanly possible, for Diem to have had them on his side in the struggle against communism.

This question is a complex one, since it is difficult to know the precise details of the attempts at negotiation between Diem and the sects in the crucial spring of 1955. All sources of information tend to be suspect. However, on the basis of the known facts, it can be concluded that, far from being the triumph it was acclaimed, the breakdown of negotiations and degeneration of the situation into open war was, at best, a failure of leadership.

Some light is thrown on the subject by subsequent events. There is evidence to show, from his authoritarian manner in later actions, that Diem's tendency is to crush rather than to lead, to challenge rather than to negotiate. He has been enabled to do this successfully because of his disproportionate resources of financial and diplomatic support. It may one day be judged, when the history of Viet-Nam is written, that Diem's regime was ruined by too much money and enthusiasm from people who were too little informed about the realities of the situation in this complicated country. One remark made, not by one of Diem's enemies, but by one of his closest friends and collaborators, is significant in this context, "It is American aid which is killing Viet-Nam".

It is a fact that in early 1955 some Western representatives in Saigon had strong reservations about the wisdom of a military defeat of the sects. But these representatives were removed from Viet-Nam because the Western powers decided to stand behind Diem in whatever action he undertook. This may prove to have been a major error. It is certainly astonishing that the sect leaders could not have been won over rather than overwhelmed. They must have known that, if it came to war, the balance of forces was completely against them. It may be that French policy at this stage, by not making it clear that the French would not support the sects in a war against Diem, was to blame. But, however the matter may be regarded, to antagonize permanently such natural and proved enemies of the Viet-Minh, and good fighters to boot, as the sects were, could only make the real situation worse, not better. The sects might be defeated, but their leaders are still there, in hiding or in exile. They may not love Ho Chi Minh, but it is certain that they hate Ngo Dinh Diem. The wave of provincial outrages in the south in 1957 could have been at their instigation, possibly on orders from Hanoi.

The whole of this question of the sects is closely bound up with the meaning of leadership. If Diem, by his own powers and the approval of his own people, destroyed the sects who were the oppressors of the people, it is legitimate to regard him as the leader that the south needed to oppose the name of Ho Chi Minh. But if Diem is merely an honest, not exceptionally able or magnetic, Vietnamese politician kept in place by Western money, he cannot be regarded as such a leader. When one looks squarely at the facts, the second picture is the truer. Diem's problem is that he is not a leader who has been merely *helped* by the West; he has been *created* by the West. The Emperor, Bao Dai, appointed him, but that was only a formal act. It was Bidault and Dulles who chose him and put him in his position. The objectionable word "puppet," so often used by both sides in the propaganda war, is in his case literally true; since it was the Western powers who put him in Saigon's Palace of Independence. The fact that he has acted against Western advice on several occasions does not contradict this.

The question of the wisdom of Diem's action against the sects is at best an open one. The desirability of his policy of eliminating the anti-Communist nationalists in the south from all participation in the country's affairs is not open; it is obviously nonsense. Diem squashed the revolutionary committees, drove the old nationalist parties underground, broke the intellectual opposition, and reserved the conduct of affairs to himself, his family, and a few political yes-men in the national assembly and administration. It is fair to assume that his reason for doing so was the impossibility to know, in Viet-Nam, where politics are so tortuous, who are Communists and who are not. Diem had reason to be suspicious of many, but not all. For if all those who claim to be nationalists in the south are Communists in disguise, whence will come the salvation of the country? This is a counsel of despair, and if it were true the West might as well withdraw its aid and pack up.

An act of a different kind, but also based on the principle of asserting the whip hand, was Diem's "nationalization" of the Chinese minority. Diem decreed that all Chinese born in Free Viet-Nam, who numbered several hundred thousand, must take Vietnamese nationality. (This is roughly equivalent to Guatemala forcing all Americans who happen to be born in that country to be Guatemalans.) It is well known that this step was taken against American advice. It is perfectly understandable that any Southeast Asian country with a large Chinese minority should try to ensure that the minority is loyal to the land it lives in. One would hardly suppose that the best way of ensuring that loyalty was to humiliate the members of a race who have always considered themselves superior to the Vietnamese, and who furthermore hold in their acquisitive hands most of the vital commerce of the country. The economic consequences of this act are already extremely serious, and even the vast American aid program may not suffice to correct them.

The political consequences are even more dangerous. The Chinese in Free Viet-Nam, though not naturally Communists, are already disenchanted with Formosa, which has signally failed to protect their interests in this matter. It is making it easy for them to turn toward Peking. Whatever happens, they are henceforth anything but Diem's loyal subjects; they are rather his certain enemies. Such a political action is explicable only on the grounds of insensate nationalism. This was even admitted by one of the topmost members of the Vietnamese government, who said, "We are determined to go through with this Chinese policy, even if it ruins the economy of the country." This is what it may well do.

Pessimism aside, facts must be reported and realities faced. The first fact is that the United States is making a great effort to support an unpopular and repressive regime in Viet-Nam, and, what is worse, a regime which does not exist by any natural strength of its own. The second fact is what this small nation is doing with the enormous amount of American aid. Is the 250 million or more dollars a year that Viet-Nam is receiving being spent in the best way?

Most of the United States aid administrators are able technicians, doing their best to help Viet-Nam. Therefore, no criticism is aimed at them, but rather with the policy they must administer. There are many positive sides to this policy. The magnificent resettlement of the refugees from the Communist north was one of the best-planned and executed operations of its kind anywhere in the world. On the economic side, one of the great successes of the aid program has been the prevention of inflation. So many regimes have slid to ruin down that slippery road. Apart from this, there are innumerable activities, both on the material and spiritual plane, which are valuable to any country—the spreading of American ideas, the building of roads, the struggle against disease, anthropological and ethnological research, welfare of all kinds. It is not these excellent activities, but the main lines of the aid program, which seem mistaken.

During the years since the establishment of Free Viet-Nam, two thirds of all the aid given to the country has been military—the direct use of the counterpart fund to pay the salaries of the army. In so far as this form of aid replaces economic aid, it can be questioned. Undeniably, there is a need for an army in a place so threatened as Free Viet-Nam, but must it be maintained at the present strength of 150,000 men? Such an army is not strong enough to resist the Communists, if the latter really decided to launch an attack, but it is too large by far for the resources of the country, if the country is to make economic progress. One does not make countries richer by giving them armies; one makes them poorer.

What are the military justifications for so large an army? The Viet-Minh army, north of the 17th parallel, is presumably much larger than that of Free Viet-Nam. Actually, the figures are doubtful, but even so, that is not the point: For, even if Ho Chi Minh's forces were small, there is the Chinese army behind him, and the threat is constant. But is it necessary, in every part of the world to match army with army? Do NATO's armies in Europe match, man for man, the one hundred and seventy Russian divisions reported to be stationed in the West? If they did, Europe would be bankrupt. In Viet-Nam's case, there is another point. What is the real deterrent to Communist aggression across the 17th parallel? Is it really the south Vietnamese army, a most uncertain weapon, for who knows how many of its men would fight again in civil war against their northern compatriots? Is not the real deterrent the power of the West, particularly the United States, as expressed in the SEATO treaty? Is it not the memory in Communist minds of what happened in Korea?

If American aid to Free Viet-Nam could be raised to so vast a figure that it could both finance an army at the present level, and at the same time develop the country's economy in the way it needs, such a policy would be rational. But such aid is quite unthinkable. It would mean increasing the assistance from 250 million to about 600 million dollars a year. If the aid figure is diminished, and military support is maintained at its present level, the southern regime will become economically even more static than it is at present.

Perhaps the most damaging critique that can be made of the American aid program is its failure to introduce industry. For some incomprehensible reason the Americans have set their face against it. (Meanwhile, the Communist north is industrializing rapidly—perhaps too rapidly.) This, when the battle for this part of Southeast Asia is at its height, seems a capital error. If there is one thing that is absolutely certain in this modern world, it is that all newly independent countries have a passion for industries. No arguments by economists, however sane they may be, can dissuade them. And why? The reason is clear. Industrialization gives two important things—material wealth and economic independence. Both are justifiable goals.

True, there are difficulties in bringing new industries to Free Viet-Nam. There is the problem that the existing industry, what there is of it, is in French hands. There is the problem that the necessary capital is not forthcoming. There is the problem of free enterprise versus state control. And there are a thousand other problems. One of the worst is the lack of capital. There is not much Vietnamese capital forthcoming, and foreign investment does not flow freely into such places as Free Viet-Nam. This is only natural. What Western capitalist, looking around for somewhere to invest his money, would choose a part of the world of which the only thing he knows is that it is constantly threatened by communism, and has for fifteen or more years been the scene of war and confusion? It is hardly a business proposition.

But why, one may enquire, are industries necessary in such a place? Why should one of the great rice-growing nations of the world not remain true to its agricultural vocation? Many economists argue in this fashion, asserting that the revival of the rice exports of Cochinchina to their level of before the Indochina war would be the most profitable form of capital investment for Viet-Nam. However, they forget that this is a purely economic argument, and, unless they are Marxists, they should know that economic arguments do not run the world. What they forget in their reasoning is the force of modern nationalism. They naturally dislike nationalism, because it so often goes against economic good sense. But, however sensible their arguments may be, it is simply useless to talk to Asian nationalists in this way. Viet-Nam is not simply a piece of territory for which one can prescribe rational economic policies from Washington. It is the country of a people who have fought for many years for their political independence, thought they had won it, and then woke up to find that they still had no *real* independence.

The substance of real independence is economic independence, as anybody struggling to earn his living knows well. Three fourths of Free Viet-Nam's imports are at present paid for, not by its own exports, but directly out of the treasury in Washington. This is an undignified situation for even the most torpid and backward colonial people. It is insufferable for the highly sensitive and independence-conscious Vietnamese. With most of its trade and the whole of its army paid for by a foreign power, Free Viet-Nam can hardly be called an independent country. In fact, it is one of the most dependent countries to be found anywhere in the world.

Taking the whole argument into the realm of politics, it is pertinent to ask: what are the ingredients of real independence for Viet-Nam? Most Vietnamese would agree that there are two—the unification of their country and its economic independence. These two things hang together; for Viet-Nam is one of those states which divided is not viable, but which united makes an economic whole. Its industries are in the north, its agriculture in the south. And apart from the economic desirability of unity, it is something which the people deeply want.

Yet there is no policy in the West for unifying Viet-Nam, and the present state of the world makes it difficult. The "free elections" prescribed by the Geneva Agreement are universally considered impossible of execution; not for the oversimple reason that "there is no freedom in the Communist north," but because elections almost anywhere in Asia are usually run on behalf of the government in office. One should not allow oneself to be too much tied to the political clauses of Geneva, perhaps, but a Western policy which makes no provision whatever for the unification of Viet-Nam is in for trouble. It is giving away a trump card to the Vietnamese Communists, who have always been adroit enough to stand for the unification of their country.

To sum up then, the criticism of Western—that is mainly American—policy in Viet-Nam, is threefold. *First,* the United States is putting a vast amount of money behind an incompetent, repressive, and unpopular regime. *Second,* this huge financial assistance is adding nothing appreciable to the capital equipment of Free Viet-Nam, whereby alone the standard of living of such a country can ever be perceptibly uplifted, and whereby alone economic independence from the United States can ever be achieved. Does Washington expect to subsidize these distant countries for ever and ever? Even if the White House does, it is doubtful whether Congress would agree! *Third,* neither Diem, nor his American supporters, seem to have any policy whatever for unifying the country, by elections or by any other means. Certainly, this state of affairs will not be tolerated for long by a nation which has sacrificed so much for its independence through so many bloody years.

The bomb outrages against Americans in Saigon were almost certainly a symptom of deep discontent with these policies. In addition to this, there have been, according to reports made by the Free Viet-Nam government itself, several hundred assassinations, or attempts at assassination, against government officials in the south during the last few months. Whatever this may mean, it cannot be a sign that all is well. Whether or not it is the Communists who are doing it, it is serious.

The Americans should not make the mistake which the colonial nations made in their time—the mistake of growing out of touch with the people who inhabit the dependent territories. It is fatally easy to do this. As long as Free Viet-Nam is simply considered as a bastion, a purely strategic piece of territory, a mere salient in the cold war, this mistake is being made. One simple fact should not be overlooked. Twelve million people live in this particular "bastion of Southeast Asia." They are not Americans, and may have ideas of their own. In fact, they do have ideas of their own. It might be worth while for Washington to find out what those ideas are. If it does not, sooner or later it is in for trouble. What is more, such a policy is most undemocratic.

Commentary: PEGGY DURDIN[169] *on* HOTHAM

HOTHAM does not fully understand the character of the sects, their role in political life, and their relationships with the French. One cannot lump the sects: They had differing characters, aims, as well as ties to the French. For example, some sect leaders could not have been "won over" as long as they had active French support.

Additionally, Hotham's criticisms of the present situation are, in a sense, made in a vacuum. Agreed that Diem's government is repressive and inefficient and that American aid money is largely ill-directed, these criticisms would have been more valid if made within the framework of what the author thinks is possible. At the time Diem came to office, there seemed to be no better possible alternatives to the steps he took; nor did there seem to be any alternative to American support of him.

In the light of present facts in Free Viet-Nam, what can Washington do politically and economically? Simple, negative criticism is too easy. Assuredly, new practical policy lines could be adopted by Americans, but the difficult question is what are they.

Commentary: JOHN M. MECKLIN[170] *on* HOTHAM

DIEM, of course, is repressive and, what is worse, almost totally impervious to advice; and this, in turn, makes it difficult, if not impossible, for other leaders to emerge. But if Diem will not change—and a good

[169] *New York Times* correspondent.
[170] *Time-Life* correspondent.

many dedicated Americans have tried to make him change—should the United States simply withdraw its support and accept chaos? It is not good enough in this unhappy day and age simply to dismiss a man such as Diem as an imperfect leader unless somebody better can be found.

Hotham credits the United States and France for Diem's "creation," and it is true that the French and Americans did collaborate in his choice after Dien Bien Phu. However, within a matter of months the French withdrew their support and persuaded the United States ambassador to do likewise. During the Binh Xuyen rebellion in the spring of 1955 the French were actively plotting on the side of the Binh Xuyen. It is to the credit of the United States that it stood by Diem at this time—when the Vietnamese army decisively defeated the rebels at the very moment that French officials were saying Diem was lost.

Subsequently, after a great deal of soul searching, the United States also overruled the French in their support of Bao Dai. Perhaps it should also be noted that, thanks largely to Malcolm MacDonald, the British tended to favor Bao Dai. If the United States is now supporting an unpopular Diem, let it be noted that it was American initiative that led to the dumping of this vastly more unpopular, and unbelievably corrupt, puppet of French imperialism. Anyone who was in Indochina after Dien Bien Phu will agree that this was one of the brightest moments of postwar American foreign policy.

Viewed in the light of the utter despair that prevailed everywhere during the months after Dien Bien Phu, the simple fact that Diem is still in business today is a miracle. Hotham notes this, but his discussion skips over much of what has been accomplished, as to be in balance unfair and distorted. The United States, however ineptly and inexpertly, *did* something about Free Viet-Nam, while the rest of the Free World did little.

Hotham suggests that Diem somehow should have retained the support and friendship of the sects—a worthy thought, but again quite impossible. In the case of the Binh Xuyen, they mortared the presidential palace, making it difficult to negotiate. All the sects at one time or another had betrayed the French or the Viet-Minh. Confronted with Diem's determination to put his country in order, they refused to give up an iota of the absolute, feudalistic control they had exercised over a large part of Viet-Nam for years. Diem had no choice but to destroy them or to give up all hope of creating a modern state.

In his discussion of the Vietnamese army, Hotham overlooks the root problem of communism in Southeast Asia, and especially in Indochina. The army is too large (one reason is the flat rejection by Diem of American advice that it be reduced), but its mission, at least as of 1955, was not primarily to oppose a massive Viet-Minh assault across the 17th parallel. Under exceptionally imaginative American guidance, the army was being trained not only to fight guèrrillas but also to work among the people to discourage Viet-Minh infiltration. In one particularly dramatic example of this, the army sent teams through one area of the country to rebuild schools and bridges, repair highways, lecture to the villagers on the army's role as their friend. It was trying to use the same principle exploited so successfully by the Communists in both China and Indochina: That "the people is the water and the army is the fish."

If the Communists resort to military action in Viet-Nam again, it is a certainty, short of World War III, that they will not attempt a frontal attack. They learned the futility of this in Korea, where they exposed themselves to the West's greatest strength: a war of machines backed up by Western industrial power, on a defined front where massive man power superiority becomes almost useless. The future war technique will be guerrillas, just as it was before. One of the paramount principles of guerilla fighting, as noted repeatedly in Mao Tse-tung's writing, is the requirement of support from a large segment of the people. By working among the people, the Vietnamese army has tried to deny this to the Communists. One cannot testify as to its success, but it is certainly significant that the Viet-Minh so far has not felt strong enough to kick off another civil war.

In fact, the bombings that Hotham deplores may possibly reflect the Viet-Minh's failure to win enough popular support for a new rebellion. The terror bomb, planted secretly, is often a trademark of revolutionary futility when it is not accomplished by a general uprising. A handful of plotters can set off bombs, embarrassing the government, with no need for any popular support. In any event, investigation of the bombings, I understand, indicated that they were done by remnants of the sects to embarrass the Diem government during the Colombo Conference.

The record also suggests doubt of Hotham's remark that the Vietnamese army might not fight against a Communist army of other Vietnamese. It fought well against the sects. In scattered, but highly impressive, cases, it also fought well against the Viet-Minh under the French. If fault must be found with the army, a great deal more attention could be paid to the state of its training, its mission, and its relationship to the people.

In regard to American failure to encourage industrial development, I believe that United States aid programs are, by law, limited to capital investment only in the public sector, e.g., dams, irrigation projects, highways. There have also been some highly exceptional economic problems in Viet-Nam, for example, the need to generate piasters through high imports to maintain such hangovers of French rule as the very high pay of the Vietnamese army. Also, Diem's stubborn refusal to heed advice may be a factor in the shortcomings of the American aid program. A significant body of Western expert opinion holds, in any case, that industrialization should be undertaken very slowly. Like political progress, industrialization requires a degree of intellectual development. In the case of an assembly plant for Italian motor scooters established after the French withdrawal, workmanship has been so consistently poor that the Vietnamese prefer imported scooters.

Finally, Hotham recommends that the United States should see about unifying Viet-Nam "by elections or by any other means," and suggests that Americans check into the "ideas" of the Vietnamese people.

About 90 percent of the Vietnamese are illiterate. And illiteracy means much more than inability to read and write; it also means a mind that functions at close to the five-year-old level, an utter absence of comprehension of even the most primitive political concepts, almost no capacity for logic. Whatever "ideas" the Asian peasant may have are imposed upon him by propaganda, usually backed up by force, as in the case of the Chinese under Mao. In 1955 I accompanied a Vietnamese army patrol occupying a village deep in the southern wilderness of Viet-Nam, which for more than a decade had been a Viet-Minh headquarters. It was reasonable to expect that the villagers —forty miles by boat and then five miles on foot from the nearest road or airstrip—would be thoroughly indoctrinated in communism. I spent two days in the hut of the village headman. He was sixty-six years old and had never traveled more than ten kilometers from his village. He had never heard of France, China, Russia, or the United States. He knew about Ho Chi Minh as a good man. He hated "the men of the noisy birds," i.e., the French fliers who had bombed the village repeatedly, but he did not know them as French, nor even as foreigners. Everyone who lived more than ten kilometers from the village was a foreigner. The concept of a nation was beyond him. Yet this was a respected village elder after a decade of Communist rule!

The aspirations of educated Asian nationalists are real enough, and not to be ignored, but they are an infinitesimally small minority. The problem of winning the masses pinpoints to such things as bringing a well or a batch of penicillin to the village. To express it cynically, it is also the problem of keeping out the Communist lie: that you can have more wells and more penicillin simply by supporting communism. The will of the people of Asia is an imposed thing. However, illiberal it may sound, the cruel fact is that the villagers I visited are incapable of judging what is going on in Saigon.

Democracy is an utter impossibility, a contradiction in terms, in a country that is 90 percent, or even 50 percent, illiterate. It is, of course, the long-term ideal, but it cannot work until the people can think. One of the most cynical, vicious evils of communism is its appeal to the illiterate peasant, laboring like an animal simply to stay alive and completely incapable of useful political opinion, in terms of "self-government." This fraud, unfortunately, has an attraction even today, when the reality of Communist tyranny stands exposed as a thing of horror unparalleled in human history, to fuzzy-minded liberals the world over who hope so pathetically that somehow there may be an easy solution, that the Communists really do stand for the principles of enlightenment that they mouth so flowingly. There can be no solution, other than disaster, in Viet-Nam or at any other focus point of freedom's deadlock with communism except in strength. Diem has created strength miraculously, in a vacuum of despair. That he has done so through excessive repression is regrettable, but relatively irrelevant.

The Geneva Agreement provided for free elections to unify Viet-Nam. Diem flatly, and rather unimaginatively, refused even to negotiate such a thing, on the grounds an election in an area under Communist control can never be free. A good many people thought that he would have been smarter to announce that he was in favor of an election and then insist on such intimate supervision by outsiders that the Communists would never agree. But again he would not listen. As Hotham points out, this gave the Communists a propaganda advantage by default. However, anyone who has read the newspapers during the last few years must certainly appreciate that the Communists are not being honest when they talk about unification. On any political issue, this is their typical line, and it is recklessly naive to suggest that Viet-Nam can ever be unified by any force other than the sword. Diem could certainly make useful propaganda by talking more about unification, but he does not do so because he believes it is dishonest—which indeed it is.

Hotham's article suffers from failing to balance the shortcomings of Diem and the United States against the harsh realities of a typical deadlock with a Communist foe, and in failing to give proper emphasis to the far worse situation that might have been.

Commentary: HOTHAM *on* MECKLIN

MECKLIN seems to belong to that school of *realpolitik,* becoming more and more fashionable among Americans, which goes to all lengths to avoid falling into the naivete of Graham Greene's *Quiet American,* and for whom the word "liberal" seems equivalent to an insult. "Being stuck with a dictator" is a phenomenon which demands deeper discussion than Mecklin has considered necessary to attribute to it, if only because the discrepancy between what the West preaches and what it practices in countries such as Viet-Nam is getting Westerners—and particularly Americans—hated the world over. Nor does Mecklin's remark that "Democracy is a contradiction in terms" in countries such as Free Viet-Nam make a good slogan for the Free World.

I did not suggest changing Diem, but merely changing his policy. By the same token, I hold no brief whatever for French policy after Dien Bien Phu, or for Bao Dai. In fact, I am much more concerned with the present and the future, than with the past. The only point connected with the past I should like to return to is that of Diem's war with the sects. Mecklin dismisses the idea that there could have been negotiation as "a worthy thought, but again quite impossible," because the Binh Xuyen sect mortared the presidential palace. Since they mortared the palace *after* negotiations had broken down, the point is quite irrelevant to the question of *why* the negotiations broke down.

As for the efforts of the Vietnamese army to root out the Viet-Minh, there is no evidence whatever that it has been successful. The opposite is far more probable, to judge from the wave of assassinations of provincial officials in the south in the winter of 1957 and spring of 1958. This is something quite different to sporadic bombs in Saigon. The activities of the army are, moreover, notorious, and if their "pacification" methods are similar to those used by the French in Algeria (where the same word "pacification" is used), they are undesirable even by the depreciated standards of the Free World. Furthermore, they are useless. They consist of killing, or arresting without either evidence or trial, large numbers of persons suspected of being Viet-Minh or "rebels." To condemn this sort of activity does not make one either a fuzzy-headed liberal or a Communist.

Things would be much better if Diem were strong in his own right. He is not. His repressiveness would be more acceptable if it came from strength, but it comes patently from weakness. The difference between Franco, Adenauer, Tito, Syngman Rhee, and Diem is that whereas the first four men were the product of *some* kind of internal process in their respective countries, Diem was simply pulled out of a hat by Dulles and Bidault in a crisis. He has no natural roots in the south. While Ho Chi Minh was fighting the French, Diem was living piously in a seminary in New Jersey. Mecklin does not challenge my point that the October, 1955, referendum, which ostensibly gave Diem a democratic basis in the south, was a trumped-up afterthought done to make things look right.

To be realistic about the miracle of Diem's being still in power, the Vietnamese army had five times as many troops as all the sects put together (and they were never united), as well as 250 million dollars a year where its opponents had no regular source of income. Similarly with the Viet-Minh. The reason why the Communists have not attacked the south is the SEATO Treaty behind Diem, the Communist experience in Korea—in a word the deadlock of the cold war. But it is no miracle; it is the natural function of the deterrent. Those are the facts and they are presented without derogation to Diem, who is a courageous and able man.

As for the people in the south, Mecklin's estimate of the illiterate peasant's mentality is not to the point. Admittedly, solutions are imposed on the illiterate masses, but unless one makes some sort of attempt to capture the imagination of these same masses, one loses out to the Communists, who are particularly adept, as Mecklin stresses, at doing just that. What has been done in the south to capture the imagination of the masses there? Almost nothing! Four years after Dien Bien Phu, three years after Diem's rout of the sects, and with 250 million dollars a year pouring into the country, scarcely a single house has been built, land reform has hung fire, not a new industry has been created to speak of. The most imaginative operation was the resettlement of the refugees from the north—especially at Cai San in west Cochinchina. But this operation, though most efficiently and sympathetically carried out, has not tended to endear Americans or Diem to the people of the south.

The economic question is one of the most important. If American law somehow prevents Americans from doing what is needed in Free Viet-Nam, a most sensitive and vital area, then the law should be changed. In Free Viet-Nam the West is competing daily with the Communists in the north, where, on the grim pattern of China, the Russians are creating new industries fast. The battle for Indochina, still undecided, let it not be forgotten, will be won by whichever zone develops its economy most quickly.

American economic aid experts have argued against using American aid to introduce industry to Free Viet-Nam: "No importer will order capital goods because there is no popular demand for them." Of course there isn't! And no underdeveloped country can really be industrialized in this way. The Americans are hamstrung by their own ideology of private enterprise, which worked very well on their own continent, where there was almost unlimited private capital; but this ideology could never work in Viet-Nam, where private capital in any quantity is simply not forthcoming. The obvious solution, taking a leaf from the Communist book, is to give economic aid to the south in the form of whole factories, to be set up by American technicians. The process must be started off by state-owned industries, not merely left to the hazards of supply and demand. This method was used in Turkey, and what country today could be more in ideological agreement with the West than Turkey?

If the need for industry and economic development generally is questioned, the answer is this. In every newly independent country the urge toward economic independence is a function of nationalism. The Vietnamese educated classes—restless, neurotic, oversensitive—are, above all things, unsatisfied nationalists. The story of Viet-Nam for thirty years has been its national struggle for independence from France, which started long before the cold war was dreamt of. The Indochina war was *not* a Korea-type war, i.e., a straight fight between communism and the Free World; it was a colonial war of independence, led unfortunately by the Communists. How many Americans know today that the United States was openly supporting Ho Chi Minh and his Viet-Minh *against* the French in 1945? An uncomfortable fact, but true! The motive was good—anticolonialism.

After an eight-year war, the Vietnamese emerged from the jungle to find their country partitioned into two zones, each dependent on one or other of the power blocks: not a very satisfactory result after so long and bloody a struggle. The overriding motive in Free Viet-Nam is not, and has never been, anti-communism; it is nationalism. By imposing the cold war strategy on Viet-Nam, making it a Free World communism issue, the West has fitted it with a pattern which is against the whole drift of Viet-Nam's recent history. It is like putting mushrooms under cement to stop them growing, but in the end they grow through.

Agreed, this is a typical deadlock with a Communist foe, but it is different to many other positions the West is holding. If the United States were to pull out of West Germany, Turkey, Siam, the Philippines, Japan, even South Korea, it would not mean chaos. The position is naturally strong in these places. But can anybody foresee what would happen if aid to Free Viet-Nam were reduced, or withdrawn altogether? The United States has a prime interest in unifying Viet-Nam on the best terms it can get while it is still there in a position of strength. If ever the American position weakens, it is only too likely that the country will be unified by some upheaval from which the Communists will emerge the victors. In this case, not merely a part but the whole of Viet-Nam might disappear into the maw of China, and the rest of Southeast Asia be endangered.

 If the United States could be certain of maintaining the position in Free Viet-Nam for ten years, during which the south can be developed economically until it stands on its own feet by an imaginative program which fires the southern masses, unification could perhaps be postponed. What the south will never accept is neither economic independence *nor* unification. The present American policy stands flatly against both. It seems like madness, if only from the propaganda viewpoint, to have no policy at all for unification, other than the sword. If that is Diem's honesty, then honesty can be overdone.

 The negative concept of merely holding Free Viet-Nam as a "bastion" against communism is Maginot-mindedness at its worst. One does not win a siege by saying: "Look how clever we are! The enemy has not captured the fortress!" Either the siege must be raised from outside, or one must make a rally. It is sheer weakness to cling to the *status quo* like a drowning man to a raft. Two things are necessary. First, a really dynamic economic policy in the south, which includes industry, land reform, and house-building—all stillborn up to now. Secondly, at least a *policy* for unification.

 What policy? Not by elections, for no one but the Communists believes in them. Hard bargaining between Diem and Ho Chi Minh, while Diem has the full strength of the West at his elbow, is the answer. If the West waits, it may be too late. Who can say how long Congress will continue aid to Free Viet-Nam at 250 million dollars a year? Or at even half that figure? When I was in Saigon in October, 1957, I got the feeling that things were deteriorating, that time was not on the West's side. The south must take the initiative on unification. What is there to lose? If Ho Chi Minh refuses to bargain, he loses face, both with his own people and with neutralist opinion. Diem correspondingly gains. The south should have more confidence in itself. Subversion can work in both directions if the frontiers are opened.

INDEX

Acheson, Dean, 28, 28n
Annam, 6, 37n, 49, 62n, 309
Asia Foundation, 160

Bac Lieu, 79, 184, 195
Baie d'Along, 69, 70
Banque de l'Indochine, 260, 260n, 270, 281
Ben Tre, 100, 107, 181n
Bidault, Georges, 13, 349, 360
Bien Hoa, 82, 89, 99, 107
Binh Dinh, 218-20
Binh Xuyen, 60, 92, 213, 333, 342, 355, 359
Blao, 84, 91
Blao School of Agriculture, 148, 149, 191, 191n, 337
Bloomfield, Arthur I., 259n, 267
Bui Chu, 67-69, 97
Buttinger, Joseph, ix, 2, 9, 42

Ca Mau, 57, 59, 183, 184, 195
Cambodia, 2, 4, 5, 5n, 26, 28, 28n, 57, 62, 79, 91, 106, 112, 126, 176, 183, 259, 274, 275, 303, 304, 309, 338
Cao Dai, 21, 92, 94, 213, 333, 342
Cai San, 90, 95, 100, 184, 195, 337, 360
Can Tho, 79, 100, 113, 260
Cap St. Jacques, 64, 97, 248
Cardinaux, Alfred, 52n, 86, 87, 101, 102
CARE, 46, 47, 50, 160
Carroll, M. J., 95, 101
Casey, R. G., 332, 333, 339, 341-44
Catholic Auxiliary Resettlement Committee, 78, 79, 86
Catholic Relief Services (National Catholic Welfare Conference), 50, 57, 60, 77n, 78-87, 101, 102
Cholon, 79, 82, 92, 99, 107, 108, 114, 118-123, 154, 155, 185, 189, 191, 206, 259, 260, 339
Churchill, Winston S., 13

Cochinchina, 6, 309, 310, 342, 352, 360
Cogny, General, 12, 71, 74
Cole, David C., xi, 174, 176, 190, 314
Collins, J. Lawton, 68, 200
Columbo Plan, 159, 325, 338, 339, 356
COMIGAL, 50-56, 60, 61, 78, 79, 83-95, 96n, 98, 101, 102, 135, 135n

Dai, Bao, 7, 8, 15, 21-27, 27n, 29, 30, 37, 40-44, 128, 200, 252, 349, 355, 359
Dalat, 60, 123, 135, 152, 157
Dang, Nghiem, 162, 166, 169
Dan Him, 195, 197
de Jaegher, Father Raymond J., 107, 111-15
Diem, Ngo Dinh, ix, x, 15, 20, 27-31, 37, 40-44, 48, 54, 73, 75, 78, 90, 92, 93, 108-16, 133, 166, 167, 170, 189, 189n, 200, 203, 204, 208, 241, 242, 310, 332-34, 339-50, 353-55, 358 62
Dien Bien Phu, 2, 8, 10, 11, 11n, 12-15, 27, 28, 55, 60, 138, 288, 289, 346, 348, 355, 359, 360
Dong Cam, 218, 219, 227
Dulles, John Foster, 13, 28, 28n, 349, 360
Durdin, Peggy, 332, 354

Eden, Anthony, 13
Eisenhower, Dwight D., 48, 81, 200
Ely, Paul, 200

Fall, Bernard B., 48n, 54, 58-61, 92, 101, 108n, 111, 113n, 135, 137n, 138n, 185n
Fox, Guy, 166
French Cultural Mission, 160

Geneva Agreement, 14, 28, 29n, 48, 55, 60, 214, 218, 245, 255, 264, 288, 304, 333, 340, 342, 343, 353, 358
Geneva Conference, 2, 4, 9, 10, 11, 13, 14, 15, 27, 29, 40, 290
Gia Dinh, 82, 99

363